JANE AND DOROTHY

JANE AND DOROTHY

A True Tale of Sense and Sensibility:
The Lives of Jane Austen and Dorothy Wordsworth

MARIAN VEEVERS

PEGASUS BOOKS
NEW YORK LONDON

JANE AND DOROTHY

Pegasus Books, Ltd.
148 West 37th Street, 13th Floor
New York, NY 10018

ISBN: 978-1-68177-678-1

10 9 8 7 6 5 4 3 2 1

Printed in the United States of America
Distributed by W. W. Norton & Company, Inc.

For Peter, with love.

This book is his because he has consistently believed in it and in me, even when I have had doubts about both.

Contents

Acknowledgements

I should like to thank the Society of Authors and the Authors' Foundation for their kind grant which made research for this book possible.

My thanks are due to everyone at Jane Austen's House Museum at Chawton who made my visit there so enjoyable and interesting, and particularly to Annalie Talent for tea and answers to my questions. Thanks also to the staff at Winchester Record Office.

I am very grateful to all my friends and colleagues at the Wordsworth Trust, particularly Jeff Cowton, Rebecca Turner, Anna Szilagyi, Barbara Crossley and Dean Hines for their advice and assistance, but also everyone else who has patiently listened to me and discussed ideas as *Jane and Dorothy* took shape. However, I should like to mention that any mistakes are entirely my own, and the opinions and theories expressed in the following pages are also my own and do not necessarily reflect the views of the Wordsworth Trust.

Thanks too to my agent Laura Longrigg at MBA, also to Moira Forsyth, Bob Davidson and everyone at Sandstone Press for their patience and support.

And finally, many thanks to my husband, Peter, for his endless reading, rereading, discussing and checking of the manuscript, and for resolving all my technical crises.

Marian Veevers, Grasmere

The Inward Secrets of our Hearts

Elinor ... possessed a strength of understanding, and coolness of judgement ... She had an excellent heart; – her disposition was affectionate, and her feelings were strong; but she knew how to govern them ... Marianne's abilities were, in many respects, quite equal to Elinor's. She was sensible and clever; but eager in every thing; her sorrows, her joys, could have no moderation. She was generous, amiable, interesting: she was every thing but prudent ... Elinor saw, with concern, the excess of her sister's sensibility.
(Sense and Sensibility, Chapter One.)

In the story of the two Dashwood sisters which Jane Austen proceeds to tell from this beginning, Elinor's concern proves to be well-founded. Marianne's 'excess of sensibility' almost destroys her reputation, her health and her happiness, while Elinor's more guarded behaviour is rewarded.

But that is fiction; what of real life?

Eager in everything, knowing no moderation in her sorrows or her joys: this might be a description of the young Dorothy Wordsworth, sister of the Romantic poet William Wordsworth, who was destined to become her brother's beloved companion, muse and housekeeper – and a talented writer herself.

At fifteen years old Dorothy was far from happy, and the letters she wrote then might have been penned by Marianne Dashwood.

Dorothy was an orphan and had been separated from the brothers she loved. The children were poor because of an ongoing lawsuit with the unscrupulous Lord Lonsdale, and she was living with her austere grandparents in the Cumberland town of Penrith, in a gloomy house of parsimony and long silences. It was a house in which the drawing room carpet was only laid down for favoured visitors, a house in which long dead ancestors stared forbiddingly from the walls.[1] Dorothy's grandfather did not speak to her except to scold, and she endured long hours sewing shirts under the critical eye of her grandmother without a word spoken. It was enough to make any teenager feel sorry for herself.

In July 1787, in the oppressive silence of this dull home – alone, late at night by a guttering candle – Dorothy wrote the earliest of her letters that has survived.

Her fifteen-year-old voice bursts from the page, eager and emotional. 'Has not my dear [friend] accused ...me of neglect? Believe me I am not deserving of these repro[a]ches. However great may have been my dear Friend's disappointment at not having heard from me it cannot equal my distress at being prevented writing to her ...'[2]

Dorothy found exquisite relief from her misery in pouring out her feelings to her friend, Miss Pollard. 'What is uppermost in my mind I must write', she declared, and promised that she would, 'ever lay open the secrets of my heart...'[3]

It is the same language of unrestrained emotion that Marianne uses. And both Dorothy and Marianne would have learned this form of expression from the novels that were popular at the time. In fact, as Pamela Woof has observed, Dorothy, in her earliest letters seems sometimes to step outside herself and identify herself as a character in a story. 'Imagine me', she wrote, 'sitting in my bed-gown, my hair out of curl and hanging about my face, with a small candle beside me, and my whole person the picture of poverty ...'[4]

As a teenager Dorothy Wordsworth was a keen reader of fiction, and she had particularly enjoyed Samuel Richardson's *Clarissa*[5] – a vast narrative of unmitigated misery. Its nine volumes detail the trials of the eponymous heroine as she is pressured by her family to marry a man she dislikes and, upon escaping them, is pursued by the libidinous Lovelace who tricks her into trusting him, imprisons her in a brothel and finally rapes her; after which Clarissa takes the only action possible for a truly 'virtuous' female and dies.

Dorothy was not quite in such dire straits but, orphaned and impoverished, and living with unsympathetic grandparents, she certainly saw similarities between herself and the heroine she admired. She relished being an object of pity. 'You cannot think how I like the idea of being called poor Dorothy', she wrote, '...I could cry whenever I think of it'[6].

She was (in her own mind, at least) as thoroughly persecuted as any novel heroine, and not only by her grim grandparents. Like Clarissa, who suffers surveillance and rudeness from, 'that bold creature Betty Barnes, my sister's confidant and servant',[7] Dorothy was convinced that her grandparents' entire household was ranked against her. '[T]he servants,' she confided to Miss Pollard, 'are every one of them so insolent...as makes the kitchen as well as the parlour insupportable.'[8]

All nine volumes of *Clarissa* (which is one of the longest novels in the English language) are written in letters, many of them sent by the heroine to 'Miss Howe, [her] most intimate friend, companion and correspondent'.[9] Indeed, there are so many letters that, had she been real, poor Miss Howe might have become a little impatient with having to pay for them all, for at this time the recipient, not the sender, paid postage.

Letter writing was so common in novels of the eighteenth century that, if a young woman was to be persecuted, it was all but obligatory for her to have an intimate friend, companion and correspondent in whom she could confide her troubles. Dorothy had determined that Miss Pollard should fill this role, and her account of herself reveals just that 'excess of sensibility' which makes Elinor Dashwood apprehensive about her sister's future.

Just four years younger than Dorothy Wordsworth, Jane Austen also enjoyed *Clarissa* and, by the time she was fifteen, she too had read her share of the fashionable novels which gloried in an extreme depth of feeling – but their effect on her was *very* different from their effect upon young Dorothy. From the age of about ten Jane had been writing stories, and, just a few months short of her fifteenth birthday, she penned her most ambitious tale to date. The voice which emerges from this story is far removed from the earnest Dorothy's.

It came from a very different place. Steventon Rectory in Hampshire, nearly 300 miles south of Penrith, was filled with Jane's brothers, her good-humoured parents, her sister, and the pupils whom her father taught. For her there was no sitting over a candle late into the night, pouring out her sorrows. In fact there would have been little space or peace in which to do that.

Even Jane's earliest work was written for publication, to be shared by as large an audience as she could get. At fifteen, her family was the only available audience, so, sitting under the low beams of the crowded rectory parlour, she confidently read out her new tale, *Love and Friendship*,[10] beginning with an exaggerated version of that interesting background every heroine ought to have:

> 'My father was a native of Ireland & an inhabitant of Wales; My Mother was the natural Daughter of a Scotch Peer by an italian *(sic)* Opera-girl – I was born in Spain & received my Education at a Convent in France ...'

This opening would have been enough to signal to her audience the kind of novel she meant this to be – except *Love and Friendship* is not exactly a novel of sensibility; it is a parody of such a novel.

It is the tale of Laura, a woman who, like Clarissa, has suffered 'the determined Perseverance of disagreeable Lovers and the cruel Persecutions of obstinate Fathers'[11] – or so at least she believes. The plot of this short satirical novel is preposterous, Laura's sufferings entirely self-induced; she marries a man upon a first meeting and he, with 'heroic fortitude', refuses to be reconciled to his father. In her ensuing poverty Laura and her companions are persecuted for such virtuous behaviour as 'majestically removing' banknotes from one of their hosts.

Far from imaginatively entering into the experience of a heroine, Jane set out to mock the whole business of sensibility and those novels in which a girl's emotions were all-important. The tone is set early in the story as Laura describes her own refined feelings, claiming that she had, in her youth, 'A sensibility too tremblingly alive to every affliction of my Friends, my Acquaintance and particularly to every affliction of my own'. But Laura finds that, after all she has gone through, 'Tho' indeed my own misfortunes do not make less impression on me than they ever did, yet now I never feel for those of an other.'

Jane Austen's meaning is clear. She distrusted claims to deep feeling, suspecting that they might be an excuse for selfishness.

The heightened language of sentimental friendship, which Dorothy was happy to adopt for her correspondence, is mercilessly ridiculed in *Love and Friendship*. Here is Laura meeting for the first time Sophia, a woman who is 'all Sensibility and Feeling': 'We flew into each others arms and having exchanged vows of mutual Friendship for the rest of our Lives, instantly unfolded to each other the most inward Secrets of our Hearts.'

The satire is cutting – and seems especially so when we consider the sensitive lonely girl in Penrith finding relief and a way of understanding her own wretchedness as she wrote late into the night beside her small candle. Dorothy Wordsworth's determination to 'ever lay open the secrets of my heart' was just the kind of language Jane was targeting in her mockery.

Dorothy was probably not alone among the young women of her time in interpreting her own experiences through the vocabulary and sentiments of the novels she read. There were, no doubt, self-indulgent girls who gloried in a show of sensibility, pretending to emotions they did not experience and putting on airs of sensitivity. But there must also have been many other young women like Dorothy Wordsworth, who (though they might not have been subjected to the extreme trials of novel heroines) suffered real loss and misery. It is not surprising that those girls should use the style of popular novels to express their woes in a language which at least legitimised and made them bearable.

Dorothy had already begun to experience the insecurities and the injustices of the world in which she lived. Jane knew nothing of them yet.

But, by the time they were fifteen years old, Jane Austen and Dorothy Wordsworth had identified themselves with those two different approaches to life – Sensibility and Reason – which Jane would dramatise in the Dashwood sisters.

How would things turn out for these two very different girls, poised on the edge of womanhood, preparing to encounter all the difficulties and excitements of life in a society which offered women little opportunity for independence, creativity or self-expression?

Jane and Dorothy never met, though they came close to doing so and, had circumstances been just a little different, they might have become acquainted. If they had met they probably would not have liked each other very much, but there are several important parallels in their lives: financial insecurity, a reliance on the support of brothers, intelligence, a certain rebelliousness and, of course, literary talent.

They did inhabit the same troubled, unequal world. The years through which they lived have been called an Age of Revolution. During their lifetimes America won independence, the Bastille fell and idealistic men talked of radically changing the British government – but there was no revolution in the lives of women.

'Family life,' wrote one observer in 1779, 'makes Tories of us all...see if any Whig wishes to see the beautiful Utopian expansion of power within his walls.' The historian Amanda Vickery has concluded, after an extensive study of letters and journals from the period, 'I have yet to encounter a single gentleman musing on whether it might be possible to reconsider his domestic rule in the light of the new political ideas.'[12]

Most women remained under the control of men all their lives: fathers, husbands, brothers. For women like Jane and Dorothy, born into genteel families, there was little hope of living independently. 'Few are the modes of earning a subsistence,' wrote Mary Wollstonecraft in 1788, 'and those very humiliating.'

Marriage was considered to be a woman's only proper career. It was, according to Anne Donnellan, 'the settlement in the world we should aim at, and the only way we females have of making ourselves of use to Society and raising ourselves in this world.'[13] The problem, as Lady Mary Wortley Montagu pointed out, was that men believed 'the end of creation of women is to increase and multiply', so 'Any woman who died unmarried is looked upon to die in a state of reprobation.'[14] It was an enormous challenge for any woman to find a meaningful life outside that prescribed destiny.

This is the story of two very different young ladies who tried to do just that. It is a story of the world they shared. It is a story of how women, as they grow up, negotiate a passage through an unjust society: the different ways of opposing, of complying and of simply surviving. It is a testing of the vision Jane Austen had when, at just nineteen, she began to write *Sense and Sensibility*. Her intuition was that exposing her feelings and acting upon her emotions put a woman in danger, while exercising a strict control would steer her more safely through the perilous waters of Georgian society.

Was she right?

The following chapters trace the growth to womanhood of that impetuous fifteen-year-old, Dorothy Wordsworth, and set it beside the more cautious youth of Jane Austen. The story follows their trials and triumphs and takes us into their thirties to discover the remarkable individuals they became. Parts One and Two trace the joys and challenges of their young days and compare their experiences of that crucial rite of passage in a woman's life: falling in love. Both young women are betrayed by men they love and trust. But their reactions to that betrayal are very different, setting them off on widely diverging courses. In Parts Three and Four Jane and Dorothy are grown women and the four-year difference in their age is less significant. Now the women are living with the decisions they have made, and both begin to see the things that matter most to them slipping away. Jane loses her ability to write, and, possibly, her ability to love, while a cruel twist of fate destroys the peace of the home Dorothy has established with her beloved brother.

Part Five looks forward a little to the events of Jane and Dorothy's later lives. It considers the changes that have taken place in the two women and the legacy they will leave behind. This study focuses on the decisions and aspirations of these two exceptional characters, paying less attention to family and friends than biographies often do. By exploring the different ways in which they responded to the obstacles which Georgian society threw in the way of all intelligent women, it places Jane Austen and Dorothy Wordsworth firmly in the context of their time. It also aims, by establishing the extent of their shared experiences – the experiences common to women of their class and time – to throw into relief the *choices* that they made, to find a new way of understanding their characters, their achievements and their griefs.

Perhaps Sense and Sensibility cannot be neatly divided. It may be that the two opposites which are set up for examination in Jane Austen's novel are ideals to which a young woman aspires, rather than absolutes which entirely define her. For sometimes, no matter how tightly it is reined in, emotion will get the better of prudence and, perhaps more significantly, there are circumstances under which the most impulsive, spontaneous woman can find herself forced into heart-breaking silence and restraint.

PART ONE

ONE

Gentlemen's Daughters

In *Pride and Prejudice*, when Lady Catherine De Bourgh suggests that in marrying Mr Darcy, owner of the vast Pemberley estate, Elizabeth Bennet will be quitting the sphere in which she has been brought up, she gets a sharp reply.

'I should not consider myself as quitting that sphere,' says Elizabeth. 'He is a gentleman; I am a gentleman's daughter.'

However, while admitting the truth of this statement, Lady Catherine follows up with a merciless attack on Elizabeth's family, folk who will, in her memorable phrase, pollute 'the shades of Pemberley.'[1]

This dignified skirmish in the little wilderness at Longbourn is one of the book's most enjoyable passages, and it highlights the very real complexity of Georgian society. The claim to gentility was a broad one, and there was a great deal of room for manoeuvre – and refined insult – within it.

Where would Jane Austen and Dorothy Wordsworth – both indubitably the daughters of gentlemen – have fallen within that general term? If they had lived in the same neighbourhood, would their families have visited one another?

To employ the brisk terminology of *Emma*'s heroine, 'what' the two women were to become is the study of this book, but to establish 'who' they were may be attempted straight away.

A comparison of the houses in which they were born is interesting.

Unfortunately the rectory at Steventon in Hampshire – the house in which Jane Austen was born on 16th December 1775 – was demolished not long after her death. But family recollections reveal that it was more than large enough for gentility, consisting of 'three rooms in front on the ground floor ...behind these were Mr Austen's study, the back kitchen, and the stairs; above were seven bedrooms and three attics.'[2]

With its wide front of nine windows, the house that is now known as 'Wordsworth House' in Cockermouth, Cumbria is on a similar scale. When Dorothy was born there on 25th December 1771 it was the grandest house in the main street of the little market town – and it still is. There is a broad facade facing the street and a grand porticoed entrance. In those days this house lay 'at the outskirts of the Town', and there was a garden behind it, 'bordering on the River Derwent ...', with a beautiful hedge where 'roses and privot (sic) intermingled'[3]. Nikolaus Pevsner in *The Buildings of England* describes it as 'quite a swagger house for such a town'.

Steventon rectory was definitely not a swagger house. Anna Austen's sketches of 1814 show it to be crowded round by trees, with jutting wings at the back, plain chimneys and irregular roofs: a pleasantly rambling, rather than a grand house. It was not very far removed from the kind of country parsonage which Henry Crawford disparages in *Mansfield Park*: 'a scrambling collection of low single rooms, with as many roofs as windows.'[4]

It was not a place built for show: Jane's nephew, James Edward Austen-Leigh, in his memoir of his aunt, remembered that inside, 'No cornice marked the junction of wall and ceiling; while the beams which supported the upper floors projected into the rooms below in all their naked simplicity, covered only by a coat of paint or whitewash'.[5]

In the house on Cockermouth's main street, elaborate Georgian cornices which would have gladdened the heart of Mr Austen-Leigh still survive in both dining room and drawing room. There is no 'naked simplicity' here.

But the houses were alike in the affection with which they were remembered. Dorothy's brother, William, would write in his autobiographical poem, *The Prelude*, of how

'...the fairest of all rivers, loved
To blend his murmurs with my nurse's song.'[6]

Dorothy, in her letters, habitually referred to her first home as 'my father's house' – the biblical term suggesting Christ's 'father's house' with its many mansions, and lending an air of lost paradise to her recollections.

Jane's niece Anna wrote fondly of the 'enclosed garden ...and terrace walk of turf' at Steventon and 'the lower bow window looking so cheerfully into the sunny garden'. And here too there was a sound-track to the memories of childhood. There was not the music of running water, but Anna recalls – 'How pleasant to childish ears was the scrooping sound of [the] weathercock'.[7]

The depth of Jane's attachment to this first home was to be demonstrated when, after twenty-five years, she learned that she must leave it. She was 'greatly distressed'[8] when the news burst upon her and there is even a family tradition that she fainted (the only account of her ever succumbing to such a display of emotion).

However, if it had been Jane or Dorothy facing that chilling interrogation in the Longbourn wilderness, Lady Catherine would have cared little for such a trifle as happy memories. While she might have rated the grandeur of the Cockermouth pillars and cornices over the rambling rooms and whitewashed beams of Steventon, she would soon have looked further and asked – as she asks Elizabeth – 'But who was your mother? Who are your uncles and aunts?'

In the last decades of the eighteenth century everyone was still judged by their 'connections', and, though Dorothy might have been born in a grander house, Jane boasted a slightly more prestigious heritage.

Her father, George Austen, the son of a surgeon, had been orphaned as a boy. His father had left him little money but George had retained the status of gentleman through a poor young man's usual resource: education. He had acquitted himself well at St John's College Oxford, gained a fellowship and, in 1755, become a priest. Then, through the intervention of more wealthy, powerful relations, he acquired the living, not only of Steventon, but also of the neighbouring parish of Deane.

Jane's mother – the daughter of another clergyman – brought some prestige to the marriage: her grandmother was sister to the Duke of Chandos. But it was a large family and Mrs Austen (Miss Cassandra Leigh) was not descended from one of the grander or more prosperous branches. According to her marriage settlement, the money she brought to the marriage 'consisted of some lease-hold houses in Oxford and a prospective sum of £1,000 to which she would become entitled, by her father's will, on the death of her mother.'[9]

Dorothy's mother brought only £500 to her marriage and that was got through trade – a damning word in the vocabulary of Lady Catherine and her real-life counterparts. Dorothy's maternal grandparents were linen drapers, living above their shop in the town of Penrith, thirty miles away.

Dorothy herself occupied a slightly ambiguous position in society, reminiscent of George Wickham's in *Pride and Prejudice*. Like Wickham's father, Dorothy's father was trained in the respectable profession of the law; but, just as Mr Wickham senior 'gave up every thing to be of use to the late Mr Darcy, and devoted all his time to the care of the Pemberley property'[10], John Wordsworth had become steward, or law-agent, to a very wealthy man.

His employer was Sir James Lowther, one of the greatest land-owners in England, who was to become First Earl of Lonsdale in 1784 and Viscount Lowther in 1797. In fact the 'swagger house' was his property and declared to the world the importance of the Lowthers rather than the Wordsworths. The Wordsworth family would certainly have had some status in Cockermouth where John's position made him Bailiff and Recorder of the borough – but Lady Catherine would have been scornful.

On the death of his stepmother in 1768 Mr Austen inherited property in Tonbridge, Kent, to the value of more than £1,280 to add to his wife's capital; but the bulk of his income came from his clerical livings and from the farm which had been apportioned to him as his 'glebe land'. They were poor livings, Steventon yielding about £100 per annum, Deane £110. And in 1800, Jane reported to her sister that their father's farm 'cleared £300 last year.' (Though this may have been a particularly unprofitable year because she described her father's feelings as 'not so enviable' on the occasion.[11])

John Wordsworth's income (which came from his salary and some business interests of his own) was probably comparable, or even slightly larger, since it was sufficient to maintain the smart town house in Cockermouth; and the complement of servants there was large enough to include a nursemaid – as William's recollections reveal.

When John died he did not leave any money to his children, but that was on account of his affairs being (to borrow a useful Austen phrase) 'sadly involved'. He had lent money to his employer and James Lowther would not honour the debt – behaviour quite in keeping with the general character of a man who was to earn himself the local title of 'The Bad Earl'. There was a protracted court case to recover the money and the matter was not settled until after James Lowther's death in 1802. However, when the final claim was made by the Wordsworth family, it amounted to a total of £10,388 6s 8d[12]. This sum would have included interest accrued, but it does suggest that, had he died at a more propitious time, John Wordsworth would have left a respectable – though not a large – legacy to his children.

The financial circumstances into which the two girls were born were not dissimilar.

So, if they had been neighbours, would the Austens and Wordsworths have visited each other? On the evidence available, I would tentatively suggest, yes; they might have exchanged morning calls and drunk tea together. They would certainly have met at public assemblies and balls, though the taint of Dorothy's linen-draper grandparents might have prevented their dining in the same company.

However, one circumstance united these two little girls from the very beginning, a circumstance which was to darken their lives as it did the lives of thousands of women as the eighteenth century drew to a close and the nineteenth century began: chronic insecurity.

The poverty which Dorothy experienced in her early life was, in part, the result of her father having spent his own money on his employer's business and not having recovered the sum at the time of his death. But in any case, John Wordsworth's sudden death at the age of forty-two – when Dorothy was just twelve years old – would have been a heavy blow.

Both Dorothy and Jane were born into families which, though wealthy enough to live comfortably, were almost entirely dependent on the income of the head of the household. Families like theirs – a class which has been called the 'pseudo-gentry'[13] – owned no significant landed property and yet aspired to 'the manners, the education, and the same markers of station as their landed-gentry neighbours'[14].

Such families possessed the horses, the servants and the spacious homes that marked them out as gentry but it was a precarious prosperity. The death of the household's head could plunge his dependents into sudden, life-changing poverty. This was a crisis which Jane and Dorothy would both experience – at different times in their lives. Even the homes that they loved were tied to their fathers' professions and could be snatched away without warning.

As the two babies lay in their cradles – one with the 'scrooping' of the weathercock ringing in her ears, the other with the sound of running water – they were surrounded by brothers. Dorothy had two older brothers, Richard and William, and two more boys, John and Christopher were to be born after her. Jane's family was larger: she had already five brothers: James, George, Edward, Henry and Francis, as well as her sister, Cassandra, and there was to be another brother, Charles, born three and a half years later.

These brothers, of course, shared the precarious existence of the 'pseudo-gentry': they, like their sisters, were 'exposed to …the kind of sudden and irreversible fall in fortune implicit to their station in life'[15]. But the little girls were particularly vulnerable.

Events in the previous generation of the Austen family illustrate this.

Jane's father, George Austen, had two sisters: Philadelphia, who was a year older than him, and Leonora, a year younger. When their father, William, died in 1737, his surgeon's income was lost and the three children – aged seven, six and five respectively – were plunged into a 'sudden and irreversible fall in fortune'. Their stepmother retained the family home and the children were left, under the terms of their father's will, to the care of their uncles Francis and Stephen. It was for these uncles to decide how the children should be educated and prepared for the world.

The way in which they carried out this trust is instructive. Leonora was taken into her Uncle Stephen's home and sank into obscurity. It is doubtful whether her niece, Jane, ever knew of her existence; she is not mentioned in family correspondence. It is possible that she had learning difficulties. She never married and spent the later part of her life in lodgings in London.

George was sent to school at Tonbridge where, 'The knowledge ...of his almost destitute circumstances joined to energy of character and very superior abilities, might naturally lead to success.'[16] His hard work paid off – he went on to St John's College, Oxford, gaining a degree and an exhibition which funded seven years study of divinity. When he eventually took holy orders his future was secure.

By contrast, when Philadelphia was fifteen, as her brother studied to regain the life-style of a gentleman, she was apprenticed to a milliner. Forty-five pounds was paid to a Mrs Cole of London to give the teenager five years' training in the art of making hats.

Stephen and Francis Austen perhaps felt this was the best option available. Higher education, such as her brother was undertaking, was not open to a girl, while, according to Bridget Hill, 'Throughout the eighteenth century the trades of milliners, mantua-makers, seamstresses and stay-makers continued to carry some prestige.'[17] But Philadelphia's life would have been very different from her brother's. She would have been labouring long hours and earning her keep from the beginning of her apprenticeship.

Working with her needle in the manufacture of clothing was more or less the only way a young woman could maintain herself, unless she was well-educated enough to become a governess or a teacher in a girls' school. But not everybody considered the occupation of milliner to be entirely respectable.

Thomas De Quincey (a very observant, though rather gossipy, writer who was to become a close friend of Dorothy Wordsworth) would, in the 1830s, recall Lord Byron's scornful comment that Samuel Taylor Coleridge had married 'a milliner', and go on to say, 'Everyone knows what is *meant* to be conveyed in that expression'.[18]

Considering the vulnerable and unprotected state of many of the women forced into the profession – and the poor living it provided – it would be surprising if some young milliners were not tempted or betrayed into prostitution, as De Quincey's sly hint suggests. The unkind gossip about the trade was nurtured by such popular fictions as John Cleland's 1748 bestselling work of pornography, *Fanny Hill,* which features the madam of a brothel (curiously, another Mrs Cole) masquerading as the head of a millinery establishment.

The job was not financially rewarding either. Milliners were said to 'give but poor mean wages to every person they employ' and a wage of between five and ten shillings a week was all that might be expected when the apprenticeship was completed.[19] Such an income – of around £20 a year – was comparable with the amount a labouring-man might expect to earn, but was a world away from the gentleman's income of £500 a year which Philadelphia's brother would draw from his church livings.

Low paid and barely respectable, millinery left Philadelphia with nothing to look forward to but a life of tedious, unremitting labour. She was, no doubt, as aware of her 'almost destitute circumstances' as her brother, but there was no 'natural' route to prosperity for her in the career her guardians had chosen.

Perhaps Philadelphia regarded her training as the preparation for marriage which Bridget Hill suggests was often one consideration when girls entered into the more prestigious kind of apprenticeship. For – displaying quite as much 'energy of character' as her brother – in 1751 she applied to the British East India Company for permission to sail to India. Though she claimed that her plan was to join 'friends' at Fort St David, she almost certainly had matrimony in mind. In the British community in India – with its preponderance of men – 'no girl, though but fourteen years old, [could arrive] without attracting the notice of every coxcomb in the place.'[20] So it would have offered excellent marriage prospects for a poor, pretty girl, providing she kept her wits about her. Philadelphia reached Madras on 4th August 1752, and six months later she was married to a prosperous surgeon.

Her scheme seems to have been based on a popular philosophy of the eighteenth century, one which her niece would, more than forty years later, put into the thoughts of Charlotte Lucas in *Pride and Prejudice*: 'marriage…however uncertain of giving happiness must be [a woman's] pleasantest preservative from want.'[21]

In escaping to India, Philadelphia was also avoiding another fate: that of becoming dependent on her brother once he had established himself in life. Her guardians may well have felt that in educating George they were also providing, indirectly, for his sisters. Family duty was a powerful force in Georgian times.

The tacit expectation that brothers would provide for their unmarried sisters was recognised by the radical writer Mary Wollstonecraft, and she drew attention to the underlying injustice which made such provision necessary. In 1792 she complained that girls 'are often left by their parents without any provision; and …are dependent on …the bounty of their brothers. These brothers are, to view the fairest side of the question, good sort of men, and give as a favour, what children of the same parents had an equal right to.'[22]

In the uncertain world of the 'pseudo-gentry', family resources were often not distributed evenly between the sexes, and the integrity and affection of her brothers could be crucial to a woman's happiness, particularly if, like Jane and Dorothy, she was not going to embrace that 'pleasantest preservative from want'.

Their brothers were to play an important role in both girls' lives – for good and ill.

TWO

Little Prattlers Among Men

With insecurity and the injustices of Georgian family politics all still hidden in the future, Jane and Dorothy's early years were tranquil. But the little we can trace about their childhoods suggests that they may have already begun to incline towards those opposites of *eagerness* and *prudence*.

The home into which Jane was born was based on a successful and happy marriage. Mrs Austen was a thorough country-woman, writing after a visit to London that the city was ' ...a sad place, I would not live in it on any account: one has not time to do one's duty to God or Man,' and turning to the subject of her cows with great enthusiasm: 'What luck we shall have with those sort of Cows I can't say. My little Alderney one turns out tolerably.'[1] She was well suited to be the wife of a clergyman in a rural parish. News of their farm is prominent in her letters: 'The wheat promises to be very good this year, but we have had a most sad, wet time getting it in, ... we want dry weather for our peas and oats'[2].

She was a practical, down-to-earth woman, discussing recipes as well as agriculture in her letters; but the character revealed in her correspondence does not suggest that her younger daughter inherited her powers of perception and imagination from the maternal line.

Mr Austen missed his wife badly in 1770 when she was absent at her sister's lying-in, complaining, 'I don't much like this lonely kind of Life, you know I have not been much used to it ...'[3]

He was a clever, handsome man who was generally admired: 'What an excellent & pleasing man he is,' wrote his niece Eliza, 'I love him most sincerely'[4]. And there is about the Austens' marriage something of that air of shared interests and shared enterprise which their daughter would capture years later in *Persuasion*'s Admiral and Mrs Croft, who have hardly been apart throughout their married life.

The Austens' family of eight was not exceptionally large, judging by the substantial size of surviving Georgian rectories and the remarks of contemporaries such as Jane's cousin Eliza who believed that 'a parson cannot fail of having a numerous progeny.'[5] However, some of their more cautious relations disapproved as their nursery began to fill up. 'That my brother and sister Austen are well, I heartily rejoice,' wrote Tysoe Saul Hancock – the surgeon husband that Mr Austen's enterprising sister, Philadelphia, had found in India – 'but I cannot say that the News of the violently rapid increase of their family gives me so much pleasure ...'[6]

At that point the Austens had only four children, but Mr Hancock had a particular reason to be concerned. He continued: ' ...especially when I consider the case of my godson who must be provided for without the least hope of his being able to assist himself'. This godson was George, the Austens' second son, born in 1766 (and thus nine years older than Jane); he was six years old when his godfather wrote this letter. Exactly why George was unable to assist himself is not clear. He may have been deaf and he certainly suffered from fits. 'I am much obliged to you for your wish for George's improvement ...' wrote Mr Austen to his sister-in-law, when the child was four, 'but from the best judgement I can form at present, we must not be too sanguine on this Head; be it as it may, we have this comfort, he cannot be a bad or a wicked child.'[7] This insistence on the boy's innocence suggests quite severe learning difficulties.

George did not grow up with his brothers and sisters; he was sent away to live in a village at some distance, where he survived to the age of seventy-two. After his very early childhood, he was not mentioned in family correspondence and following generations were either misinformed, or else joined in the conspiracy of silence. In her *Family History* Jane's great-niece Fanny Caroline reported that Mr and Mrs Austen 'had six sons and two daughters.' She then lists these children, beginning: 'Their sons were James born 1765 ... George born 1766 died ...'[8]

This disappearance of young George Austen is just one of many instances we shall come across, as we follow Jane and Dorothy's stories, of children who are not where we would expect them to be. Jane's Aunt Leonora who vanished into lodgings; Dorothy herself who was taken from her family at the age of six; Jane's brother Edward who was given away to rich relations; poor little Basil Montagu for whom Dorothy cared in Dorset and Somerset. The lives of these two women were to be woven through with the tales of displaced and disappearing children, children who sometimes – as in the cases of George and Leonora Austen – grew into invisible adults.

Family ties were to be crucial in the lives of both our subjects, but they were not the ties of simple affection that are idealised in the twenty-first century. Affection played its part, naturally, but the Georgian family was a unit of survival in a society with no welfare system. Vulnerable members must be cared for, but they could not be allowed to stand in the way of their brothers and sisters; rich relatives must be placated for the sake of the money they could bestow, the influence they could exert; children must sometimes be put out of the way so that their parents could earn money.

It is in this context that we should understand an aspect of Austen family life which seems a little odd and callous to us today. Mrs Austen – according to Jane's nephew, James Edward Austen-Leigh – 'followed a custom, not unusual in those days ...of putting out her babies to be nursed in a cottage in the village.'[9]

'I suckled my little girl [Cassandra] thro' the first quarter;' wrote Mrs Austen, 'she has been wean'd and settled at a good Woman's at Dean just Eight weeks.'[10] The practice was for the children to be visited daily by their parents, and to return to the rectory when they were old enough 'to run about and talk.'[11]

There is no record of Jane being fostered in this way, but it is likely that she was. Biographer Claire Tomalin has suggested that the breaking of the mother-child bond in infancy may have been the cause of 'the emotional distance between child and mother [which] is obvious throughout [Jane's] life.'[12] This is an interesting theory, and it is certainly impossible to read Jane's letters without noticing that 'emotional distance' from her mother. When, in adult life, she was parted from her mother, she did not write frequently. 'I am not likely to write there [i.e. to Mrs Austen] again these ten days,' [13]she told her sister, Cassandra – to whom she wrote every two or three days when they were apart. On another occasion, there is this decidedly chilly remark: 'I suppose my mother will like to have me write to her. I shall try at least.'[14]

However, it is difficult to identify the cause of this coolness. Mrs Austen's practice of putting her children out to nurse – which was probably an efficient way of running her household – does not suit our twenty-first century ideas of child care, but the children's experience of it cannot have been very different from that of many middle and upper class children of the time, who, though remaining under the parental roof, were cared for in separate apartments by nurses and nurserymaids.

Looking back from the mid-Victorian era, Austen-Leigh was himself a little uncomfortable with Mrs Austen's system which, he said, 'seems strange to us'. But his concern was not for the removal of the child from its mother, but rather the placing of a genteel infant in a mere cottage, for he reassures his readers thus: 'It may be that the contrast between the parsonage house and the best class of cottages was not so extreme then as it is now, that the one was somewhat less luxurious, and the other less squalid.'[15]

His priorities seem wrong to us, but they are a reminder that the notion of a mother being always a child's primary carer did not take hold until well into the twentieth century. Austen-Leigh himself – and many of his original readers – would have spent little more time with their mothers as infants than Jane and her siblings did. It may be that the degree of reserve caused by being sent out to nurse was no more than that which was common in a woman of Jane Austen's time and class, and the roots of that more particular coldness which pervades her letters must be sought later in her life, in differences of opinion and temperament between mother and daughter.

Mrs Austen was loving and enthusiastic about her children when they were small, urging one friend to visit because 'I want to show you my Henry & my Cassy, who are both reckoned fine children.'[16] But a distance would develop between her and her talented daughter, and it is likely that Jane looked elsewhere for what we would now term 'role models' as she grew into a woman.

Nor could Dorothy's mother have had very much influence on the woman that her daughter became. Anne Wordsworth (née Cookson) died when her daughter was only six, in March 1778. Anne is a rather shadowy figure, remembered by both William and Dorothy with a kind of unspecific affection such as Dorothy expressed in a letter of 1805: 'Our Mother, blessed be her Memory! Was taken from us when I was only six years old. From her I know that I received much good that I can trace back to her.'[17] She does not give any more detail about the good she received from Anne and though she continued to lament her loss throughout her life, the memory of it was always inextricably mixed with another, more intense grief – the loss of her brothers' company.

It is from William, the brother who was just eighteen months older, that we gain our best knowledge of Dorothy's character as a child.

In his poem *The Sparrow's Nest* he would recall:

'The Sparrow's dwelling, which, hard by
My Father's house, in wet or dry
My sister Emmeline and I
Together visited.'

Emmeline (or Emma) is a name which he often gave to his sister in his poems. (Perhaps it falls more readily into metre than Dorothy.) The poem continues with her reaction to the nest:

'She looked at it and seemed to fear it;
Dreading, tho' wishing, to be near it:

Such heart was in her, being then
A little Prattler among men.'

The same cautious sensitivity is displayed in a memory Dorothy herself recorded in her *Grasmere Journal*. She wrote of how, as a child, she used to chase butterflies 'a little but ...I was afraid of brushing the dust off their wings, and did not catch them.'[18] William also remembered how Dorothy, when very small, displayed 'the sensibility for which she was so remarkable' by bursting into tears at her first sight of the sea.[19]

These scraps suggest that Dorothy, the child, already had the extremely sensitive feelings of the writer of the *Grasmere Journal* who, after parting with her brothers in May 1800, 'sate a long time upon a stone at the margin of the lake, and after a flood of tears my heart was easier', the woman who was so upset by the breaking of a swallows' nest by her window that – 'Poor little creatures they could not themselves be more distressed than I was.'[20]

As an adult, Jane Austen does not seem to have valued this kind of behaviour in children. She sternly adopted the voice of reason when she described the childhood of Catherine Morland in *Northanger Abbey*, insisting that the young Catherine displayed no excess of tenderness towards people, animals or nature. She had no taste for 'the more heroic enjoyments of infancy, nursing a dormouse, feeding a canary bird, or watering a rose-bush.'[21] Catherine's childhood, her creator insists, was not a typical preparation for the role of a novel heroine; though Dorothy's – as it is described by herself and her brother – might well be. Catherine Morland is definitely not the sort of child who would approach a birds' nest with caution or worry about the careless handling of a butterfly. She is 'noisy and wild, hated confinement and cleanliness, and loved nothing so well in the world as rolling down the green slope at the back of the house.'[22]

It is tempting to read this down-to-earth portrayal of childhood as a description of Jane's own early years, and biographers have even identified a 'green slope' behind Steventon rectory down which she might have rolled[23]. But Catherine's infancy may be entirely fictitious.

There is, in fact, only one quality which Jane attributed to her own childhood self: shyness. When she was thirty-one she enjoyed the visit of a friend's young daughter and wondered at the little girl's confidence. 'What is become of all the shyness in the World?' she mused. But she admitted that the change might be for the better. '[S]he is a nice, natural, openhearted, affectionate girl, with all the ready civility which one sees in the best Children of the present day; – so unlike anything that I was myself at her age, that I am often all astonishment & shame.'[24]

Shy, rather cautious and not given to displays of feeling in company: this is our best glimpse of little Jane's character, while sensitive and easily moved to tears must be our clearest idea of Dorothy's.

If Jane Austen had written about the childhoods of Elinor and Marianne Dashwood, her description may not have been very unlike this.

We know little of how either of the children looked, but Dorothy was probably a small child, for she was small as an adult. It was, perhaps, this which prompted William's slightly odd description – 'a little prattler among men' – which presents the Wordsworth brothers, though still children themselves (the eldest, Richard, not four years older than Dorothy), as 'men' in comparison to their sister, and emphasises solemn male wisdom in the face of the little girl's talkativeness. Dorothy was certainly a chatty little girl. '[Y]ou are well acquainted that I was never remarkable for taciturnity',[25] she wrote, at fifteen, to Miss Pollard, who had known her for nearly ten years.

The description, 'a little prattler among men' might also have been applied to the young Jane. Her eldest brother, James, was ten years her senior and, by the time she was three, the spacious old rectory was crammed full with lads who may well have appeared 'men' in her eyes. Mr Austen, finding his income insufficient for the support of his growing family, had begun to take paying pupils, boarding them in his own house. In 1779 there were four boys – probably all teenagers – besides Jane's brothers, sharing her home, and other pupils came and went over the years.

The little girl was surrounded by 'men', the house devoted to the serious masculine business of studying the classics in Latin and Greek, the whitewashed beams echoing with the earnest reading of lessons and translations.

Though Homer and Ovid may have been passing over her head, little Jane had begun to learn a lesson which would be very important in her life and in her work: she was learning about the true nature of the opposite sex, and she had the opportunity to develop easy familiar relationships with boys.

At a time when boys and girls were usually educated separately; when young men hunted and shot while ladies sewed and pursued mainly sedentary hobbies, the contact between the sexes in adult life could be confined to the dance floor and the dinner table. To girls who had not lived closely with brothers, the male sex might appear almost an alien species. Jane was particularly fortunate in this respect. Her brothers remained at home for their schooling, and, from her very earliest days, she was used to living on intimate terms, not only with them, but also with young men unrelated to her.

By the time she began to write her mature novels in her late teens, she was aware of how inadequate the conventional interaction of men and women could be when it came to the important business of choosing a marriage partner. In *Pride and Prejudice*, the pragmatic Charlotte Lucas argues that Jane Bennet should do her best to 'fix' the highly eligible Mr Bingley. Elizabeth Bennet is, however, much more cautious: the couple, she believes, do not really know one another. Four dances, four dinners and one morning visit, she maintains, are 'not quite enough to make her understand his character.'[26]

The exploration of friendships between men and women was to be a major concern of Jane's work. Her characters struggle to achieve satisfying relationships even as they socialise in the restricted world of dinners and visits and balls – the world with which Jane Austen's name is most often associated.

Later in her life, Dorothy, through her closeness to her brother William, would have opportunities to forge meaningful friendships with men in much less restricted situations. However, there is one glimpse to be had of little Dorothy Wordsworth in the very formal setting of a ballroom.

It would seem that at a very young age Dorothy began to take lessons from a Cockermouth dancing master, Mr Hadwin; for in the summer of 1777 he gave a children's ball to demonstrate his pupils' proficiency, and the 'ball was opened by Master Lucock and Miss Wordsworth (both under 5 years old) who notably performed the Minuet, Cotillion, and Country Dance.'

Master Lucock was the grandson of the High Sheriff of Cumberland and, as John Worthen has pointed out, 'The pairing of the Wordsworth daughter with the grandson of a great local landowner and magnate suggests the circles in which the Wordsworth family moved.'[27]

Children's balls were sufficiently common in the last decades of the eighteenth century to draw several pages of condemnation from the moralist and educational reformer, Hannah More. 'Baby-balls' as she contemptuously termed them, were a 'conspiracy against the innocence, the health and the happiness of children.' She complained that 'instead of bounding with the unrestrained freedom of little wood-nymphs, over hill and dale...these gay little creatures are shut up all the morning acquiring a new step for the evening.' The result, she believed, was the creation of 'Lilliputian coquettes'.[28]

Little Dorothy with her sensitivity and impulsive feelings certainly seems more like a bounding wood-nymph than a Lilliputian coquette. It is intriguing to think of her leading a dance and, in particular, performing the stately minuet. This dance – to which Austen-Leigh draws attention in his description of Jane Austen's dancing days – 'was a slow and solemn movement, expressive of grace and dignity, rather than merriment' and its many 'complicated gyrations' were 'executed by one lady and gentleman, amidst the admiration, or criticism, of surrounding spectators.'[29] Quite a challenge for a sensitive five-year-old![30]

This fragment of Dorothy's very early education suggests the kind of life her parents expected her to lead, and offers a tantalising glimpse of what the social world of Miss Wordsworth of Cockermouth might have been. If she had not been orphaned so

young, she might have grown up as a young lady of some consequence in the little market town. Perhaps the honour of opening
balls would have frequently fallen to her. And if it had, would she
have sought it jealously as *Emma*'s heroine does, or dreaded and
tried to avoid it as Fanny Price does in *Mansfield Park*?

It is impossible to know, because, little more than a year after
this social triumph, Dorothy's young life was shattered by the
death of her mother. At six years old she left Cockermouth, and
was never again to step inside the 'swagger house' by the River
Derwent.

When Mrs Wordsworth was dying of pneumonia – at the age of
only thirty – she begged her cousin, Elizabeth Threlkeld, to give
a home to her daughter. Perhaps she felt that, unlike the boys,
six-year-old Dorothy would need a mother figure in her life, and
her choice of foster-mother was certainly an excellent one. For
the next nine years 'Aunt Threlkeld' would provide a secure,
happy home for her cousin's child, and Dorothy came to love her
dearly. This new home was in Halifax, however, over a hundred
miles from Cockermouth and, for reasons which are not clear, her
father did not allow her to return, even for a visit, to the house in
which she was born.

Not much is known of Dorothy's father. He seems to have been
diligent and honest in business, though he earned himself some
unpopularity by being associated with a man so disliked as James
Lowther, and it is impossible not to conclude that he felt little
affection for his only daughter. There can be no other reasonable
explanation for poor little Dorothy's unrelieved exile.

It was a separation which, she would say, 'I cannot think of
without regret from many causes, and particularly, that I have
been thereby put out of the way of many recollections in common
with my Brothers ...'[31]

Sending his daughter to a foster-family might have been
expedient, and travel was not easy in the eighteenth century, but
Dorothy's lack of contact with her family between the ages of six
and sixteen is remarkable. If John Wordsworth had cared for his
daughter's company, travel arrangements could have been made.

Maybe this thought occurred to Dorothy as she grew older, for, though she never wrote disrespectfully of her father, it was not the opportunity of being with him which she regretted losing, only that of being with her brothers.

Shared memories and jokes are such an important ingredient in the cement that binds families that it is easy to understand Dorothy's regret and sense of exclusion. It is just these kinds of recollection – these memories that brothers and sisters hold in common – that Jane Austen was to celebrate in *Mansfield Park*. 'Children of the same family ...with the same first associations and habits,' she would write, 'have some means of enjoyment in their power, which no subsequent connections can supply; and it must be by a long and unnatural estrangement ...if such precious remains of the earliest attachments are ever entirely outlived.'[32]

Despite the long years in which she was denied her brothers' company, Dorothy's earliest attachments never were outlived. 'I have at all times', she wrote, 'a deep sympathy with those who know what fraternal affection is'.[33]

When tragedy or poverty struck, the Georgian family had to regroup and survive as best it could. Children's feelings could be overlooked and Dorothy's experience rather resembled that of poor little Fanny Price (*Mansfield Park*'s heroine). Like Fanny, Dorothy was parted from her siblings by adults who may have believed they were acting for the best but who seem not to have understood the importance of her daily companions in the life of a child, nor the grief and trauma that might result from being suddenly removed from them.

As a mature writer in her thirties, Jane Austen would recognise the hurt caused by such a separation, but it was something Dorothy experienced while she was still young. The sense of loss would colour her whole life.

THREE

Original Sin

Dorothy's removal, at the age of six, to her foster home at Halifax not only separated her from her brothers, it took her from an old-fashioned market town to a rapidly growing industrial community.

Dorothy, who would later write so beautifully about the natural world, was not a child of the countryside; she spent her early years in urban environments. The towns in which she lived – Cockermouth, Halifax and Penrith – were smaller than they are now and it was possible, even in Halifax, for a determined walker to escape into fields, but she did not grow up, as Jane did, attuned to the rhythms and habits of rural life. Dorothy was not surrounded by the earnest concerns over cows and barley and hay which fill Mrs Austen's letters; she did not, for example, learn the names of birds and wildflowers in the natural, almost unconscious way that country children do. Years later she would long for a book on botany in order to identify the flowers she saw around her at Grasmere.

The move to Halifax also placed Dorothy under the influence of a strong, determined woman. Elizabeth Threlkeld, the cousin she would always call 'aunt', the woman of whom she was to say, 'she has been my mother',[1] was a positive and rather unusual female role model for this displaced child.

Family letters reveal Elizabeth Threlkeld to have been a dynamo of a woman who, 'will not allow herself time to grow fat'.[2] When

Dorothy arrived in Halifax Miss Threlkeld was already taking care of two nephews and three nieces (all older than Dorothy) as well as running the business left by their dead father. Her obituary hints at a strength of mind and a determination to do what she believed was right. '[W]hilst a young, and admired Woman,' it says, she ' ...took upon herself the charge, and Maintenance of five Orphan Children ... relinquishing the Society of her Relatives – amongst the Gentry of Cumberland, to place herself in a small Haberdashers Shop ...'.[3]

In her young adult life Dorothy would demonstrate a capacity for hard work and a lack of concern for genteel expectations very similar to Miss Threlkeld's. She admired her foster-mother and thrived in the busy household attached to the haberdasher's shop. She was fond of her older cousins and it was here too that she met her life-long friend and confidante, Jane Pollard, a little girl of just her age who lived on the opposite side of the street.

The move also brought another very significant influence into Dorothy's life, and it was one which may have deepened the difference in character between her and Jane, for they were now on opposite sides of an important religious divide. The home in which Dorothy found herself was a dissenting household, while Jane Austen lived all her life among traditional Anglicans.

This was a time when to be born English was considered, almost by definition, to be born Christian, but conventional Christianity had got very worldly. It was a time when *Pride and Prejudice*'s Mr Collins might congratulate himself on being advantageously settled in his 'humble parsonage'[4] by a great patron such as Lady Catherine De Bourgh, or a well-meaning, shy young man such as Edward Ferrars of *Sense and Sensibility* might be made 'comfortable as a bachelor' in a rectory of £200 a year, by a kindly landowner interested in his welfare.[5]

A clergyman with the right friends frequently held more than one living. He was not obliged to live in the parish from which he drew his income, and might not even be seen by his parishioners – the weekly services often being read by a badly-paid curate. Jane's father held two church livings and when he was first appointed to the living of Steventon in 1761, he neither moved to the village nor took services there, though the tithes would have begun to be paid to him. It was not until he was preparing for his marriage in 1764 that he took up residence and began to do the duty of a clergyman.

This was not an unusual practice but dissenting churches such as the one to which Dorothy's new foster-mother, Aunt Threlkeld, belonged, challenged this laxity.

At the time when Dorothy began to attend its services, the Northgate End Chapel in Halifax was strongly influenced by the Unitarian beliefs of its Minister, John Ralph. Unitarians rejected as unbiblical the established church's doctrine of Original Sin: the doctrine which taught that all men and women were intrinsically evil, tainted by the first sin of Adam and Eve in the Garden of Eden. So Mr Ralph's sermons may well have encouraged Dorothy's belief that her own feelings were right and that they could be trusted as a guide to behaviour.

The opposition of character which Jane Austen sets up at the beginning of *Sense and Sensibility* was part of a wider debate in Georgian society. Elinor's *prudence* and Marianne's *eagerness* relate to two very different approaches to life: the rationality championed by the Enlightenment and the cult of feeling which had grown up as a reaction against it.

Philosophers asked the question: which is the more virtuous, the 'natural' man who acts honestly on his emotions, or the schooled, controlled individual who allows himself to be governed by external rules of behaviour? Religion played an important part in this discussion.

Anglicans such as the Austens, with their orthodox belief in Original Sin, believed that, since all human beings were naturally sinful, feelings should be controlled by external laws. On the other hand, the Unitarian idea that man was naturally good – untainted by Original Sin – encouraged a belief that subjective feelings were of value and should be trusted and acted upon.

However, it is not the case that Dissenters always championed sensibility over sense. Reason was more important than ritual to them and they promoted a personal quest for truth, rather than unquestioning adherence to the teachings of the established church. The chapel's policy when choosing books for the library it provided for the poor was this: 'As it behoveth us to try all things, it is not intended to exclude the writers upon any doctrinal system, provided their books breathe the spirit of that religion they are designed to teach.'[6]

This ethos of open-minded discussion, which she encountered in Halifax, would remain, for many years, an ideal of Dorothy's. Describing her dream home in 1793, she conjured up a picture of friends gathered about a fireside, reading together, and 'at Intervals we lay aside the Book and each hazard our observations upon what has been read without the fear of Ridicule and Censure.'[7]

Dissenters were, in many ways, outsiders; by the Corporation Act of 1661 they were excluded from holding any civic or municipal office because they had not taken communion in the Church of England. This was, inevitably, a source of grievance, and many Dissenters were critical of the Establishment. It is likely that Dorothy encountered political as well as religious debate in Halifax.

Jane's early experience was at the opposite end of the Georgian religious and political spectrum. Orthodoxy would have been in the very air of Steventon parsonage.

'Moderate Toryism,'[8] was the political creed which prevailed in her family, though this was 'rather taken for granted ...than discussed,'[9] and religion too was probably more taken for granted than discussed. The daughter of an Anglican clergyman would certainly not have been expected to 'try all things' in the spirit of Reverend Ralph.

Jane's opinions 'accorded strictly with those of our Established Church'[10] – or so said her brother Henry when he wrote the very earliest account of her life, shortly after her death in 1817. Henry's idea of how a woman *should* be remembered – the way in which her family *wished* Aunt Jane to be remembered – is as a very conventional Anglican lady. But Henry's almost hagiographic summary of his sister's life is not to be trusted entirely, and Kathryn Sutherland has observed that Jane's novels 'offer little evidence' that her opinions were in accord with Anglican doctrine.[11] And yet, there is a sense in which the early novels do accurately reflect the moribund Georgian church from which Jane's father drew his livelihood – and that is the very scarcity of religious references.

It is only in times of crisis that God impinges on the bright young lives of *Sense and Sensibility* and *Pride and Prejudice*. Thus, Marianne's life-threatening illness produces 'serious recollection' and a wish for 'atonement to my God'.[12] When Lydia's elopement threatens herself and her family with disgrace, Elizabeth obliquely refers to religious morality as she regrets that her sister 'has never been taught to think on serious subjects.'[13] But, once the crises are over, the Almighty soon passes out of the narratives, and He has no place in the happy denouements.

Anglican religion of the kind Jane knew as a little girl was like a trusted bottle of medicine: always on the shelf, to be reached for when needed: accepted, ever-present, and not much talked about. The Austen family appears to have been particularly adept at avoiding controversy. According to Jane's niece, Caroline, the 'family talk' among the adult brothers and sisters was 'never troubled by disagreements as it was not their habit to argue with one another.'[14]

Caroline was writing about the last decade of her aunt's life, but the habit seems to have been firmly established by then. In 1816 Henry Austen's financial problems lost his brothers many thousands of pounds, but this 'produced no quarrels and created no permanent estrangement'[15] among them. By then their reticence was an established part of family life, and it had probably begun under the parental roof at Steventon. It was certainly a peaceable little community that Mary Leigh (wife of Mrs Austen's cousin) found there when Jane was about five years old. She remarked upon 'the simplicity, hospitality, and taste' of the Steventon household.[16]

It sounds like a pleasant, happy home but not one filled with the discussion of dangerous or uncomfortable ideas. It was a home in which the young Jane might have had little opportunity for open-minded enquiry – that rigorous search after personal truth which cannot help but lead to disagreement – that Dorothy enjoyed among the dissenters of Halifax.

FOUR

Fashionably Educated and Left Without a Fortune

It is not possible to read the works of Jane Austen without gaining the impression that their author disliked schools. In *Persuasion* Anne Elliot has been unhappy at her school in Bath and her friend, Lady Russell, believes that the simple fact of her having been 'three years at school there,' is sufficient reason for her prejudice against the city. [1]

'I would rather be a teacher at a school (and I can think of nothing worse) than marry a man I did not like', declares Emma Watson in Jane's unfinished novel *The Watsons*. But her more realistic elder sister replies: 'I would rather do anything than be a teacher at a school ...'[2] Real women echoed this view. 'A teacher at a school,' wrote Mary Wollstonecraft, 'is only a kind of upper servant, who has more work than the menial ones.'[3]

It is only Mrs Goddard's homely little school in *Emma* that gets any praise in Jane Austen's fiction, and this is approved because it is unlike other schools of its time. It is not 'a seminary, or an establishment ...where young ladies for enormous pay might be screwed out of health and into vanity.'[4]

Jane herself attended two schools, but we know too little about either to be sure whether they resembled the despised seminaries and establishments or were more like Mrs Goddard's comfortable little school. However, one line in her novels may have been

26

influenced by experience, and that is the remark about young ladies being 'screwed out of health'. The first school to which Jane and her sister, Cassandra, were sent in the spring of 1783, when Jane was just seven years old, was run by a Mrs Cawley. When the Austen girls first joined Mrs Cawley she was based in Oxford but, later in the same year, she and her pupils removed to Southampton. Here an epidemic of typhus fever struck. Jane became dangerously ill and was saved only by the intervention of her cousin Jane Cooper, another of Mrs Cawley's pupils, who wrote to warn her mother of the situation. The girls were taken home and Jane recovered but the misery and terror of a seven-year-old experiencing severe illness away from home, together with the later realisation of the danger she had been in, would be enough to account for a lifelong bias against boarding schools.[5]

Since Jane had been entrusted to Mrs Cawley's care at the age of seven, it is rather surprising that, two years later, when the subject of school was next mooted, Mrs Austen considered that 'Jane was too young to make her going to school at all necessary'.[6] The plan this time was to send twelve-year-old Cassandra on her own but Mrs Austen had reckoned without the determination of her younger daughter: Jane insisted on accompanying her sister. '[I]f Cassandra's head had been going to be cut off,' said Mrs Austen. 'Jane would have her's *(sic)* cut off too'[7].

This is clearly an early demonstration of the sisters' deep attachment (an attachment that was to last all their lives), but Jane's motives and feelings remain obscure because we do not hear Cassandra's voice. How did she feel about being sent away again? After the Southampton debacle, the prospect of going alone to another strange school may well have been terrifying. Jane's insistence on being included in the scheme might be not just an attempt to stay together, but an act of defiant self-sacrifice not so very far removed from Mrs Austen's flippant – and, in view of Jane's near-death experience, rather tasteless – metaphor.

There seems, at the very least, to be a lack of understanding between mother and daughter here. The down-to-earth Mrs Austen was perhaps capable of insensitivity and baffled by her young daughter's strong feelings. This may be one of the places at which that distance, so painfully evident in the later letters, began to open between them.

The Austen girls were now to be educated at the Abbey House School in Reading. This establishment was presided over by a Mrs La Tournelle (real name Sarah Hackitt, but a suggestion of Frenchness was useful in the field of girls' education). She was, by one account, a far from academic woman and fit only for 'doing the work of a housekeeper': her talents being limited to supervising laundry, ordering dinner and making tea. But her assistant Miss Pitts and a few other teachers provided lessons in 'writing, spelling, French, history and geography, needlework, drawing, music and dancing'.[8]

This was a fairly typical curriculum for girls at the time. After learning the basics of reading and writing, a girl's education diverged from that of her brothers and, while they began to concentrate upon the study of the classics (with some time devoted to mathematics), she would be expected to focus on the more ornamental 'accomplishments': modern languages, embroidery, drawing and music.

However, the Austen sisters profited from the Abbey House School's instruction for little more than a year. At some time during 1786 they returned home to the crowded rectory where their father was engaged in the more serious business of educating young gentlemen. It is not clear how their education continued from this point: whether they were left simply to their own devices, whether masters were provided, or whether their mother found time in the midst of running the large household to teach them. It is unlikely that a governess was employed. At this time 'a governess was unknown in Parsonage Houses...'[9] according to Jane's niece Caroline.

The girls' formal education was at an end.

We do not know whether Jane enjoyed her school days or not, because her letters hardly mention them. The majority of Jane's surviving letters were written to Cassandra and, according to their great-niece Fanny Lefroy, Jane and Cassandra's 'full feelings and opinions were known only to themselves,'[10]. So we can hope that these letters bring us as close to their writer as it is possible to come two centuries on. However, the collection is far from complete.

'My Aunt [Cassandra]' wrote Caroline, 'looked them [the letters] over and burnt the greater part, (as she told me), 2 or 3 years before her own death.'[11] Even some of the surviving letters have had passages cut out of them. It may be that some censoring was done during Jane's lifetime and at her request. 'Seize upon the scissors as soon as you possibly can on the receipt of this,' she wrote towards the end of a letter of 1798 which had ranged freely – and not uncritically – over various family concerns.[12] Sometimes it is possible to see where comments have been obliterated. For example, in one letter of 1814, a tantalising, 'Edward is quite ...' remains, but the rest of the sentence has been excised.[13]

Such a precaution would be necessary in a family which was determined not to argue. 'Known only to themselves' Jane's comments to Cassandra were safe, but they could not be allowed to escape to a wider audience. Like fossils, Jane Austen's letters must be approached with caution. There are large gaps in the record; conclusions must be tentative.

So it is impossible to know what this silence about school signifies. Ten years after leaving Mrs La Tournelle's establishment, Jane wrote, in praise of a funny letter Cassandra had sent, 'I could die laughing at it, as they used to say at school.'[14] This one passing reference to the idiom of their companions is the only time the subject is mentioned. Maybe schooldays were just not memorable, or maybe Cassandra destroyed references to them. Neither possibility argues for Jane enjoying the small amount of formal education she received.

Dorothy Wordsworth, however, does seem to have enjoyed her school days. As an adult she reminisced enthusiastically about school and seems to have made many friends there. She attended two schools while in Halifax. At nine years old she was sent to a boarding school in Hipperholme, near Halifax. Very unusually for the day, it seems to have taken both boys and girls, for Dorothy later wrote of a Mrs Wilkinson as 'teacher of the girls'. She remembered this lady as 'a most excellent-tempered, motherly and sensible woman'[15]. This brings to mind the fictional Mrs Goddard who 'gave the children plenty of wholesome food ...and ...dressed their chilblains with her own hands',[16] but does not suggest academic brilliance.

Dorothy stayed only three years in the motherly care of Mrs Wilkinson. On 30th December 1783 she endured another devastating, life-changing loss – the death of her father. At twelve she was an orphan, and an orphan with very little fortune. Her uncles,[17] who were now responsible for the care of her and her brothers (and for trying to extract the outstanding debt from the reluctant Lowther), clearly felt that economy was necessary – and a girl's education was not a priority. William's education at Hawkshead grammar school continued uninterrupted by his father's death, but in 1784 Dorothy was removed from the Hipperholme establishment.

However, the five-shilling entrance fee was found to take her to a day school in Halifax and, since her friend Jane Pollard was also a pupil there, Dorothy was probably not unhappy with the change.

This school was run by the two Misses Mellin, who were, like Aunt Threlkeld, members of the Northgate End congregation and, considering Mr Ralph's enthusiasm for 'trying everything', their curriculum might be expected to be a little broader than that of girls' schools in general. So it is quite disappointing to read, in an advertisement for Miss Mellin's school which appeared in 1788, that, 'the greatest Care and Attention will be paid to the Health, Morals and Accomplishments of the young Ladies.'[18]

It does not sound like an extensive education, but Dorothy's health, morals and accomplishments were cared for by the Misses Mellin until she was fifteen, when the need for further economy took her away from Halifax altogether.

Dorothy had spent six years in schools, which was longer than many girls of her time and class. But when Thomas De Quincey met her twenty-three years later, although he found her to be 'a person of very remarkable endowments intellectually', he did not consider her well-educated. 'Her knowledge of literature was irregular,' he said, 'and not systematically built up. She was content to be ignorant of many things.'[19]

Perhaps Jane's low opinion of girls' schools was well founded.

Jane and Dorothy's experiences draw attention to the weaknesses in girls' education at the end of the eighteenth century. There was a purpose to a boy's schooling: he must acquire the grounding in classics which prepared him for university. For girls – to whom higher education was closed – there was no such aim, and the decisions taken by the Austen and Wordsworth elders demonstrate that a girl's schooling could be a rather desultory affair, very much at the mercy of family crises and contingencies.

'Everybody knows,' wrote Jane's niece Caroline (in the middle of the next century), 'that a hundred years ago, there was not much trouble taken with the education of young ladies.'[20]

What a girl learned, and how thoroughly she learned it, depended, to a large extent, on the individual herself. 'Such of us as wished to learn, never wanted the means ...' says Elizabeth Bennet, describing the education of herself and her sisters. 'Those who wished to be idle certainly might.'[21] This may also have represented the situation at Steventon after Jane and Cassandra returned from Reading.

There was a great deal written about the deplorable state of female education at the time, and much of it focused on girls like Jane and Dorothy: girls whose fortunes were negligible, and whose futures were, as a consequence, extremely uncertain. Since girls were not being prepared for university, what was their education for?

Laetitia Matilda Hawkins raised a remarkable argument against women undertaking exacting intellectual study – it tended to make them frown and look ugly. 'That we are not designed for the exertion of intense thought,' she reasoned, 'may be fairly inferred from the effect it produces on the countenance ... The contracted brow ...the motionless eye-ball ...can give nothing to soft features that is not unpleasant.'[22] The conclusion suggests that Laetitia Matilda herself was not so careless of her appearance as to undertake much intense thought.

Most writers agreed that it was private, domestic life for which a woman should be prepared, and that, of course, meant marriage. Hannah More believed female education should consist of more than the conventional 'accomplishments' such as music and drawing, because 'when a man of sense comes to marry, it is a companion whom he wants and not an artist ...it is a being who can comfort and counsel him ...one who can assist him ...soothe his sorrows and educate his children.'[23] For conservative writers like More a woman should set a moral and spiritual example to her husband and family. Therefore, the purpose of a girl's education was 'to enable her to regulate her own mind, and to be useful to others.' [24] Restraint and service were the guiding principles of a woman's life.

Even the radical Mary Wollstonecraft believed that a young woman should be prepared for marriage. 'A woman may fit herself to be the companion and friend of a man of sense,' she wrote, 'and yet know how to take care of his family.'[25] But Wollstonecraft acknowledged that not all girls were heading towards a guaranteed marriage, and she lamented the difficulties faced by 'Females, fashionably educated, and left without a fortune'[26]: women who had little chance of securing that highly desirable, but rather elusive, *man of sense* (whose sense too often prompted him to look for a wife with money). Mary Wollstonecraft pointed out that, apart from being a companion, teacher or governess – all three of which careers she tried herself and heartily disliked – 'The few trades which are left [for women to follow] are now gradually falling into the hands of the men, and certainly they are not very respectable.'[27] There is a reminder here of Philadelphia and her training in millinery.

Priscilla Wakefield went further. She put forward the innovative idea that, properly prepared, genteel women would be capable of supporting themselves, and she was delightfully practical in her suggestions of the professions they might take up in order to 'procure for themselves a respectable support by their own industry.' The trades of literature, miniature painting, the making of patterns for calico, and landscape gardening, were all, she suggested, suited to impoverished gentlewomen, though acting certainly was not.

Wakefield also had a surprisingly modern-sounding solution to the problem of men appropriating all the respectable crafts: female solidarity allied to the power of the consumer. Women 'of rank and fortune', she suggested, 'should determine to employ women only, wherever they can be employed: they should procure female instructors for their children: they should frequent no shops that are not served by women: they should wear no clothes that are not made by them.'

Unfortunately, most of the professions in her list remained closed to women until the latter decades of the nineteenth century. But it is interesting that the first possible employment that she mentioned was literature, which, she said, 'affords a respectable and pleasing employment, for those who possess talents and an adequate degree of mental cultivation.' Female writers were becoming increasingly conspicuous during the eighteenth century and Jane and Dorothy, as they grew up, would have become aware that this was a possible occupation for women, though it had its limitations. The problem, as Priscilla Wakefield pointed out, was that 'the emolument is precarious, and seldom equal to a maintenance.' However, it might still be useful to a lady in straitened circumstances, for 'it may yield a comfortable assistance …and beguile many hours, which might otherwise be passed in solitude or unavailing regret.'[28]

Writing would never make a woman's fortune, but it might earn her some pocket money and take her mind off her problems.

Jane and Dorothy were to be among those women 'left without a fortune' upon the death of their fathers. Dorothy would, belatedly, gain a little money of her own when the Lowther case was finally settled, but Jane's father made no provision for her in his will and she had no *expectations* from any other source. To what extent could the education that these two girls received be expected to help them? Did it supply any means of supporting themselves? Did it prepare them for dependence and life on a restricted income?

It seems likely that both girls learned languages to some extent. A Mr Martin, teacher of French, Italian and Spanish, is recorded as being employed at Miss Mellin's school.[29] Dorothy certainly owned and was reading French books in her twenties. 'I should like to read French with you' she wrote to Jane Pollard in 1794[30]. However, it is unlikely that she learned much Italian at school for, in the same year, William Wordsworth wrote to a friend: 'My Italian studies I am going to resume immediately, as it is my intention to instruct my sister in that language.'[31]

In 1815 Jane described herself as 'a Woman who...knows only her own Mother-tongue.'[32] However she was probably being over-modest: according to her nephew, she 'read French with facility, and knew something of Italian.'

Austen-Leigh goes on to remark: 'In those days German was no more thought of than Hindostanee (*sic*), as part of a lady's education.'[33] However, Dorothy Wordsworth *did* think of German as part of a lady's education. At the age of twenty-six, believing (probably erroneously) that 'translation is the most profitable of all [literary] works,'[34] Dorothy would set about learning the German language in order to work as a translator – going to the length of accompanying her brother to Germany in an attempt to complete this part of her education.

Dorothy was one of those women who 'wished to learn', and she did not consider that the time for learning was past when she had outgrown the schoolroom, though her understanding might have seemed irregular to a university-educated man.

There were gaps in Dorothy's education which she did not attempt to fill, even though she was aware of them. Some of these gaps were the more ornamental *accomplishments*. 'You expect to find me an accomplished woman and I have no one acquirement to boast,'[35] she wrote when she was 18. Music never played much part in her life and, writing to Lady Beaumont in August 1805 and trying to convey something of her home's appearance, she attempted a drawing, warning that it 'will make you smile at my little skill.'[36] Evidence of that little skill survives in an endearingly childlike sketch of Dove Cottage.

This lack of the more artistic acquirements reflects the practical, dissenting ethos of Dorothy's education. She regretted her lack of artistic skill, writing that, 'I scarcely ever take a walk without lamenting it'.[37] With training and practice, she might have become a competent artist, as, in her journals, she frequently considered landscape with an artist's eye.

Jane, in her comfortable Anglican vicarage, became the more accomplished of the two girls. Henry Austen reported in his brief Biographical Notice that his sister had both taste and skill in drawing. And 'I believe that a music Master attended at Steventon...' wrote Jane's niece, Anna Lefroy.

In *Sense and Sensibility* it is partly through the arts that Marianne Dashwood assesses sensibility in others. Music is a passion with her and when she judges Edward Ferrars' suitability as a husband for her sister, her greatest hope is that he will learn to share Elinor's love of drawing. She also forces poor Edward to read poetry aloud in the drawing room – the poetry of William Cowper.

Cowper, according to her brother Henry, was a favourite writer of Jane's.[38] Dorothy too seems to have had read this very popular poet when she was young, and to have approved his championing of simple rural life. The vision of her ideal home which she would describe in 1793 was almost certainly influenced by Cowper's poem *The Task*. 'When I think of the winter', wrote Dorothy, 'I hasten to furnish our little Parlour, I close the Shutters, set out the Tea-table, brighten the Fire.'[39] It is an echo of Cowper's lines:

'Now stir the fire, and close the shutters fast,
...
And while the bubbling and loud-hissing urn
Throws up a steamy column, and the cups,
That cheer but not inebriate, wait on each,
So let us welcome peaceful evening in.'[40]

Poetry would be pre-eminently important in Dorothy's life, but her willingness to pass over the conventional 'accomplishments' by which many young ladies self-consciously defined their sensibility suggests that her particular brand of deep feeling was not an off-the-peg affectation, rather something genuine to be expressed in her own way.

Both these talented girls learned for their own purposes, not for show.

Anna Lefroy recalled that Jane Austen's piano was sold when the family removed from Steventon, but, 'when settled at Chawton she bought a Pianoforte and practised upon it diligently…in order to recover that facility of fingering, which no doubt she had once possessed.'[41]As she used to do most of her piano-playing in the early mornings before the rest of the household was awake, it would seem she played for her own enjoyment, not for the kind of display which motivated Mary Bennet and many real women who spent long hours acquiring all those *accomplishments*.

This ability and willingness to follow up on subjects that interested them, and to adapt the heterogeneous content of female schooling to suit their own interests and ends was, undoubtedly, the most useful skill which both Jane and Dorothy acquired from their various teachers. An intelligent and determined young woman could – to a large extent – become her own schoolmistress.

Untrammelled by the need to learn all that Latin and Greek, girls of the gentry class had time to read a great deal, though, since family libraries were generally collected by men, they might find themselves restricted by the taste of their fathers and grandfathers.

References in Jane's novels and letters reveal that throughout her life she read very widely indeed. She began exploring books early, with her father's collection of over 500 volumes, and during her lifetime her reading was to include a large number of contemporary novelists such as Samuel Richardson, Frances Burney and Charlotte Lennox; travel books by Joseph Baretti and Lord Macartney; political histories such as that written by Dorothy's friend, Thomas Clarkson; French works by Madame de Genlis and German ones (presumably in translation) by Johann von Goethe. She particularly admired the prose of Samuel Johnson.[42]

In Halifax Dorothy would have had access to that wide-ranging library established by Mr Ralph, but when, in 1787, she was summarily removed by her uncles from Aunt Threlkeld's care, and sent to live in Penrith with her Cookson grandparents, the opportunities for reading became much more restricted.

Her brothers seem to have done their best to help. In addition to the works of Milton and Goldsmith 'I have a pretty little collection of Books from my Brothers' she wrote soon after her removal, and listed the *Iliad* and the *Odyssey* (most probably in Alexander Pope's 1715 translations), Fielding's works, and the poems of William Hayley (a friend of Cowper). There was also *Gil Blas*, a picaresque novel in French, and, rather surprisingly, 'Gregory's Legacy to his Daughters.'[43]

Dorothy did not say which brother had given her this last book, which was a dreary conduct manual advising young women in all the conventional proprieties. Surely it was not William! The young man who was so deeply impressed by his sister's spontaneous expressions of feeling could hardly have wished her to heed the solemn warning of Dr Gregory who maintained that a lack of reserve 'would make you less amiable as women.'[44]

There is, however, one piece of advice in this volume which William might have approved and which Dorothy may have taken to heart. By confiding in your brothers, Gregory told his daughters, 'you will receive every advantage which you can hope for from the friendship of men, without any of the inconveniences that attend such connections with our sex.'

In one way, Dorothy was very well prepared for her role as William's future friend and housekeeper. At some time before she reached her mid-twenties (perhaps from her Aunt Threlkeld) she learned the practical skills necessary to manage a household on a limited income. When she set up home with William she would confidently tackle laundry and the making of curtains; baking bread and broiling steaks; as well as preparing what was to become almost her 'signature dish' – giblet pie.

The very notion that his Aunt Jane might have acquired such knowledge seems to have embarrassed James Edward Austen-Leigh. He grudgingly admitted that, in the days of his aunt's youth, ladies 'took a personal part in the higher branches of cookery', but he hastened to assure his readers: 'I am sure that the ladies there [in Steventon rectory] had nothing to do with the mysteries of the stew-pot or the preserving pan.'[45]

So it seems likely that Jane's initiation into the 'mysteries' of the kitchen was limited to the theoretical understanding necessary for a supervisory role. Later in life, as her circumstances contracted, she would show signs of irritation at the increasing demands of domestic life on a small income. Dealing with the infuriating 'Joints of Mutton & doses of rhubarb'[46] that kept her from writing in 1816, cannot have been made easier by the attitude of such people as Austen-Leigh who found something to be apologised for – something shameful – in a daughter of the house knowing too much about what was going on in the domestic 'offices'.

Any hope that her biographer's stance was a later, Victorian affectation – an attitude which Jane would not have encountered, or been hurt by – is undermined by the fact that a character in one of her own novels can be heard voicing the same disdain for domestic work. When, in *Pride and Prejudice*, the tactless Mr Collins asks 'to which of his fair cousins, the excellence of [the dinner's] cookery was owing ... Mrs Bennet ... assured him with some asperity that they were very well able to keep a good cook, and that her daughters had nothing to do in the kitchen.'[47]

As Jane and Dorothy entered their teens they could not help but think about their futures – and, like other intelligent women of their time, such as Wakefield, Wollstonecraft and More, they would have come to recognise the particular difficulties faced by women like themselves: genteelly educated, but possessed of no fortune to supply either a dowry or a future support.

With both her parents dead, Dorothy was taken from her happy home in Halifax to her grandparents' grim house at Penrith, and there, separated from everyone she cared about, she sat down beside her small candle to write to her friend, Miss Pollard. Her future was not looking bright. The court case to recover money from her father's old employer, Lowther, was not progressing well. Unless the debt was repaid, Dorothy would have practically nothing.

She was not despondent, but at this trying time, when the insecurity of her position was painfully apparent, her optimism rested chiefly on her brothers' affection, and the kind of informal understanding which Mary Wollstonecraft deplored. 'I am sure,' she wrote, 'as long as my Brothers have a farthing in their pockets I shall never want.'[48]

In the rectory at Steventon, still surrounded by her own brothers and their friends, Jane's life seemed much more secure. However, she was already turning to the occupation of Literature and finding that it might indeed 'beguile many hours'.

PART TWO

FIVE

Love and Friendship

Much of Dorothy's unhappiness as she sat writing her first letter to Jane Pollard was caused by the ill-success of the family's efforts to recover the money Lord Lonsdale (formerly Sir James Lowther) owed them. Dorothy insisted that she was resigned to whatever might happen in this long-running court case – which, with its delays and complications, calls to mind Dickens' 'Jarndyce and Jarndyce' in *Bleak House* – but she frequently reverted to it in her letters and her comments show that she understood the implications of the dispute.

'Our fortunes will I fear be small,' she wrote in July 1787, 'as Lord Lonsdale will most likely only pay a very small part of his debt ... My Uncle Kit (who is our guardian) having said many disrespectful things of him ... I fear we shall feel through life the effects of his imprudence'.[1] She was aware that young men of little fortune such as her brothers – young men who must make their way in trade or professions such as law – could not afford to have enemies in high places.

At fifteen, Dorothy was not simply emotional and sentimental; she had a shrewd grasp of the way in which 'pseudo-gentry' families like hers were dependent for their prosperity on the 'real' landed gentry and aristocracy. In the same way, Jane Austen, in her early novels, would create characters like the servile Mr Collins (of *Pride and Prejudice*) and his benefactress Lady Catherine, demonstrating *her* understanding of how patronage worked in the world she and Dorothy shared.

Poor Dorothy! (To give her the title she liked to imagine.) Her natural optimism was put to a severe test during her time in Penrith. Evenings with her grandparents must have seemed endless. '[O]ur only conversation,' she complained in her letters, 'is about *work*, *work*, or what sort of a servant such a one's is, who are her parents, what places she lived in, why she left them, etc etc. What ...can be more uninteresting than such conversation as this? Yet I am obliged to set upon the occasion as *notable* a face as if I was delighted with it ...'

Dorothy's impatience with chit-chat about work (i.e. sewing) and the neighbours – topics which would have been staples in most gentry parlours – suggests that conversation in Halifax had been more stimulating.

Certain expressions of her grandmother's set the teenager's teeth on edge. That repeated 'notable' was so irritating!

'[N]otability is preached up to me every day,' she wrote – and, more than two hundred years later, we detect the suppressed irritation in her voice. '[S]uch an one is a very sedate clever, notable girl says my Gr[andmothe]r. My Gr[andmother]'s taste and mine so ill agree that there is not one person who is a favorite (*sic*) with her that I do not dislike ... I now see so many of those *useful* people, in their own imaginations, the *notables*, that I have quite an aversion to everyone that bears that character.'

The 1803 edition of Johnson's dictionary defines 'notable' as 'memorable, bustling, careful', with 'notableness' meaning 'diligence, contrivance'. This gives some idea of the practical, thrifty qualities which old Mrs Cookson valued in her neighbours and which, no doubt, she wished to foster in her granddaughter.

Dorothy's years at the Halifax schools had not prepared her for this kind of life. She felt herself better educated than her new acquaintances:

'I could bear their ignorance well enough,' she wrote of the Miss Custs, some young ladies her grandmother particularly admired, 'if they did not think so exceedingly well of themselves; for it cannot be expected that those who have not had the advantages of Education can know so much as those who have.'[2]

Perhaps this irritated adolescent made her feelings of superiority too evident and her grandmother believed her to be educated above her station. It may have been Mrs Cookson, rather than Aunt Threlkeld, who instilled in the young Dorothy those practical skills which would later prove so useful when she and William dedicated themselves, for the sake of poetry, to a simple rural life in Somerset and the Lake District.

Her grandmother evidently disapproved of Dorothy neglecting the all-important 'work' in order to read. For, though Dorothy told Jane Pollard that 'I am determined to re[ad] a great deal now both in French and English,' it had to be done by subterfuge. Her grandmother, she explained, 'sits in the shop in the afternoons' but it seems Dorothy was expected to sew for all the time she was absent. So she planned to work very hard for one hour, thus making time to read for an hour, and hoped that she would not be 'discovered'.[3]

Despite the dramatic complaints in her letters, Dorothy's life was not uniformly miserable. Most importantly, she was now able to see her brothers when they came to the Penrith house for school holidays. 'They are charming boys,' she enthused to Jane Pollard after they had left her in August 1787, and then made an interesting qualification: 'particularly the three youngest'. Even at this early age there seems to have been a little distance between Dorothy and her eldest brother, Richard, who was already articled as a clerk to his lawyer cousin and beginning to make his way in the world.

These three youngest – William, Christopher and John – were all 'just the boys I could wish them ...so affectionate and so kind to me as makes me love them more every day.'[4] William, the brother who was to become all-important to Dorothy, was about to go to university at Cambridge, funded by his uncle, Richard Wordsworth, and was hoping to be a lawyer 'if his health will permit'. He had not yet become the centre of Dorothy's attention and affection, but there was already a hint that he was regarded as troublesome by his guardians. 'My uncle Kit ...has taken a dislike to my brother W[illia]m'[5] Dorothy reported – a prejudice for which the loyal sister 'absolutely dislike[d]' Uncle Kit.[6]

The boys' presence animated Dorothy and, even in their absence, she had time for the little matters which concern most young women. The hair which in her pathetic picture of herself was 'hanging about my face' was to be curled before she could go to sleep. She described the style of it: 'curled about my face in light curls friz'd at the bottom and turned at the ends.' She was eager to know how her friend wore her hair, and fascinated to hear of her high-heeled shoes.

There were balls too, though these were not very satisfactory, for Dorothy encountered a problem which Jane Austen also lamented in her letters. 'There was [an assembly] on Wednesday evening,' Dorothy wrote in December 1787, 'where there were a number of Ladies but alas! Only six Gentlemen, so two Ladies are obliged to dance together.'[7]

Here was a young woman not quite so taken up with her own sorrows as to be indifferent to fashion, or not to regret missing a little physical contact with the opposite sex.

There were friends to walk with when she could escape from the tedious shirt-sewing, including Mary Hutchinson who was eventually to become her sister-in-law. And it was while she was living with her grandparents at Penrith that she formed a friendship with another woman who would influence her life, providing a more passive and conventional role-model than the energetic Miss Threlkeld.

A neighbour, Miss Dorothy Cowper, was attached to Dorothy Wordsworth's uncle, William Cookson (her grandparent's second son who was nine years younger than her guardian, Uncle Kit). By 1786, an engagement official enough to authorise the couple's correspondence had existed for six years.

It was a relationship which required a large degree of patience. 'I was calculating the other day,' wrote Miss Cowper to her beloved, '...how many months we have spent together during the course of six years, and found they amounted to nearly eleven – Ah my friend! who would have thought at the commencement of our attachment that we should at this day be under the necessity of conveying our sentiments to each other upon paper.'[8]

It says much for the tenacity and determination of this lady that the long-distance relationship had survived. Less than a sixth of their time spent together with only the slow, unreliable medium of letters to connect them!

This was not an unusual experience among those gentry classes who inherited little property and depended on trade and professions to make their fortunes. Sensible women such as *Persuasion*'s Mrs Croft and Mrs Musgrove might deplore long engagements, but they were frequently unavoidable. Like many other young men, William Cookson had his fortune to make before he could reward himself with a respectable marriage. He was at present away at Windsor working as a tutor to the young princes. The appointment sounds grand – and it certainly provided him with useful connections – but it was not a suitable basis for marriage and the couple must wait. Their best hope lay in his taking holy orders if he could secure, from a wealthy patron, one of those much sought-after good livings.

His gentle, loyal, long-suffering lady, holding tenaciously to her engagement through such a prolonged separation, appealed to the younger Dorothy much more than her acerbic grandmother or the self-important Miss Custs. 'I often go to Mr Cowper's,' she wrote, 'and like Miss D.C. better than ever. I wish my uncle and she would but get married.'[9]

William Cookson was a little at variance with his parents and his brother, Christopher, at this time. 'I have written to Kitt to tell him that if I thought I should meet with a welcome at Penrith I intend to visit it,' he told Miss Cowper in 1786.[10] This state of exile would almost certainly have endeared her younger uncle to Dorothy, but she probably had no idea how important a role he and 'Miss D.C.' were to play in her life.

Unlike Dorothy, Jane had her brothers always with her. Steventon rectory was full to overflowing with family and pupils during her childhood and early teens. In May 1786, when Jane was ten years old, cousin Eliza had to seize her chance for a visit there because, 'my uncle informs us that Midsummer and Christmas are the only seasons when his mansion is sufficiently at liberty to admit of his receiving his friends.'[11] These would have been the times when the pupils went home for their holidays and, at Christmas in particular, the family took the opportunity to fill the place with lively entertainment, the favourite being amateur theatricals. 'My uncle's barn is fitting up quite like a theatre,' reported another cousin, Philly Walter, at Christmas 1787, 'and all the young folks are to take their part.'[12]

These family productions, which took place nearly every winter from the time Jane was seven years old until she was thirteen, were organised by James, the eldest of the Austen sons. In the winter of 1787, the family was alive with acting.

Eliza was paying another long visit to Steventon and she wrote to Philly, pressing her to join them, but she warned her cousin that she could only come to the rectory if she would agree to take a part in the plays, 'for my Aunt Austen declares that "She has not room for any *idle young* people"'.

There was certainly parental support for the scheme, but Philly's remark that 'all the young folks' were participating in the performance of 1787, is the only evidence that Jane herself took part in any of these plays[13]. If she did, she may not have enjoyed the experience, and this might be one of the subjects on which she and her mother were not in accord.

In *Mansfield Park*, Jane would present a very negative picture of the kind of amateur theatricals which were fashionable during her lifetime. The novel portrays them as dangerous, introducing 'licence' among the actors, breaking down barriers which are necessary to keep young people safe from their own passions. This has made many commentators on the book uncomfortable. Acting seems to us such a harmless pastime and the notion of Jane Austen as a puritanical killjoy does not agree with what we see of her elsewhere in her work and letters.

Back in 1966 Tony Tanner (in his introduction to the Penguin edition of the novel) offered an explanation in which many people have found comfort ever since. 'We know that amateur home theatricals were popular in her family,' he wrote soothingly, 'and by no means disapproved of as they are in the book'. He insisted that the Mansfield theatricals should be seen merely symbolically.

There is, however, no reason to conflate the individual's opinion with that of her family – on this subject, or any other. The Austen family was large and loud, sprawling and exuberant. Jane's life was lived out within its affectionate, but restricting, boundaries. She would be buried simply as a member of it under an epitaph which described her only as a Christian and the 'youngest daughter of the late Revd George Austen, formerly Rector of Steventon', mentioning the family's affection and sense of loss, and omitting entirely any reference to the extraordinary achievements of her life.

Yet, Jane Austen was more than simply a part of her family, and the fact that theatricals took place around her when she was a child is no reason to suppose that her own opinion was at odds with the unequivocally disapproving authorial voice of *Mansfield Park*.[14] However many layers of symbolism it may have, the description of Mansfield's theatricals is fundamentally *real*. No modern-day member of an amateur dramatics company could deny that it lays bare the dark underbelly of his or her chosen hobby.

Jane Austen gives an unflinching insider's view of everything that is worst about amateur acting, from the concealed, but overwhelming, self-interest of Julia and Maria Bertram who each hope to have the best part in the play 'pressed on her by the rest'[15], to the self-indulgent over-rehearsal of favourite scenes by some actors, and the insidious, self-gratifying criticisms of others' performances – 'Mr Yates was in general thought to rant dreadfully ...Mr Yates was disappointed in Henry Crawford ...Tom Bertram spoke so quick he would be unintelligible ... Nobody would remember on which side they were to come in – nobody but the complainer would observe any directions'.[16]

There can be no doubt that this detailed understanding of what can happen among a group of people – even people who are fond of one another – when 'the inclination to act was awakened'[17] came from real observation. It would seem that brother James's annual productions in the Steventon barn were riven by jealousy, bad-feeling and unkindness. They were far from universally happy events, and his highly observant younger sister had reason to disapprove of them.

Jane's distrust of amateur theatricals, rather than being founded on prudery, seems to have arisen from a much more humane concern that the opportunity to perform released a tide of self-obsession which could temporarily render even kindly people insensitive to the feelings and needs of others. As Fanny Price, the quiet observer of Mansfield's theatre, notices, 'selfishness...more or less disguised, seemed to govern them all.'

Any doubts which the young Jane might have felt about the goings-on in the Steventon barn were unlikely to have been expressed, and there is no reason to suppose that, if they were, any attention would have been paid to the opinion of such an insignificant member of the family.[18] Any resistance to the expectation that *all* the young people would take their part in James's plays would have been dismissed impatiently by Jane's mother who regarded non-participation as idleness. But the young girl may have been supported – and, perhaps, influenced – by another woman who arrived in the neighbourhood when she was eight years old.

Anne Lefroy, wife of the Rector in the nearby parish of Ashe, was twenty-five years older than Jane Austen, but she would be a close friend until her untimely death in a riding accident in 1804. That Jane admired this dynamic woman is evident from the poem which she wrote on the anniversary of Mrs Lefroy's death, praising her 'Genius, Taste & Tenderness of Soul'. Other members of the family testified to the importance of this friend in young Jane's life. She was one of the older women who provided an example and a template for Jane as she grew and developed her own ideas: a model of what a woman could be and an example of what a woman could achieve in life.

Mrs Lefroy was a forceful, active, popular lady; she was elegant and well-read with a particular love of poetry, but, unlike Mrs Austen, she was no enthusiast for amateur dramatics. In 1787, when asked by her friend, Lady Bolton, to take part in a theatrical party at Hackwood Park, she declined firmly, tempering her refusal with a tactful, witty piece of verse in which she asked:

'Can I a Wife, a Mother, tread the Stage
Burn with false fire & glow with mimic rage...'[19]

Her objection is similar to the one Edmund Bertram would make in *Mansfield Park* when he protests that acting requires 'more exertion and confidence'[20] than a lady could be supposed to have. Perhaps it was a point of view which Jane internalised and recalled many years later.

Anne Lefroy presented an attractive role model for a bright young girl. Her letters conjure up a clever woman with strong, sometimes contradictory opinions. Conventionally pious, as befitted a clergyman's wife, she was sure, when a French invasion threatened in 1803, that God would favour the religious British. But she could also be superstitious and had an interest in some of the odder claims of quack medicine. She was fond of animals, and once rescued a donkey from neighbours, claiming: 'they really both starve & overwork him & I cannot bear he should be so ill used.' But she could describe the human suffering of naval life with equanimity. 'Charles Austen told me that Bob Simmons had behaved very well since his whipping which was uncommonly severe,' she wrote in March 1802, adding cheerfully, 'he had the honour to suffer in the presence of Prince Augustus who chose to stay upon deck and be a spectator of his punishment.'[21]

Anne Lefroy held a great deal of power and influence, not only in her own family, but also in the wider community. However, she did not break the rules of decorum by engaging in trade or stepping down the social ladder as Dorothy's Aunt Threlkeld had done. She gained her status rather by being the ideal gentlewoman. Although devoted to her family she was also very active in the parish. She worked among the poor, ran a Sunday and a weekday school and undertook the inoculation against smallpox of just about everyone she could get her hands on.

Mrs Lefroy had, in effect, created a fulfilling career for herself out of the activities which were deemed proper for a virtuous lady and it was all based on a philosophy of 'usefulness' such as Hannah More's. '[T]o be permitted to be of essential service to any fellow creature,' she wrote, 'appears to me the best blessing that can be bestowed upon us.'[22]

In her activity and energy Mrs Lefroy was not unlike Mrs Austen, yet her dislike of acting and her love of literature indicate a degree of refinement, a capacity for abstract thought, which the young Jane may have found lacking in her mother. The discovery of such a friend may also have increased the emotional distance between Jane and her mother. This friendship, by providing her with a point of reference outside her own family, would have helped Jane to develop her own opinions. *Love and Friendship* – and the other early stories which are now collected together as Jane Austen's *Juvenilia* – reveal a determination to think for herself which is remarkable in a teenage writer.

Jane Austen and Dorothy Wordsworth were alike in their close observation of their fellow men and women. Maybe it was a suspicion that she was being scrutinised and judged by her younger cousin which alienated Philly Walter when she first met her cousin Jane in July 1788. She much preferred fifteen-year-old Cassandra to twelve-year-old Jane. Cassandra, was 'very pretty,' but Jane was 'not at all pretty & very prim, unlike a girl of twelve.' A few days later, having spent more time in their company, she added: 'Jane is whimsical and affected.'[23]

Perhaps, up in the parlours of Penrith, the Miss Custs and the other 'notables' equally resented Dorothy's critical stare. Or perhaps they detected in her a 'sensibility too tremblingly alive' to her own afflictions, and distrusted it.

Jane was learning another very useful lesson at this time. In the way of teenagers, she was testing the limits in her early stories, finding out just what it was allowable to mention. Oddly enough, quite a lot was allowable as she read out her work to the assembled Austen family. In the very opening lines of *Love and Friendship*, there is a reference to bastardy – 'my mother was the natural daughter of a Scotch Peer by an Italian opera-girl' – and, later in the story, the subject recurs when two cousins calmly explain that, 'our mothers could neither of them exactly relate who were our fathers'. Confused identity was a device on which the plots of many novels turned, for it opened the possibilities of noble heritage and sudden legacies. Here, however, Jane adds her own twist, snatching away the glamour by making the probable fathers, 'Philip Jones a Bricklayer' and 'Gregory Staves a Staymaker'.

In *Love and Friendship* there are also sudden deaths with corpses 'weltering in their blood' and elsewhere in Jane's early tales there are horrible injuries in man-traps and serious alcoholism (in *Jack and Alice*) and even cannibalism (in *Henry and Eliza,* when the heroine's children become so hungry they gnaw off their mother's fingers). Yet none of it is shocking, because it is all completely ridiculous.

Humour, the young Jane was discovering, was a useful way of avoiding direct argument. It was very effective if one was surrounded by a large family and wished to make oneself heard without causing offence. Humour was both a weapon and a stalking-horse. Under its cover it was possible to say things which would have been unacceptable if they had been pronounced in a serious voice. Jane was learning the advantages of speaking obliquely, of *not* laying open the secrets of her heart, but instead expressing herself with caution and ambiguity.

SIX

Ladies of the Rectory

Dorothy's delivery from the dull house in Penrith came suddenly and from an unexpected quarter. In October 1788 William Cookson – now reconciled to his parents and brother – at last married Miss Cowper. And the sixteen-year-old Dorothy was invited to make her home with them.

She was delighted. As always at emotional moments, tears streamed from her eyes when the offer was made. She 'cried and laughed alternately' at the thought of living 'in the country and with such friends.'[1] It was as well she was pleased with the arrangement for, in truth, she probably had little choice. The family seems simply to have decided that it would be convenient.

The trio left Penrith immediately after the wedding and so were rid of the 'awful forms' of receiving congratulatory visits. Dorothy found this a great relief, seeming to share in that bashfulness which Jane Austen allows brides in *Emma*. Dorothy was playing a third party in this marriage; it was a role she would repeat fourteen years later when her brother married. This was the first of two honeymoon journeys that Dorothy, the life-long spinster, would take.

The country to which she now removed was very different from the mountainous terrain of Cumberland. Her uncle had been appointed rector of Forncett, a parish in Norfolk, about two hundred and fifty miles from Penrith. 'The country about us,' wrote Dorothy, 'though not romantic or picturesque is very pleasing, the surface is tolerably varied, and we have great plenty of wood but a sad want of water.'[2] There was a comfortable red brick rectory built in Queen Anne's day, a Norman church and 'farmers, who,' Dorothy reported cautiously, 'seem very decent kind of people.'[3]

William Cookson had hesitated long over his decision to take orders and feared that he would make 'but a very sorry divine'.[4] But he seems to have been a conscientious parson when he first took up his living. 'My uncle will I am sure do a great deal of good in the place',[5] wrote Dorothy soon after their arrival in the parish.

For the next six years Dorothy's closest companion would be Dorothy Cookson, and she would write, towards the end of their life together, 'My Aunt is without exception the best-tempered woman I know and is extremely kind to me.'[6] The influence of this calm, quiet, domestic woman is apparent in her life at this time. 'Am I not daring?'[7] exclaimed Dorothy on one occasion when she had — like Elizabeth Bennet in *Pride and Prejudice* — walked just three miles alone. Dorothy would later stride about on her own with great confidence but, during her Forncett years, she seems to have considered such independent behaviour to be almost as shocking as Miss Bingley and her sister do.

Like Anne Lefroy, Mrs Cookson was a woman who took seriously the role of rector's wife and seems to have been motivated by a wish to be 'useful'. By the beginning of 1789 Dorothy was able to report that she and her aunt had now 'visited most of the poor people in the parish'[8]. By the summer of that year Dorothy was running a school with nine scholars drawn from the labouring families in the area.

Presiding over small charity schools such as the one Dorothy describes, where lessons were delivered between church services on a Sunday and 'those who live near us come to me every Wednesday and Saturday evening'[9], was considered a very proper undertaking for a gentlewoman. (In *Emma* Mrs Elton is proud of her sister's involvement in such a project near Maple Grove[10].) The purpose of these schools was limited, however; they were not intended to extend the horizons of the poor too far. 'I only instruct them in reading and spelling,' Dorothy explained, 'and they get off prayers hymns and catechisms.' The children were taught to read in order to be able to read the Bible and other religious material. They were not taught to write; it was not necessary for them to express their own ideas.

Jane Austen's friend, Anne Lefroy, who was an enthusiastic educator of the poor, summed up the conservative ethos of these church schools. 'My great object,' she wrote, 'is to make them [her pupils] understand their duty & to convince them it is both their interest & their happiness to follow the precepts of that most excellent religion in the principles of which I endeavour to instruct them.'[11]

Apart from her charity work it was a quiet life at Forncett, but it suited Dorothy. 'I have two kind friends,' she told Jane Pollard, 'with whom I live in retirement … I have leisure to read; work; walk and do what I please.' It sounds like an idyll, but there was already a small cloud on the horizon, a threat to all that wonderful freedom. Dorothy continued: 'We look forward to the coming of our little relation with anxious expectation. I hope to be a good nurse …'[12]

Down in the Hampshire rectory, when Jane was a teenager, Mr Austen was more occupied with supplementing his own income by teaching the sons of gentlemen than doing 'a great deal of good' to his impoverished parishioners. Interest here focused less on charity and more on entertainment. For the boys there was hunting; for Jane and Cassandra there was dancing at the monthly assemblies in Basingstoke town hall and private parties among their neighbours such as the Dewars of Enham House (where Jane probably made her first entry into society in the Autumn of 1792).

Cousin Eliza wrote of Cassandra: 'I hear her sister & herself are two of the prettiest girls in England,'[13] and 'I hear they [Jane and Cassandra] are perfect Beauties & of course gain "hearts by dozens"'[14]. Though she does not say where she has heard either report, and it has to be admitted that Eliza tended to gush.

In the neighbouring parish of Ashe, Mrs Lefroy had probably already established her school for the poor by the time Jane was in her teens, but there is no evidence that Jane or Cassandra joined in her schemes, or were inspired to emulate her example in their own village.[15] Although she admired her older friend – and would, over the years, take a proper ladylike interest in charity – Jane did not seek meaning for her life in the kind of 'usefulness' that earned Anne Lefroy her power and status in the local community.

It is likely that both Jane and Dorothy, intelligent young women with their formal schooling behind them, were looking at this age for a sense of purpose in their lives. And this could be a tortuous quest for a genteel Georgian woman. Denied higher education and a career, unable even to travel on her own, what could a well-brought-up young lady do?

The journal of nineteen-year-old Hannah Gurney reveals how difficult it was for a Georgian girl to find something worthwhile to do with her life, something which she was good at and to which she could devote her energies. In 1806 Hannah described the many ambitions which she had already gone through as she tried out the limited options open to a woman confined to the home, and discovered, either that she had no talent for them, or the limitations of solitary study prevented her from making progress. She had begun with a love of riding and then had wished to be regarded as learned – 'and for this purpose how many books did I devour'. Next it was mathematics 'and many were the castles which I built upon the fame which I expected to acquire by discoveries in this science ... This passion retired at the entrance of that for painting ... how towering were my imaginations this way; what structures, with the help of fancy, hope and ambition, I built at this period: they have vanished, and three or four wearied pieces of canvass remain to be a sorry spectacle of the result of my folly. Ambition,' concluded Hannah, '...still hovers about me, marking me for its prey'.[16]

Jane Austen's ambitions were more focused than poor Miss Gurney's; or else she was more fortunate in discovering her true talent while she was still very young. From a remarkably early age she seems to have found satisfaction in writing. Here is one of those contradictions which mark the lives of Jane and Dorothy. While the 'sensitive' Dorothy turned outward to serve the community, the 'sensible' Jane retreated into an inward, imaginative life.

Jane was honing her skills and finding ways of expressing her ideas, while still using humour to attack anything of which she disapproved. Courtship and weddings (subjects which would be central to her mature work) were beginning to interest the observant young writer, for her brothers were beginning to find their marriage partners. This seems to have occasioned an error of judgement on Jane's part which was to have far-reaching consequences.

It was her custom to dedicate each piece of writing to a friend or relative and sometime around 1791 or 1792, she presented to her third brother, 'Edward Austen Esquire, The following unfinished Novel.'[17] The fragment, which is called *The Three Sisters*, records the selfish marital manoeuvring of three sisters, particularly the mercenary Mary whose happiness depends entirely on jewels, 'settlements' and new carriages. It is a witty piece which shows that Jane's style was maturing and it includes several nice observations of character which would later find their way into the published novels. For example Mr Watts, Mary's suitor, resembles Mr Woodhouse of *Emma* insofar as 'what he hates himself he has no idea of any other person's liking', and the ambitious Mary displays Lydia Bennet's enthusiasm for being married before her sisters and chaperoning them to balls. The style of humour would have been acceptable in the rectory parlour, but Jane's dedication was tactless.

Because 'Edward Austen Esquire' was not quite a part of the Steventon family any longer. He was one of those displaced children whose stories illustrate the hard, pragmatic side of Georgian family life. He was a good-looking, easy-going young man with moderate intellectual powers and, in worldly terms, he was certainly the lucky brother in Jane's family. As a boy of twelve he had attracted the attention of his father's distant cousins, the very wealthy Catherine and Thomas Knight who owned estates at Godmersham and Chawton. They liked the lad so much they took him with them on their honeymoon tour and he began to spend a great deal of time with them. By 1783 – when he was sixteen – his parents had allowed the couple to adopt him as their heir, and given him up entirely to these wealthy relations. His home was now with the Knights at Godmersham Park in Kent – though, unlike poor Dorothy, he seems to have maintained a reasonable level of contact with the family of his birth.

This passing of a child from one family to another was not an unusual arrangement in an age when getting a son and heir was considered to be of all-consuming importance, but only four years into a marriage does seem rather early to despair of producing a child. There is perhaps a part of this tale which will never be properly understood now, but Mrs Knight never did bear a baby to oust Edward.

Distanced from the rest of his family by wealth, luxury and great expectations, Edward's relationship with his siblings must have been a delicate one, and he was not a good choice of dedicatee for a story about ambition and the unprincipled pursuit of riches. Nor, as a young man who had just married, was he the best recipient of a tale about callous marital manoeuvring. As the husband of a woman who was one of three sisters who had all just formed advantageous alliances, he was particularly badly placed to appreciate the acerbic humour of *The Three Sisters*.

Elizabeth Bridges was only eighteen years old when she married Edward Austen in December 1791, and she came from a stratum of society decidedly above the Steventon Austens. She had been educated at one of the most exclusive, fashionable girls' boarding schools in London – just the kind of establishment Jane would ridicule in her novels. The priorities of its curriculum are best summed up by the tradition that there was kept, propped up in a back room, an old coach, so that the young ladies might receive instruction in the art of 'getting in and out of it in a modest and elegant manner'.[18]

The product of this education, the modest and elegant Mrs Edward Austen, does not seem to have been a great appreciator of wit, and she never quite warmed to her younger sister-in-law. 'A little talent went a long way with the ...Bridgeses of that period;' commented Jane's niece, Anna Lefroy, '& *much* must have gone a long way too far.' Anna recalled that Elizabeth was never 'really fond of' Jane.

The dedication of *The Three Sisters* was almost certainly a blunder and a bad beginning to the relationship between the two women. The coincidence of the title with the three recently married Bridges sisters might – or might not – have been unintentional, but it cannot have gone unnoticed.

One can imagine the gently reared, proper Elizabeth shaking her head in bemusement over the manuscript, wondering at Mary's burning desire to possess a coach of 'blue spotted with silver' and her ridiculous vacillations over whether to accept the rich, but unappealing, Mr Watts: 'I won't have him I declare. He said he should come again tomorrow & take my final answer, so I believe I must get him while I can. I know the Duttons will envy me …' Elizabeth may well have formed a poor opinion of the girl who had presented this offering almost as a wedding gift.

The dynamics of every family shift as younger members marry and strangers are drawn into the domestic circle. In the eighteenth century, when family ties and connections were often crucial to material as well as emotional well-being, this would have been a particularly difficult transition to negotiate, but it seems to have been something for which Jane was not quite prepared.

Dorothy managed much better. Her open-hearted eagerness made her very ready to love and accept new friends and family members, while Jane's more cautious approach to life could make her reluctant to form new connections. There is evident in Jane's letters a tendency to draw back from people. 'I do not like the Miss Blackstones;' she wrote in 1799, 'indeed I was always determined not to like them, so there is the less merit in it.'[19]

At times she seems to have found pleasant company positively threatening. 'I spent Friday evening with the Mapletons,' she wrote, '& was obliged to submit to being pleased inspite of my inclination …'[20] But she would not allow any intimacy to develop between herself and these pleasing young women. Two weeks later she reported: 'I do not see the Miss Mapletons very often, but just as often as I like; We are always very glad to meet, & I do not wish to wear out our satisfaction.'[21]

This drawing back from acquaintances may have produced an unappealing coldness in Jane's manner; but there was a kind of safety in it. Dorothy's willingness to love people would have been more attractive, but it was an approach to life which made her very vulnerable after her move to Norfolk.

The values and beliefs of the people with whom Dorothy now shared a home were far removed from those of the folk she had grown to love in Halifax. It is only necessary to put that description of her school's Bible-reading, prayers and catechisms alongside the Northgate End Chapel's ideal of education for the poor – with its willingness to include controversial books in its library and to 'try all things' – to realise that Dorothy, isolated in an Anglican rectory, found herself in an alien world. Mrs Dorothy Cookson was a kind and gentle companion, but she represented a very different model of how a woman should behave than the assured and energetic Miss Threlkeld. There is some evidence of conflict at this time; perhaps a battle was being waged for the young Dorothy's soul.

The move to Forncett was marked by a disruption in Dorothy's letter writing. 'I believe nearly half a year has elapsed since I last wrote to you,' she wrote to Jane Pollard on 7th December 1788[22]. It was the first letter she had sent to her friend since her arrival in Norfolk and, after another letter sent later that month, there are no letters to Miss Pollard surviving until one written, more than a year later, on 25th January 1790. Dorothy then apologised abjectly for her 'apparently unfriendly behaviour'[23].

It was not only Jane Pollard that she had been neglecting. It seems she had also incurred her Aunt Threlkeld's displeasure. 'I fear she is very angry with me as indeed she has great reason,' Dorothy admitted. She may just have been as dilatory in writing to her aunt as she had been in writing to her friend, or she may have written something that had caused offence.

An unreserved contact with her dissenting friends in Halifax may have been impossible and the situation probably became more difficult in the winter of 1789 when Dorothy came under the influence of the extremely religious, politically conservative William Wilberforce. He was an old university friend of her uncle and he spent several weeks at Forncett during the time that Dorothy was at variance with her relations.

William Wilberforce is best remembered now as a campaigner

against the slave trade; and he certainly won Dorothy over to that cause. 'I hope you were an *immediate* abolitionist ...' she wrote to Miss Pollard.[24] He was also an extremely charismatic man. Madame de Staël said he, 'is the best converser I have met with in this country. I have always heard that he was the most religious, but I now find that he is the wittiest man in England.'[25]

He would have made quite an impact in a quiet country rectory and Dorothy may have fallen under his spell. Her account of him when she *did* write to Miss Pollard aroused the suspicions of her friend; by April she was teasing Dorothy about being in love with the man.

Wilberforce was an evangelical. His brand of Christianity was nothing like the easy-going, unquestioning religion which George Austen preached at Steventon, but it was equally far removed from John Ralph's earnest, open-minded search for truth. The message of the evangelicals was stark: everyone, they believed, was contaminated by Original Sin and must undergo a conversion experience. 'All men are originally of one character,' wrote John Witherspoon in his *Practical Treatise on Regeneration,* 'unfit for the kingdom of God ...and, unless a change do pass upon them hereafter, they must be for ever excluded.'[26]

Dorothy now found herself plunged deep into this belief, which may have been shared by her uncle and aunt. She was grateful for the home she had been given; her relations and their visitor deserved her respect; and she would have found the kind of honest discussion she had come to value in Halifax impossible.[27]

When Mr Wilberforce left Norfolk he made a gift of books to Dorothy. 'I am at present reading ...a little Treatise on Re-generation; which with Mrs Trimmer's *Oeconomy of Charity* Mr Wilberforce gave me,'[28] she wrote in April 1790.

The treatise was Witherspoon's and its teaching was a denial of the values of all the people in Halifax whom Dorothy loved. She may well have felt confused and found it easier not to correspond with her old friends. The very essence of evangelicalism is to make religious faith immediate and emotional. Believing as they do that the unsaved soul is destined for eternal torment, evangelicals – if they have any compassion at all – cannot help but have a deep emotional investment in their efforts to convert others. It was a matter of *feeling*; Dorothy would have been attacked at her weakest point.

Her plan to 'read the New Testament with Doddridge's exposition,' also suggests Wilberforce's influence. It was to the persuasions of the writer and preacher Philip Doddridge that William Wilberforce attributed his own conversion.

It seems Dorothy was, at this time, under pressure to confess to being *converted*. Her letters reveal nothing at all about her own thoughts on the subject, and this is the first time that it becomes clear that Dorothy *could* be reticent when she must; sometimes she just could not 'lay open the secrets of my heart' as it would be too painful for the people she loved.

The painful effect of suppressing her feelings is also hinted at. In December 1791 she wrote: 'I have, during the whole of this Summer … been less able to support any Fatigue and been more troubled with Headache than I ever remember to have been.'[29] It was the beginning of an account of intermittent illness which would run like a dark thread through the rest of her life. And, as she grew older and tried to analyse the causes of her diseases, Dorothy would acknowledge that mental strain – 'any thing that exercised my thoughts or feelings'[30] – played a part in making her ill.

It may have been an exercising of her thoughts and feelings, her conflict over the uncompromising faith in which she was now immersed, that was weakening Dorothy at the age of eighteen.

She took refuge in the more practical suggestions of the other book she had been given – Sarah Trimmer's *The Oeconomy of Charity*. 'The time is arrived,' wrote Mrs Trimmer, 'when all who have a true regard to God and Religion, should make an open profession of their faith, and endeavour to adorn it by their practice.'[31] Religion expressed in good works – *being useful* – was a philosophy Dorothy could embrace wholeheartedly. And she gained a sense of achievement by teaching her Sunday school – proudly telling Jane Pollard that one pupil who 'did not know a letter when she came to me' was now able to 'read exceedingly well.'[32]

Although she was initially enthusiastic about charity work,

Mrs Cookson seems to have lacked the energy and determination of Anne Lefroy or Elizabeth Threlkeld. Her home and growing family were soon absorbing all her attention. After the birth of her aunt's first child Dorothy's school was closed for fear that the children in it might infect the baby with the small-pox.

Aunt Cookson seems to have fallen into that very inconvenient routine which Mrs Jennings predicts for Edward Ferrars' wife in *Sense and Sensibility*: 'Then they will have a child every year'[33]. It must have been a familiar pattern, a severe drain on material resources as well as women's health. ('Lord help 'em, how poor they will be' adds Mrs Jennings.) 'We expect that my Aunt will present us with another young one early in the Spring. This is rather sooner than we could have wished', Dorothy announced unenthusiastically in December 1791.[34] However it was something which must be borne with by wives – and also by the unmarried female relatives who shared their homes.

Gone were the days when Dorothy had 'leisure to read; work; walk and do what I please'. By May 1792 she was forced to admit that a longed-for visit to her friends in Halifax was impossible because 'The birth of another little Cousin has made me more necessary than ever to my Aunt ...'[35]

The apparently kindly offer of a home – the chance of an escape from her grandparents – which had so delighted Dorothy, carried a price. In 1792 she was just twenty and unmarried, but already domesticity was closing about her like a trap. She loved the people she lived with, but, despite all her hard work, she had no income of her own. Like a child, she was provided with a home and her keep. But, when she asked her Uncle Cookson for money, he simply referred her to her guardians.

How could a woman escape such dependence?

SEVEN

A Happy Command of Language

By June 1791 Dorothy had begun to make long-term plans. She hoped that a satisfactory outcome to the Lowther case would give her something to live on and she still looked forward to a time when 'my brothers are able to assist me'; but, in the meantime, she resolutely declared to Miss Pollard, 'I am not destitute of the means of supporting myself'.

What means of supporting herself Dorothy meant to employ is unclear, but she certainly meant, once she was twenty-one, to take some independent action. She would, at least, make her visit to Halifax – 'though I would do nothing inconsistent with the duty I owe my Uncle and Aunt, yet I shall then be able to do it of myself without all the difficulty which I should have before my coming of age.'[1]

Dorothy's early loss of her parents, the financial uncertainty which the long court case against Lowther engendered, and her strained relationship with her guardians, had made her keenly aware of her own insecurity. In her plans for the future, she was already rejecting the idea of a permanent residence with her uncle and aunt, though that was what her family expected her to submit to. Much as she loved her aunt Cookson she was not prepared to be absorbed with her into a life of domesticity and child-care.

Jane Austen has left behind no such plans for her future and it is easy to assume that she made none. After all, her parents were still alive and she was living in a comfortable family home, but in fact,

Jane's future promised little more certainty that Dorothy's. By the time she reached her teenage years, it would have been evident to Jane that all the resources of the family were being channelled into the futures of her brothers. There was to be no provision for the girls in their father's will and, by this time, it was probably clear to her that no money was being laid aside to provide either marriage portions for her and Cassandra, or an income to support them as spinsters.

What did her future hold: a pragmatic marriage such as that of Charlotte Lucas in *Pride and Prejudice*? A happy – but unlikely – love match such as Elizabeth Bennet's? Or was hers to be the fate which Mary Wollstonecraft so deplored: dependence upon the arbitrary bounty of brothers? As she reached the end of her teens Jane was putting more and more time and energy into writing, developing her distinctive voice and – though she was still employing her old stalking horse, humour – handling more serious themes. Perhaps she was motivated entirely by the love of writing for its own sake; but perhaps she too was considering how she might escape a life of complete dependence.

Interestingly, the question of how a single woman might act independently was one which she set about exploring with enthusiasm. The theoretical answer at which she arrived was much more radical that Dorothy's. It was rather frightening. She created a remarkable character: Lady Susan, a woman who refuses to be bound by any of the conventions that Georgian society imposed on women. Lady Susan is a moral monster – but she is also a gloriously autonomous woman.

As Jane reached her late teens Steventon Rectory was becoming less crowded. Her brothers were off to university, or to pursue careers in the Navy. Mr Austen – now past sixty – was beginning to take life more easily and there were fewer pupils in the house. So Jane and Cassandra (though they would share a bedroom for the rest of their lives) were now given a small 'dressing room'; in effect, a sitting room of their own. This private space seems to have freed Jane's mind and helped her to write a story such as she had never written before – and would never write again.

Lady Susan – written when Jane was about eighteen or nineteen –

is an investigation into just what might be achieved if a woman set her face against the demands, not only of decorum, but also of family duty. The title character is, of course, the villain of the tale, but she is so vibrant, and the good characters are so faintly drawn, that there can be no doubt where the interest – if not the approval – of the young author lay. For this first attempt at a complete novel, Jane chose to put at the centre of her story, not a young girl like herself, but a widow of thirty-five.

Lady Susan, escaping the fall-out of a little bit of pleasant adultery with a friend's husband, imposes herself on the tranquil family of her late husband's brother, where she deliberately wins the affections of her sister-in-law's brother, not from any serious designs, but merely to cause trouble. She is a schemer and a bad mother who attempts to marry her daughter to a rich fool while pursuing any affair or flirtation which will further her own gratification. It was not a story which Jane Austen ever chose to work up for publication, but the tale is full of themes to which she would return, and Lady Susan shares some important characteristics with the more subtly drawn Mary Crawford of *Mansfield Park*. They are both selfish, mercenary and contemptuous of romantic love. But the most striking resemblance between Miss Crawford and Lady Susan is that – despite their determination to live according to their own rules – in outward appearances they both conform perfectly to the Georgian ideal of womanhood. As Edmund Bertram notes with approval, there is 'nothing sharp, or loud, or coarse,' in Mary Crawford's manner, 'She is perfectly feminine'[2] and even Lady Susan's most determined critic is forced to admit: 'Her countenance is absolutely sweet, and her voice and manner winningly mild'.

Writing away in the relative peace of the new dressing room with its ' …common looking carpet with [a] chocolate ground … scanty furniture and cheaply papered walls'[3], Jane was still exploring the limitations of her world, pushing experimentally at its boundaries. She seems already to have understood the dangers of a loud or a coarse voice. She suspected that more might be achieved by assuming a voice and a manner that were 'winningly mild', and so avoiding controversy.

Jane knew that such feminine charms – preferably allied to a pretty face and figure – represented one way in which an ambitious woman might make her way in the world. Unlike Dorothy, she had, in her family circle, women who had used their looks and their wits to very good effect: glamorous figures who would intrigue any girl as she considered her own possible futures. Aunt Philadelphia and cousin Eliza were frequent visitors to Steventon rectory. Jane would have known them and their histories well and those histories are fascinating.

As a young woman, Mr Austen's sister, Philadelphia, had certainly been very attractive, but it is impossible to be sure of the exact use to which she put her personal charms. The simple facts of the matter are as follows: Philadelphia escaped from a life of millinery, sailed to Madras and in 1753 married Tysoe Saul Hancock, a British surgeon who had various business interests. They had no children for seven years. In 1759 they moved to Calcutta and there became extremely friendly with the rich and powerful Warren Hastings, who became a widower soon after their arrival in Calcutta. Hastings was then working for the East India Company but he would go on to become Governor-General of Bengal. In 1761 Philadelphia bore a daughter, Eliza. She had no more children. Warren Hastings was godfather to Eliza, took a great deal of interest in her and, in 1772, under conditions of extreme secrecy, he offered to settle £5,000 on her. In 1775 the sum was increased to £10,000 and instead of being paid directly to Eliza it was settled on Philadelphia herself, to provide an income for her life – the capital passing to Eliza on her mother's death.

It is difficult to know now quite what to make of these facts; but the gossip-loving British community in India knew exactly what conclusion to draw from its own observations. 'In no circumstances whatever keep company with Mrs Hancock,' Lord Clive warned his wife, 'for it is beyond a doubt that she abandoned herself to Mr Hastings.'[4]

If the rumours were true, and Eliza was, in fact, Hastings' child, the strangest part of the whole business was Mr Hancock's unswerving devotion to his wife and 'daughter'. But his abject devotion is extreme in any case. His behaviour and his letters suggest that he was in thrall to his pretty wife. Their relationship is a fascinating example of how – despite all legal inequalities and social discrimination – a woman could hold power in a relationship. Though there is no evidence that Aunt Philadelphia was ever as ruthless as Lady Susan, she certainly shared with Jane's fictional creation the ability to enslave men.

By 1765 Philadelphia, Tysoe Saul and little Eliza had returned from India and settled in London, hoping that the fortune Mr Hancock had made in India would keep them in comfort for the rest of their lives. However, by 1768 it was evident that it would not. In their three years and six months in England they had spent £5,559 – twice what they could afford.

There does not seem to have been any question of Philadelphia's lifestyle being made more economical; no suggestion of giving up the expensive London house and living economically in the country. Instead her husband must return to India and earn enough money to support her and Eliza in comfort. He hoped that a three years' separation would be sufficient to restore their fortunes, but it was not, despite his own desperate economies in India: 'I have confined my diet to one dish a day,' he told his wife, 'and that generally Salt Fish or Curry & Rice.'[5]

Meanwhile, Philadelphia lived in the most expensive districts of London and kept her carriage, Eliza had lessons in music and her own riding horse. Sometimes Hancock was exasperated by his wife's irresponsible replies to his letters and her unsuitable gifts – she bombarded him with hand-embroidered waistcoats which he refused to wear and threatened to return. And sometimes he wished that she was a better manager: 'Oh Philla, had a very few of those hours which were formerly spent in dissipations been employed in acquiring the necessary and most useful knowledge of Accounts, happy would it have been for us both.'[6] But he was mortified by the very idea of his lovely wife making real economies: 'some of your economical expressions hurt me much,' he wrote in December 1774.[7]

He struggled on, trying to make money in a country which he had come to hate, becoming more ill, depressed and abject, living in a state of servitude to the woman he no longer had any hope of returning to: 'While I crawl upon the face of the Earth, I will do my utmost to make you easy ...'[8] When Hastings' gift was finally made, it was a relief for Hancock to give up the struggle. 'As you and the child are now provided for,' he wrote on 25th March 1775, 'I may venture to tell you that I am not well enough to write a long letter ...'[9] He died – probably exhausted – eight months later.

Clergyman though he was, Mr Austen was unabashed by his sister's dubious reputation, and he was not above using the connection with the influential Warren Hastings to further the promotion prospects of his sons. The example which Philadelphia set – of a woman claiming a comfortable provision as a right based on her personal attractions – would not have gone unnoticed by her observant niece.

Eliza, the product of this odd, triangular alliance, was fourteen years older than Jane, a young woman when her cousin was a child. A great deal of money had been expended on Eliza's education. In his letters Mr Hancock insisted that she should learn the ladylike accomplishments of French and drawing as well as music and riding – though he was also particularly anxious that she should acquire the practical skills of accounting and arithmetic which her mother so disastrously lacked. (However, judging from his increasingly desperate pleas, it seems unlikely that Philadelphia ever heeded his wishes on this subject.)

After Hancock's death, Philadelphia took her daughter to the continent and settled in Paris in 1779. Had he known of the move, poor Tysoe Saul would probably not have approved. Back in 1774 he had grudgingly agreed that the child should have a French companion as this was the 'shortest' method of teaching her the language, but had insisted that the arrangement should not continue after 'the Child may be old enough to imbibe the Spirit of Intrigue, without which no French Woman ever yet existed.'[10]

Now the seventeen-year-old Eliza was surrounded by dangerous French companions, and perhaps she did imbibe a little Spirit of Intrigue. Somehow, she and her mother managed to make their way into the most aristocratic and fashionable circles in Paris. Neither their income of about £600 a year, nor their Austen and

Hancock connections could have gained them their entrée into this level of society; so it is likely that they made the most of their connection with the 'fameux lord Hastings, gouverneur de l'Inde.'[11]

There is something of the air of adventuring about Philadelphia and Eliza's life in France, but this was a time of general extravagance, as the French monarchy lived out its last few decadent years, and Mrs Hancock and her daughter were not the only ones who were being less than truthful about their circumstances. In 1781 Eliza married a dashing Captain in the French army whom she believed to be the Comte de Feuillide. He had no real claim to the title and at some point Eliza must have discovered this. At some point too he would have been disappointed to find that his mother-in-law was not the wealthy woman she appeared to be.

'There is not one in a hundred who is not taken in when they marry...' observes Mary Crawford in *Mansfield Park*, 'it is of all transactions, the one in which people expect most from others, and are least honest themselves.'[12]

Eliza de Feuillide shared many of Mary Crawford's opinions, including an unromantic approach to marriage. Her marriage, Eliza explained, 'was a step I took much less from my own judgment than that of those whose councils & opinions I am the most bound to follow...'[13] All the love was on the side of her husband: 'It is too little to say he loves, since he literally adores me,' she reported happily.

Here was a woman whose personal assets, charm and confidence bought her – for a while – a brilliant lifestyle. Eliza's letters from France are full of descriptions of visits to Versailles, royal finery – all 'gauze, feathers, ribbon and diamonds' – fine equipages with 'running footmen' and 'open Clashes drawn by six horses'.

In 1786 (when Jane Austen was ten years old) this glamorous cousin returned to England to bear her first child, leaving her husband on his estates in the south of France. Eliza was kind-hearted and extremely fond of Jane. All in all, she must have made a deep impression on her younger cousin.

Growing up involves considering the examples set by older people, and trying out manners and ways of behaving. But experiments are much safer when they are confined to paper, a method of exploration which Jane had already discovered. Now, as she worked away in the luxury of her dressing-room, she was pushing her investigations in new directions, abandoning the absurd and coming closer to real life. She was beginning to deal with the questions which most interested her.

That highly developed moral sense which enabled her to detect self-interest in ostentatious displays of sensibility and danger in the freedoms of amateur dramatics must have prevented Jane from being entirely uncritical of her cousin, and she probably disapproved her rejection of romantic love. All six of Jane Austen's complete novels record the triumph of love over more worldly marital schemes, and when, in *Mansfield Park*, Mary Crawford describes how a friend considered a marriage proposal in a remarkably similar way to Eliza, asking 'the advice of everyone connected with her, whose opinion was worth having'[14], we are left in no doubt that the friend's final acceptance of the gentleman resulted in a miserable marriage.

For the same reasons, she cannot have been entirely in sympathy with Lady Susan as she wrote. But, besides giving her monstrous creation all the personal charms necessary to entrap a man, Jane bestowed on her one more very significant characteristic. Her ladyship has, 'a happy command of language, which is too often used…to make black appear white.'[15]

Though she had no desire to make black appear white, Jane cannot have been unaware by this time that she herself possessed that most potent of weapons: a very *happy command of language*. She was still experimenting with how it might be used, but it offered a way of responding to the challenges and tensions of a woman's life, a way, perhaps, of creating an independent future.

EIGHT

Considering the Future

In October 1792 Eliza de Feuillide described Cassandra and Jane as 'both very much grown ([Jane] is now taller than myself) and greatly improved as well in manners as in person ... They are I think equally sensible, and both so to a degree seldom met with'.[1]

At nearly seventeen Jane would have reached her full height and, according to her brother Henry, 'Her stature was that of true elegance. It could not have been increased without exceeding the middle height.'[2]

This 'middle height' was highly prized in contemporary assessments of female figures, and it was a quality Jane herself bestowed on the very elegant Miss Fairfax in *Emma,* whose 'height was pretty, just such as almost everybody would think tall, and nobody could think very tall'.[3]

Henry continued his description of his sister: 'Her features were separately good. Their assemblage produced an unrivalled expression of that cheerfulness, sensibility, and benevolence, which were her real characteristics.' It is interesting that Henry separates out her features and that, although he describes those features as good in this unconnected way, his final assessment does not actually include prettiness. In fact there was a difference of opinion about Jane's physical beauty. Eliza insisted that she was pretty. But her niece Anna, after listing those good features in more detail – a 'clear and healthy' complexion, and 'fine naturally curling hair, neither light nor dark; the bright hazel eyes to match, & the rather small but well-shaped nose' – ends on a slightly puzzled note, unable to understand how, 'with all these advantages she could yet fail of being a decidedly handsome woman.'[4]

Perhaps there was something in Jane's air which prevented all those good features adding up to unequivocal beauty. Mary Russell Mitford recalled her mother describing Jane as 'the prettiest, silliest, most affected, husband-hunting butterfly she ever remembers'. Laura Boyle has pointed out that, at the time of Mrs Mitford being a neighbour of the Austens, Jane was only in her early teens, so rather young to be supposed a husband-hunter.[5] It is *possible* that some of the silliness which Mrs Mitford observed at that time arose from a naïve attempt of the young girl to emulate the airs of her glamorous cousin, Eliza, but it is interesting that the accusation of affectation should appear again.

The pattern that emerges in the comments made about Jane Austen suggests that she was not a young woman whose good qualities were immediately appreciated. Those who knew her best enjoyed her company, while new acquaintances, like Philly Walter and Mrs Mitford, found her difficult to understand. There was, perhaps, something rather off-putting in her manners, something which suggested artificiality. Within her family she was remembered for her 'sunniness of temper' and for demonstrating her feelings more than the very cautious Cassandra, but her letters suggest that those feelings were not very directly expressed. Nearly every sentence has a little twist of sarcasm or satire, cynicism or exaggeration. 'I am very much flattered by your commendation of my last Letter' she told Cassandra in January 1796, 'for I write only for Fame.' On discovering that her brother Charles had faithfully carried out a commission with which she had entrusted him but which she had subsequently discovered she could not afford, she declared, 'What a good-for-nothing fellow Charles is to bespeak the stockings ...'[6]

This is a kind of half-serious address which is easily accepted within a family; but to an outsider some of her remarks could seem abrasive – or worse. 'I am sorry for the Beaches' loss of their little girl,' she wrote very properly to Cassandra in 1796 – but there then followed the inevitable twist: 'especially as it is the one most like me'.[7] That – taken at face value – is both callous and self-centred. A shield of humour has its uses in a large family, but it can keep acquaintances at a distance and prevent them from ever becoming friends.

If Jane was husband-hunting, there was no shortage of opportunities for meeting young men. 'There has been a Club Ball at Basingstoke & a private one in the neighbourhood, both of which my cousins say were very agreeable,'[8] reported Eliza. And Jane's social circle was expanded by visits to Kent to stay with Edward and his wife and their rapidly growing family.

Marriage was in the air at Steventon. In 1792 or 1793 Cassandra had become engaged to her father's ex-pupil, Tom Fowle, who was now a clergyman; though it seemed as if it would be a long engagement because the living he had obtained through his wealthy relative, Lord Craven, was not large enough to support a wife. Jane's brothers James and Edward were both now married and, though Jane might not have been hunting a husband in a worldly or mercenary way, her mind was occupied with courtship and marriage.

She had now embarked on the novels that today's readers know and love so well. It was when she was just nineteen that she wrote *Elinor and Marianne*, the epistolary novel which would evolve into *Sense and Sensibility*. No manuscript of the early version survives so it is not possible to know how much the story changed over the years, but even at this stage it was almost certainly a tale of two sisters negotiating their way to happy marriages, and of two very different approaches to romantic attachment – one a headlong fall into the unknown and one a circumspect assessment of the character of a man closely connected with the family, a steady journey through the stages of regard and esteem to love. In the story, of course, it is the latter approach – Elinor's attachment to Edward Ferrars, rather than Marianne's passionate love for Willoughby – which wins out. The dénouement is a triumph of reason over impulse.

However, when – soon after completing the first version of *Elinor and Marianne* – Jane fell in love herself, she does not seem to have gone about the business in a cool rational manner at all.

She did not come to love an old and trusted companion, though there were plenty of those to choose from. Instead she plunged headlong into love with a man she scarcely knew, thereby displaying the sensibility of a Marianne rather than the sense of an Elinor.

'[I]f ever I do form an attachment it shall not long be a secret from you,' wrote Dorothy to her confidante Jane Pollard in April 1790, but the subject of romance made her uncomfortable. Miss Pollard had been teasing her friend about being in love with William Wilberforce, and Dorothy had no shield of humour to hide behind. 'Mr W,' she wrote earnestly, 'would, were he ever to marry, look for a Lady possessed of many more accomplishments than I can boast'.

Her response, even to common raillery, was a denigration of her own merits. She also wrote that – '[N]o man I have seen has appeared to regard me with any degree of partiality, nor has any one gained my affections'[9]. But the convention of the day was that 'no young lady can be justified in falling in love before the gentleman's love is declared'[10], and maybe she had fallen a little in love with Wilberforce.

Six months later when her friend wrote again about love and attachments, Dorothy begged her not to 'say anything more to me upon the subject'[11]. Maybe she had been attracted to Wilberforce and did not wish to be reminded that he had been more interested in her immortal soul than her personal charms, for she did not abide by her own embargo. In a postscript to a letter written the following March she joked about a Mr Edward Swain: 'Ought *I* to *rejoice* at his marriage, for do I know what might have been my chance for him?'[12]

By the time she reached the end of her teens, Dorothy was – like nearly every other girl of her age – interested in love and eager to hear about weddings. She pressed Miss Pollard to tell her details of the wedding of her Aunt Threlkeld who, about this time, married (at the age of 45) a pleasant widower.

It is hard to know whether Dorothy's assessment of her own attractions was sound. Samuel Taylor Coleridge, who met her just a few years later, would remark, 'if you expected to find a pretty woman, you would think her ordinary – if you expected to find an ordinary woman, you would think her pretty!'[13] which suggests a pleasant, though not a striking, appearance. She had now arrived at the age when her looks – and how men reacted to them – would have been a matter of anxiety. With no fortune and few respectable careers other than marriage open to her, much of a woman's future depended on her appearance and attractiveness, her manner, her ability to make a good impression. These were her qualifications, and the report that other people made of her was the CV on which her career was founded.

The calculations of women's attractions which are constantly being made in Jane Austen's fiction would have been a com-monplace of real life at the time and it is surprising, when those calculations are looked at closely, how intrusive and deeply unpleasant they are. The beauty of the new bride, Mrs Elton, is to be calibrated on a sliding scale by the inhabitants of Highbury: 'it must be left for the visits in form ... to settle whether she were very pretty indeed, or only rather pretty, or not pretty at all.'[14] Fanny Price's looks are to be jealously evaluated by dozens of disappointed women when they hear that she has won the heart of the eligible Henry Crawford. She is told that 'your eyes, and your teeth, and how you do your hair,'[15] will all be enquired into.

Jane herself sometimes subjected other women to this kind of scrutiny. Reporting to Cassandra on her brother Henry's new fiancée in 1796, she wrote: 'pray be careful not to expect too much Beauty ...'[16] She became even more harsh with age: 'I never saw a family, five sisters so very plain,' she told Cassandra in 1813 when describing the unfortunate Misses Fagg. 'Miss Sally Fagg has a pretty figure, & that comprises all the good Looks of the family.'[17]

That separating out of features, which is evident in the recol-lections of Jane's relations, seems to have been a common way of assessing a woman. It appears almost as a checklist as Caroline Bingley makes her spiteful summing up of Elizabeth Bennet: 'Her face is too thin; her complexion has no brilliancy ... Her nose wants character; her teeth are tolerable, but not out of the common way; and as for her eyes ...'[18] It was a particularly unpleasant approach because it turned women's eyes, teeth, complexions and noses into commodities that could be traded on the marriage market. It must have been stressful for any young woman to know that her appearance was being measured in this way. For a girl who was at all uncertain of herself it would have been traumatic.

One cause of Dorothy's discomfort in October 1790 may have been a fear that her looks would soon deteriorate. She may well, by now, have realised that there was a severe flaw in one of her features – one which was frequently singled out for comment. Dorothy's teeth were certainly not 'out of the common way': they were not even 'tolerable'.

In an age of rudimentary – and terrifyingly painful – dentistry, how strong her teeth were made an enormous difference to a woman's appearance (and, consequently, her prospects in life). Meeting Jane Austen's mother for the first time, Philly Walter remarked: 'My aunt has lost several fore-teeth which makes her look old'[19]. Mrs Austen was then forty-nine, married with a growing family. Looking old was acceptable in her circumstances, but it was nothing short of disaster for a woman's teeth to begin to fail her while she was still young and unmarried.

Dorothy's did. Woven through the rapturous descriptions of the Lake District in her Grasmere journals there would be the heart-rending tale of Dorothy's teeth – lost and broken and aching - but it was soon after October 1790 – and Dorothy's insistence that her friend should not tease her about lovers – that this tragic saga began. By March of the following year, she was 'much troubled with the toothache' and forced to have two teeth drawn by a surgeon in Norwich.[20] She did not mention whether these were 'fore-teeth'; but it would not be long before tooth-loss began to make Dorothy look much older than she was, destroying that unobtrusive prettiness upon which Coleridge remarked.

Twenty-first century readers, looking back from the – comparative – luxury of a society in which a woman's right to earn her own living is enshrined in law, are sometimes inclined to find Jane Austen's novels trivial, because they seem to be about nothing *but* the search for a marriage partner. However this view fails to take into account the true situation of girls like the Bennet sisters of *Pride and Prejudice*. Consider for a moment the prospect which has hung before Jane, Elizabeth, Mary, Kitty and Lydia ever since they were old enough to understand the workings of their world. Their father will die; their cousin, Mr Collins, will, under the terms of the entail, inherit Longbourn; they will be homeless. While their mother lives they will have no money of their own at all; improvident as she is, they will be entirely dependent on her, and after she dies (if she has not by then gone through all the money – an extravagance of which she seems entirely capable) 'one thousand pounds in the 4 per cents' will give them £40 a year each. This tiny income – and the few resources (such as governessing) which might supplement it – would cut them off entirely from the society in which they have grown up. They would be alone with no welfare system to support them in sickness or old age and no respectable means of improving their lot.

In a sermon of 1762 a certain Dr Dodd lamented the situation of young women whose parents 'expend much on boarding schools' for daughters who, left to fend for themselves, find the world a hostile place: 'So few the occupations which they can pursue ...so small ...the profits arising from their labours, and so difficult often the power of obtaining employment ...'

It was the same problem which Mary Wollstonecraft and Priscilla Wakefield would identify; but Dr Dodd was no educational theorist. He was a clergyman, and he gave this sermon to the governors' meeting of the *Magdalen Hospital for the reception of Penitent Prostitutes*. He continued his discourse with the dire warning that many such 'virtuous and decent young women ...have been compelled to the horrid necessity ...of procuring bread by prostitution.'[21]

It is a stark reminder of the straits in which even women whose parents had been wealthy enough to afford boarding school fees could sometimes find themselves.

Little wonder that hopes of a respectable – and, ideally, happy – marriage tend to occupy the Bennet sisters' thoughts. It is the only alternative to a kind of poverty which it is hard for us to comprehend. But the girls' happiness balances on a knife's edge.

In the few years available to them before their teeth begin to fall out, or sickness dulls the 'brilliancy' of their complexions, they must find the *right* husband. There was nothing trivial about that.

Georgian England was not the world of the 'rom-com'; marriage was for life. Divorce could only be got by an act of parliament and required financial resources comparable to those of a present day multi-millionaire. A legal separation came a little cheaper, but, like those of divorce, its terms were heavily weighted against women. A man's adultery was not sufficient grounds, though a woman's was, and only a degree of violence that endangered her life was considered sufficient cause for a woman to bring a complaint against her husband. The law protected a man's right to 'chastise' his wife, and to enforce her 'marital duty'.

Time was short and girls only glimpsed eligible men in the ball-room and at the dining table. Most of a gentleman's life was lived beyond female surveillance. If a woman made a false move during this crucial period of her life she could find herself unmarried and destitute, or else imprisoned for ever in a house with a tyrant, subject to humiliation, violence and repeated rape.

No Georgian reader with a modicum of intelligence would have considered a novel about a woman's search for a husband to be trivial, but the part which love played in all this was ambiguous. To hold out for love, to believe in love, in this treacherous, dangerous world could be presented as an act of heroism and integrity, or love could simply be regarded as a messy complication which endangered a woman's prospects, rather like a twenty-first century woman allowing the mixing of her sex and work lives to spoil her chances of promotion.

Another alternative was to make love less dangerous by the means advocated in Jane Austen's first two mature novels: thorough knowledge of the gentleman. It is one of the great triumphs of *Pride and Prejudice* that it succeeds in making Elizabeth's cautious, slow grown love for Darcy appear not only safer, but also much, much more sexy than Lydia's impetuous elopement with Wickham.

It is in this crucial arena – those few, vital years of a woman's life when she was adult, unmarried and marriageable – that Jane

Austen dramatises Marianne and Elinor's different philosophies, as one falls headlong into love with a stranger and allows her love to dictate every action and speech, while the other admits gradually to the charms of a close family connection, and holds her emotions in check.

Yet Jane herself fell in love with a stranger, while Dorothy Wordsworth, the great advocate of spontaneous feeling, fell in love gradually with a man she had known all her life.

NINE

Falling in Love

Jane Austen was twenty years old when she fell in love and Dorothy Wordsworth was about the same age – though, because her love grew slowly, it is impossible to date exactly. Their letters suggest some similarity of experience: excitement, a slight loss of reason, an overwhelming need to talk about the beloved.

The ways in which they fell into love were very different, with the rational Jane surrendering her heart over a few nights spent in crowded ballrooms, and the avowedly impulsive Dorothy gradually allowing her affection for one man to develop into an exclusive devotion over several years. The two women certainly responded very differently to the obstacles which Georgian society placed in the course of true love. The decisions which they took, and the ways in which they negotiated this crucial rite-of-passage, could hardly have been more different. But the experience would have a long-term impact on both their lives.

By the time she wrote the earliest of her letters to survive, Jane was already in love – and had been, perhaps, for a week or so. Her love pulses irrepressibly through two letters which she wrote between 9th and 15th January 1796. Addressed to Cassandra, who was away at Kintbury staying with the family of her fiancé, these early letters are lively and very young. They are quite unlike any of the other letters which Cassandra allowed to survive.

The name of the beloved found its way into the second sentence of the first letter. Jane opened with her sister's birthday: 'In the first place I hope you will live twenty-three years longer', but this subject (as any other would have done) served to introduce the name which filled her thoughts: 'Mr Tom Lefroy's birthday was yesterday...'[1]

Mr Tom Lefroy suffuses this first letter, intruding again and again as Jane attempts to give a dispassionate account of the family's comings and goings and the previous night's ball at Manydown. He just cannot be kept out. After providing a list of the people attending the dance, the letter reverts to a description of Jane's own scandalous behaviour during the evening.

It seems Miss Jane Austen and Mr Lefroy had spent far too much time enjoying one another's company. 'Imagine to yourself, everything most profligate and shocking in the way of dancing and sitting down together,' wrote Jane dramatically. She was trying to use humour to ridicule her own emotions as she had mocked the sensibility of other girls in *Love and Friendship*, but that playful, ironic tone which would, in the course of her correspondence, be used again and again to conceal her own feelings, was, on this occasion, like an inadequate gown hastily let down to cover a muddy petticoat – 'not doing its office'.[2]

Mr Lefroy was so recent an acquaintance that Cassandra had not yet met him; so Jane hastened to assure her that he was 'a very gentlemanlike, good-looking, pleasant young man'. And there was comfort – of a sort – for Cassandra: 'I *can* expose myself only *once more*,' wrote Jane, 'because he leaves the country soon after next Friday'.

Thoughts of Tom Lefroy dominate this letter – but, after being introduced in the second sentence, his name is made conspicuous by its absence. All sorts of linguistic tricks are evident: Tom is 'my friend', 'my Irish friend', 'the other' or, more usually, simply 'he'. The name is only written again towards the end of the letter when, it appears, he intruded in a physical form: a visit from him and his young cousin interrupting Jane's writing.

Years later, when she came to write *Emma*, Jane would recall the disturbing potency of a beloved's name. Emma Woodhouse, fantasising that she is in love with Frank Churchill, fears she will be unable to speak his name calmly in company and is preparing to substitute such an awkward alternative as 'your correspondent in Yorkshire' – but finds, at the last minute, that it is not necessary after all. Her ability to pronounce Frank's name without embarrassment is a proof of her *not* being in love[3].

In January 1796, Emma's creator was not so heart-free, and such was her own enthusiasm for this remarkable Mr Lefroy that she believed her sister must share her interest. 'I wish Charles had been at Manydown,' she wrote, 'because he would have given you some description of my friend, and I think you must be impatient to hear something about him.'

Cassandra had probably, by now, read enough of her sister's effusions to wish very much to know more about this extraordinary man who had, apparently, 'but *one* fault, which time will, I trust, entirely remove – it is that his morning coat is a great deal too light.'

Cassandra would have been reassured to know that the delectable Tom was the nephew of their old and highly respected friend, Anne Lefroy. He was just a month younger than Jane, the eldest son of a large, respectable family in Ireland. He had recently left Trinity College Dublin where he had 'attended all the class examinations ...taking the highest prize each year'; and he was now come to England where he was spending the Christmas holidays with his relations before enrolling at the inns of court in London in order to study Law.

All this, though it might have done something to soothe Cassandra's fears, cannot explain Jane's headlong plunge into love. What was so intoxicating, so remarkable, about Mr Tom Lefroy? What did Jane see in him that was different from the Hampshire swains who surrounded her?

'My Irish friend' has, inevitably, attracted a great deal of attention from everyone interested in Jane Austen's life and work, and perhaps the impetuosity of her own letters has contributed to the image of him (most evident in the fictional portrayal *Becoming Jane*) as an attractive but disreputable figure. However, this ignores the significant body of evidence that survives about Tom Lefroy's character. Incongruous though it seems, this devastating young man who could melt a woman's heart in the ball-room was, eventually, to become the Lord Chief Justice of Ireland. A very dignified portrait of him in later life with beaky nose, vast judicial wig and a severe expression around the mouth, rather gives the impression of a man pronouncing the death sentence and, if looked at too long, might destroy any sense of romance about this episode in Jane's life. A memoir of his career was published in 1871 by his son and, there are, preserved within it, several letters which testify to the very positive impression Tom Lefroy made on others when he was a young man.

There was nothing disreputable about him. He was certainly brilliant and studious. When he was only fourteen, his great uncle, Benjamin Langlois, believed: 'He is so advanced for his years that, unless vice and bad example lead him astray he will ...be highly qualified.' On the completion of his time at Trinity College, his tutor, Dr Burrowes, wrote modestly: 'for his success at college I can claim no credit. It was entirely the effect of his own talents and judicious diligence.'[4]

He also seems to have possessed very solid virtues which endeared him to his elders. His Uncle Langlois found him to have 'as little to correct in him as ever I saw in one of his age.' And Dr Burrowes praised his 'religious principles ...his desire of knowledge and his just ambition.'[5] These were the qualities which were to make him successful in later life; but elsewhere in his tutor's account, we can glimpse the attractions which might have captivated Jane.

The Doctor himself seems to have been a little captivated by young Tom. He wrote gratefully of the young student's 'endearing attentions to me and my family,' declaring, 'Of my dear Thomas I cannot speak without emotion.' And even went so far as to say, 'I feel for his absence more than his family can do'.[6] Which, since this letter was addressed to Tom's father, seems a little excessive and tactless. There was certainly something appealing here, not something brash or false, but a charm which had remained consistent over the years in which Tom had been intimate with his tutor and his family.

Jane might have fallen headlong into love, but it would seem that her good sense had not entirely deserted her. Her well-honed skills of observation enabled her to detect suitable husband material when she saw it. For this was no unprincipled Willoughby out to ruin a girl's happiness and reputation. Tom Lefroy was a solid, honest, hard-working young man.

The 'endearing attentions' which he no doubt paid to his dancing partner during the parties that marked the Christmas season of 1795/96 would have been exhilarating and flattering – but there was more to this encounter than common flirtation.

There was no shortage of young men to flirt with in Hampshire. Writing again, four days after her first letter, Jane mentioned some of her former favourites. With her head still full of the charming Irishman, she told Cassandra to pass a message to their friend Mary Lloyd. 'I make over Mr Heartley and all his Estate to her ...' she wrote, 'and not only him, but all my other Admirers ...even the kiss which C. Powlett wanted to give me'. The reason for this magnanimity? 'I mean to confine myself in future to Mr Tom Lefroy ...' – followed, of course, by the inevitable twist of irony – 'for whom I do not care sixpence.'[7]

Intelligent and genuinely affectionate, Mr Lefroy possessed one more characteristic which would have made him stand out from the general run of beaux at the Basingstoke balls. It was a characteristic he shared with the rather flushed young woman who sat beside him as the dancers and the fiddle music of the Christmas parties swirled about them; it was that 'happy command of language' which Lady Susan puts to such dangerous use. Tom Lefroy was a skilled debater. He had revived the Historical Society at his college and shone in it as a public speaker. His great uncle Langlois acknowledged his 'talent for oratory' [8] even though he was anxious it should not disrupt the course of his studies.

For Jane, the 'sitting down together' would have been as delicious as the dancing if Tom engaged her in genuinely interesting discussion. We have no record of what they talked about; but, despite the levity of the letters, it is hard to believe that conversation was nothing but teasing about such inconsequential matters as his white coat. Jane could have joked about morning coats with any young man in Hampshire.

There is only one clue to the topics they discussed. Jane had learned that her Irish friend was a 'very great admirer of Tom Jones'. (She jokingly attributed the pale morning coat to the fact that the fictional Tom wore 'the same coloured clothes'.)[9] Novels provided a common ground of experience on which men and women could meet, and it is easy to imagine that a studious young man who had had little time to spare for socialising might resort to them when called upon to entertain his partner in a ballroom. And Jane, incidentally, seems to have been perfectly comfortable with the discussion of *Tom Jones* – a slightly risqué work. Samuel Johnson was shocked when Hannah More told him she had read this story; he said it was 'a confession which no modest lady should ever make. I scarcely know a more corrupt work.'[10]

A touch of immodesty would have added a certain frisson to a conversation made private only by the music and clamour of a ballroom, but once on the subject of novels, Jane would have had interesting, perceptive remarks to make – remarks which her companion would have had the intelligence to value.

Dr Burrowes' comments indicate that Tom was able to make himself pleasing to his companions. The common small-talk of a ballroom might not have pleased Jane particularly, but a genuine exchange of ideas – verbal sparring with a skilled debater – could soon have engendered a sense of closeness and connection such as she never achieved with any other man. Here would have been something entirely new to her; someone who was not all bland, polite agreement; someone who did not think argument should be avoided. She might have experienced something like Dorothy's ideal of discussion without fear of ridicule or censure.

All her life Jane was to struggle to find other people agreeable. Her intelligence, her talent for observation – her genius – made her impatient with people whose minds were less agile. But something significant happened during those four Christmas balls. Rapid though her fall into love was, she may not have surrendered entirely to emotion and sexual desire, nor have abandoned completely her conviction that love should be founded on friendship. Maybe, that Christmas, she came to believe that she had really found a man who could 'meet her in conversation, rational or playful'.[11]

For an intelligent woman, confined in a society which denies her a higher education and restricts her existence largely to the home, the male companion with whom she shares her life is her chief provider, not only of security and affection, but also of intellectual stimulation.

Jane Austen's fiction demonstrates a keen awareness of that evocative phrase of St Paul's, 'unequally yoked'. Poor Emma Woodhouse dragging out the long winter evenings with her father who fails to understand her conversation and becomes 'nervous' when she tries to explain herself, and sensible Charlotte Lucas doomed to pass her life with the ridiculous Mr Collins, act out on the page a fate which must have been all too common in Georgian England.

By the time she was twenty, Dorothy Wordsworth understood the misery of an uncongenial family circle. She had experienced it for herself in the dreary Penrith parlour. It seems likely that, when they came to fall in love, Jane and Dorothy's needs and preferences were very similar. Both these keen observers of human nature sought a man who could match them in intelligence, a man with whom they could talk. While Jane was drawn to the intellectually brilliant and conventionally ambitious Lefroy, Dorothy's affections settled on a young man whose remarkable talents made him a fascinating companion, but who, sadly, had not Tom Lefroy's glittering career prospects.

In the retirement of Forncett rectory Dorothy can have met few young men and probably none to equal in intelligence and interesting conversation one lad whom she already knew. William, the brother who was just over a year older than herself, had been entirely lost to her for ten years and, when he re-entered her life at the age of sixteen, her loving heart had been ready to receive him. But he was only one among the four brothers who lit up her dull life in Penrith. She was delighted by the affection which they all showed for her and – apart from a little reservation about Richard – all her brothers were equally dear to her at that time.

However, by June 1793, a deeply significant change had come about. Dorothy would write then to her friend Jane Pollard, 'the last time we were together he [William] won my Affect[ion] to a Degree which I cannot describe.'[12] After that, William was to be the emotional centre of Dorothy's world for the rest of her life. Her love was so all-absorbing, so central to everything she became, that, brother though he was, it is impossible to describe the formation of this relationship as anything but 'falling in love'. Ten years later – during their life together at Grasmere – observers would question the nature of this extremely close relationship and 'there was an unnatural tale current...of Wordsworth having been intimate with his own sister'[13].

The exact nature of Dorothy's love has been questioned ever since, but there is nothing to suggest that it was – at its beginning – a sexual attraction. It developed mainly in letters, and tracing its development reveals that there were contradictions and caution mixed with that depth of feeling for which Dorothy was celebrated.

The beginning of a special relationship between brother and sister is first apparent in a long letter of September 1790. William was spending the university vacation walking through the Alps with a college friend, and Dorothy was his only correspondent in the family: 'When you write to my Brothers...tell them I am sorry it has not been in my power to write to them,' said William. He also admitted that he had deliberately avoided Richard for some time before setting out, because this elder brother would 'look upon our scheme as mad and impracticable.'[14]

William was living up to his uncles' opinion of him as irresponsible, but he seems to have had no fear that Dorothy would disapprove of this extended jaunt across Europe. Already he was turning to his sister with an expectation of sympathy. '[N]ever have my eyes burst upon a scene of particular loveliness,' he wrote, 'but I have...wished that you could...be transported to the place where I stood to enjoy it.' This was a style of writing to appeal to a sensitive young woman, hungry for affection.

After his return to England William stayed at Forncett rectory for six weeks in the winter of 1790/91. Now Dorothy could get to know him properly as an adult. There had been only brief meetings since Penrith days – as she passed through Cambridge on her way to her new home in October 1788, and when William came for a short stay at the rectory in June 1789.

Now they walked for hours together, talking and talking, so Dorothy too might have been taking part in an exhilarating exchange of ideas. From this point on, there is certainly a change in the way she thought about William.

'I confess you are right in supposing me partial to William,' she wrote in June 1791. But she was aware it was a long time since she had seen her other brothers and she thought that 'probably when I next see Kitt, I shall love him as well.'

The same letter which describes William's visit ends with that light-hearted postscript about her chances with Edward Swain. Her affection for her brother was not yet dominating her life. Through 1791 she praised William, but was honest about his failings, particularly the failure to apply himself to mathematics which had already lost him the chance of a fellowship and a secure academic career. She was objective enough to admit that his attachment to poetry was 'not the most likely thing to procure his advancement in the world.'[15]

However by June 1793, this objectivity would be abandoned and Dorothy would begin writing of William as if he was a conventional lover, describing his 'attentions' and saying that he had won her affections. She began then to look forward to a future which sounds very much like marriage: a future in which she would be 'united to my dear William.'[16]

Brother and sister did not meet between the winter of 1790/91 and 1793. The strangest thing about Dorothy's fall into love, is not that she fell in love with her brother – but that she fell in love with a man in his absence. So who was this extraordinary young man who could – even at a distance – engender such wholehearted loyalty?

Like Jane Austen, Dorothy could not help but talk about the man with whom she was falling in love. She described this delightful brother as having 'a sort of violence of Affection ...which demonstrates itself every moment of the Day when the Objects of his affection are present with him, in a thousand almost imperceptible attentions to their wishes, in a sort of restless watchfulness…a Tenderness that never sleeps, and at the same Time such a Delicacy of Manners as I have observed in few Men.'[17]

He sounds a very pleasant companion, but, to the older members of his family, the most striking thing about young William was probably vacillation and indecision – and, possibly, a certain rebelliousness. William's biographer, John Worthen, believes it is impossible to know 'whether Wordsworth developed republican political sympathies whilst a student',[18] but points out that he was enthusiastic about the French republic when he visited it during his walking tour in summer 1790. So there may have been the first stirrings of republican ideas in the boy who came to Forncett in 1790. If Dorothy detected them, she made no mention of them in her letters.

William was certainly not popular with his uncles. He had already annoyed them by refusing to pursue a college fellowship, and by his alleged over-spending. 'I think your Bro[the]r W[illia]m very extravagant,' wrote a grumpy Uncle Christopher to Richard Wordsworth in December 1789, 'he has had near £300 since he went to Cambridge w[hi]ch I think is a very shameful sum for him to spend, considering his expectations.'[19] His guardians were clearly watching William carefully – and they had reason to. They had advanced the money for his education, and they were probably already beginning to worry about when and how it would be repaid.

William caused more offence by gaining an undistinguished degree in January 1791 and by then hesitating over his choice of career, a choice which seemed obvious to his elders. Since he had destroyed his own chances of an academic appointment, he *must* become a clergyman. His uncle Cookson and his father's cousin John Robinson, MP for Harwich, were both willing to help him get a curacy. But William was unenthusiastic about the scheme.

He equivocated with his relations, pointing out that he could not, in any case, take holy orders until he was twenty-three. His Uncle William Cookson proposed (for unfathomable reasons) that he should fill in the time by studying Oriental languages at

Cambridge. William made a feint of complying, returning briefly to Cambridge; but soon he had removed to London and, by the end of the year, had changed the subject of his studies to French. In November he set sail for France, protesting to his anxious relatives that residence in a family there was the cheapest and most effective way of learning the language.

However, a fluency in French was not to be the most significant result of William's twelve month sojourn in that country.

TEN

Betrayal

Even affectionate, well-meaning young men can have secrets – as Elinor Dashwood discovers when news of Edward Ferrars' previous engagement bursts upon her. Before long, both Jane Austen and Dorothy Wordsworth would learn that the men they loved were not being entirely honest with them.

Although these two young women had read widely and scrutinised their fellow human beings intently, their experience was limited. Theirs was the female existence which Anne Elliot describes to Captain Harville in *Persuasion*: 'We live at home, quiet, confined, and our feelings prey upon us.'[1] Jane had lived in one home all her life with only short visits to friends and relations; Dorothy, though she had had four different homes, had mixed even less in 'society'. For both of them the beloved was a meteor shooting through that quiet, confined home and lighting it up. These young men did not belong in the domestic world; they were en-route between unknown masculine territories: universities, law-courts and London lodgings.

This partial understanding of their lovers was an experience Jane and Dorothy shared with hundreds of other well-brought-up girls at a time when men and women were expected to occupy the separate spaces of public and private life. Their perception and intelligence could protect both girls to a certain extent: neither of them succumbed to the charms of a villain or a fool. But they both took their young men on trust, and both were betrayed.

Tom Lefroy left Hampshire soon after Jane's second letter was written, and there is no evidence that she ever saw him again. The imminent departure was announced with characteristic melodrama: 'At length the Day is come on which I am to flirt my last with Tom Lefroy, & when you receive this it will be over – my tears flow as I write, at the melancholy idea.'[2]

Did Jane, when she wrote that letter, expect to hear from, or see him again? Almost certainly she did: the hurt pride she would later demonstrate suggests that there was hope mixed with the melancholy of the parting.

Tom had probably given her reason to hope. Mrs Anne Lefroy thought that the young man had misled Jane; her own sons remembered many years later that 'their mother had disliked Tom Lefroy because he had behaved so ill to Jane Austen.'[3] Then there is the testimony of Tom himself. In later life the staid Lord Chief Justice of Ireland confessed to a nephew that he had once felt a 'boyish love' for Jane Austen.[4]

'Mrs Lefroy sent the gentleman off at the end of a very few weeks, that no more mischief might be done,'[5] wrote Jane's niece Caroline. The reason for Mrs Lefroy's determination to end the affair is often said to have been mercenary: Jane's lack of fortune made the union impossible. Tom, the eldest son of a large and not very wealthy family, was being educated at the expense of his great-uncle Langlois, who, having seventeen great nephews and nieces, was calculating that, 'On such a sure total, the chance is great that one or two should rise into distinction and there haul up the rest'.[6] Tom – it is usually believed – was one of those who must do the hauling.

Caroline certainly seems to have believed that the cause of Anne Lefroy's intervention was the financial imprudence of an attachment for, in her account, she adds a comment which might have strayed from the pages of *Persuasion* and describe the disappointment of Anne Elliot rather than her creator. 'If his love had continued a few more years, he might have sought her out again – as he was then making enough to marry on ...'

However, the ponderous prose of the memoir written by Tom's son reveals another reason why the growing affection between these two young people had to be abruptly terminated. This is what the memoir says about young Tom Lefroy's love life:

'A warm friendship which existed between him [Tom Lefroy] and one of his fellow students, during their college course [at Trinity College Dublin], opened the door to him as an acquaintance and guest in the family of Jeffry Paul Esq of Silverspring, in the county of Wexford, the father of his fellow student, and, very soon, an attachment sprung up between him and Mr Paul's only daughter.'

That 'very soon' strongly suggests that this attachment was formed during Tom's days as a student in Ireland, thus pre-dating his introduction to the captivating Miss Jane Austen in Hampshire. This dating is made more certain by what follows in the memoir:

'During his stay in Ireland in 1797, when he came over from London to be called to the Bar, but only to return again for his further study of Law, he was engaged to be married to Miss Paul.'[7]

This would have been his first meeting with Mary Paul since his visit to Hampshire the previous year, so it is highly unlikely that their 'attachment' had not been formed before Jane and Tom met.

When Mr Lefroy arrived at Ashe for Christmas 1795 he was not a free man.

The existence of an informal 'attachment' which would arouse expectations in the young lady and her family, but the absence of an actual engagement, would have placed Tom Lefroy in a very delicate position indeed. He was in the same situation as Captain Wentworth of *Persuasion*, who, after paying attentions to Louisa Musgrove, acknowledges that, 'I was no longer at my own disposal. I was hers in honour if she wished it.'[8]

Out of consideration for Miss Paul, he could not explain his true dilemma when he found himself attracted to another lady. It would not be proper – in the absence of a positive engagement – to imply that Miss Paul was attached to him. A rapid removal from temptation, such as his Aunt Anne recommended, was the only way of salvaging his honour, and Tom Lefroy seems, in the end, to have acted honourably.

This explanation of his sudden departure accords well with Jane's subsequent behaviour. A hint of a previous attachment (given to her in strict confidence by Mrs Lefroy) would explain her dignified withdrawal from and her subsequent avoidance of Tom. He is mentioned no more in her surviving letters until November 1798 – more than two years after their meeting. She reported then that Anne Lefroy had visited her, and there seems to have been some anxiety on her part to talk privately with that lady, which was very natural. Tom had recently been staying again with his relations at Ashe and Jane would have been anxious to hear any news of him, but Mrs Lefroy was not forthcoming. '[O]f her nephew she said nothing at all…and I was too proud to make any enquiries', wrote Jane.

That *too proud* suggests that there had been cause for hurt or offence and it seems Mrs Lefroy was being cautious. Jane would have discovered nothing if it had not been for her father's intervention: '[O]n my father's afterwards asking where he was, I learnt that he was gone back to London in his way to Ireland, where he is called to the Bar and means to practise.'[9]

The hurt feelings resolutely hidden here accord well with a separation made necessary by a previous understanding. It seems less likely that she would have responded so patiently to a purely mercenary motive. Why could not she – like her sister – form an engagement and wait for the young man to work his way to success and fortune?

The idea that an alliance between the two was quite out of the question – that Tom and his family were so desperately poor he *must* marry for money – was something of which niece Caroline had certainly heard no rumour, or she would not have suggested that he might have returned to court Jane after he had established his career. The notion that he was honour-bound to make his fortune for his family's sake has been furthered by the fact that his marriage did, in the end, prove very advantageous. However, this could not have been foreseen. He did not choose a great heiress, he simply chose a fairly well-endowed lady. When Tom married Miss Paul she had a brother – Tom's student friend – who was the heir to her father's estates. It was only the subsequent death of this young man that made Tom's wife rich.[10]

If Tom was to haul his relations into prosperity, it was more likely that he should do it by success in his career: a success which would not have been blighted by his marriage to the penniless daughter of a respectable, well-connected clergyman. There is another indication that Jane's disappointment was caused less by money concerns than the insuperable objection of a previous attachment. She does not seem to have resented Mrs Lefroy's intervention. The warm friendship between the two women continued unabated.

In her novels Jane shows scant respect for people who consider money of paramount importance in marriage. If Anne Lefroy had persuaded her to give up Tom for financial reasons alone it seems unlikely that she would have continued to hold her friend in such high regard.

Jane yielded to the older woman's persuasion, though, in truth, she might have found it difficult not to. Anne Lefroy's letters to her son, Edward, reveal her to have been an expert at emotional manipulation when she was determined to carry her point.

Edward trained to be a lawyer, but it was not the career he wanted, and only emotional pressure from his mother kept him from giving it up. 'Continue what you now are & you will always be one of the best comforts of your anxious and affectionate mother,'[11] is a typical comment from her letters. When the restless young man had thoughts of joining the army, she became more forceful: 'should you...plunge yourself into all the dangers & misery of a marching regiment,' she wrote, 'any suffering you undergo will be doubled by the reflection that you have brought it upon yourself & that the pangs you feel are still less than what your parents endure on your account; how my beloved Child...will you be able to endure this thought?'[12]

Anne Lefroy was a woman with an unshakable faith in her own opinions, and she certainly knew how to use other people's affection for her to achieve what she felt was desirable. It is easy to imagine the kind of emotive arguments she might have put forward to separate her young friend from her nephew.

The capitulation would have caused Jane pain. The young man whom she had seemed to know, to whom she had seemed to be drawing close as she sat in the Christmas ballroom, had a life filled with plans and ambitions about which she knew nothing, and in which she could take no part. She withdrew with dignity, but, if she had chosen to, she could have behaved differently. It is evident from the letter quoted above that she had seen nothing of Tom during his second visit to his Hampshire relatives. She could have seen him if she had chosen to, and done it without behaving at all improperly. A morning call on her friends at Ashe – which was within walking distance – would not have been out of place at any time. But she seems to have behaved fairly towards Tom himself, and honourably by another woman she did not know. She kept away from Ashe and waited for Mrs Lefroy to bring her news.

The anxiety of that wait would have been torture, but a reading of Tom Lefroy's later letters must raise a doubt of their happiness together had they married. The liveliness to which Jane responded so wholeheartedly in the Christmas ballroom seems to have been an attribute of youth which was lost in the process of aging. There is certainly no evidence of the captivating dance partner in Tom's surviving correspondence.[13]

Perhaps Jane had fallen a little too precipitously into love. Solid, respectable and 'eligible' Tom Lefroy might have been; but he was probably not a suitable life-partner for a woman of genius. The letters of his middle age reveal a clever, religious but didactic man, whose views were conventional, unimaginative – and *extremely* long-winded. 'The comfort and security,' runs one typical passage in a letter to his wife, 'are inexpressible which result from no longer considering ourselves merely as our own, depending on our own puny strength or foresight, but as objects of Almighty care ...'[14] And so it goes on for pages – not only in this letter, but in many others, rarely breaking out an original thought, but displaying a complacency and a leaning towards evangelicalism which Jane, with her quiet, understated piety, could not have relished.

It is to be hoped that Mrs Mary Lefroy was happy to read

dutifully through pages of doctrine she had heard before in a hundred sermons. Had there been a Mrs *Jane* Lefroy in the case, she would probably have soon been reaching for her pen to write a satiric portrait of the man she had once found captivating.

Jane Austen seldom wrote about her own beliefs when she was a young woman, but the core of her morality was consideration for others. She found it difficult sometimes to live up to her own ideals, and, particularly in her letters to Cassandra, the sharp, critical comments would slip out, but her abhorrence of selfishness disguised as deep feeling made her ridicule novels of sensibility and distrust amateur theatricals. In the end, she applied this ethic of reason and caution even when her heart was broken. She did not let her feelings dictate her actions. Her happiness could only have been pursued by risking the misery of another woman whose disappointed hopes would have exposed her to ridicule.

Jane's passion for Tom Lefroy proved that her feelings were deep and that she *could* be impetuous. On the first publication of *Sense and Sensibility* she received a congratulatory verse from her brother James which contains these lines:

'On such Subjects no Wonder that she shou'd write well,
In whom so united those Qualities dwell.'[15]

James knew that saying his sister possessed both sense and sensibility would be an acceptable compliment. Jane certainly valued the ability to feel deeply. But it was not all-important to her; the head as well as the heart must be involved in deciding what was the *right* way to behave. Her novels suggest that there was something essentially pragmatic about her; she was less concerned with absolute ideals – with the way things *should* be – than with what was considerate and fair within the boundaries of society as she found it. There was a certain coldness in all this, but there was safety too.

Dorothy Wordsworth, living a quiet and confined life at Forncett rectory, had no better understanding of her brother's world than Jane did of Mr Lefroy's. When William left her in January 1791, he returned to Cambridge to take his degree – a qualification to which he was so indifferent he apparently spent the days leading up to the examinations reading *Clarissa*. (Perhaps the novel had been recommended by his sister.)

There followed a restless, aimless few months that ended in his eventual escape to view the revolutionary regime which had been established in France. Some of this in-between time was spent in London, where his radical ideas developed. His biographer, Stephen Gill, says that, at this time: 'Wordsworth was becoming politically aware, by associating with men who cared passionately about certain ideas and causes and who were hostile, from varying standpoints, to the present order of society.'[16]

Dorothy seems to have had no inkling of any turmoil in her brother's mind. '[William] is going, by the advice of my uncle Wm to study Oriental languages',[17] she confidently informed Miss Pollard in the autumn of 1791, even as William was plotting his escape to France. For all their talking in the wintry garden of the rectory there was surprisingly little understanding between brother and sister.

While William moved in the world of politics and big ideas, Dorothy – removed now from the free-thinking ethos of her Halifax home – occupied the narrow world considered proper for a woman, concerning herself with 'the minutiae of domestic affairs',[18] living within a family, absorbing and conforming to the attitudes of those in authority over her.

Read together, William and Dorothy's letters from this period form an eerie, disquieting counterpoint and dramatise the dislocation between male and female experience.

By May 1792 William's discussions in London and his own observations in France had brought about a definite dislike of monarchy and the established order. Writing from Blois to his friend, Matthews, at a time when it seemed that the patriot army defending the new French republic would soon be defeated by foreign forces, he reflected with satisfaction that outside intervention could not now reverse the changes of the Revolution: 'It will be ...impossible to reinstate the clergy in its ancient guilty splendour, impossible to give an existence to the noblesse similar to that it before enjoyed, impossible to add much to the authority of the King.'[19]

Ironically, just as William's radical ideas began to blossom, Dorothy was drawn to the very heart of 'noblesse' and monarchy's power. Her uncle William Cookson's former role as tutor to the sons of George III now brought him an appointment as a Canon of Windsor. The whole Forncett family visited Windsor in the autumn of 1792, and Dorothy was uninhibited by any suspicions of her brother's radicalism as she responded to her first sight of court life. 'When I first set Foot upon the Terrace I could scarcely persuade myself of the Reality of the Scene. I fancied myself treading upon Fairy-Ground ...'

She was as wholeheartedly Royalist as her uncle and aunt. 'I think it is impossible to see the King and his Family at Windsor without loving them ...' she wrote. 'I own I am too much of an aristocrate or what you please to call me, not to reverence him because he is a Monarch more than I should were he a private Gentleman'.[20]

Perhaps she was aware of William's opinions and paid them no heed; but it seems more likely that he had not shared his thoughts with her, for all through 1792 and 1793 the misunderstandings were deepening. By the time Dorothy made her curtsey to the King at Windsor, she was happy in the expectation of her brother taking holy orders. On 19th May 1792 William had given in; he wrote to a friend, 'It is at present my intention to take orders in the approaching winter or spring. My Uncle the Clergyman will furnish me with a title.'[21]

When the news reached Dorothy nine days later she was delighted and she began to plan a home in the comfortable rectory where she would keep house for her brother. But William's strain runs counter to her joy. His decision seems to have been forced on him by financial necessity. 'Vegetating on a paltry curacy', is how he described such a life to his friend,[22] while Dorothy wrote of the 'happiness of receiving you [Miss Pollard] in my little parsonage.' While Dorothy envisaged a blissful life in which 'we do not sigh for any Pleasures beyond our humble Habitation', William would write, 'all professions I think are attended with great inconveniences, but that of the priesthood with the most.' [23]

Neither Dorothy's rosy dream of parsonage life, nor William's nightmare of vegetation were to become reality, but their letters show that brother and sister were not only separated by distance during these years when Dorothy's love was growing and taking over her whole being, they were inhabiting different worlds.

Why was Dorothy falling in love with a man she only half knew?

There were his letters. William was always a reluctant letter-writer, frequently leaving his friends for months with no news, but he seems to have made an exception for his sister at this time. '[William] writes to me regularly, and is a most affectionate brother' Dorothy remarked in December 1792. It is almost as if he was 'courting' his sister at this time, trying to win her affection.

He wrote to her of 'that sympathy which will almost identify us when we have stolen to our little cottage!' He expressed a lover-like yearning for their reunion: 'I assure you so eager is my desire to see you that all obstacles vanish. I see you in a moment running or rather flying to my arms.'[24]

William loved and needed his sister, and his warm assurances of affection would have been extremely acceptable to Dorothy, whose unsettled life had made her very anxious to be reassured that other people cared about her. She loved him for loving her.

Her need for affectionate reassurance was painfully apparent in June 1793. She had had her twenty-first birthday the previous December and was now planning the long-delayed visit to Halifax. Her aunt and uncle had consented to the visit (note that their permission was still needed, even though Dorothy was now of age) and the momentous news was announced to Miss Pollard in a short, excited letter. But eleven days later no reply had been received and Dorothy felt rejected. She had hoped for expressions of joy from her friend. 'I am much disappointed ...' she wrote, 'I know not why it is, except that one cannot hear Truths of a pleasing nature repeated too often, particularly by those one loves.'[25]

William's letters certainly repeated 'truths of a pleasing nature', and his reference to 'our little cottage' in particular would have answered Dorothy's need for assurance and security. She had longed for a home of her own ever since 'my father's house' was lost to her at the age of six.

The desire for a home – a household in which she could take centre-stage and not be marginalised and despised as a dependent – was an important factor in a Georgian woman's desire for marriage. An awareness of this permeates Jane Austen's fiction; home and marriage are inextricably entwined, particularly for women of very small fortune, from Charlotte Lucas's acceptance of Mr Collins in *Pride and Prejudice,* 'from the pure and disinterested desire of an establishment'[26], to Mrs Weston's transition in *Emma* from a dependent governess to a matron 'in the centre of every domestic comfort'[27].

The conflation of marriage with home, spinsterhood with insecurity, was no mere fiction. Amanda Vickery has traced the stories of many Georgian spinsters such as Marthae Taylor, who wrote to her niece, 'you see how lightly regarded I am by kindred, how I have been tossed from wig to wall as ye phrase is …'. Vickery's conclusion, from her study, is that 'Few spinsters sighed aloud for the lost opportunity of marriage, or for plump babies they would never hold, but lament for a safe haven was recurrent.'[28]

It would seem that – for all his own fears of 'vegetation' – William was encouraging Dorothy's dream of a shared home during the years they spent apart from 1791 to 1793, promising the kind of permanence and safety which women usually found in marriage. Since this beloved brother was associated with Dorothy's memories of the only home in which she had ever felt secure, it seems likely that these shared daydreams contributed to her fall into love for him. But when William wrote to Dorothy about a shared home he was not being entirely honest. To steal away to a little cottage with his sister would not be honourable. Like Tom Lefroy, he had committed himself elsewhere – and rather more deeply.

By May 1792, when William wrote to accept his uncle's offer of a curacy, he had already met, at Blois, a French Catholic woman, Annette Vallon, and she had fallen in love with him. Maybe he was influenced by the heady ideas of the Revolution which, at the time, were questioning the restriction of sexual love to the bounds of marriage, for, by May, Annette was two months pregnant. Their daughter, Caroline, was born in December of that year.[29]

It is impossible to know exactly what William's feelings were for Annette but at the time he decided to take holy orders, he cannot have been intending to marry the woman with whom he was sleeping. English law was vehemently anti-Catholic; an Anglican clergyman could not have a Catholic wife. He did not marry Annette even when her pregnancy became obvious – though it would have been possible to do so. They had no money, but marriage would not have made their financial situation worse, and it would have saved Annette from facing the shame and ridicule of childbirth with no ring on her finger.

William returned to England a few days after Caroline's birth. If he meant to raise some money and go back, he was prevented by the outbreak of war between Britain and France in February 1793.

The existence of William's lover and child was known to Dorothy by March 1793. It must have been a great shock, but she kept any hurt or disappointment to herself. Eager, as always, to love and feel herself beloved, she responded with an open-hearted acceptance of the situation. She assumed that marriage was inevitable and began to include a wife and child for William in the dream home she was still planning to share with him. It seemed she could not, after all, be the centre of her brother's home, but she had no choice but to accept the situation. She wrote affectionately to Annette and a warm correspondence ensued.

William urged his sister to break the news of his daughter's birth to their Uncle Cookson, and Annette deeply regretted that she should have to undertake such a difficult task. She begged William: ' ... to invite her not to say anything to your uncle. It will be a hard fight she will have to engage in. But you deem it necessary.'[30]

It was indeed a hard fight Dorothy had to engage in! William's reliance on her indicates his emotional need, and Annette's letter to Dorothy shows how compassionately Dorothy had responded to the distress of a woman she had not met: 'Your last letter gave me such a powerful feeling,' Annette wrote. 'In every line I saw the sensibility of your spirit and that interest, so touching, you take in my sorrows ...'[31]

Dorothy had involved herself emotionally even in this most intimate aspect of her brother's life and she did her best to help the couple. She broke the bad news to her uncle, but the result was as disastrous as they had all foreseen.

The Reverend Mr Cookson was indignant; William's passionate interlude with a woman he scarcely knew must have appeared particularly self-indulgent to the man who had waited more than six years to be respectably married to the woman he loved.

All offers of a curacy were withdrawn. William was not welcome at Forncett rectory; the puritanical Mr Cookson probably feared that his company would corrupt his innocent sister. The painful communication had been made by 16th June 1793 because Dorothy then wrote sadly to Miss Pollard: 'I cannot foresee ...the Day in which I am once more to find a Home under the same Roof with my Brother ...'[32]

William now had no prospect of an income. He was in disgrace with all the relations who might have helped him. His conduct in France made him resemble the dastardly lover of a romance. Yet it was now that Dorothy committed herself to him.

Reverting in her letter to the time she had spent with her brother over two years ago, she declared 'his Attentions to me were su[ch] as the most insensible of mortals must have been touched with.' Rather oddly, she described to Jane Pollard those winter walks in the rectory garden as if they had only just taken place: 'Nothing but rain or snow prevented our taking this walk. Often have I gone out when the keenest North wind has been whistling among the trees over our heads ..I never thought of the cold when he was with me.'[33] In Dorothy's memory even the weather was conspiring to give significance to the occasion with snow and a keen north wind. When she described the walks soon after they happened, the weather had been 'unusually mild'.

William's outspoken affection for her seems to have first aroused a reciprocal love in Dorothy; but it was his fall from grace, his isolation and his need of a friend, which provided the final catalyst that raised her gradually deepening affection into wholehearted, single-minded devotion. Dorothy did not think of caution; she did not think of herself; she did not consider what the world would think of her. She demonstrated that talent for sympathy which was the very heart of her 'sensibility', and responded immediately to her brother's *need* for love, even though she knew that she was not the only woman in his life.

Her passion threw her once more into the role of a novel heroine. By the time she wrote her next letter to Miss Pollard, the innocent visit to Halifax had turned into a clandestine plot. William was to join her in Halifax, but in secret.

Dorothy began her letter with a dramatic warning: 'None of this is to be read aloud, so be upon your guard!' and she once more set herself into a scene as she had years ago by her small candle in Penrith. 'The evening is a lovely one,' she wrote, 'and I have strolled into a neighbouring meadow where I am enjoying the melody of Birds and the busy sounds of a fine summer's evening … But oh how imperfect is my pleasure! I am *alone* …'

In this extremely long letter – much of which was written with the paper resting on her knee as she sat in that meadow – Dorothy set out the plan which she and William had evidently devised together. With no employment in view, William had agreed to act as travelling companion to a wealthy friend, William Calvert but, as soon as he was sure Dorothy was in Halifax, he intended to make his way there.

In between the detailed planning and a lengthy detour in praise of her beloved ('but enough he is my brother, why should I describe him? I shall be launching again into panegyric') Dorothy made only a brief reference to the disastrous events in France. 'I have not time or room to explain to you the foundation of the prejudices of my two Uncles against my dear William;' she wrote, 'the subject is an unpleasant one for a letter, it will employ us more agreeably in conversation, then, though I must confess that he has been somewhat to blame, yet I think I shall prove to you that the Excuse might have been found in his natural disposition.'

Instead of offering further explanation, she turned to a quotation from James Beattie's popular poem *The Minstrel, Or The Progress of Genius* (see Appendix 1).

'"In truth he was a strange and wayward wight fond of each

gentle etc etc.["] That verse of Beattie's Minstrel,' she wrote, 'always reminds me of him'. [34] Dorothy's use of Beattie's poem to excuse William's treatment of Annette is enlightening. Edwin – the minstrel whose progress is related in the poem – belongs to the distant past, to what Beattie, in his preface, calls 'a rude age'. So Dorothy, while asserting her belief in her brother's calling to be a poet, was also placing him outside eighteenth century expectations of morality and respectability, in a world of wildness and emotion.

Jane Austen would have ridiculed this affectionate attempt to claim moral impunity for a sensitive soul. It comes dangerously close to *Love and Friendship*'s heroines 'majestically removing' banknotes from their host.

Dorothy's generous excuse for her brother seems to be a gesture of freedom, a protest against the restrictive morality of the time. However, challenging Christian sexual morality at this time did not prove liberating for most of the women who had the courage to attempt it.

Annette bore her child in disgrace. Soon after the birth she had lost not only her lover but her daughter too, for the baby must be sent away to nurse to avoid bringing shame on the family. Seeing her child carried away by another woman 'caused me a whole day of tears' Annette confided to Dorothy. Her letters reveal the heartbreak of a mother divided from her baby. She wrote that, if William would but come back and marry her – even if he must, for safety's sake, leave immediately afterwards – 'her [Caroline's] poor mother might enjoy the delight of always having her near. I should myself give her the care I am jealous to see her receive from other hands. I should no longer cause my family to blush by calling her my daughter ...'[35]

Annette and her family lived through the violent aftermath of the Revolution in poverty and danger. After her brother came close to losing his life on the guillotine, Annette seems to have embraced a passionately Royalist stance and to have risked her own safety in helping others condemned by the revolutionary government to escape execution. The turmoil of the times at least seems to have allowed her to pretend to a marriage which she never achieved. She adopted the name of Madame Williams, regained her daughter and struggled to bring her up according to her own standards of respectability.

Stories like hers were common. In 1793 – just after William abandoned Annette – another English radical, adrift in the revolutionary chaos of France, acted upon the new ideas that advocated an end to the institution of marriage, and quickly formed a passionate alliance. But, for this individual, it was not possible to flee the consequences, nor to retreat into a more conventional lifestyle as William did.

When Mary Wollstonecraft's love for the American, Gilbert Imlay, ended in pregnancy, she was, of course, left holding the baby. Imlay, like William, decamped, and Mary waited for her lover at Le Havre – as Annette waited at Blois – with fading hopes and a broken heart, so emotionally damaged that she would go on to make two suicide attempts. Unable, like William, to simply catch the next packet back to Dover and pretend to friends that the affair had never happened and the child did not exist, Mary had somehow to deal with the situation and support herself and her daughter.

This affair not only ruined Mary's happiness, it tainted her reputation as a writer. Although her work had originally been respectfully received, when the details of her personal life became known after her death, public opinion turned violently against her. Her ideas were mocked; Horace Walpole called her a 'hyena in petticoats'. Richard Polwhele opined that 'a woman who has broken through all religious restraints [as Wollstonecraft had] will commonly be found ripe for every species of licentiousness', and took a sadistic satisfaction in her agonising death from puerperal fever after the birth of her second child.[36] 'I cannot but think, that the Hand of Providence [i.e. God] is visible...in her death...as she died a death that strongly marked the distinction of the sexes, by pointing out the destiny of women, and the diseases to which they are liable...'[37] Or – in more modern terms – Mary was a mouthy woman who had got her comeuppance.

No such opprobrium ever attached to William Wordsworth;

no-one ever questioned the validity of his ideas because of perceived moral failings. He was able to keep his French affair a secret beyond a very close circle of family and friends, but had it become known it is highly unlikely that it would have impacted at all on his career. Men's work and private lives were allowed to be separate. Jean-Jacques Rousseau's philosophy was respected despite his cruel, irresponsible treatment of the children he fathered and, although the world loved to gossip about and be scandalised by Byron's colourful sex-life, it still bought his poetry.

Though Dorothy was never to suffer the humiliation that Mary Wollstonecraft endured, her love for William pitched her into a risky disregard for the proprieties which defined a Georgian woman's life. Her love had been a long time growing, but now that it was established it would rule her actions for the rest of her life, and make her vulnerable in surprising ways.

Just getting to the rendezvous at Halifax presented difficulties. The plan was long delayed by the problems which always beset a single female when she attempted to move from one place to another. A young woman was not supposed to travel alone, and Dorothy's plans depended upon the movements of an acquaintance, Mr Griffiths, who would, at some uncertain time, be making a journey in the right direction and would be able to provide the necessary escort.

However, Dorothy's love made her rebellious. In the end she became impatient with waiting and probably dispensed with the services of Mr Griffiths altogether, thus taking the daring step of travelling alone. She had begun to think and act for herself and, by the time she arrived in Halifax in 1794, she could dismiss her Uncle Cookson – who had once been a 'dear friend' – as 'extremely indolent and does not blend much instruction with his conversation ...'[38]

The passive home-building example of her Aunt Dorothy Cookson had, in the end, failed to appeal sufficiently to the young Dorothy Wordsworth. Inspired by love, she was taking matters into her own hands, more in the manner of her Aunt Threlkeld, and doing what she believed to be right. She would never return to Forncett. The rest of her life would be lived with, and for, William.

With her love impetuously launching her into unguarded behaviour (and a plot which was almost an elopement) Dorothy Wordsworth resembled Marianne Dashwood. In the novel her passion almost kills Marianne and, over the years to come, Dorothy's devotion to William would test her gift for self-sacrifice to its very limits. She would struggle to supply all the love and support that his genius demanded, until, at last, a cruel twist of fate defeated her.

ELEVEN

Journeys, Brothers, Freedom and Confinement

There was no elopement for Jane. After Mr Lefroy's departure, she continued to live in the heart of her family, socialising in the neighbourhood and travelling to visit relations, but something had changed. Never again, in any of her surviving correspondence, would she write as she had written in those first two letters. No ball would ever be remembered with the same thrill, no dancing partner would ever produce the same excitement as 'my Irish friend', never again would there be any hint of romantic or sexual turbulence. Two years later, she was too 'proud' to even mention Tom's name to his aunt.

Jane's family did not wish her acquaintance with Tom to be discussed. 'I think I need not warn *you* against raking up that old story of the still living Chief Justice'[1], wrote Caroline Austen to her brother when he was collecting material for his memoir of Aunt Jane. But, more than fifty years after Jane's death, the story was still remembered and, much to Caroline's alarm, freely canvassed by some members of the Lefroy family. Tom himself admitted to having loved the girl he partnered at those Christmas dances and Anne Lefroy was angry with him for using her young friend ill. Jane could only have been hurt by his behaviour if that love was mutual.

In sharp contrast to those first two letters, the rest of her correspondence with Cassandra during 1796 is muted, with little to suggest her feelings. The letters are, however, outwardly cheerful.

She was probably determined to keep up her sister's spirits for in January of that year Cassandra was forced to bid farewell to her fiancé, Tom Fowle. An opportunity had arisen for him to sail as private chaplain to Lord Craven on an expedition to the West Indies and, fearful of offending so rich and powerful a patron, Tom had accepted the appointment without revealing his engagement.

Such a journey in a time of war was dangerous, and one of its purposes was brutal in the extreme – to put down a slave uprising. It is hard now to envisage just what the role of chaplain could be in this violent mission which succeeded in restoring the institution of slavery in St Lucia, but the Austen family – with their wide naval connections – probably found nothing disquieting about a young couple's future domestic happiness resting on such an ugly foundation. It was hoped that the appointment would improve Tom's future prospects and Cassandra could only wait and hope.

In the meantime, Jane continued to live the life of a young woman in search of a husband: dining and dancing and making prolonged visits to relations in other parts of the country in order to form new acquaintances. But now she knew what it was to love a man and this may well have made her more exacting in her choice, less willing to give her heart and risk it being broken again.

In August she was in London and by 1st September, she had begun a long visit to her brother Edward, his wife Elizabeth and their three children at Rowling in Kent. There were balls and dinner visits and the interminable sewing of shirts which occupied so much of Georgian women's days. This time the shirts were for Edward and Jane was 'proud to say that I am the neatest worker of the party'.[2]

There was also some rather unenthusiastic attention to her youngest nephew – 'I have taken little George once in my arms since I have been here, which I thought very kind.' Such a cool response to the new baby cannot have endeared Jane to Elizabeth. The relationship between the sisters-in-law was probably not improving.

Like Dorothy waiting upon the convenience of Mr Griffiths,

Jane found herself unable to make her own plans. Everything depended upon the wishes of her brothers, Frank and Henry, who were also staying in the house, and there was no predicting what they would do. 'Since I wrote last, we have been very near returning to Steventon so early as next week,' she told Cassandra. 'Such was our dear brother Henry's scheme, but at present matters are restored, not to what they were, for my absence seems likely to be lengthened still farther. I am sorry for it but what can I do?'[3]

What indeed, could she do? Jane's situation at Rowling that September is an example of the way in which her life was constrained by the bonds that Dorothy had shaken off in her escape from Forncett. With no money of her own to hire a chaise and restricted by the perceived need for a male travelling companion, a spinster could only wait upon the convenience of other family members. Jane tried to be patient about her brothers' insistence on the proprieties of the business. 'As to the mode of our travelling to town,' she wrote at one point, '*I* want to go in a Stage Coach, but Frank will not let me.'[4]

It must have been frustrating to have so little control and she admitted that, 'I should be glad to get home by the end of the month.'[5] In fact, Henry was pursuing an agenda of his own as the travel arrangements were discussed. He had recently become engaged to a Miss Mary Pearson who lived at Greenwich and who had not yet been introduced to his parents. It was *his* plan that Jane should return home via Greenwich so that Mary could travel with her back to Steventon. Then Jane's visit was thrown into confusion by the plans of Frank, who was now a captain in the Navy and who, on 18th September, received orders for his new posting to HMS *Triton*. He must leave to join his ship almost immediately. Jane now wrote urgent letters, hoping to make arrangements so that she could travel with him when he left.

These arrangements depended upon her being able to stay with the Pearson family in Greenwich. Frank would be leaving her to join his ship and it was unthinkable for a young lady to spend a night alone at an inn. But there was no reply to assure her that the Pearsons would be at home to receive her.

Jane was very keen to return to Hampshire (as we shall see, there was perhaps a particular reason for her needing to get home) and, at one point, she was prepared to throw caution to the wind: 'I had once determined to go with Frank tomorrow and & take my chance...' she wrote. Her family succeeded in dissuading her from 'so rash a step'. She allowed herself to be talked out of travelling without the assurance of respectable overnight accommodation, and her actual feelings on the occasion were – as usual – veiled by humour.

'[F]or if the Pearsons were not at home,' she observed wryly, 'I should inevitably fall a Sacrifice to the arts of some fat Woman who would make me drunk with Small Beer – '

The image Jane is conjuring here is the first in Hogarth's popular series of pictures, *The Harlot's Progress*, which shows a young innocent girl arriving in London (with, presumably, no respectable accommodation arranged). In the picture the girl is being tempted into prostitution by a leering fat woman. This preposterous exaggeration of her brothers' fears for her safety was a way of defusing potential conflict with them, but it was also an expression of Jane's own impatience.

With the spectre of the malevolent fat woman – and the threat that she posed to young ladies' reputations – throwing Jane upon the goodwill of her family, the return to Steventon was not made until the end of the month. Then it was probably brother Edward – the leisured man of property, free to come and go as he wished – who took her home.

This whole episode demonstrates how the wishes and plans of her brothers (with their careers and wider interests) must always take precedence over Jane's own desires. She might almost have joined in Marthae Taylor's lament: 'you see how lightly regarded I am by kindred, how I have been tossed from wig to wall ...' Like Miss Taylor, she was vexed by her lack of autonomy. Her letters to Cassandra for this month contain a great deal of veiled, irritated criticism of her family.

Besides the impatient references to Frank and Henry there are cynical remarks about the prosperous Edward. 'Farmer Clarinbould died this morning,' Jane wrote on 5th September. 'I fancy Edward means to get some of his Farm if he can cheat Sir

Brook enough in the agrement *(sic)*.'[6] Ten days later she returned to the subject with another preposterous fancy: ' …Edward had some idea of taking the name of Calringbould (sic);' she wrote, 'but that scheme is over, tho' it would be a very eligible as well as a very pleasant plan, would any one advance him Money enough to begin on.'[7]

The joke against Edward was not only that he was a little grasping (poor Mr Clarinbould had died very recently) but also that he was prepared to change his name for financial gain. This was not an uncommon practice at the time. The adoption of the surname that had traditionally belonged to an estate was frequently made a condition of inheritance when property passed to a distant branch of a family. Edward had probably already consented to such an arrangement (he would abandon the Austen surname and become Knight when he took over the estates of Godmersham and Chawton two years later) but Jane's cynicism suggests she did not approve and that she was exasperated by the ease with which a man might acquire a comfortable fortune.

These letters show that she could be critical of the brothers who were already beginning to exercise control over her life.

The meeting between brother and sister in Halifax was rapturous. They remained six weeks at Mill House, the comfortable home of Aunt Threlkeld, Dorothy's foster-mother, who had recently married a prosperous Mr Rawson.

They must have talked about Annette, though it is unclear what plans William had for marrying, for returning to France, or for supporting his child. He now had no prospect of employment and neither he nor Dorothy had any money. What should they do? Where should they go? Their decision demonstrates the priorities of their early life together, and it must have baffled and infuriated their more prudent relations.

They set off on a walking tour. Unwilling to give up the joy of being in each other's company and eager to return to the countryside they had loved as children, they took the stagecoach to Kendal (how Frank Austen would have disapproved!) and then walked thirty miles through the Lake District to a farmhouse called Windy Brow, near Keswick, the home of William's friends, the Calvert brothers.

Dorothy gloried in her own ability to walk so far and in the freedom of the journey. Years later she would recall little details of the adventure: stopping to wash her tired feet in a mountain stream, drinking milk at the door of a public house: little pleasures very far removed from the constraints of her previous life (and from the kind of journey the Austen brothers thought suitable for their sister).

Every step she took was bearing her further away from her dutiful life at Forncett rectory but, though the open-minded Rawsons had been accepting of her behaviour (while probably not entirely approving it), there were other members of her family who were outraged. Dorothy's guardian, her uncle Christopher Cookson, had, like Edward Austen, changed his name for the sake of a fortune, becoming Mr Crackenthorpe when he inherited his estate in 1792. He had also taken a wife, and it was this wife – the formidably named Aunt Crackenthorpe – who disapproved most strongly of her niece's gallivanting. Her ideas of the proper way for ladies to travel were similar to those of the Austen family, and her letter of protest which reached Dorothy at Windy Brow must have been strongly worded. 'I am much obliged to you for the frankness with which you have expressed your sentiments upon my conduct,'[8] wrote Dorothy in her reply.

It is a delightful letter which Dorothy composed on 21st April 1794, dignified and icily polite, but completely uncompromising. She would not admit that she had done anything wrong, nor make any undertaking to amend her conduct and the pleasure of defying this critic must have been greatly increased by the fact that Aunt Crackenthorpe had been – before her marriage – one of the *notable* Miss Custs who had made Dorothy's life miserable in Penrith seven years earlier.

'As you have not sufficiently developed the reasons of your censure,' wrote Dorothy, 'I have endeavoured to discover them, and I confess no other possible objections against my continuing here a few weeks longer suggest themselves, except the *expence* and that you may suppose me to be in an unprotected situation.'

She then defended herself against the first objection by describing the frugality of her life (no tea and a diet consisting mainly of milk, bread and potatoes) before turning with energy to the more significant point.

'I affirm,' she said, 'that I consider the character and virtues of my brother as a sufficient protection ...' It is such a positive assertion, it seems likely that Aunt Crackenthorpe's 'frankness' had extended to giving an opinion on the character and virtues of that brother, based on his recent conduct in France. Dorothy's defence of William – her insistence that he was, despite his fall from grace, a suitable chaperone to guard her reputation – was very brave. She was defying the sexual rules of society and religion, and her vocabulary reflects the seriousness of the moment. 'I affirm' was a formula used to preface solemn undertakings by those dissenters who found the swearing of oaths repugnant.

Having committed herself unreservedly to her brother's protection, Dorothy made a spirited defence of her mode of travel. '[Y]ou speak of my "rambling about the country on foot". So far from considering this as a matter of condemnation, I rather thought it would have given my friends pleasure to hear that I had courage to make use of the strength with which nature has endowed me ...'

She completed her letter with a particularly pointed description of her own ongoing education. 'I not only derive much pleasure but much improvement from my brother's society,' she wrote. 'I have regained all the knowledge I had of the French language some years ago, and have added considerably to it, and I have now begun reading Italian ...'

Seven years earlier, smarting under her grandmother's praise of the Miss Custs, Dorothy had comforted herself by dismissing those young ladies as 'those who have not had the advantages of Education'. In her letter from Windy Brow she seems to be reminding the erstwhile Miss Cust of her deficiency while pointing out that she herself had received an education in the past and was still conscientiously pursuing her own improvement.

Despite this hint of smugness, it is a glorious letter that Dorothy wrote as she enjoyed William's company in the Cumberland farmhouse. And the significance of this fraternal elopement should not be underestimated. Dorothy was, in one way, very fortunate to have fallen in love with her brother. 'Rambling about the country on foot' with a slightly disreputable brother might bring down the censure of her more conventional relatives, but it was a good deal safer than rambling about with a man who was *not* a brother. At about the same time that Dorothy made her daring bid for freedom, another young lady was rambling with another poet and getting herself into more serious difficulties.

Miss Sarah Fricker of Bristol had recently fallen in love with Dorothy's future friend, the poet, Samuel Taylor Coleridge. Together with her sister, Edith, and Coleridge's friend, Robert Southey, Sarah had been indulging in the vices of walking tours and unchaperoned overnight stays at inns. The result was such a severe loss of reputation as could, in her family's opinion, have only one remedy and 'marriage was believed to have been rather hurried on, in consequence of some hostile breath of rumour ...'9 The Fricker girls had been living for years among radical ideas in Bristol and may well have read Mary Wollstonecraft's *Vindication of the Rights of Woman*; they shared the new-fangled doctrines of the young fellows who paced at their side.

Dorothy's act of rebellion was different, it was inspired simply by love and personal integrity. When put to the test, she trusted her feelings and believed that by following them, she was not being selfish, but was doing the *right* thing. It was a very different approach to morality from Jane's with its insistence on self-control. Dorothy would probably have said, as Marianne Dashwood does when she is charged with behaving improperly with Mr Willoughby, 'if there had been any real impropriety in what I did, I should have been sensible of it at the time, for we always know when we are acting wrong.'10 Elinor, on the other hand, argues steadily in favour of restraint and propriety, for she is all too aware of how dangerous spontaneity can be in the society which she and her sister shared with their creator – and Dorothy Wordsworth.

By leaving her relations at Forncett, Dorothy was committing herself to the life she had been happy to foresee at the age of fifteen: dependence on her brothers. She heartily disliked the idea of 'living upon the bounty of one's friends'; but the prospect of living with a brother – of being supported by a brother – was never abhorrent to her. At the age of fifteen she had taken comfort in the idea that 'as long as my Brothers have a farthing in their pockets I shall never want.'

To live with a brother, she believed, would be freedom. However, a recent study shows that being supported by a brother and sharing his home – though it was a very common fate for unmarried women – was by no means always the happy independent life of which Dorothy dreamed.

Amanda Vickery's research into the letters and journals of unmarried women from this period has shown that a brother's support was often given grudgingly, and unmarried sisters were frequently made to feel as if they were a burden on family resources. Gertrude Savile, for example, while living with her brother at Rufford Abbey, felt 'the very Walls look'd inhospitably upon me and everything frown'd upon me for being an Intruder'. Vickery's conclusion is that, 'A household headed by a brother was one of the least congenial for an ill-endowed sibling, if the letters and diaries of resentful sisters are anything to go by.'[11]

This summary would have struck a chord with the Dashwood sisters of *Sense and Sensibility*. Elinor, Marianne and Margaret are made to feel like intruders in the family home at Norland Park by their brother and his wife, and are driven out to take refuge with more distant relations.

Elinor and Marianne, the novel in letters which would later be converted into the straightforward narrative of *Sense and Sensibility*, was written, according to Cassandra's recollections, sometime during 1795. So some version of the story already existed by the time Jane Austen was fretting about how she would get home from Rowling and turning her irritation into jokes about ludicrous name changes and malevolent fat women.

It was Jane's first complete novel and its preoccupations shed some light on the situation and thoughts of the young woman who loved and lost Tom Lefroy, the young woman who was now expected to continue the life of a dutiful daughter in her round of family visits and discreet husband-hunting.[12]

The opening of this story would have made uncomfortable hearing when it, like Jane's previous work, was read aloud in the Steventon drawing room, since the narrative is set in motion by a rank injustice which is uncompromisingly laid bare to the reader. An estate passes to a son who is already wealthy while his three half-sisters are left to survive on slender means. Henry Dashwood – father of the girls, and of their brother John – is unable to help his daughters because of legal limitations laid upon him when he inherited the estate so, when he is dying, he begs John to assist his sisters. John agrees. But when he tells his wife that he intends to give the girls a thousand pounds each, 'Mrs John Dashwood did not at all approve.'[13] There then follows what is probably the most horribly believable portrayal of family cruelty seen in English Literature since Goneril and Regan drove King Lear out into the storm, mad and homeless.[14]

John's wife, Fanny, works slyly upon him. Why, she asks, is 'he to ruin himself, and their poor little [son] Harry, by giving away all his money to his half-sisters?' Three thousand pounds is a considerable sum, she argues – despite the fact that their income has just increased by more than four thousand pounds a year. She undermines his sense of duty and affection by making it seem extravagant: 'what brother on earth would do half so much for his sisters', she argues. She wears away at the amount to be given until it is nothing but 'a present of fifty pounds, now and then', which she finally succeeds in reducing to 'presents of fish and game …whenever they are in season.'

The passage is a damning indictment of the way selfishness and the abuse of power could operate within a family, and it presented a situation not uncommon in eighteenth century England. Others had also noticed the same phenomenon. Mary Wollstonecraft's factual depiction of the fate of spinster sisters at the hands of their brothers and their brothers' wives is remarkably similar to Jane Austen's representation of John and Fanny Dashwood. This is her description:

' ...when the brother marries ... she [the sister] is viewed with averted looks as an intruder, an unnecessary burden on the benevolence of the master of the house ... The wife, a cold-hearted, narrow-minded, woman, and this is not an unfair supposition; for the present mode of education does not tend to enlarge the heart any more than the understanding ...she is displeased at seeing the property of *her* children lavished on a helpless sister ... The consequence is obvious, the wife has recourse to cunning to undermine the habitual affection which she is afraid openly to oppose ...till the spy is worked out of her home, and thrown on the world ...'[15]

Wollstonecraft maintained that, 'These are matters of fact, which have come under my eye again and again'. It would seem that Jane Austen – the so-called 'moderate Tory' – had made the same observations, and experienced the same sense of outrage, as the radical writer of *The Vindication of the Rights of Woman*.

By the time she was nineteen, Jane Austen – who had once mocked the extravagant woes of novel's heroines – was becoming aware of the very real injustices that often lay at the heart of Georgian family life. It was an awareness which had been forced on Dorothy Wordsworth at a younger age because of the more obvious insecurity in which she lived.

The subject was important enough to Jane to become the driving force of her first mature novel. She spent time thinking about how this kind of unfairness operated, examining motives and the ways in which they might be articulated and defended. It is not surprising that the subject interested her; she knew that, unless she somehow managed to marry without a dowry, it would be *her* fate to be dependent on her brothers all her life.

What did her family think as she sat in the old rectory parlour reading aloud her account of the Dashwood family's politicking? There would have been laughter, of course, for Jane wrapped up the unsavoury subject with comic characters and delightfully clever dialogue. She had learned in this very room how to make the unacceptable acceptable. A few years ago drunkenness, cannibalism and casual sex had passed safely under the distraction of

121

humour. Now she was writing about something which her family was probably even less willing to hear.

The laughter may not have been entirely comfortable: not from Mr Austen who was aware that the rosy-faced, sharp-eyed girl reading from her manuscript might one day find herself dependent for her very livelihood on just the kind of informal, unenforceable understanding which is set aside by John and Fanny Dashwood; nor from the Austen brothers who knew that they would eventually be required to somehow balance the competing claims of sisters, wife and children to their limited incomes.

Twelve

A House of My Own

Dorothy had no fears that a brother would be selfish or use her badly in the way that Jane Austen and Mary Wollstonecraft described. Her reliance on her brothers predated her exclusive love for William; the ideal home she had carried in her head since she was fifteen was a house shared with a brother.

This is a testimony to the empathy which existed between the siblings who had been separated so long ago. Now, at twenty-three years old, Dorothy could talk of those relations with whom she had hitherto shared a home as affectionate but, 'not positively congenial in pursuits and pleasures ... and with separate and distinct views.'[1]

She longed to be free of the notables of Penrith and the evangelicals of Forncett. She wanted to be in a home where she could be herself, where she could hazard her own observations without fear of ridicule or censure. By 2nd September 1795, it seemed that this dream was at last within reach.

'I am going now to tell you what is for your own eyes and ears alone ...' she wrote dramatically. She was once more entering into a bit of thrilling plotting: the one-time Miss Pollard – recently married and translated into Mrs Marshall – must again play the part of confidante to the narrative of her life. That narrative had now taken a happy turn and, at last, Dorothy might have, 'at least for a time a comfortable home, in a house of my own ...'[2]

It was over a year since Dorothy strode boldly through the Lake

District to Windy Brow, and the intervening time had been an unsettled one. Lack of money had meant that she could not sustain an independent life with her brother. They had been forced to separate and Dorothy had travelled about the North of England, visiting friends and relations, but showing no inclination to return to what her family considered her home – Forncett rectory.

There had been a visit to the Crackenthorpes where Dorothy began to suspect that she – like the Dashwood sisters – was the victim of a selfish wife who had set her husband against his impe-cunious relations. Her Uncle Christopher was remarkably kind to her on this visit; she warmed to him and came to believe that all his apparent hostility was the result of his wife's malevolence.

This, by the way, might seem slightly unreasonable since her uncle's marriage had taken place after the time in Penrith when Dorothy had begun to dislike him. But a letter of Dorothy Cowper's indicates that Christopher Cookson was courting Charlotte Cust as early as 1786, and the couple were spending a good deal of time together[3]: so perhaps, in 1787 when Dorothy decided that she 'absolutely disliked Uncle Kitt', that notable lady had already begun to poison the mind of her lover against relations she feared would be a drain on family resources.

Dorothy had also visited her old Penrith friends Mary and Peggy Hutchinson, who were now keeping house for *their* brother on a farm at Sockburn, near Darlington. This household seems to have been a pleasant place and she enjoyed her time in a home where the usual occupations of reading, walking and sewing were sup-plemented by the rather less ladylike 'playing at ball'. The happi-ness of the Hutchinson sisters could not help but remind her that, though orphaned like her, they had achieved the kind of home for which she longed: 'very different indeed is their present situation from what it was formerly when we compared grievances and lamented the misfortune of losing our parents at an early age and being thrown upon the mercy of ill-natured illiberal relations.'

'When shall I have the felicity of welcoming you my earliest friend to such a home?' she wrote. '…but these are airy dreams.'[4]

Dorothy was sensitive to other people's joys and sorrows but there was a part of her which could never quite let go of her own preoccupations. The fortunes, or misfortunes, of others tended to remind her of her own troubles and grievances. The way in which her mind turned so readily from her friends' concerns to herself is evident in several letters. She wrote, for example, in 1788: 'Poor Miss Priestly! She is much to be pitied, the loss of a mother ...but still she has a father, and while he lives, how much less pitiable is her situation than ours!'[5]

However, the contentment of the Hutchinsons must have contrasted painfully with her own rootless state. The wish that she herself might obtain a home like theirs had been repeated for many years, but she had no more power to make the dream come true at the age of twenty-three than she had had at fifteen. Despite her brave bid for freedom she was still as helpless as Jane Austen as she waited at Rowling for her brothers to agree on how she should be conveyed home.

It was a series of circumstances entirely beyond her control which, by the beginning of September 1795, turned Dorothy's airy dream of a home into a real possibility. The first step had been taken back in June 1794 when Raisley Calvert, the younger of the two brothers who had lent their house at Windy Brow, became convinced of William Wordsworth's genius. At the age of just twenty-one Raisley was dying of tuberculosis, and he determined upon leaving a legacy of £900 to William so that he might be able to pursue a career as a writer. It was an astonishing act of generosity. This young man's devotion indicates the deep impression which William Wordsworth could make on people and the belief in his genius which he was able to inspire. It helps to make Dorothy's own unswerving commitment to him appear less eccentric.

Dorothy announced Raisley's death to her brother Richard in January 1795 in a sentence which does no credit to the sensitive feelings for which she was celebrated: 'No doubt William has informed you of the death of his poor friend Raisley Calvert, and that he has made no alteration in his will by which he bequeathed to him the sum of nine hundred pounds.'[6] There is no pause even for a few conventional words of regret on the ending of this young life, no praise of the lad's character or mention of his sufferings;

there is not even a new sentence begun before she rushes on to the pressing question of the legacy.

The money was of vital, life-changing importance to Dorothy. In her excited letter to Jane Marshall, she wrote: '[William] means to sink half of it[the legacy] upon my life, which will make me always comfortable and independent ...' However, it does not seem that this arrangement was ever carried out, for, seven years later, when William married, Dorothy had no such comfortable independence and was obliged to ask her other brothers for support.

Dorothy was full of exuberant optimism. 'Wm finds,' she wrote, 'that he can get 9 per cent for the money upon the best security'. But William would never achieve anything like this rate of return, and the Calvert legacy was very far from producing the financial security which Dorothy anticipated. William was not good at handling money. A considerable amount of the legacy was spent rather than invested and Wordsworth's attempts to raise higher returns by lending to his friends were disastrous. Much of the interest was never paid and some of the capital was lost.[7] But for now it seemed that things were beginning to go right for the young Wordsworths. Soon after the legacy had been secured, two other pieces of good fortune occurred.

William remained in Cumberland with Raisley Calvert until Calvert died in January 1795, but he did not enjoy this prolonged stay in the county of his birth. He wrote to his friend William Mathews, who was in London working as a journalist: 'I begin to wish much to be in town; cataracts and mountains, are good occasional society, but they will not do for constant companions.'[8]

It is a surprising comment from the man whose name has come to be so inextricably linked with cataracts and mountains, and it hints at the transitional, unformed persona of the brother to whom Dorothy had committed her future. He had at this time published only two pieces of poetry, *An Evening Walk* and *Descriptive Sketches,* and, though his sister and some of his friends had begun to regard him as a poet, it is evident that William himself had not yet started to identify himself solely as such. 'This is a country for poetry it is true;' he wrote to Mathews, 'but the muse is not to be won but by the sacrifice of time, and time I have not to spare.'

He was planning a different future. He eagerly picked up an encouraging comment from his friend Mathews: 'You say that a newspaper would be glad of me;' he wrote, 'do you think you could ensure me employment in that way on terms similar to your own?' Politics and the great questions of the day interested him much more than mountains and cataracts and his political ideas bordered on the revolutionary.

'I am of that odious class of men called democrats, and of that class I shall for ever continue ...'[9] he wrote to Mathews in May 1794, and again, the following month: 'Hereditary distinctions and privileged orders ...I think must necessarily counteract the progress of human improvement. Hence it follows that I am not amongst the admirers of the British constitution ...'[10]

These were dangerous views to hold in England during the last decade of the eighteenth century when the terrifying example of revolution just across the channel had prompted the government to take repressive measures and radicals were being summarily imprisoned. 'I hope you will be cautious in writing or expressing your political opinions,' wrote brother Richard anxiously to William in May 1794, 'By the suspension of the Habeas Corpus Acts the Ministers have great powers'.[11]

The only surviving reply to this brotherly concern is not from William himself, but from Dorothy. 'I think I can answer for William's caution about expressing his political opinions,' she replied within a few days. 'He is very cautious and seems well aware of the dangers of a contrary conduct.'[12]

Dorothy's intervention on this point raises two questions. To what extent did she ever share William's radical political opinions? And what role did she play in turning him and his writing away from the political to the personal, from polemic to poetry? The letters and journals written during her twenties and early thirties, while showing compassion for what she termed 'the lower classes' and an interest in them as individuals, do not demonstrate that conviction of the need for social upheaval which her brother's letters to Mathews display.

Dorothy was pro-French enough to avoid paying the tax on

hair powder which the government had imposed to raise funds for war, believing that 'every individual …should avail himself of every fair opportunity of declaring his disapprobation of the present destructive war …' [13] But that gesture was being made even in a Tory family like the Austens. In 1799 Jane's brother, Charles, cropped his hair short and stopped using hair powder. His more conservative brother Edward was shocked. 'I thought Edward would not approve of Charles being a crop, and rather wished you to conceal it from him …'[14] wrote Jane to Cassandra, attempting, as usual, to preserve that all-important family harmony.

Dorothy declared no actual support for the French Republic, nor did she recant the views of that 'aristocrate' who had felt reverence was due to King George's rank and title. Set against this, there is her belief that sharing a home with William would be fundamentally different from living with relatives who had 'separate and distinct views', which suggests that her own views were not 'separate and distinct' from William's.

In her forties and fifties, when William had retreated to a position of staunch conservatism, Dorothy would not hesitate to endorse his opinions in her letters. But the writing of the young Dorothy seems rather to sidestep political questions, focussing on the personal and small-scale.

Despite the expectation that women would confine themselves to the domestic sphere and leave politics to men, some women, as they matured and began to take note of the world around them, trespassed into male territory. Several contemporary women writers, such as Helen Maria Williams, Mary Wollstonecraft and Anna Seward, engaged directly with the ideas of the French Revolution. This however was something which Dorothy Wordsworth would never choose to do, even when she was settled in a home where she was free to express herself. Instead she sought meaning, as Jane Austen did, in the world of family and local community. It was an approach which suited her taste for retirement, but she may also have felt that all the 'big issues' could be left to her brother's pen.

As for Dorothy's influence on her brother and his work: William believed that her influence was crucial. He wrote in *The Prelude* about this period of their lives:

> 'She, in the midst of all, preserv'd me still
> A Poet, made me seek beneath that name
> My office upon earth, and nowhere else.'

It could, however, all have been very different.

After Calvert's death, William went to London and renewed his acquaintance with the radical men he had met before his trip to France. He hoped that Dorothy would join him.

'Dorothy and William Wordsworth have now a scheme of living together in London, and maintaining themselves by their Literary talents, Writing and translating,' wrote Dorothy's 'aunt', Elizabeth Rawson, in March 1795. ' ... We think it a very bad wild Scheme.'[15]

It is unlikely that Dorothy approved wholeheartedly of the scheme herself; but her determination to do something for herself, her conviction that 'it is painful when one is living upon the bounty of one's friends,' would almost certainly have carried her to London if an alternative more suited to her own taste for the countryside and a retired life had not presented itself. In the eighteenth century other women, such as Charlotte Lennox, Mary Wollstonecraft and Charlotte Smith, finding that they must do something to support themselves, did earn a living of sorts in London, writing and translating.

It would have been a hard life for Dorothy. Wollstonecraft suffered almost continually from exhaustion and depression, and Smith, who wrote poetry and fiction to support herself and her children when her husband was imprisoned for debt, died destitute after her brief popularity as a novelist came to an end. But if Dorothy Wordsworth had been called upon to live by her talents, there might now exist a substantial body of published work with her name on it and, since her brother would have been taken up with politics and journalism, there might have been very little poetry attributed to William Wordsworth.

It was chance that decided it all.

Struggling – and failing – to make ends meet in London, William received two offers which seemed too good to refuse. An old Cambridge friend, Basil Montagu, was studying law and supporting himself by taking pupils. Montagu was a widower with a young son (another Basil) about two years old, for whom he had no time to make a home. It was suggested that this little boy should be entrusted to William and Dorothy's care in return for fifty pounds a year.

At just about the same time, William was offered a house rent free – Racedown Lodge in Dorset. This offer came from two rich young men, the Pinney brothers, pupils of Montagu. The young Pinneys seem, like Raisley Calvert, to have been a little dazzled by Wordsworth's promise of genius and were eager to help him in any way they could.

Maybe it is not surprising that two privileged young men, just entering upon adulthood, should be aware of no contradiction in admiring a supporter of liberty and equality while continuing to enjoy all the advantages that their father's large fortune – made in the West Indies – bestowed upon them.

It is harder to understand the apparent unconcern with which William and Dorothy accepted their offer. The extremely comfortable Racedown Lodge had been financed by the slave trade, which ought to have been repugnant both to the radical William and to Dorothy who had been so outspoken in her support of Wilberforce's Abolition Bill. Amazingly, Dorothy was able to report in her long letter of September 1795: 'William is staying at Bristol, at present, with Mr Pinney and is very much delighted with the whole family, particularly Mr Pinney the father...'

William Wordsworth was on this occasion a very bad judge of character. He was almost certainly blinded by gratitude. Even by the standards of his day, John Pinney senior was not a delightful man. He had restored the fortunes of the ailing estate he had inherited on the West Indian Island of Nevis through a judicious combination of sound business sense and hypocrisy. Active in the anti-abolition campaign, Mr Pinney helped to organise three petitions to parliament which played a major role in delaying the ending of the slave trade until 1807. In 1765, he had produced a particularly unpleasant justification for the exploitation of one race by another: 'surely God ordained them [i.e. the entire population of Africa] for the use and benefit of us,' he argued, 'otherwise His Divine Will would surely have been made manifest by some particular Sign or Token.'

Such was John Pinney's reliance on his maker's generous provision of other human beings to be exploited for his profit, that he felt no qualms about employing subterfuge to protect his grotesque enterprise. When Tom Wedgwood, son of the anti-slavery campaigner Josiah Wedgwood, visited the Nevis estate in 1800, Pinney ordered his manager not to allow 'a negro to be corrected in his presence or so near for him to hear the whip.'[16]

This was the man with whom William Wordsworth was delighted. In fact, contrary to William and Dorothy's belief, old Mr Pinney was not a man who willingly provided free accommodation either. His sons had omitted to mention to him that the new tenants of Racedown Lodge were to pay no rent and he was furious when he discovered the truth.

The patronage of richer men was an integral part of life for members of the pseudo-gentry, and this may be one reason why the Wordsworths expressed no doubts about accepting the offer of a home. They were prepared to build their future on this offer just as the conventionally Tory Austens accepted that Cassandra's domestic happiness could be furthered by the brutal suppression of a slave revolt.

Dorothy's letter to her friend is full of the advantages of the new project, but many of the advantages she listed were never to be realised. There was, she hoped, to be another child in the household – the illegitimate daughter of a cousin – and 'with these two children and the produce of Raisley Calvert's legacy we shall have an income of at least 170 or 180£ per annum.'

This second child never arrived at Racedown, nor did the teenage son of Mr Pinney of whom Dorothy also had great hopes in September 1795. If this boy was entrusted to William as a pupil, 'then his income would be large, as he would have a very handsome salary. A Friend of Williams had the care of one of his brothers in his own house and had two hundred a year with him.'

These really were 'airy dreams'. In the end William and Dorothy found themselves struggling to live in Dorset on Montagu's £50, which was not regularly paid, and the Calvert legacy which came to them only a little at a time and much of which was, of necessity, used to pay off pressing debts rather than invested. Yet Dorothy was realistic about the responsibilities that lay ahead of her. 'It will be a very great charge for me I am sensible,' she wrote, 'but it is of a nature well suited to my inclinations. You know I am active, not averse to household employments, and fond of children... I shall also have a good deal of work, [sewing] to do – and I am determined to take the whole care of the children such as washing, dressing them etc upon myself.'

In fact, the domestic labour and childcare that lay ahead of Dorothy were almost indistinguishable from the duties she had escaped at Forncett rectory. But now she was to be living in a home she had (to some extent) chosen, with a man she loved. At Forncett she had felt herself to be 'living upon the bounty of one's friends', but at Racedown she believed she would be an independent woman.

On 22nd September 1795 she joined William in Bristol, having travelled all the way from Halifax on the public coach – probably on her own! Four days later the pair arrived at Racedown. Here, in a grand Georgian mansion founded on slavery, Dorothy Wordsworth began her experiment in liberty.

PART THREE

THIRTEEN

An Experiment in Liberty

Dorothy's life at Racedown, a fashionable red-brick house with four parlours and formal gardens decorated with statues, began much as she had expected[1]. Housework was her first concern.

She had 'one of the nicest girls I ever saw' for a maid and, once a month, a woman came to help with the washing. 'I give her ninepence for one day to wash,' wrote Dorothy, the novelty of keeping her own house seeming to prompt detailed descriptions. '[O]n the next [day] we have got the clothes dried and on the third have finished ironing.' This, she reported, was the only time that she had 'any thing to do in the house'. But she was keeping to her resolution of doing all the sewing herself. She was busy making 'frocks, shirts, slips etc' for little Basil. She also had 'a good deal of employment in repairing his clothes and putting my brothers (sic) into order.'[2]

She seems to have been enjoying herself. She was an adult now running her own house, with no aunt or grandmother to direct her. But her pleasure must have been marred by William's gloom. 'My brother handles the spade with great dexterity,'[3] Dorothy wrote proudly as William toiled in the garden, but William himself took little pleasure in his new accomplishment. 'We plant cabbages,' he told his friend Mathews, sounding resigned but glum, 'and if retirement ...be as powerful in working transformations as one of Ovid's Gods, you may perhaps suspect that into cabbages we shall be transformed.'[4]

He was returning to his theme of vegetation.

Dorothy's routine of household management and childcare was just as she had expected it to be, while William had looked forward to a life of tutoring and studying – not digging. But, with the slow payment of the Calvert legacy and the non-appearance of the young Pinney with his £200-a-year price-tag, there was no choice but to make use of the large kitchen garden and be as self-sufficient as they could.

Some biographers have suggested that William Wordsworth suffered a mental breakdown after his return from France. If that was the case, this was the period of his recovery. It would certainly seem that at this time Dorothy was caring for two needy, vulnerable people: a deeply unhappy man, and a very young child traumatised by bereavement and dislocation. The way in which she responded to the double challenge is revealing.

She had probably read the work of Jean-Jacques Rousseau, particularly his *Emile* with its ideas about raising a child in a state of nature; for she described teaching Basil nothing 'but what he learns from the evidence of his senses,' and endeavouring to answer his questions as fully and truthfully as possible. 'Our grand study,' claimed Dorothy, 'is to make him happy'. All this sounds as if it was inspired by the French philosopher. Rousseau's ideas would have had an emotional appeal to Dorothy, who valued naturalness and spontaneity. 'You are afraid to see [a child] spending his early years doing nothing,' wrote Rousseau. 'What! is it nothing to be happy, nothing to run and jump all day? He will never be so busy again all his life long.'

This attractive vision of childhood would help educationists break away from the brutal tradition of rote learning enforced by punishment, but Rousseau had not trialled his ideas before he let them loose on the world, and he knew very little about real children, for he had abandoned his own offspring to be brought up in an orphanage.

There was also a darker side to Rousseau's teaching, which, surprisingly, Dorothy seems to have embraced. 'To endure is the first thing that a child ought to learn,' he wrote, 'and that which he will have the most need to know.' He advocated an extremely hardy, bracing regime and a surprising number of parents at the end of the eighteenth century attempted to put the theory into practice. The parents of poor little Princess Sophie of Württemberg were disciples of Rousseau and they insisted the four-month-old baby be bathed in a cold fountain every morning and then left outside naked. Fortunately, Dorothy did not go quite so far in her treatment of the lonely grieving toddler who had been taken away from everyone he knew to live in an unfamiliar house with strangers, but her treatment of this child is odd and disquieting. It suggests that her brand of sensitivity could, at times, be surprisingly indifferent to the feelings and needs of others.

'At first when he [Basil] came he was … perpetually disposed to cry,' she explained to Jane Marshall – as if this was remarkable behaviour for such a young child in an unfamiliar environment. She then proudly described the system she had devised to deal with this nuisance, even suggesting that her friend might find the example useful in raising her own new baby. 'Upon the[se] occasions …' she said, 'w[e] used to tell him that if he chose to cry he must go into a certain room where he cannot be heard, and stay till he chose to be quiet, because the noise was unpleasant to us.' She reported with great satisfaction that the system had been entirely successful: '[A]t first his visits were very long, but he always came out again perfectly good-humoured. He found that this mode was never departed from, and when he felt the fretful disposition coming on he would say, "Aunt, I think I am going to cry" and retire till the fit was over. He has now entirely conquered the disposition.'[5]

It is hard to understand how Dorothy, who had suffered homesickness herself as a girl and who continued to lament her orphaned state all her life, could have been so indifferent to a lost, uprooted child; nor how she could suppose that the mere suppression of tears could genuinely help little Basil overcome his unhappiness. How could the woman who would write of her own adult weeping, 'I could not keep the tears within me,' use such a cruel, unperceptive phrase as 'chose to cry' about a little boy who was not yet three years old when he was entrusted to her care?

How could Dorothy Wordsworth – whose family and friends defined her by her 'ready sympathy' – resist the powerful human instinct to cuddle and comfort a weeping toddler? Dorothy's sensibility was not an affectation, but there were situations in which, while remaining 'tremblingly alive' to her own afflictions, she could fail to enter into those of another. Reading her Racedown letters it is hard not to conclude that little Basil fell outside the compass of Dorothy's sympathy. Though she dutifully reported that he was a 'charming boy' and expressed pleasure in watching 'his little occupations', she seems to have been able to maintain an emotional distance from him which contrasts sharply with the endless enthusiasm with which she would write about William's children when they began to appear on the scene. Then her detailed accounts to her friends could rival a mother's in doting admiration and shameless prejudice.

At Racedown, Dorothy was not playing a mother's role. She was, primarily, a *sister*. She was establishing the priorities which would dominate the rest of her life. William must be the focus of her sympathy – but William was not happy. There is an air of petulance in his letters written at this time. He appears to have found less pleasure than Dorothy in Basil's society. Contradicting Rousseau's insistence on a child's essential innocence, he fell back on more traditional ideas of sin, suspecting that there was much to fear for Basil's morals; 'among other things,' he reported gloomily, 'he lies like a little devil.'[6]

An instance of this deplorable moral degeneracy was that on one occasion the child fancied he saw a cow in his bedroom. Wordsworth solemnly 'expostulated with him on the unreasonableness of the idea',[7] which suggests that he did not adhere wholeheartedly to the principles outlined in *Emile*, for Rousseau believed that childhood was 'the sleep of reason'. Reasoned arguments about the likelihood of cows appearing in bedrooms should have been postponed until Basil was at least twelve. Certainly Wordsworth's response to this mysterious cow is disappointing. One might expect a budding Romantic to enter more readily into a three-year-old's imaginative world.

Dorothy and William were perhaps too absorbed in one another to be very conscientious, consistent or affectionate guardians of the child in their care. Basil himself later complained that they had treated him cruelly, saying that he 'was constantly employed in the most menial occupations: and but for the pity of the poor villagers…he should have been starved.'[8]

William was frustrated by his inability to write anything that pleased him. He acknowledged that his only compositions had a tinge of unkindness: 'I attempt to write satires!' he told Mathews, 'and in all satires…there will be found a spice of malignity.'[9]

Poverty and the lack of any prospect of an improvement in his fortunes would have been making him miserable; indecision and guilt over Annette would have made things worse too, for it is likely that it was clear to him now – if it had not been before – that he did not *wish* to marry the mother of his child. He would also have been reminded of another anxiety when, on a walk he saw, 'the West India fleet sailing in all its glory…'[10] This was Sir Ralph Abercromby's expedition – the expedition which Cassandra Austen's fiancé had joined[11] – and this glimpse of massed white sails caught from the peaceful Dorset hills may well have raised mixed feelings in William. The war between England and France, which he had once opposed as a cruel attack by a tyrannical nation on a fledgling democracy, was now taking on a very different meaning with the beginnings of Napoleon's rise and France's attempts to expand her power. One of the worries occupying William's mind as he dug morosely in his garden was probably one which puzzled many of his contemporaries: how could a man be a democrat and a patriot?

William's greatest torment was his uncertainty about what he *should* be doing, where his talents really lay and how he should try to make a difference in the world. 'We are now surrounded by winter prospects without doors,' wrote Dorothy in her first letter to Mrs Marshall from Racedown, 'and within have only winter occupations, books, solitude and the fireside.'[12] It sounds cosy, but it would take determination to remain cheerful in such an isolated situation if the beloved face on the opposite side of the hearth was haunted and troubled.

Dorothy had that determination, and William found the strength and support he desperately needed in his sister. Her love and her unswerving belief in him played a vital part in forming the man – and the poet – that he began to be from this time onward.

Wordsworth's biographer, John Worthen, who defines his subject as a 'peculiarly self-possessed but needy figure',[13] is convinced that 'It was Dorothy's presence and influence at Racedown which meant that he came back to being a poet.'[14]

To direct and form genius in this way would have been an exhilarating experience for a young woman and the way in which Dorothy said nothing about the process herself – her failure even to mention to her friends that William was troubled – was a part of that sacrificing of herself to William's needs which would become more and more marked as her life progressed.

Her motives in determining that William should be a poet were probably complex. She believed firmly in his talent, but she was probably also anxious about the dangers of a more political career and knew that poetry could draw him towards a retired life in the country such as suited her own tastes. In exerting her influence in this way, she was making this beloved man her own. She was providing a kind of support which no-one else had given him – not even Annette.

William and Dorothy were now truly sharing their lives. They had, in William's words:

'... found means

To walk abreast, though in a narrow path,

With undivided steps.'[15]

William was no longer the half-stranger whose adventures had been only imperfectly reported to his sister. His endeavours were all carried out within the home they shared. They were engaged upon a shared enterprise and their love could mature into solid friendship.

Dorothy was also making plans for the future. Somehow, she found time amidst the sewing and the washing and the providing of moral support to study Italian, reading Ariosto and Davila – challenging writers of the sixteenth and seventeenth century. In her letter to Aunt Crackenthorpe from Windy Brow Dorothy had described her study of Italian as providing not only future 'entertainment', but also 'advantage', and Aunt Rawson's letter about the London scheme indicates that as early as March 1795 Dorothy was seriously considering working as a translator. So her Italian studies may have been part of a plan to earn money for herself. Perhaps she had realised by now that William was not a very reliable bread-winner.

FOURTEEN

My Own Darling Child

I believe there is evidence to suggest Jane Austen was also striving for some degree of independence at this time. She was certainly developing a serious approach to her own work: an approach which could be described as professional.

According to the memorandum which Cassandra made of her sister's writing, Jane set about writing *First Impressions* – the first version of *Pride and Prejudice* – just after she returned from the prolonged visit to Rowling in October 1796, working through the particularly cold winter that followed and completing the book in August 1797. (That is during the time that Dorothy and William spent at Racedown.) This brief note of Cassandra's is one of the most revealing facts that survive about Jane Austen's life: she wrote the novel in ten months and it was not a short book: the finished *Pride and Prejudice* is around 130,000 words and this first draft was probably longer, for Jane would talk of 'lopping and cropping' the text when she later came to revise it.

To write in ten months a full-length novel which would be enjoyed by everyone who read it or heard it read, required inspiration and talent, to be sure, but it also required sheer hard work. It required the author to sit down at her desk, not only when the whim took her and she had nothing more pressing to do, but regularly, for long periods. It required an input of time and effort comparable to that of a full-time job.

Brother Henry's earliest *Biographical Notice* set the tone for the way in which Jane's family would choose for her writing career to be remembered. 'She became an authoress entirely from taste and inclination,' he wrote. 'Neither the hope of fame nor profit mixed with her early motives.' [1]

Since Henry wrote those words in 1817, reading her letters has made many people question this ladylike, dilettante picture. 'I am never too busy to think of [*Sense and Sensibility*]' she wrote in 1811, 'I can no more forget it than a mother can forget her sucking child'[2]. And 'I cannot help hoping that many will feel themselves obliged to buy it,' she would write of the same novel in 1813. And, after the publication of *Sense and Sensibility* and *Pride and Prejudice* she wrote to her brother Frank, 'I have now written myself into £250 – which only makes me long for more'.[3]

This does not sound like the refined disinterest which her family chose to portray. In the same way, it is worth noting, Henry's sugary assessment of his sister's character must surprise anyone who has read Jane's letters. 'Faultless herself, as nearly as human nature can be,' he eulogised, 'she always sought, in the faults of others, something to excuse, to forgive or forget ... She never uttered either a hasty, a silly, or a severe expression.'

This, however, was the woman who not only admitted that she had difficulty finding other people agreeable, but who could also pen the infamous line which has shocked and delighted generations of her admirers: 'Mrs Hall of Sherbourne was brought to bed yesterday of a dead child, some weeks before she expected, oweing to a fright – I suppose she happened unawares to look at her husband.'[4] And 'Only think of Mrs Holder's being dead!' she exclaimed in another letter. 'Poor woman, she has done the only thing in the World she could possibly do, to make one cease to abuse her.'[5]

Even in her published work, she could describe a young boy killed at sea as 'a troublesome hopeless son' whose family had had 'the good fortune to lose him before he reached his twentieth year.'[6] The evidence contradicts the panegyric. However, Henry was not simply retailing conventional platitudes; he was representing his dead sister as she might have wished to be remembered. A prayer written by Jane Austen (which survives in a manuscript that may have been partially copied out by Henry) contains these lines: 'Incline us oh God! to think humbly of ourselves, to be severe only in the examination of our own conduct, to consider our fellow-creatures with kindness, and to judge all they say and do with that charity which we could desire from them ourselves.'[7] But conscientious people pray for help in overcoming their faults, not in celebration of their virtues.

Henry's kind representation of Jane as the mild, uncritical person she prayed to be was very natural in a recently bereaved and loving brother and Jane's ideas of justice, of what people owed to one another in everyday social interaction, were certainly very strong. Her ideal of behaviour can be found in *Sense and Sensibility* when Elinor scrupulously pays to the tedious Mrs Jennings the polite attentions which she feels are her due and which Marianne neglects to pay.[8]

However, it seems that at times Jane's emotional reaction to people could get the better of this reasoned, moral stance. Sometimes she fell (quite far) short of her own ideals, and readers of her fiction have reason to be thankful that she never did overcome that fault of severity towards her fellow-creatures without which such wonderful characters as Mr Collins, Mrs Elton and Aunt Norris could never have been created.

The tragedy is that, by making Jane into the ideal Christian lady he wished to remember, Henry was denying her genius. Maybe Henry was also trying to describe Jane as he thought she would wish to be remembered when he said that, in her work, she was indifferent to fame and profit. Jane wrote enthusiastically about her novels – particularly in the excitement of first publication – but mostly this was in letters to Cassandra and this may have been one of those subjects on which the true feelings of the sisters were known only to each other.

In a letter written to Cassandra in January 1813, Jane was full of excitement: 'I want to tell you that I have got my own darling Child from London.' The darling child was the first printed copy of *Pride and Prejudice* and she filled more than a page of her letter with all the natural concerns of an author at such a moment – typographic errors, the distribution of her free copies, the reactions of her friends, and minor errors of her own that she had detected ('a "said he" or a "said she" would sometimes make the Dialogue more immediately clear'). After a while, though, she pulled herself up. 'Now I will try to write of something else,'[9] she said firmly. She had talked long enough of her own concerns.

James Edward Austen-Leigh believed that his aunt 'wrote upon small sheets of paper which could easily be put away or covered with a piece of blotting paper', and that, in her last home at Chawton, 'There was, between the front door and the offices, a swing door which creaked when it was opened; but she objected to having this little inconvenience remedied, because it gave her notice when anyone was coming.'[10]

This suggests that she was reluctant to let people know about the work she was engaged in.

Perhaps Jane did not want to seem self-important, a fault for which she mocked others, and it is understandable that her family should wish her to be remembered as quiet and self-effacing, for these were qualities much admired in women (particularly spinsters) at the time. Professional excellence was a virtue proper only to men.

However, Jane was certainly professional and business-like over the writing of *First Impressions*. She must have taken to her dressing room and her writing desk very soon after Edward delivered her from Rowling. The novel had perhaps been coming to fruition in her head during her prolonged visit, and the pressing need for space and time in which to write may have played its part in her impatience to return home.

Imagine having the germ of *Pride and Prejudice* inside you, demanding to be written, and being forced to waste time sewing shirts and being polite about someone else's baby!

Perhaps Henry was not so far wrong in his praise of his sister's good nature. Jane would have required a fair amount of patience in order to confine her irritation to jokes about leering fat women and barbed comments about Edward's eagerness to make money.

Jane's new book returned to the central concern of her previous novel: a family of financially insecure sisters in search of suitable husbands. She was establishing herself in the fictional territory which she would make her own and, like the territory which Dorothy chose, it was confined, rooted in the everyday. However, her motives for limiting the scope of her subject matter appear to have been different from Dorothy's, for, without engaging in political debate, she wrote again about some of the most insidious social injustices of her age while quietly avoiding controversy. Her novel was witty, but neither coarse nor unfeminine.

Pride and Prejudice (and we can only judge the earlier version of the story by the published book, for there is no surviving copy of *First Impressions*) begins light-heartedly with its famous line pronouncing the 'truth' that a rich man needs a wife. It is a snappier, livelier beginning than the description of the Dashwood girls' misfortunes with which *Sense and Sensibility* opens, but, as the tale progresses, a darker bass theme develops beneath the sparkling melody of Lizzy's witty dialogue and hilariously dire relations. The Bennet sisters are living more precariously than the Dashwoods. Their situation is made worse because they have no brother to share his last farthing with them as Dorothy fantasised, no brother even to feel the faint guilty pangs of neglected duty as John Dashwood does.

The Bennet girls' misfortunes are revealed gradually. It is not until the beginning of the seventh chapter, when the lighter theme is well established with Miss Bennet and Mr Bingley already falling in love and Mr Darcy gradually admitting to Elizabeth's charms, that we learn: 'Mr Bennet's property consisted almost entirely in an estate of two thousand a year, which, unfortunately for his daughters was entailed in default of heirs male, on a distant relation.'[11] After that the threatening shadow of future poverty is dramatised by Mr Bingley's sisters' disdain of Elizabeth and her sister, and Mrs Bennet's determination to marry one of her daughters to the ghastly Mr Collins (the distant relation who will inherit Mr Bennet's property), until, at last, in Chapter Nineteen, it is put into harshly accurate terms in Mr Collins' insulting proposal speech: 'I am well aware,' he tells Elizabeth, 'that…one thousand pounds in 4 per cents which will not be yours until after your mother's decease, is all that you may ever be entitled to.'[12]

This bald statement – entirely in keeping with the character of Jane Austen's most repulsive clergyman – ensures that readers understand the situation exactly as the heroine and her sister struggle to achieve happiness in the genteel world from which they may, all too soon, be excluded. But, though the early part of the novel has been dominated by the embarrassing behaviour of Mrs Bennet, as the story progresses, Mr Bennet's role in this dysfunctional family becomes apparent.

It is Mr Bennet who, though he recognises Lydia's vulnerability, fails to prevent her endangering her reputation and her future happiness by visiting the militia camp at Brighton. And finally, Mr Bennet, shut away in the library in which he has habitually hidden from his responsibilities, contemplates the only way in which his daughters' futures might have been made more secure. 'Mr Bennet,' Jane wrote, 'had very often wished that instead of spending his whole income, he had laid by an annual sum, for the better provision of his children, and of his wife, if she survived him.'[13]

Mr Austen might have taken the same precaution.

This passage – which could have caused uneasiness as it was read out in the rectory parlour – is immediately followed by a humorous comment: if Mr Bennet had saved money, the author reflects, 'The satisfaction of prevailing on one of the most worthless young men in Great Britain to be [Lydia's] husband, might then have rested in its proper place.'

This trick of following a critical remark with a disarming joke is a device used again and again in Jane's letters, so maybe it was employed here to the same purpose – to keep the peace and sidestep the controversy which the first statement had provoked.

The fact was there had been no such provision made for the Austen women, nor did it seem likely that it would be made. Jane's recent experience with Tom Lefroy may well have made her less hopeful of ever finding a suitable marriage partner. Now she was spending hours away from her family, shut away in her dressing-room, behaving like a professional writer. She may have been attempting to make that provision for her future which her father had failed to make.

The plots of both *Pride and Prejudice* and *Sense and Sensibility* hinge on the inequitable distribution of family resources; and an injustice two generations back in her own family may have been in Jane Austen's mind as she devised them. If Jane's great-great-grandfather's will had been more even-handed, she and her immediate family would have occupied a more privileged place in society.

John Austen, who died in 1705, was a very wealthy man, but his money came from trade. He had made his fortune as a clothier, supplying wool to the home-based handloom weavers and collecting and selling their finished cloth. In pre-industrial days it was a lucrative trade, but John was ambitious for his only son, determined that he should take a step up the social ladder and become a gentleman, rather than a tradesman.

However, this son died a year before his father, leaving a widow, a daughter and six sons.

After his son's death, old John Austen seems to have been worried that the money he had amassed might be divided and he made a will which would be a source of bitterness for several generations to come. He left almost his entire fortune to his eldest grandson, John. To his granddaughter he left only £400 and to the younger boys just £200 each. In addition he left to each of these boys the sum of £40 to be used, when they were 14 years old, 'towards putting and placing them out to Trades or Employments'.[14] The allowance for these apprenticeships made it very clear that the younger boys were to remain tradesmen, and only the oldest brother was to be made into a gentleman.

Jane's grandfather, William Austen – one of those boys who had inherited just £200 and an apprenticeship (to a surgeon, in his case) – seems to have felt his grandfather's injustice deeply for, when he came to make his own will nearly thirty years later, he insisted that his trustees should divide his possessions between his son George and his daughters, Philadelphia and Leonora, 'in as equal manner as possible having no respect to sex or Eldership'.[15]

He chose to make his daughters equal sharers in everything he had.

Despite the social prejudices against women at the time, this was a choice which any father was free to make, if he was not restricted by entail arrangements imposed by earlier generations. And Jane Austen's early novels reflect this crucial element of choice.

This very important distinction is often lost in adaptations of the books as script-writers struggle to compress complex narratives into the two hours' traffic of the screen. Explaining their poverty to her youngest sister, Margaret, in Emma Thompson's film script of *Sense and Sensibility,* Elinor says it comes about because 'estates pass from father to son, not father to daughter', but the book goes to some length to show that this is not the problem. The Dashwood sisters' uncle *could* have provided for his nieces, but chose instead to leave everything to their brother's little boy simply because he had 'gained on the affection of his uncle'.[16] Though, in *Pride and Prejudice*, the imposition of the entail which makes the Bennet girls' futures insecure lies further back in family history, it is not inevitable; as Lady Catherine condescendingly observes, such a measure 'was not thought necessary in Sir Lewis De Bourgh's family'.[17]

When it came to inheritance, the stories Jane Austen told were not about the big picture, the widespread legal discrimination against women (for example, the laws which put a wife's property into her husband's control). Instead, she concerned herself, as usual, with the actions of individuals and the choices they made within the limitations of their society.

The story of the very different choices made by her great-great-grandfather and by her grandfather was certainly well-known to Jane.

The fortunate gentleman created by old John Austen's will had one son who inherited his estate. This son lived until he was 91, surviving his only child (an unmarried daughter). When he died in 1807, the entire fortune was inherited by a great-nephew and passed well out of the reach of the Steventon branch of the family. Jane announced this news in a letter to Cassandra beginning with:

'We have at last heard something of Mr Austen's will ...' which suggests there had been a great deal of interest (and perhaps a little hope) in the subject. Having broken the bad news that none of the money was to come to Steventon, she commented sourly: 'Such ill-gotten wealth can never prosper!'[18]

More than a century after John Austen wrote his will, Jane still felt its injustice – as her grandfather had when he divided his (very limited) fortune without regard to 'sex or eldership'. But maybe Jane's father was less impressed by the memory. For he does not seem to have been determined to establish all *his* children equally well in life.

Jane's rapid composition of *First Impressions* was disrupted by two family events in the early months of 1797. Her eldest brother, James – now a clergyman – had lost his first wife two years before and been left alone with a small daughter, Anna (who would become one of the nieces closest to her Aunt Jane). Now, on 17th January, James remarried. His new bride was Mary Lloyd – described by cousin Eliza as 'not either rich or handsome, but very sensible & good-humoured'. The Lloyd sisters, Mary and Martha, had been friends of Jane and Cassandra's for many years and it was to Mary – whose face was scarred by smallpox – that Jane had entrusted her former lovers when she committed her own heart to Tom Lefroy.

'Jane seems much pleased with the match,' Eliza reported of James's marriage, 'and it is natural she should be having long known & liked the lady'[19]. But time was to prove that a good friend does not necessarily translate into a good sister-in-law.

Surprisingly, Henry Austen described the author of *Pride and Prejudice* – that classic tale of altered opinions – as someone who 'seldom changed her opinions', but about Mary Lloyd Jane certainly would change her opinion over the years to come. As friends Jane and Mary had been equals but now there had been a significant shift of status in their relationship.

Jane Austen was sensitive to the customs which gave wives precedence over single women. In *Pride and Prejudice* Lydia Bennet displays her silly selfishness when, after her marriage, she insists on taking her eldest sister's place at table, '…because I am a married woman.'[20] When, in *Emma*, Mrs Elton must be given the honour of opening the Westons' ball, Emma herself – who has always protested her intention of remaining single – finds 'It was almost enough to make her think of marrying.'[21]

Now Jane saw her friend Mary take precedence in all these little matters. Now Mary would have the kind of power over Jane and Cassandra which Fanny Dashwood exerts over Elinor and Marianne.

According to his granddaughter, James's second marriage was, 'more to the taste of his family than the first'.[22] Mrs Austen welcomed her new daughter to the family with a kind, affectionate letter; but, even as she praised Mary who would be 'a real comfort to me in my old age', there was a hint of mystification or exasperation towards her youngest daughter. Looking forward to her own old age, Mrs Austen foresaw a time when Cassandra would be 'gone into Shropshire' (where, it was hoped, her fiancé would eventually get a church living). '& Jane–' she supposed, would be gone, 'the Lord knows where.'

Poor Mrs Austen! Her (perhaps limited) imagination seems to have failed her when she considered Jane's future. What was to become of this odd girl? She had been discontent in the social whirl of her brother's comfortable Kent home and, after all, what were such visits for but to give a young lady the opportunity of widening her circle of acquaintance and meeting possible husbands? And now that she had returned home she had shut herself away in an upstairs room, just writing and writing!

Then, as the bitterly cold winter gave way to a slow, reluctant spring and the pages of finished manuscript gradually stacked up beside Jane's writing desk, Cassandra's future became as uncertain as her sister's. The second, much more disturbing, family event to draw Jane away from the developing passion of Lizzy and Darcy in the spring of 1797 was the death of Cassandra's fiancé, Tom Fowle. In April, just as there began to be some hope of the young man returning, news reached Steventon that he had died of yellow fever off St Domingo.

'Jane says that her sister behaves with a degree of resolution &

propriety which no common mind could evince in so trying a situation,'[23] reported cousin Eliza. Even in this extreme situation, we glimpse the qualities Jane admired in another woman's behaviour.

Despite her air of proper resignation, Cassandra's love for Tom appears to have been very deep; she was never to marry anyone else and her family would describe her as sinking into a premature middle-age from about this time. Jane was probably the only person with whom Cassandra could talk unreservedly of her grief. Time must have been given to the necessary business of support and comfort.

Yet Jane kept on writing. Even in the midst of her sister's grief her novel remained important. It is another mark of her professional attitude towards the work she had undertaken. Any interruption to her writing routine cannot have been a long one, or she could not have achieved a finished novel by August – certainly not one which would entertain its first audience as well as *First Impressions* did. Despite its uncomfortable references, the story was thoroughly enjoyed by the Austens and their friends. Even three-year-old Anna liked listening as it was read aloud, until it was decided that it was not suitable for her to hear and she was excluded from the readings. Martha Lloyd must have read it several times because in 1799 Jane joked that one more reading of the manuscript would enable her to know it by heart and she would be able to 'publish it from memory'[24].

As the novel was read and enjoyed and praised, from somewhere, there came the idea of publication. The book entertained everyone who heard it, so perhaps a wider audience would appreciate it. It is impossible to know with whom this idea originated. Mr Austen is usually credited with starting it because it was he who, three months after the book was completed, wrote a letter to the publisher, Thomas Cadell. But no matter who first made the suggestion, Mr Austen would have been considered the proper person to take that action. Although Jane was now twenty-one, she was still a dependent and her father had authority over her. Just as Dorothy asked her uncle's permission to travel, Jane would not have expected to act independently in such an important matter as this (and she never did make an initial contact with a publisher herself). If an approach was to be made to a publisher, then her father ought to make it.

It is possible that Mr Austen determined upon seeking a publisher himself, but it is also possible that he yielded to the persuasions of other friends or members of the family – or pressure from Jane herself. This may have been the end to which she had been working over the last ten months of intense effort.

The letter that Mr Austen wrote is decidedly lacklustre. He does not sound enthusiastic about the book himself; he might well have been acting on someone else's wishes rather than his own. 'I have in my possession,' he wrote, 'a manuscript novel, comprised in three Vols. About the length of Miss Burney's Evelina.' There is nothing there likely to make any publisher wish to read it. He continued though with a little flattery, such as he used on patrons he hoped would advance his sons' careers, writing, 'as I am well aware of what consequence it is that a work of this sort should make it's first Appearance under a respectable name I apply to you.' He then went on to ask what would be the cost of publishing the book at the author's expense and how much Cadell would pay for it, if he liked it well enough to buy it outright.

These two suggestions reflect alternative ways of publishing at the time. Either a publisher bought the copyright of a work and took the profits from it, or the author invested his or her own capital in the venture and took the proceeds of sales.

Unsurprisingly, Mr Austen's brief missive failed to persuade Cadell to consider either option. 'Declined by return of post' was written across the top of the letter. Thomas Cadell did not even look at the manuscript. It was the letter that failed, not the book, but Mr Austen does not seem to have made any approach to other publishers.

This one short, ineffectual letter is often considered as evidence that Mr Austen was supportive of his younger daughter's work, but it was a limited kind of support which produced no more effort to find a publisher for *First Impressions,* and no attempt to sell the two books which followed rapidly as Jane remained dedicated to the hard work of writing. His query about the cost of publishing at 'the author's risk' does suggest he may have considered – or been persuaded to consider – putting forward money for publication, but this offer never became more concrete.

This single attempt to promote the career of his brilliant daughter pales into insignificance when set against the time and effort Mr Austen devoted to forwarding the fortunes of his sons. In 1794 his attempts simply to get Frank moved from one ship to another involved canvassing the interest of Warren Hastings, Admiral Sir Edmund Affleck and Mr Pybus (a Lord of the Admiralty).[25] Four years later he and his sons were still pestering potential patrons – 'The Lords of the Admiralty will have enough of our applications,' quipped Jane.[26]

Mr Austen was certainly not unusual in considering his sons' careers to be more important than his daughter's, and he did not actively *discourage* Jane from writing. But it was not unknown for aspiring female authors to be more actively encouraged by their fathers at this time. There is evidence that Maria Edgeworth, Amelia Opie and Susan Ferrier all received more paternal support than Jane did.

Although there were no more approaches to publishers, Jane's next move was that of a dedicated, professional writer: she took out the manuscript of *Elinor and Marianne* and began to rewrite it, converting it from an epistolary novel into a straightforward narrative. Again there were distractions as she tried to work. In November Jane, Cassandra and their mother accompanied their aunt and uncle Leigh-Perrot to Bath and stayed for a month. This visit – which seems to have been Jane's first experience of a town she was to come to thoroughly dislike – was made for the sake of her mother's health.

Though Mrs Austen's early married life had been characterised by hard work and energy with a home, a farm and a school of boys to oversee, now that she had less to think about, she seems to have become rather preoccupied with her own health, an interest which would sometimes irritate her younger daughter. Jane was impatient with anything approaching hypochondria; she would hold the subject up to merciless ridicule in her last, unfinished novel, *Sanditon,* even as the illness that would end her own life was taking hold. So Mrs Austen's new hobby may well have been another cause of friction between mother and daughter – particularly when it took Jane away from the peace of the Steventon dressing room and her work.

Soon after the ladies returned to the rectory there was the distraction of another family engagement. Cousin Henry, having broken his previous engagement to Mary Pearson, had now formed a new attachment. His fiancée – whom he married on the last day of 1797 – was none other than his cousin, the glamorous widow, Eliza de Feuillide.

Jean-François de Feuillide was now dead, having fallen foul of the new revolutionary government of France. His wife described him in one letter as 'a strong Aristocrate or Royalist in his Heart'.[27] There is an echo here of Dorothy's description of herself: 'I own I am too much of an aristocrate or what you please to call me ...'. It seems that, in this Age of Revolution, the term 'aristocrate' was used, not just to refer to titled folk, but also as a kind of shorthand to indicate allegiance.

Sometime in 1793 de Feuillide was arrested for an attempt to save the Marquis de Marboeuf from execution and, early in 1794, he himself perished on the guillotine. These events would, of course, have provided Jane Austen's personal experience of the French Revolution, in marked contrast to the account that would have been mediated to Dorothy through the observations of her brother.

Eliza – who had remained in England since the birth of her son[28] – recovered rapidly from any grief she felt at her husband's death, and showed every sign of enjoying her widowhood. She was not prepared to admit, even now, that she might marry for love. '[I]ndependence and the homage of half a dozen are preferable to subjection and the attachment of a single individual' she had written earlier that year; and Henry's greatest attractions lay in his 'steady attachment' and his readiness to let her have her own way.[29] However, Eliza was to prove a much more congenial and kindly sister-in-law to Jane than James's bride.

With the distraction of the wedding out of the way, Jane continued with her task of turning *Elinor and Marianne* into *Sense and Sensibility*. The translation from epistolary form to third person narrative would have been hard, often tedious, work, a honing of her craft much more than an exercise of the imagination. What was the impetus for such a labour?

The tale had already reached as wide an audience as she could expect without the manuscript being circulated as a printed book. There would have been little satisfaction in reading it again – even in a revised form – to the same circle of family and friends. It is difficult to see what her purpose can have been if she was not aiming for publication.

FIFTEEN

A *Small Revolution*

Like Jane's writing, Dorothy's study of Ariosto was constantly interrupted. The cold winter of 1796/97, which Jane spent ensconced in her dressing room conjuring into being Lizzy Bennet and Mr Darcy, produced money worries at Racedown.

Uncle Richard Wordsworth – who had financed William's studies at Cambridge – had died in 1794; but the debt of about £400 was still outstanding and now his son, Robinson Wordsworth, was – not unreasonably – asking that at least some of it should be repaid. Up in Cumberland gossiping folk were saying that young William Wordsworth had 'used his Uncle's children very ill.' Dorothy and William, unable to deny the justice of their cousin's claims, were upset.

'We are very anxious to know what you have done respecting Robinson Wordsworth's claims upon us'[1], wrote Dorothy to their lawyer brother, Richard. Poor Richard! William and Dorothy always looked to him to sort out legal and financial problems. Perhaps, on this occasion, they hoped he might put up some money. But Richard probably felt that William should make more effort to earn something for himself.

There were, however, visitors to distract Dorothy. At Racedown she first experienced the long-anticipated pleasure of welcoming friends to a home of her own. Mary Hutchinson came in the spring of 1797. She and Dorothy worked happily together, making fair copies of the poems William was now composing and sewing shirts for both William and Richard.

If his brother and sister were a little unreasonable in their demands on him, Richard also seems to have expected unpaid labour from Dorothy, and his attitude towards the construction of these shirts was unhelpfully cavalier. His answer to the question of how long they should be was 'a tolerable length' and when the first four shirts proved too tight around the neck, Dorothy wrote testily, 'It is a great pity you did not send me an accurate measure.' Relations with this eldest brother were never easy.

Mary Hutchinson left Racedown on 5th June 1797 and the following day produced a visitor who put shirts and money troubles – and pretty much everything else – out of Dorothy's head.

Coleridge arrived.[2]

'You had great loss in not seeing Coleridge,' Dorothy enthused in a letter to Mary Hutchinson. 'He is a wonderful man. His conversation teems with soul, mind and body.' She described him as 'pale and thin, has a wide mouth, thick lips, and not very good teeth, longish loose-growing half-curling rough black hair ...' But, like Maria and Julia Bertram of *Mansfield Park* who think Henry Crawford plain at a first meeting only to be won over by his charming ways, Dorothy soon did not notice Coleridge's looks. '[I]f you hear him speak for five minutes,' she assured Mary, 'you think no more of them.'[3]

Dorothy knew before she met Coleridge that he was a married man and there was never any wavering in her devotion to her brother. She would certainly not have said that she was in love with her new acquaintance. But she would also have rejected such commonplace words as *respect* or *esteem*. 'Eager in everything', Dorothy immediately gave this charismatic man a unique place in her affections. It was a dangerous thing to do. Everybody who loved Coleridge was, sooner or later, hurt by him.

The reason why there was no conflict in her feelings for her new friend and her brother was because they too were, for a while at least, infatuated with each other. Wordsworth and Coleridge – who had met, briefly, before – read their work to each other and talked. And Dorothy talked with them.

Coleridge had intended to stay at Racedown for only ten days, but it was not until the beginning of July that he returned to his home at Nether Stowey (about thirty-five miles away, in Somerset), and when he did return he took his new friends with him. None of them could bear the thought of parting, and Dorothy seems to have had no hesitation in leaving little Basil behind with the maid, Peggy. Her intoxication with Coleridge's company entirely overcame her determination to take all the care of the child upon herself.

Coleridge's little cottage on Lime Street in Nether Stowey, with its cramped parlour, three small bedrooms and an open drain running within yards of the front door, was a world away from the gracious mansion that had been the Wordsworths' home for the last year and a half. The place did not dampen their spirits – though it did perhaps drive them out into the fresh air as much as possible. Leaving behind his wife, Sarah, and nine-month-old son, Hartley, Coleridge took Dorothy and William rambling for hours – days – in the Somerset countryside which delighted them all. Dorothy wrote to her friends of, 'sea, woods wild as fancy ever painted, brooks clear and pebbly as in Cumberland ...'[4]

They walked and continued to talk. They talked about philosophy and poetry, they talked about the meaning of life and how to change the world. Dorothy was now joining in a conversation far removed from the usual chit-chat that genteel women shared with their men-folk in drawing-room and ballroom. This was that delightful sharing of thoughts without fear of ridicule or censure, which her 'elopement' had made possible.

It would take a whole book to summarise all that might have been discussed during those walks in Somerset; the meeting of Coleridge and Wordsworth laid the foundations of English Romantic Poetry as they both 'sought to define what would be for them the most appropriate field of endeavour.'[5] The two men may well have talked about events in France, for they would both, later, date their disenchantment with political radicalism to about this time. They certainly discussed the work of the philosophers Coleridge was reading: David Hartley, Joseph Priestley, George

Berkeley and others. Gradually, William's faith in political revolution was replaced by an almost mystical belief that 'love of Nature...must lead both to a perception of the harmony of all things and to acceptance "of human suffering or of human joy"'.[6]

In this new way of looking at the world deep feeling – sensibility – was of paramount importance. Summing up the ideas formulated at this time William would explain that, 'the feeling therein developed [i.e. in his poems] gives importance to the action and situation, and not the action and situation to the feeling.'[7] But feeling was not an end in itself: 'For our continued influxes of feeling are modified and directed by our thoughts, which are indeed the representatives of all our past feelings'. So 'our feelings will be connected with important subjects', and this would have a profoundly moral influence.

It was a deep, complicated, exciting discussion, a welcome relief from housework and childcare! It must have been exhilarating for Dorothy, but we can only know the ideas distilled from it; the conversation itself is lost. We cannot know whether Dorothy merely listened, or whether she contributed.

Dorothy never returned to Racedown. By mid-July the Wordsworths had moved themselves, Basil, and Peggy, into Somerset. Their 'principal inducement was Coleridge's society'. And, though they had begun with 'some dreams of happiness in a little cottage', the house they took was no cottage; it was even larger than Racedown Lodge. 'Here we are in a large mansion, in a large park, with seventy head of deer around us,'[8] Dorothy announced to Mary Hutchinson on 14th August 1797 – as if she had just woken up to find the move accomplished.

Alfoxton House, about three miles from Nether Stowey, had been discovered by William and Dorothy on one of their walks. Built in the early eighteenth century, it had nine bedrooms, several living rooms and the full complement of kitchens, cellars, attics, stables and pleasure grounds required of a true gentleman's residence.

Three adults and a child would barely have filled a corner of it. During their life there, Dorothy would write of gathering firewood in the neighbouring woods, evoking an odd picture of her and William returning to the grandeur of Alfoxton House to light a makeshift fire of twigs and dead branches in an elegant drawing-room fireplace.[9] They can have done little more than set up camp in the house; their lives would have failed to fill the many empty rooms; there would have been unopened doors ranked along corridors, and voices must have echoed in the vastness of the place.

The rent was £23 a year, a price they certainly could not afford, but this seems to have been the only house available to rent. The Wordsworths loved it and, of course, they urgently needed to be near Coleridge.

The creative result of their year's stay at Alfoxton would be impressive. This extraordinary alliance (which Coleridge would describe as: 'tho we were three persons, it was but one God'[10]) was the beginning of Dorothy's journal writing and produced, from the two men, the ground-breaking volume of poetry, *Lyrical Ballads*. But the Wordsworths' decision to move into Somerset cannot have seemed wise to their family and more prudent friends.

Brother Richard must have been horrified by their abandoning a rent-free home for one which would absorb half their income for the coming year. Their cousin, Robinson Wordsworth – still waiting for his money to be repaid – would have been unlikely to accept the necessity of their occupying a vast mansion in glorious countryside while he struggled to find enough money on which to marry.

In this triangular love-affair – the 'Concern' as they called themselves – feelings were considered to be all important. A few years later Coleridge would describe the trio of himself, Wordsworth and Dorothy as having 'seen a great deal of what is called the World, & yet have formed a deep conviction that all is contemptible that does not spring immediately out of an affectionate Heart.'[11] But Dorothy's affection, though it endowed her with an extraordinary capacity for self-sacrifice, seems to have had its blind-spots. At this time it certainly did not include poor Robinson Wordsworth – nor Sarah Coleridge.

Just as Marianne Dashwood is contemptuous and inconsider-ate towards the dull, kindly Mrs Jennings because she believes her to lack sensibility, so Dorothy could be dismissive of those she believed did not share her own depth of feeling. Coleridge's wife, Sarah, did not win Dorothy's approval or affection; she believed her to be lacking in sensibility. Sarah was excluded from their walks and discussions, but she was an interesting character who would play a significant role in Dorothy's life. It was a mistake to underestimate her – as Dorothy consistently did.

Just a few years earlier it had been Sarah tramping about the countryside with Coleridge having interesting conversations. Together with her sister Edith and Coleridge's friend Robert Southey, they had – during those shockingly unchaperoned excursions – planned nothing short of Utopia. They meant to found an ideal society in America where about twelve men and twelve women would live a simple rural life, holding all property in common, all joining in the cultivation of the soil, all studying and educating their children.

The project, which they called Pantisocracy, was more than a theory. They really intended to carry it out until it foundered on a lack of money and disagreements between Coleridge and Southey. It drew on Rousseau's ideas about the virtues to be found in nature and the vices that inevitably follow from an urban existence. It also incorporated William Godwin's radical teachings on shared ownership of property. Her willingness to join in this scheme says a great deal about the young Sarah; it would have required extraordinary courage for a woman of her time to consider such an undertaking.

Perhaps the inclusion of Sarah and Edith in the discussions had the effect of introducing an element of what we would now call feminism into Pantisocracy. Perhaps they were able to point out to their idealistic lovers that women could only achieve the freedom to study if they were not tied entirely to domestic duties, for, unlike most radical and revolutionary philosophies of the time, Pantisocracy embraced a degree of gender equality. This is how Coleridge himself foresaw the division of labour in their community:

'Let the married Women do only what is absolutely convenient and customary for pregnant Women or nurses. Let husbands do all the Rest – and what will that all be? Washing with a Machine and cleaning the House. One Hour's addition to our daily Labor ... An infant is almost always sleeping and during its slumbers the Mother may in the same Room perform the little offices of ironing Cloaths or making Shirts.'[12]

As her life progressed, Dorothy Wordsworth was to find herself increasingly restricted by the burdens of domestic life, a fate she shared with Jane Austen and thousands of other intelligent women in a time when simply maintaining a modicum of comfort in a home and getting meals on the table involved incessant labour: when fires must be lit and maintained to heat ovens, when every drop of water must be carried from a pump or well, when chamber-pots must be emptied, when shirts must be sewn and sheets washed by hand. (Most Georgian housewives seem to have had no access to that mysterious washing machine which Coleridge meant to use in America.)

It was widely accepted at the time that such work was a woman's lot. However, while it is wise, as we consider the past, to remember the differences in attitudes that belong to different ages, and important not to judge too freely by our own standards, it is also worthwhile to note that sometimes those in possession of a privilege may recognise its injustice and yet retain it. Notions of equality *had* emerged among the people with whom Dorothy lived, but had been deliberately discarded when they proved inconvenient. A redistribution of chores was one revolutionary idea which could have changed her life entirely.

When he laid the plans for his Utopia, Coleridge clearly knew little about housework or babies. In fact, he and his friend seem to have been remarkably ignorant about physical labour of any kind. 'When Coleridge and I are sawing down a tree,' fantasised Robert Southey, 'we shall discuss metaphysics: criticise poetry when hunting a buffalo, and write sonnets whilst following the plough.'[13]

However, Coleridge's ideas about equality in marriage outlived

the Pantisocratic American Dream. After the project was abandoned and he and Sarah moved into their little cottage, there was
enough idealism left to keep him from Wordsworth's fear of vegetation. His marriage – though it might have been 'hurried on' by
gossip – began very happily and he intended 'to work very hard as
Cook, Butler, Scullion, Shoe-cleaner, occasional Nurse, Gardener,
Hind, Pig-protector, Chaplain, Secretary, Poet and Reviewer ...'[14]

How fortunate Sarah must have thought herself to have won
such an enlightened, considerate husband! However, by the
time Dorothy Wordsworth came into their lives, Sarah had seen
alarming changes in the man she loved: changes in his ideas, and
changes in the man himself. A married man now, with a baby,
a vegetable patch and a pig, Coleridge had a more realistic view
of all kinds of physical labour and he was much less enthusiastic
about undertaking it. His ideals were not substantial enough to
stand against the rigours of real life. Maybe this is an indication
that it *was* Sarah who had urged the rights of women in their
discussions, and Coleridge fell out of love with the ideals as he fell
out of love with the woman who had inspired them.

As the three members of the Concern rambled about and talked,
on the hills and in the wooded coombes of Somerset a literary
revolution began to grow. Meanwhile, down in the damp cottage
by the village sewer, Sarah Coleridge nursed her baby and got
on with the housework. But she also nursed a secret, of which
Dorothy was to remain ignorant for many years.

The change in Coleridge that had taken place since the heady
days of Pantisocracy was, in a large part, due to the lethargy of a
drug addict. Opium – probably first given to him during a teenage
attack of rheumatic fever – was becoming more and more necessary and was beginning to produce the ill-health, the irritable
temper, the inability to work and the dishonesty which commonly
accompany opiate addiction. The loyal Sarah said nothing of this
to his new friends, even though Coleridge could not help making
comparisons between the two young women with whom he now
shared his life.

Thomas de Quincey, in his *Recollections of the Lakes and the*

Lake Poets, would claim that Dorothy's advent had a detrimental effect on the Coleridges' relationship. He said that Dorothy's 'superiority ... when made conspicuous by its effects in winning Coleridge's regard and society, could not but be deeply mortifying to a young wife.'[15]

De Quincey believed that that superiority was intellectual, but it seems unlikely that there was much wrong with the intelligence of the woman who had shared in the birth of Pantisocracy. Also, years later, wishing her extremely clever daughter to learn Italian, Sarah set about learning the language herself so that she might teach it to her; and she was much more successful in her efforts than Dorothy ever was in her desultory assaults on German.

Dorothy would herself identify Mrs Coleridge's 'radical fault', not as stupidity, but as 'want of sensibility'[16]. There was certainly a reserve, a lack of spontaneous friendship, about Sarah Coleridge, not dissimilar to Jane Austen's avoidance of intimacy, and the relationship between these two women gives us a hint of how Dorothy and Jane might have got on if they had ever met.

The difference between Sarah and Dorothy is captured in a story that was told about this period in Dorothy's life. It seems that sometimes, when she had been caught in the rain on a walk, Dorothy would help herself to dry clothes from Sarah's wardrobe without asking her permission and 'make herself merry with her own unceremoniousness and Mrs Coleridge's gravity. In all this, she took no liberty that she would not most readily have granted in return; she confided too unthinkingly in what she regarded as the natural privileges of friendship.'[17] (Perhaps Sarah would not have found the communal ownership of property as easy as she had imagined!)

It is likely to have been Dorothy's capacity for unreserved friendship which won her Coleridge's 'regard and society', for he was now moving away from the intellectual radicalism which had inspired him when Sarah first found him irresistible, and, like William, he was finding meaning instead in an emotional response to nature and his fellow-men.

Dorothy would have been a devoted friend, listening closely to everything William and Coleridge said. Sarah, struggling to care for her child and her visitors with only the help of a not very effective maidservant[18], had not time – or perhaps inclination – to listen as avidly to the men around her as Dorothy had. She could not, or would not, leave little Hartley as Dorothy left Basil, in order to join in those extended rambles.

De Quincey would describe Dorothy as a highly skilled listener. 'The pulses of light,' he said, 'are not more quick or more inevitable in their flow and undulation, than were the answering and echoing movements of her sympathizing attention.'[19] She would have been a delightful companion to any man who liked to talk, and Dorothy's new friend certainly liked to talk. ('C[oleridge] will let nobody talk but himself', remarked Lady Beaumont in 1812)[20]. Perhaps Dorothy had heeded the advice that she had read long ago in John Gregory's *A Father's Legacy to his Daughters*. 'The art of pleasing in conversation consists in making the company pleased with themselves,' Dr Gregory explained. 'You will more readily hear than talk yourselves into their good graces.'

It was very good counsel if a young lady's aim was to please the male sex (and pleasing the male sex is the end of all Gregory's advice). Coleridge enjoyed Dorothy's rapt attention as much as Dr Gregory, and other writers of conventional conduct manuals, knew a gentleman would enjoy the company of a woman who listened rather than talked.

Soon – with the neediness common to drug addicts – Coleridge would come to wish he might have such a charming, self-deprecating woman for his own constant companion. His wife had, of course, married in the expectation of a rather more equal partnership; all that talk of shared housework and equal opportunities to study, had not led her to expect to have to listen constantly to her husband. But Coleridge had already abandoned Wollstonecraft's proto-feminism and he would eventually conclude: 'The perfection of every woman is to be characterless. Creatures who, though they may not always understand you ...always feel with you.'[21]

This is a chilling, derogatory assessment of a woman's role and value, but it is not original. It was a recurring refrain of conduct literature of the time that women should suppress their own ideas and allow men to hold forth on Big Issues uninterrupted. Laetitia Matilda Hawkins, who was distressed by Helen Maria Williams publishing her reflections on the French Revolution, said 'I do not ask women to have no opinion on the subject; but, for decorum's sake, do not encourage them to a tilting match'. Wetenhall Wilkes went further, advising that a sensible wife should perform an astonishing feat of self-obliteration and 'be sure never to have any private opinions of her own'.

Dorothy was far from characterless, but Coleridge's enthusiasm for her company, when it is placed in the context of his developing notions of femininity, raises the disquieting possibility that the Concern was founded on rather conventional gender roles, and that Dorothy may have been regarded – by one of her companions at least – as a means of furthering his own ends, affirming his own sense of self, rather than as an individual in her own right.

If an important part of Dorothy's role during those long walks on the Quantock Hills was passive and supportive, the journal which she began to keep at Alfoxton proves that she was also finding time to observe for herself and develop her own response to the things that she saw around her.

The *Alfoxton Journal* opens on 20th January 1798 and is, apart from her letters, Dorothy's first literary effort: or, at least, the earliest to survive. It begins confidently with a vivid description of the scene:

'The green paths down the hill-sides are channels for streams. The young wheat is streaked by silver lines of water running between the ridges, the sheep are gathered together on the slopes. After the wet dark days, the country seems more populous. It peoples itself in the sunbeams ... The slanting woods of an unvarying brown, showing the light through the thin net-work of their upper boughs. Upon the highest ridge of that round hill covered with planted oaks, the shafts of the trees show in the light like the columns of a ruin.'

Dorothy was a meticulous observer, giving equal attention to everything, from the sunbeams and the oaks to the wet sheep gathering on the hill. She was simply being in nature, both seeing it and attempting to be a part of it.

We do not know why Dorothy started this journal. Maybe she began to write down her impressions because Coleridge was away from Stowey at the time and she wished to be able to share with him the scenes he had missed. Four years later she would begin her *Grasmere Journal* when William left on a journey and say that part of its purpose was to 'give William pleasure'. Perhaps she hoped that this journal would give Coleridge pleasure when he returned on 9th February.[22] But she seems to have enjoyed the experience of recording her impressions enough to continue after the constituent parts of the Concern were reunited.

The journal records almost daily meetings with Coleridge. To take one week in February for example: 'I walked to Stowey before dinner' (19th) 'Coleridge came in the morning...' (21st) 'Coleridge came in the morning to dinner.' (22nd) 'William walked with Coleridge in the morning.' (23rd) 'Coleridge came in the morning' (26th).

Most of Dorothy's journal is taken up with observation of the world around her. 'Brown fallows, the springing wheat, like a shade of green over the brown earth, and the choice meadow plots ...of a soft and vivid green; a few wreaths of blue smoke, spreading along the ground; the oaks and beeches in the hedges retaining their yellow leaves ...' (February 24th).

She observed every detail and, with her companions, attempted to lose herself in the scene. 'We lay sidelong on the turf,' she wrote of the 26th February, 'and gazed on the landscape till it melted into more than natural loveliness. The sea very uniform, of a pale greyish blue, only one distant bay, bright and blue as a sky ...'

Even at this moment of oneness, with the scene melting into supernatural loveliness, Dorothy was capable of looking with the eye of a painter, or a student of the picturesque, for she found the prospect of the sea not quite complete. 'Had there been a vessel sailing up it, a perfect image of delight,' she concluded. There was, perhaps, little of the mystic in Dorothy; she does not – either in the *Alfoxton Journal* or elsewhere in her writing – touch upon that 'perception of the harmony of all things' which was her brother's end in observing nature.

Her wish to compose pictures, to somehow improve upon the scene that she saw, would appear much more frequently in her later travel writing. Most of the *Alfoxton Journal* is simply a faithful and vivid record of the world that she experienced: 'A duller night than last night:' she wrote on 24th March, 'a sort of white shade over the blue sky. The stars dim...Some brambles I observed to-day budding afresh and those have shed their old leaves. The crooked arm of the old oak tree points upwards to the moon.'

It is as if she wished to capture an essence: to fix not just the beauty, but the reality of the scenes she saw by pinning them down with words, by remembering them exactly.

William's poetry would constantly seek for the significance of the natural world and his response to it.

'Come forth into the life of things,
Let nature be your teacher.'

And:

'One impulse from a vernal wood,
May teach you more of man
Of moral evil and of good
Than all the sages can.'[23]

Also, in the preface to *Lyrical Ballads* (poems which he was composing at this time) William would write that though he had given descriptions of 'situations from common life' it had been his aim to 'throw over them a certain colouring of imagination whereby ordinary things should be presented to the mind in an unusual aspect.'

In her journal, Dorothy did not seek beyond the veil of nature for universal truths, nor attempt to colour with the imagination. She rarely ventured beyond description. It has been said, 'In her writings, the natural world, in all its delicate detail stands as the end point of vision.'[24] However, it is hard to know whether, at this time, Dorothy's observations were finding their way into the visions – and the poems – of the two men who shared her walks. There are tantalising echoes. On 4th February, for example, she noted in her journal a fence: 'The moss rubbed from the pailings by the sheep, that leave locks of wool, and the red marks with which they are spotted, upon the wood.' In William's poem *The Excursion* (which was begun at this time[25]) there is this description:

'The corner stones, on either side the porch,
With dull red stains discoloured, and stuck o'er
With tufts and hairs of wool, as if the sheep,
That fed upon the common, thither came ...'

And, on 7th March, Dorothy described how 'Only one leaf upon the top of a tree – the sole remaining leaf – danced round and round like a rag blown by the wind.' In his poem *Christabel*, Coleridge would write of:

'The last red leaf, the last of its clan
That dances as often as dance it can
Hanging so light, and hanging so high,
On the topmost twig that looks up at the sky.'[26]

It is tempting to think that both men referred to Dorothy's descriptions when they wrote their poems. But we can only be sure that ideas were shared. For, even if Dorothy's account was the first to be written down, there is a part of the creative process now entirely lost: there is no recapturing the *conversations* that took place on the Quantocks during that slow cold spring. By the time the trio returned, breathless and windblown, to the grand drawing room of Alfoxton, or the overcrowded, stuffy parlour at Nether Stowey, they had probably already forgotten who had started which idea, created which metaphor, or noticed which detail of the natural world.

Dorothy was not walking, thinking, or writing alone. She was an essential part of the Concern.

Sixteen

Poetry and Prose

It was not in Jane's nature to share every thought as it arose in her mind. She was alone in the dressing room at Steventon. There were no geniuses around her to walk with and listen to, to spark ideas or to influence her opinions, to encourage her – or, by comparison, to undermine her confidence in her own abilities.

She continued to write although still interrupted by family visits. August and September of 1798 were passed at Godmersham Park where her brother Edward had recently moved his family. Mrs Knight, now a widow, had given up the house to her adopted son and moved to Canterbury.

Godmersham was a vast Palladian mansion with pleasure grounds including two summer-houses, a river walk and bathing house. Jane described a later visit there as comprising 'Elegance & Ease & Luxury'[1], with the luxuries including eating ice and drinking French wine. This – unlike Dorothy and William's occupation of Alfoxton – was country house living in style. Edward's observant sister would have been reminded of just how much a man might achieve by agreeing to change his name.

Jane knew nothing like the constant three-way conversations that Dorothy was experiencing at this time, but were the Austen family supportive of her writing?

The question is a complicated one. Her habit of writing, providing it did not absorb too much of her time, would have been entirely acceptable. Writing was a family pastime. Jane's mother was said to be, 'a quick witted woman ... who could write an excellent letter either in prose or in verse, the latter making no pretence to poetry, but being simply playful common sense in rhyme ...'[2] Mrs Austen could turn the most mundane material (such as the squeaking of the garden weathercock) into rhymed and metrical verse.

Literary activity was part of family life, and Jane was permitted (or encouraged) to read her stories aloud. But encouraging a young lady to read her work in the drawing room was as far removed from wishing her to expose herself in print as encouraging her to play pretty tunes upon the pianoforte was removed from wishing her to be a concert performer. The witty versifying and writing which was common in the Austen household – and in other literate families – was very different from the dedicated labour of the professional author Jane was becoming. It is possible, however, that her family – for many years at least – saw her work as nothing out of the ordinary, and perhaps that is why Mr Austen made no more approaches to publishers.

Mrs Austen is reported to have said of her son James, 'he possessed in the highest degree classical knowledge, literary taste and the power of elegant composition'.[3] Yet no-one in the family recalled her saying anything at all about her younger daughter's extraordinary talents. Perhaps she really did not believe *Pride and Prejudice*, or *Emma* to have as much merit as James's competent, unremarkable verse.

Cassandra, who was privy to her sister's true feelings, is likely to have known her ambitions and supported them as much as she could. After writing for some time about *Sense and Sensibility* in one letter, Jane remarked: 'I cannot tire *you* I am sure on this subject, or I would apologise.'[4]

The death of Tom Fowle brought the sisters closer together, with Cassandra gradually taking on a supporting role, sparing Jane, as far as she could, from some of the more trying tasks that the daughters of a family were expected to perform: tasks such as writing condolence letters.

'As Cassandra is at present from home,' Jane wrote to her bereaved Cousin Philly Walter in April 1798, 'You must accept from my pen, our sincere Condolance ...'[5]

Another task which only fell to her lot when Cassandra was absent from home, was tending Mrs Austen's illnesses. 'I had the dignity of dropping out my mother's laudanum last night,' Jane announced with mock pride in October, after she had returned from Godmersham with her parents, leaving Cassandra behind to help Elizabeth with the latest baby. There were domestic responsibilities too while her mother deemed herself indisposed. 'I carry about the keys of the Wine & Closet;' she continued, '& twice since I began this letter, have had orders to give in the Kitchen.'[6]

It is easy to imagine the relief with which she relinquished the keys and laudanum bottle to Cassandra whenever possible, and escaped to the manuscripts in her dressing room. Her family – though they provided an audience for her finished work – were probably little help in the creative process. Even such a friend as Anne Lefroy, who may have been supportive and understanding of the young Jane, can have had little real empathy with the extraordinary woman she was growing into. Mrs Lefroy – always secure in the rightness of her own opinions – seems to have felt that Jane needed a man and almost any man would do.

In November 1798 she promoted a match between her young friend and the Reverend Mr Samuel Blackall. She urged this acquaintance to visit Hampshire, somehow contriving to suggest to him that Miss Jane Austen – whom he had met the previous year – would make him a suitable wife. Jane, however, was not impressed by Mr Blackall's Fellowship of Emmanuel College, Cambridge, nor his expectations of soon acquiring a lucrative college living; she would sum up his pompous, talkative personality as 'a piece of Perfection, noisy Perfection'.[7]

For his part Mr Blackall seems to have been as enthusiastic about the possibility of a romance as his ponderous, self-important manner would allow. 'It would give me particular pleasure to have an opportunity of improving my acquaintance with … [the Austen Family] with a hope of creating to myself a nearer interest,' he wrote to Mrs Lefroy. 'But,' he regretted, 'at present I cannot indulge any expectation of it.'

Unsurprisingly, Jane was glad to hear that there was no danger of him creating a nearer interest. '[O]ur indifference will soon be mutual ...' she commented, 'unless his regard, which appeared to spring from knowing nothing of me at first, is best supported by never seeing me.'[8]

Mrs Lefroy's choice seems disastrously inappropriate, and Jane may well have been insulted by the suggestion she could be attracted to (or, at least, be prepared to marry) a man she found ridiculous.

'Oh Lizzy!' cries the highly principled Jane Bennet, 'do anything rather than marry without affection.'[9] When Jane Austen wrote that line in *Pride and Prejudice* she may have been no more than twenty-one years old[10]; but it was a tenet based on more than youthful fancy. Seventeen years later, advising her niece, Fanny, on affairs of the heart, she would voice the same sentiment: 'nothing can be compared to the misery of being bound *without* love.'[11]

Jane held a very high ideal of marriage. This bungled, ill-considered bit of match-making is likely to have been deeply unpleasant for her. Her hurt could be soothed by returning to work. She finished the rewriting that produced *Sense and Sensibility* sometime during 1798. But there is no evidence that her father made any approaches to publishers on this occasion.

Perhaps Mr Austen was preoccupied with other matters; 1798 was a troubled year for the whole country. The war against France was not progressing well. After great successes in Europe the previous Autumn, the twenty-eight-year-old Napoleon Bonaparte had been given command of an invasion force massing on the northern shores of France. Fearful rumours were rife in Britain by the Spring of 1798, with fevered imagination sometimes getting the better of common sense.

'I suppose you have seen a print of the rafts on which they mean to reach us,' Henry Austen's new wife, Eliza, wrote to her cousin Philly. 'It seems these rafts are to be worked with wheels which have the effect of oars, that they are to be bordered with cannon & support a tower filled with soldiers.'

Eliza was sceptical about the monstrous craft. 'I can hardly believe,' she continued, 'that they seriously mean to trust to such a contrivance...however I do believe that they will make an attempt on this country, & Government appears convinced of it...'[12]

The government was indeed convinced of the danger. 'His Majesty', reported the *Hampshire Chronicle* on 3rd January 1798, 'sent a message on Thursday to both houses of parliament on the subject of the preparations now making by the enemy to invade the country'. And here, in her local newspaper, Jane could have read King George's speech in which he said that he was 'greatly relying on the zeal and on the courage of his faithful people who are struggling for everything most dear to them ...'

In April 1798, the Defence of the Realm Act prepared for able-bodied men to be drafted into fighting forces, and demanded that evacuation plans should be drawn up, with places appointed where villagers could gather and routes arranged along which they could drive their livestock to keep them from the marauding French. In order to carry out these plans vast quantities of information had to be gathered. Lists were to be made of all the able-bodied men in the country, and the oxen, sheep, goats, pigs, horses and wagons etc of every parish must be counted. The Lords Lieutenant were in overall charge of gathering this data, but, at a local level, respon-sibility fell upon the literate men of the parish – the schoolmaster and the clergyman.

It was not only filling in government forms that would have kept Mr Austen busy. Henry Dundas, Secretary for War, also wrote to clergymen urging them to interpret and explain the government's plans, to convince their parishioners of the necessity of comply-ing, and to calm their fears. We do not know in what way Mr Austen carried out this order. Perhaps he preached such a sermon as the diarist Mary Hardy recalled hearing in her Norfolk village on 29th April in which the vicar 'harangd the people on taking up arms in defence of the Country, an Invasion being apprehended from the French.'[13]

With two sons – Francis and Charles – in the Navy, and one – Henry – an officer in the Oxfordshire Militia, Mr Austen would certainly have felt himself deeply involved in the defence of his country. No letters survive from the early months of 1798 to give any idea of Jane's own feelings; but in December she hailed Francis's promotion from Lieutenant to Commander with unequivocal joy, giving no hint of any anxiety over the danger that his profession entailed in these dark days of war. With so many family members in the armed forces, she was inured to the dangers, her fears at least controlled.

Down in Somerset, the national anxiety over the French invasion made Dorothy and William homeless.

It all began with a dinner-party. The dinner – probably the first they had ever given – had taken place in July 1797 and it included, among its fourteen guests, a radical acquaintance of Coleridge's, John Thelwall, who was staying in Nether Stowey. Thelwall had recently been arrested under the Treasonable Practices Act for subversive opinions; and, although he had been acquitted at his trial, he was a marked man and a dangerous man in many people's opinion. 'To what are we coming?' cried one respectable local woman when she heard of his visit. Thelwell was known for his toasts and speeches and at the Wordsworths' dinner he 'talked ...loud and was in ...a passion ...' – according to one Thomas Jones, a local man who had been employed to act as a waiter for the evening.

With an invading army camping just across the channel, any talk that hinted of revolutionary ideas was considered unpatriotic. Soon there were rumours circulating against the Wordsworths via a servant called Mogg and a former Alfoxton cook who was now living in Bath.

The tenants of Alfoxton were said to wander about by day and night, writing in notebooks and sometimes sitting on camp stools – which was obviously, highly suspicious behaviour. They had 'contrived' to get hold of Alfoxton House – they must have looked too poor to have any rightful claim to be its tenants. They were an 'emigrant family' – in other words they were French, and clearly not to be trusted. 'The master of the house,' it was said, 'has no wife with him, but only a woman who passes for his sister' – and it was generally accepted that immorality and radical, anti-British sentiments went together.[14]

If the rumours had remained among servants and the poorer folk they would have done little harm, but by August they had been picked up by Dr Daniel Lysons of Bath who now employed the gossiping cook. Lysons was concerned enough to write to the Home Office. Within a few days James Walsh, a government agent, had arrived to check on the odd goings-on at Alfoxton House.

He quickly noticed that the Wordsworths were not French and concluded that they were instead 'a mischiefous gang of disaffected Englishmen.'[15] This was a dangerous enough conclusion in these edgy days of war and fear, and by now the rumours had reached Mrs St Albyn – from whom the Wordsworths rented Alfoxton House. Their one year lease was not renewed. The notion of having revolutionaries for tenants was too much for this good lady, though the equally shocking rumour that Dorothy had been seen 'washing and mending their Cloaths all Sunday'[16] also played a part in her decision.

Ironically, Walsh was wrong in concluding that Wordsworth and Coleridge were 'disaffected', for, by now, both men were abandoning radical politics. The inescapable outcome was that Dorothy's 'house of her own' was lost. Just as she had begun to find expression in her new journal, she was in danger of having to return to her uncongenial relations. Her new life did not have very secure foundations.

There was anxious debate over what they should do, where they should go, the only certainty being that they must remain in close contact with Coleridge. By March 1798, an exciting plan had evolved: the Coleridges, the Wordsworths and some of their friends would go for a few years to Germany (where they believed they could live cheaply) to study and learn the language.

It must have been deeply disappointing for Dorothy to lose the home in which everything had been going so well. William was writing more fluently than he had ever done before and 'his ideas flow faster than he can express them.'[17] 'Tolerably industrious,'[18] was his description of himself. However, Dorothy entered into the new plan with characteristic enthusiasm, trying her best to represent it to her relations as reasonable and prudent. She made a virtue of necessity as she wrote to her Aunt Rawson: 'as we are now determined upon going into Germany with Mr and Mrs Coleridge…we are glad that we are not shackled with the house.'[19]

There was one thing which Dorothy was very pleased to

announce to her relations. '[William] is about to publish some poems,' she told her brother Richard triumphantly. 'He is to have twenty guineas for one volume.'[20] This was the first edition of *Lyrical Ballads* and, although Dorothy wrote as if the work was entirely William's, it was, in fact, a collaboration with Coleridge: the brilliant outcome of their time spent together.

Dorothy explained to her family that they meant to learn a new language in order 'to make some addition to our resources by translating from the German, the most profitable of literary labour, and of which I can do almost as much as my Brother.'[21]

Although she had begun to write, although she shared her life with two writers, Dorothy was not thinking of making money by her own, original composition. Whatever the conversations on the Quantocks had achieved they had not supplied her with either that ambition, or that confidence. Instead, financial gain only seemed possible if she first struggled through the arduous task of learning a new language, in order to labour over the translation of other peoples' words and ideas. It was only in this that she hoped to *almost* equal her brother.

Coleridge would say, towards the end of his life, that 'but for the absorption of her whole Soul in her Brother's fame and writing [Dorothy] would, perhaps, in a different style have been as great a Poet as Himself.'[22] He certainly believed her to have talents of her own, though he does not seem to have regretted the loss of the poet which she might have been, placing that primary virtue of women – the ability to 'feel with' their menfolk – above the pursuit of her own creativity.

The Alfoxton journal appears to be a search for that 'different style', but it was a style which never developed into poetry as Coleridge assumed it should. So far Dorothy had written only prose, and she would, in her lifetime, compose only a very few poems. The concern of the Concern was, of course, poetry – that was the expression it sought for all the myriad experiences that the three persons with one God shared as they walked in the Somerset countryside. This may have created in Dorothy a sense that her work was only a part of a process – merely the sketches from which great paintings were to be composed – and prevented her from considering as an end in itself the beautifully lucid prose which she was so well able to write.

Jane Austen, on the other hand, lived in a community which valued prose. In December 1798 the Austen ladies were invited by a Mrs Martin to subscribe to her new library, and 'as an inducement' they were told that the 'Collection is not to consist only of Novels, but of every kind of Literature ...' Mrs Martin might, Jane observed to Cassandra, 'have spared this pretension to *our* family, who are great Novel-readers & not ashamed of being so.'[23] This was one way in which Jane's family would have been a great support: she never seems to have had any doubt about the value of the novel form.

Northanger Abbey, the first draft of which was written (according to Cassandra's recollections) sometime during 1798 and 1799, contains Jane Austen's spirited defence of her chosen genre. In an unusually long intrusion of the authorial voice, she counters the low opinion of novels held by such people as Mrs Martin with an unequivocal statement of her belief in the value of the work she was undertaking.

She calls novels works 'in which the greatest powers of the mind are displayed, in which the most thorough knowledge of human nature, the happiest delineation of its varieties, the liveliest effusions of wit and humour are conveyed to the world in the best chosen language.' Novels she claims bravely 'have afforded more extensive and unaffected pleasure than those of any other literary corporation in the world.'[24]

She had support in this opinion: although she had no contact with the fashionable literary world of London, she did live in a literate society. The writing and publishing of novels was by no means unknown among her acquaintance. In 1798 Cassandra Cooke, wife of Jane's godfather, published *Battleridge, an historical tale founded on facts,* and an erstwhile neighbour, Samuel Egerton Brydges, produced *Arthur Fitz-Albini.* [25]

Mr Austen was disappointed in this last work, but Jane was not for, she said, 'I expected nothing better.' Her critical comments on the book demonstrate how she was thinking about the skills of her chosen profession. 'Every sentiment,' she noted with exasperation, 'is completely Egerton's. There is very little story and what there is told in a strange, unconnected way. There are many characters introduced, apparently merely to be delineated.'[26]

Three things Jane Austen seems to have valued in a novel were clear, memorable characterisation, a balance of viewpoints, and a strong narrative thread. They were certainly all qualities she was developing in her own work. Jane was a natural storyteller. Her nieces recalled her telling children 'long circumstantial stories' which were 'woven as she proceeded out of nothing, but her own happy talent for invention.'[27] It is no surprise to find that in Jane's fairy-stories the 'fairies had all characters of their own',[28] and it is delightful to imagine a fairyland peopled with, say, fairy versions of Miss Bates or Mrs Bennet or Harriet Smith – or perhaps Mrs Norris as a wicked godmother!

With that 'happy talent for invention' and a similarly 'happy command of language', novel writing was a natural choice for her. But, being a thoughtful young woman, she would not have undertaken her work lightly. There was a belief current in the eighteenth century that novels had the power to 'excite the actions they describe' and their influence was 'likely to be considerable both on the Morals and the Taste of a nation.'[29] Samuel Johnson – a writer Jane admired so much she referred to him as 'my dear Dr Johnson'[30] – was very concerned about the influence novels could have upon their readers. Novels, he said, 'are the entertainment of minds ... not informed by experience, and consequently open to every false and partial account.'[31]

This brings to mind Catherine Morland, the heroine of *Northanger Abbey* who easily follows the current of *her* fancy, turning Northanger Abbey – the comfortable home of her friends Eleanor and Henry Tilney – into a place of horror and adventure in her imagination, and transforming their father, the mundanely unpleasant General Tilney, into a villain of gothic romance.

However, while Jane explored the danger of a too literal reading of far-fetched romances such as Ann Radcliffe's *The Mysteries of Udolpho* and Francis Lathom's *The Midnight Bell,* Dr Johnson and other literary men worried about novels that exhibited 'life in its true state, diversified only by accidents that daily happen in the world,' – in short, the very kind of domestic tale that Jane herself was writing. Johnson believed that their closeness to real life made Jane's kind of novels particularly influential, because the readers of such stories identified too closely with the characters. This placed a great responsibility on a novelist, for, he said, 'that which is likely to operate so strongly, should not be mischievous or uncertain in its effects.'

Jane had almost certainly read Johnson's opinion on the subject. She would have been aware of the great significance that he and others ascribed to fictions. It is unlikely that she regarded her own work as trivial or unimportant. And though it was not yet earning her money, there was no reason why it should not in the future.

SEVENTEEN

A Maid Whom There Were None to Praise

As Jane worked away quietly in her dressing room, Dorothy, sailed for Germany. This appears to be a much bolder step towards independence, but the reality of the trip did not much resemble Dorothy's ambitions. She believed that they would *all* develop new skills. She and William were to equip themselves to become translators. She was to study alongside her brother and Coleridge.

Making money by translating was something she had been considering for the last few years, and it was not an unreasonable ambition. Mary Wollstonecraft moved to London in 1787, disillusioned with the career of governess, and taught herself enough French and German to support herself by translation.

Things began to go wrong with Dorothy's plan before she even left England. The projected 'community' of friends living together was given up. Coleridge and his wife (who had borne a second son, Berkley, in May) had decided that he should travel alone while Sarah remained at home with the children. Only one other companion, a young man called John Chester, had agreed to accompany the travelling party.

Dorothy began her first journey abroad sick and miserable. She was 'consigned to the cabin' for the entire crossing and emerged only when they arrived at the mouth of the Elbe. As the ship made its way up river to Altona and Hamburg she was able to take note of the alien scene and to write in her journal the kind of meticulous description which she had developed in the quiet safety of Alfoxton: 'the houses scattered over the sides of three hills...half-concealed by, and half obtruding themselves from, the low trees.'

However, she did not relish her first taste of foreign parts. She seems to have been intimidated by the strangeness of the place and the people. Hamburg they found to be an expensive place to live and Dorothy considered the inhabitants to be dishonest. After an argument with a baker over the price of bread she wrote bitterly, 'I am informed that it is the boast and glory of these people to cheat strangers'.[1] William was in agreement. '[T]he inn-keepers, shop-keepers etc are all in league to impose upon strangers.'[2] he reported.

Coleridge was more relaxed. He was naturally gregarious and he was rather better off than his friends, for, not long before they left home, he had been given an annuity of £150 by the wealthy Wedgwood family.

The pressures of foreign travel and unequal finances broke up the Concern. At the end of September Coleridge and Chester left Hamburg for the fashionable island resort of Ratzeburg where Coleridge passed the winter skating and partying in high society. Meanwhile Dorothy and William sought out a cheaper place in which to learn the German language, settling on the medieval city of Goslar in Lower Saxony.

Differences were becoming apparent between the Wordsworths and Coleridge. Writing to his wife, Coleridge was critical of William's 'unseeking manners' which prevented him from mixing with the local inhabitants. There are also some lines of verse written by Coleridge in December 1798 which indicate that he already felt a sense of exclusion, a touch of jealousy perhaps, at the closeness of the brother-sister relationship: 'You have all in each other; but I am lonely, and want you!'[3] he wrote.

Goslar did not suit the Wordsworths any better than Hamburg had done. The town had a palace and a cathedral built in the eleventh century, but it had come down in the world since then and was, according to William, 'now the residence of Grocers and Linen-drapers.' [4] It was with the widow of one of those drapers that Dorothy and William took lodgings, unable to afford rooms in a higher-class household. The place was cheap but, complained Dorothy, 'We are not fortunately situated here with respect to the attainment of our main object, a knowledge of the language ... there is no society at Goslar, it is a lifeless town.'[5] They spent most of their time alone and met hardly anyone with whom to converse in German.

Maybe it was those 'unseeking manners' of William's that kept them isolated, but Coleridge had another explanation for their solitary life. In Germany, as in Somerset, Dorothy and William's intimacy was suspected. Coleridge believed that Wordsworth's 'taking his sister with him was a wrong step' because, in Germany, 'Sister is considered as only a name for Mistress'.[6]

Coleridge's dismissal of Dorothy as an encumbrance – his belief that William should have travelled alone – is a telling insight into what *he* thought the Concern was all about. It is another indication that he regarded Dorothy's role as supportive only: she was dispensable. He believed that the true purpose of the German expedition was the furthering of his and William's learning.

And all Dorothy's own hopes of learning a skill which would enable her to earn an independent living began to fade as the freezing continental winter set in, making travel impossible and imprisoning her and William in the lifeless town where they had only their landlady and her apprentice to talk to, their society occasionally supplemented by visits from a French priest and a deaf neighbour.

This was not a situation in which to gain a knowledge of German, certainly not the kind of knowledge William advocated, a knowledge which involved 'having your mind in such a state that the several German idioms and phrases without any act of thought or consideration shall immediately excite feelings analogous to those which are excited in the breasts of the natives.' Without attaining this, William proclaimed – with a typical confidence in his own opinion – 'what we call knowledge of languages is a wretched self-delusion; words are a mere dead letter in the mind.'[7]

This was a level of competence which could only be achieved through a year or two's residence in a country and continual use. Since Mary Wollstonecraft had gained a perfectly adequate grasp of German by studying quietly in London, this advanced level of linguistic skill cannot have been necessary to achieve Dorothy's modest aim of earning a bit of money as a translator. But if this was the standard being insisted upon – if any slighter acquaintance with a language was being disparaged as self-delusion – the task of equipping herself to be financially independent must have been a daunting one for Dorothy. It would be hard for her ever to achieve the confidence necessary to do the job, and the possibility of earning her own living would have been receding further into the distance.[8]

The weather was extreme. '[T]he cold of Christmas day', wrote Dorothy, 'has not been equalled even in this climate during the last century'[9]. Even wrapped in heavy furs they could walk out for no more than an hour a day, so Dorothy was denied the intimate connection with nature that had sustained and inspired her at Alfoxton. She does not seem to have kept a journal during her time at Goslar.

However, this was by no means a dead time for William. 'William works hard, but not very much at the German,'[10] Dorothy reported in November. In fact he wrote poetry, poetry which had nothing to do with Germany. 'He might as well have been in England as at Goslar,' commented Coleridge. During the dark cold days, as he and Dorothy sat beside the black iron stove in their cheap lodgings, William continued to be the poet which Dorothy had called into being. Possibly depressed by his surroundings, he turned inward, considering not the present and the new culture in which he was supposed to be immersing himself, but the past – his own past.

In the same notebook in which Dorothy's fragment of journal was written at Hamburg, William began to draft lines about childhood memories. As he recalled bathing in the Derwent when he was four years old, rowing on Ullswater, and birds-nesting as a schoolboy, he dwelt upon the 'pure organic pleasure' which he gained from nature even when he was very young.[11] He had completed 400 lines by the time they left Goslar and, by the end of December, Dorothy was engaged upon the ongoing task which would occupy so much of her adult life – making fair copies of his verses. Her copies were to be sent to Coleridge and, as Dorothy laboured over them, William was out 'walking by moonlight in his fur gown and a black fur cap'[12] – probably creating more poetry, as walking and reciting was always his preferred method of composition.

This odd, confined time at Goslar, during which William and Dorothy were, in the most complete sense, 'all in each other', also drew from Wordsworth, some other, stranger verses – beautiful, sad, short poems that are filled with a profound sense of human loss. The poems describe a dearly loved woman called Lucy. In one, *Strange Fits of Passion Have I known*, the narrator describes visiting his beloved and being overcome with presentiments of doom as he approaches her cottage:

> 'What fond and wayward thoughts will slide
> Into a Lover's head!
> "Oh mercy!" to myself I cried.
> "If Lucy should be dead".'

While in another, *She Dwelt Among the Untrodden Ways*, the dreaded bereavement has already taken place.

> 'She dwelt among the untrodden ways
> Beside the springs of Dove,
> A maid whom there were none to praise
> And very few to love.
>
> A violet by a mossy stone
> Half hidden from the eye!
> Fair as a star, when only one
> Is shining in the sky.
>
> She lived unknown, and few can know
> When Lucy ceased to be;
> But she is in her grave, and, oh,
> The difference to me!'

What lay behind these strange, impassioned and deeply anxious poems? Coleridge believed that 'in some gloomier moment [Wordsworth] had fancied the moment when his sister might die.'[13] And no-one was better placed to understand Wordsworth's work – or his relationship with his sister – than the third member of the Concern.

Perhaps Wordsworth was fantasising about Dorothy's death, feeding and dwelling on dark and rather destructive thoughts in order to produce that intensity of emotion which he believed necessary for the creation of poetry. What did Dorothy herself think as she sat in the lonely little lodging room making fair copies of these poems? She may well have believed that her own relationship with her brother had produced this storm of rather morbid emotion; there had been no other love in William's life, except for Annette – abandoned now for six years.

Whether or not she believed Lucy to be herself, Dorothy would certainly have read in the lyrics a clear description of what William valued, what he loved most, in either herself or a fictional, idealised woman.

Lucy's greatest glory lies in her obscurity. It is an attractive obscurity, but one from which she seems to have no escape, except through death, for even the few people who love her cannot – for some unexplained reason – praise her. Perhaps this is because she shrinks from praise and attention herself. That violet half-hidden by the mossy stone rather suggests it.

Lucy, in her rural retreat, may seem a wild and natural creature, and it has been said that 'Wordsworth found Dorothy (as Coleridge did) a help in locating what wildness and naturalness in an adult might ...be like.'[14] But sometimes that 'wildness' is hard to distinguish from the unworldliness and lack of ambition expected of a genteel woman. Lucy is suspiciously like Henry Austen's picture of his sister: a conventionally correct, modest and retiring spinster, shrinking from unladylike fame.

William's love had become necessary to Dorothy; her whole life now centred on him and she seems to have internalised his image which linked female modesty with the beauty of flowers.

Three years later she would herself observe some columbines, 'sheltered and shaded by the tufts and Bowers of trees,' and reflect that, 'It is a graceful, slender creature, a female seeking retirement and growing freest and most graceful where it is most alone. I observed that the more shaded plants were always the tallest.'[15]

Neither William's sweet violet half-hidden by her mossy stone, nor Dorothy's 'female seeking retirement' seem much like women intent on pursuing their own education in order to earn an independent living. In the street outside the lodging-house window Dorothy would have heard the language which she had travelled five hundred miles to learn: the language which was to have given her an income of her own. But, on the papers spread before her for copying, she would have seen the woman that William admired: the woman he needed: a woman made beautiful by obscurity and self-effacement.

By the time the brother and sister returned to England, their love had become more intense than ever. The isolation in which they had lived had confirmed, and changed, their bond. It is impossible to know exactly why William had begun to fantasise about losing his idealised woman. Perhaps he feared that his very love and need would stifle the frail, ephemeral creature that Lucy seems to be. Or perhaps he was afraid that she might escape, through her own efforts, into a life that was independent of him.

Independence for a creative mind does not necessarily require a great deal of space in the physical world. Hamlet declares that, if his mind was untroubled by bad dreams, he could be 'bounded in a nutshell, and count myself a king of infinite space.'[16] And a little dressing room with a chocolate coloured carpet and cheaply papered walls might have served the Prince of Denmark quite as well as a nutshell.

If a woman keeps an emotional distance from the people around her, if she contrives to have no responsibilities which she cannot hand over to someone else, retreat into her own imaginative world – that 'infinite space' within the head – is always a possibility. Even when other duties press upon her, the space remains with its writing desk, its satisfying piles of manuscript, a tenuous promise of future freedom.

Through much of 1799 Jane's retreat into her dressing room was impossible. When she and her parents returned from Godmersham in October 1798, Cassandra remained behind and did not come home until March of the following year. Jane was alone at home to see her mother through five weeks of illness and take care of the house – with a little 'experimental' menu-making. Ox-cheek, ragout and haricot mutton all appeared on the Austen dinner table as Jane made the most of this rare opportunity to choose her favourite dishes.

There was an element of play in Jane's housekeeping. 'I always take care to provide such things as please my own appetite,'[17] she explained. She never seemed to regard looking after the house as her job – she was just holding the fort until Cassandra came home. In the same way, her cousin Philly 'must accept from my hand' the family condolences because the *real* Miss Austen was not there to write. In all these matters Jane seems to have been content to be a surrogate only.

It was the same outside the home. 'Dame Tilbury's daughter has lain-in,' she reported to her sister. 'Shall I give her any of your Baby Cloathes?'[18] Cassandra had also taken charge of the charitable work which would have been expected from the daughters of the rectory. There appears to have been an understanding developing between the sisters of the roles they should play. It was an arrangement which would be crucially important in the years to come. Jane was fortunate, for, as William Wordsworth was discovering at about the same time, it is incredibly useful for a creative mind to have a devoted supporter.

One of the little luxuries which Jane allowed herself as she ordered meals at Steventon that autumn was some little dumplings to accompany the ox-cheek, and she chose them, 'that I may fancy myself at Godmersham.'[19] Steventon – indeed the whole of Hampshire – seemed dull and impoverished compared with the luxuries of Edward's grand home, and the comparison made Jane discontent. She noticed such things, unlike Dorothy who would have been almost ashamed to admit to enjoying luxuries. 'People get so horridly poor and economical in this part of the World,' Jane complained ' ...I have no patience with them, Kent is the only place for happiness. Everybody is rich there.'[20]

Dorothy had chosen a simpler way of life, because it was the means of being with the man she loved. Poverty made her independent of her relations, but Jane felt both dependent *and* poor.

She had little patience with her mother's illnesses. 'My mother's spirits are not affected by her complication of disorders ... nor are you to suppose that these maladies are often thought of,'[21] she wrote on 24th December; but, since her previous letter had contained a list of the multitude of colourful disorders Mrs Austen *had* recently thought of – unsettled bowels, asthma, dropsy, water in her chest and liver disorder – the remark was almost certainly ironic.

'She does not like the cold weather, but that we cannot help,'[22] Jane reported briskly in the same letter. A few weeks later, as a new complaint was added to the asthma, dropsy etc: 'She would tell you herself that she has a very dreadful cold in her head at present; but I have not much compassion for cold in the head without fever or sore throat.'[23]

Poor Mrs Austen! A writer longing to return to her work does not make the most sympathetic nurse. A woman who thought less and responded from the heart would have been, not only a more satisfactory carer, but a more satisfactory daughter as well. Sometimes that coldness and reserve which made Jane draw back from intimacy with the pleasant Miss Mapletons seems to have operated even within her own family; empathy for others' suffering was not one of her strengths.

There were dances that winter. 'We are to kill a pig soon. There is to be a ball at Basingstoke next Thursday,'[24] ran one line as her thoughts tumbled into her letter. Her attitude to these balls was a little equivocal. One, at Manydown, which she expected to be 'stupid' exceeded her expectations and she was pleased to find herself 'capable of dancing so much and with so much satisfaction as I did.'[25]

She did not say why she was surprised. Maybe she was beginning to feel – now that she was approaching twenty-three – that she was getting too old to be enthusiastic about balls, that she had at least grown up over the last seven years and no longer suffered under 'the insatiable appetite'[26] for dancing which she ascribed to girls of fifteen in *Sense and Sensibility*.

She was certainly beginning to be impatient with the labour of dressing well, a labour which was considered the duty of every young lady still in search of a husband. 'I cannot determine what to do about my new Gown,' she wrote in the same letter. 'I wish such things were to be bought ready-made.' Her wish would not become a reality for another century, but she found other ways of saving time and effort. 'I have made myself two or three caps to wear of evenings since I came home,' she wrote in December – just two weeks before her twenty-third birthday – 'and they save me a world of torment as to hair-dressing, which at present gives me no trouble beyond washing and brushing...'

Matrons and women past marriageable age generally wore caps; young girls went bare-headed indoors, their hair usually elaborately curled. It is likely that Jane's caps were intended for wear at a time when only family would see her, but their creation was a first concession to advancing age. Perhaps this sense of increased maturity gave her new confidence. 'I enjoyed the hard black frosts of last week very much, and one day while they lasted,' she reported proudly to Cassandra, 'walked to Deane by myself – I do not know that I ever did such a thing in my life before.'[27] It was probably very refreshing to get out of the house.

While Cassandra was away from home, there can have been little opportunity to write. Another distraction was the arrival of James and Mary's first baby in November 1798[28]; and then, soon after Cassandra returned home to take over the housekeeping keys and the laudanum bottle, Edward and some of his family arrived to take Jane and her mother to Bath. The wealthy, fortunate Edward had been unwell of late, and his sister's sympathy was mixed with a large helping of sarcasm. 'Poor Edward!' she commented. 'It is very hard that he who has everything else in the World that he can wish for, should not have good health too.'

191

She did go on to concede that 'I know no one more deserving of happiness without alloy than Edward is.'²⁹ But she could never quite forget those inequalities of fortune.

She seems to have enjoyed Bath on this occasion. A visit paid with Edward and Elizabeth would have involved good lodgings and the best entertainments. She may have used the visit to gather background details for the Bath episodes in *Susan,* the novel on which she was now engaged (and which would eventually become *Northanger Abbey*). She may even have managed to get some writing done during the visit since she had the luxury of a room of her own in their lodgings.

Even so, she was soon missing the peace of her dressing room. 'I feel tolerably secure of our getting away next week,' she wrote on 11th June, betraying the desire for a return that is nearly always detectable in her letters when she was away from home, 'tho it is certainly possible that we may remain till Thursday the 27th.'³⁰

She was also impatient with the idea of other visits which were being suggested for the coming months. 'I wonder what we shall do with all our intended visits this summer?' she wrote. 'I should like to make a compromise with Adlestrop, Harden and Bookham that Martha's spending the summer at Steventon should be considered as our respective visits to them all.'³¹

Jane seems nearly always to have resented journeys and visits and to have preferred being left peacefully at home, where it was possible to escape to the manuscripts in her dressing room. And Martha Lloyd was one of the few friends whose company seemed to give her pleasure. 'I love Martha better than ever,'³² she wrote, in a rare expression of decided, straightforward affection. A long visit from Martha would be a positive pleasure; and this was a friendship which would deepen over the years. But there was already a rift opening between the Austen girls and Martha's sister, Mary, who was now James's wife. 'I am heartily glad that You have escaped any share in the Impurities of Deane,' Jane remarked at the beginning of this letter – apparently congratulating Cassandra on having avoided a visit to James and Mary.

Tensions had been building since James's second marriage and one cause of ill feeling may have been Mary's resentment of her husband's family: a feeling that he paid them too much attention. Back in October 1798 Jane had remarked, 'James seems to have taken to his old trick of coming to Steventon inspite of Mary's reproaches.'[33]

A wife ill-disposed towards her husband's relations did not bode well for Jane's future.

EIGHTEEN

Homecoming and Exile

On May Day 1799 Dorothy and William Wordsworth arrived in England, having spent two months walking back through Germany. They were very glad to be on English soil once more. They had found 'living in Germany, with the enjoyment of any tolerable advantages, much more expensive than we expected.'[1] They had no money and no better prospect of earning any than when they set off. 'My progress in German considered with reference to literary emolument is not even as dust in the balance',[2] reported William.

They were also homeless but, fortunately, they had good friends. Mary Hutchinson welcomed them as warmly to her home at Sockburn as they had welcomed her to Racedown, and it was on this farm where Mary was living with brothers Tom and George, and sisters Sara and Joanna, that William and Dorothy passed most of the rest of the year.

Coleridge did not return to England until July – despite the fact that his infant son Berkley had died in February. Poor Sarah, grieving on her own at Stowey, heartbroken and exhausted with nursing, had been longing and pleading for his return. Coleridge's attempt to distance himself from this tragedy, his deliberate procrastination over going home and his reluctance to witness his wife's grief certainly did not reflect well upon the man who claimed to value an affectionate heart above all else. But Dorothy does not seem to have been surprised by his behaviour.

Even after his return from Germany Coleridge did not remain

long with his sadly diminished family. By the end of October he
and his friend, the publisher Cottle, were in Sockburn with the
Wordsworths and Hutchinsons. On 27th October Coleridge,
Cottle and Wordsworth set off from Sockburn for a walking-tour
of the Lake District. And, on this walk, William made a discovery.
On 8th November he wrote to Dorothy, 'There is a small house
at Grasmere empty which perhaps we may take, and purchase
furniture but of this we will speak.'³ This small house was the one
that is now known as Dove Cottage. William and Dorothy moved
into it in December 1799.

By the end of 1800 Coleridge had moved himself and his family
north to be near the Wordsworths, occupying a part of the large
Greta Hall in Keswick – just thirteen miles from Grasmere. The
Concern was re-established; and Dorothy was settled in the house
that was to be more completely her *home* than any other.

Soon after Dorothy achieved this longed-for home, Jane found
herself an exile, cast out from Steventon Rectory, the only home
she had ever known.

It seems likely that those visits to Adlestrop, Harden and
Bookham had been forced upon her, so her working life would
have been sadly disrupted during the summer of 1799. However,
she had not been called upon to pay another, stranger visit.

In August Jane's wealthy aunt, Mrs Leigh-Perrot (wife of Mrs
Austen's brother), 'a ladylike little old woman' who was 'not at
all a stupid person'⁴, was accused of shoplifting in Bath.⁵ Though
her accusers probably expected to be bought off, she staunchly
maintained her innocence and allowed the law to take its course.
She spent the following seven months confined in the jailer's
house at Ilchester and in March 1800 stood trial at Taunton
Castle, facing a charge which could have carried a sentence of
deportation. But she was, to the great rejoicing of her family,
found innocent.⁶

During Mrs Leigh-Perrot's imprisonment her sister-in-law, Mrs
Austen, wrote very kindly offering the services of either of her
daughters if Mrs Leigh-Perrot would like some company in jail,
or moral support at the trial. Jane was never very fond of her

aunt, but she was probably grateful to that lady for declining Mrs Austen's generous offer. '[T]o have two Young Creatures gazed at in a public Court would cut one to the very heart,'[7] wrote Mrs Leigh-Perrot in explanation of her refusal.

An unmarried daughter's hold on her own time was extremely fragile. By comparing the situations of Jane and Dorothy at this point in their lives, it appears that what Dorothy had achieved in her escape from Forncett was, in effect, adulthood.

Jane had very little control over her own life. She could be made use of in any crisis, transported against her wishes to socialise at Adlestrop or Bookham, or sent, just as easily, to endure the squalor of Ilchester jail. As she approached her twenty-fifth birthday, she was still in the position of a child, provided with her keep and pocket money, but taking no part in family decisions, even those which concerned her most closely.

In December 1800, while she was staying with her friend Martha at Ibthorpe, and Cassandra was once more paying a long visit to Edward's family at Godmersham, their parents took the momentous decision to move from Steventon, give up the rectory, and settle in Bath. Jane knew nothing of such a plan. Just weeks before announcing their decision, Mr and Mrs Austen were buying furniture for their home and making improvements to their grounds. 'Our improvements have advanced very well;'[8] Jane wrote on 25th October, and on 8th November she reported: 'The Tables are come, & give general contentment ...'[9] And then, on 20th November, eleven days after a great storm had felled three elm trees in the rectory grounds, the improvement plans were still developing. 'A new plan has been suggested concerning the plantation of the new inclosure ...'[10]

It seems unlikely that Mr and Mrs Austen would have been pursuing these schemes and spending money on a home which they were considering giving up. So their decision to move was probably taken suddenly. That they should have failed to take either of their adult daughters into their confidence is astounding. It says a great deal about Mrs Austen's attitude towards Jane and Cassandra – the little importance she placed upon them as young women. And such a lack of respect offers a more credible explanation for Jane's coldness towards her than the child-care arrangements she made.

When Jane returned from Ibthorpe, in December, she was immediately greeted with the news – and in the most unfeeling way. Mrs Austen met her daughter in the hall with the bald statement, '…it is all settled we have decided to leave Steventon…and go to Bath.'[11]

'The resolution to leave Steventon took all their relations by surprise,' Jane's great-niece reported, 'and as there did not seem any sufficient reason for it in the health of either, some secret motive was suspected.'[12]

Mr and Mrs Leigh-Perrot believed that the secret motive might be a growing attachment between Jane and neighbour, William Digweed, but none of the closer family gave credit to this idea, for there was no particular reason why such an attachment – if it existed – should be disrupted. It is more likely that other family members had persuaded Mr and Mrs Austen into the removal during their daughters' absence. This seems to have been what Jane suspected.

There are no surviving letters from Jane to Cassandra between the visit to Ibthorpe and January of the following year – although Cassandra was still away at Godmersham during that time. Letters destroyed by Cassandra may well have included criticism of James and Mary, and the accusation that they had persuaded Mr and Mrs Austen to make a move which they had not been planning a few weeks earlier.

Jane's eldest brother and his wife were to benefit considerably from Mr Austen's retirement: they would take over the Steventon house and the curacy of the parish. As the arrangements for the transfer carried on, Jane definitely detected inordinate greed in their actions. 'My father's old ministers are already deserting him to pay court to his son;' she wrote ironically, turning this passing on of a country rectory into a state coup and so implying intrigue and dark plotting: 'the brown Mare, which as well as the black was to devolve on James at our removal, has not had patience to wait for that, & has settled herself even now at Deane…& everything else I suppose will be seized by degrees in the same manner.'[13]

'My Aunt was very sorry to leave her native home,' recalled Jane's niece Caroline in a letter to James Edward Austen-Leigh when he was gathering material for his memoir. ' ...My mother who was present said my Aunt Jane was greatly distressèd – all things were done in a hurry by Mr Austen & of course this is *not a fact* to be written and printed – but you have authority for saying she *did* mind it – if you think it worth while.'[14]

The fact that Mary (Caroline's mother) was present when the retirement was announced would have been an extra aggravation. It cannot have pleased Jane to find that her sister-in-law was privy to a plan of which she knew nothing. It may well have seemed that the malevolent power of the married woman over her spinster sisters-in-law – a power which she had imagined in her fiction – was becoming a reality in her life.

It is clear from Caroline's letter, not only that Jane was greatly upset by the news, but also that her family felt her reaction should be covered up in the interests of that peaceableness and solidarity on which they wished all their interactions to be founded. Decades later, when Austen-Leigh was composing his memoir, this subject *still* had to be avoided. Maybe that is not surprising, for the subject does raise questions about the darker aspects of family life. Jane's distress on hearing of the move may not have been caused entirely by grief at losing her home. The change also impacted on her in another way: it meant that her long-term future was even less secure than it had seemed to be.

Though, in the early months of 1801, Mr Austen did 'all in his power to encrease (sic) his Income ...', the move to Bath could not help but impoverish him. He must now pay two curates to perform his duties at Steventon and Deane. Even at the very lowest rates of pay (similar to the miserable income of £50 a year which Mrs Jennings foresees Edward and Lucy 'setting down on' in *Sense and Sensibility*) that would cost £100 a year. The family would also lose their rent-free rectory and be obliged to pay for very expensive accommodation in Bath. The modest town-house in which they finally settled in May 1801 cost £150 a year. Comparing this figure – which was advertised as a 'very low' rent in the *Bath Chronicle* [15]– with the £24 that the Wordsworths paid for a great mansion in parkland at Alfoxton demonstrates the extremely high cost of living in a fashionable resort town. Food, brought in from the countryside, would have been relatively expensive too, particularly to the Austens who had been used to being almost self-sufficient on their glebe lands.

It was, in real terms, a severe cut in the family income. Mr Austen would receive nearly £600 a year after the move, but the new expenses he was incurring would eat up almost half that money. Jane would not have been so narrow minded (or *illiberal* as she would have put it herself) as to deny her father's claim to retirement. But the decision to move would have made clear to her that there would definitely be no money set aside to settle on her or Cassandra. Now he had set his sons up in the world and given them the best start in life he could manage, Mr Austen considered his duty to his family to be over.

After all, his retirement need not have entailed a costly change of abode; he could have hired curates and continued to live in the rectory. Perhaps the move was all for the sake of Mrs Austen's health, which might have been pure hypochondria, since her relations did not consider her ill enough to necessitate a residence in Bath. Or perhaps it was all done to provide James and his wife with a better income and a larger home. If Mary resented her husband's frequent visits to his family, perhaps she wished to get them out of the way.

There may have been no arguments in the family, but that does not mean that injustices were not felt. It would have required the temperament of a saint for a woman not to care at all about her own future poverty – and Jane Austen never pretended to sainthood.

Nor did she believe that a woman should give up her own opinions in submission to others' judgement. Elinor sums up the approach of a 'sensible' woman when she says, 'My doctrine has never aimed at the subjection of the understanding. All I have ever attempted to influence has been the behaviour.'[16] Jane may have held her tongue, but she could maintain an opinion of her own.

Another subject on which Jane Austen was noticeably reticent was one which must have made her removal from Steventon particularly painful: that is her love of the countryside. '[H]er delight in natural scenery,' recalled her great niece, 'was such that she would sometimes say she thought it must form one of the joys of heaven.'

This same niece was surprised by 'how little there is in her writings to indicate this taste ... there is not what could be called a picturesque description to be found in any one of her novels. No word pictures no elaborate accounts of wind and storm ...or even of the fair meadows and winding hedgerows ... in which her youth was passed ...'[17]

It is an omission which must strike many readers of the novels. Many of Jane's characters – most notably Fanny Price of *Mansfield Park* – share her delight in all things rural; but – apart from a short passage in *Persuasion* praising the countryside around Lyme – there is nothing like a 'picturesque' description. Perhaps she held back from effusions on the subject because she associated them with an over-emotional approach to life. She makes them a characteristic of Marianne Dashwood's conversation: Marianne can wax lyrical on everything from 'bold' hills to dead leaves. But perhaps Jane had heard too many of her contemporaries making a parade of being nature lovers and did not wish – when she spoke in the author's voice – to give the impression of false enthusiasm.

However, the 'sweet retired bay, backed by dark cliffs ...' and 'green chasms between romantic rocks ...' of the *Persuasion* passage, give some support to brother Henry's remark that, 'At a very early age [Jane] was enamoured of Gilpin on the Picturesque'[18].

William Gilpin, a clergyman from Cumberland, encouraged travellers to view landscape, not as something to be lived in, but as material which could be formed into pictures. The fashion for touring Britain – encouraged by improvements in roads and the closing off of foreign travel by the wars with France – made his writings very popular during Jane's girlhood. Tourists travelled between recommended viewpoints, admiring rocks, chasms and waterfalls (the 'cataracts and mountains' which William Wordsworth had once damned with faint praise), valuing the countryside for the way it looked rather than for its usefulness.

Jane Austen certainly knew how to compose a picture (her drawing lessons at Mrs La Tournelle's school would have taught her that): 'the prospect from the Drawingroom window...is rather picturesque' she wrote once from lodgings in Bath, 'as it commands a perspective view of the left side of Brock Street, broken by three Lombardy Poplars in the Garden of the last house ...'[19] But she does not seem to have been entirely comfortable with Gilpin's vocabulary. Apart from that uncharacteristic description of Lyme, her most notable use of it is in *Sense and Sensibility* when Edward Ferrars gently ridicules the jargon, insisting that, 'I have no knowledge in the picturesque ... I shall call hills steep, which ought to be bold; surfaces strange and uncouth, which ought to be irregular and rugged ...' His ideal countryside does not have 'crooked, twisted trees' or 'ruined tattered cottages', it simply 'unites beauty with utility'; it features 'a snug farmhouse' and 'tidy, happy villagers.'[20]

Jane may have inclined towards his view. The taste of Fanny Price – her most outspoken enthusiast for the countryside – coincides with Edward's. On a drive through the country Fanny is entirely practical, finding entertainment in 'the bearings of the roads, the difference of the soil, the state of the harvest, the cottages, the cattle, the children ...'[21]

These were perhaps the things which Jane noticed herself on a journey, for she had lived all her life in a farming community, attuned to country matters. While she was living at Steventon her letters conveyed questions about pigs and hay from one farmer (her father) to another (her brother Edward), and, in the years leading up to the removal, she sometimes referred to arrangements on the family's farm. 'John Bond,' she wrote to Cassandra in December 1798, 'begins to find himself grow old ...a man is therefore hired to supply his place as to labour, and John himself is to have the care of the sheep.'

However, she maintained an air of detachment from these affairs; like housekeeping, farming was something which she could not quite take seriously. She finished this account with: 'I fancy so at least, but you know my stupidity as to such matters.'[22]

Her letters are certainly not like her mother's, with their

enthusiastic discussions of the merits of Alderney cows and the getting in of barley. This same letter ends with a message conveyed on behalf of Mr Austen. 'My father is glad to hear so good an account of Edward's pigs, and desires he may be told, as encouragement to his taste for them, that Lord Bolton is particularly curious in *his* pigs, has had pigstyes of a most elegant construction built for them, and visits them every morning as soon as he rises.' The eccentricity of the aristocrat may well have interested Jane more than the pigs.

Mrs Austen, bemused by Jane's detachment from important farming matters, might almost have agreed with those observers who thought her 'affected', and this may have been another subject which distanced mother and daughter. Yet, despite this air of disengagement, Jane *was* deeply rooted in the country. It was perhaps a connection she did not fully appreciate herself until she was called upon to break the tie, to give up the deep rural rhythms and routines of Steventon for the superficial pleasures of Bath: the 'littleness of the town' as she would describe it herself in *Persuasion*.

Her niece's recollections, her hatred of Bath, her joy at her eventual escape from that town, all testify to Jane being, in her heart, a countrywoman. For twenty-five years she had taken a home in the countryside for granted, now, when she was about to lose it, she understood its importance.

By the time she arrived at her home in Grasmere, Dorothy had experienced both town and country life and was able to make comparisons. While staying with friends in Bristol, after the enforced move from Alfoxton, she wrote, 'After three years' residence in retirement a city in feeling, sound, and prospect is hateful.'[23]

Yet, oddly, the effect of Dorothy's urban upbringing seems to have lingered long after she was living in a rural setting. Her six years in a Norfolk village did little to put her at ease with country life. Her 1795 account of her visit to her friends the Hutchinsons at their farm in Yorkshire still betrays the naïve wonder of a born townswoman: 'It is an excellent house,' she reported, 'not at all like a farm-house and they seem to have none of the trouble which I used to think must make farmers always in a bustle ...' Like a student of Gilpin, she was more interested in the scenic aspect of the farm than its utility. 'It is a grazing estate, and most delightfully pleasant, washed nearly round by the Tees (a noble river,) and stocked with sheep and lambs which look very pretty, and to me give it a very interesting appearance.'[24]

Her new home at Grasmere, with its lake, its soaring mountains, its waterfalls, woods and unpredictable weather, was at the very heart of the picturesque landscape Gilpin described. Just thirty miles from her birthplace, Grasmere was still, essentially, a traditional rural community, though it was just beginning to attract tourists and a few big houses had been built by wealthy folk from the industrial towns.

Curiously, the descriptions Dorothy started to write of the scenes she saw around her at Grasmere seem to be those of an outsider – a woman still feeling her way into country life. For example, she described, 'a little bird with a salmon coloured breast – a white cross or T upon its wings, and a brownish back with faint stripes',[25] which she had seen pecking at dung on the road. This sounds like a male chaffinch, a bird common throughout the British countryside. But Dorothy described the bird as though she had never seen one before, with a sense of wonder at the exquisite beauty of this common little creature. It is this freshness of vision which makes many of her descriptions so arresting. But it is strange that she does not say 'we saw a chaffinch' – or give it its local name of skoby. She knew that name. Earlier she had written that 'the skoby sate quietly in its nest rocked by the winds ...'[26]

There is sometimes evident in Dorothy's writing a struggle for names as she looked about her at the natural world. She could, on one occasion, name wild strawberries, geraniums and primroses, but was at a loss over a 'grassy leaved, Rabbit toothed white flower'[27] which was almost certainly the very common stitchwort. 'Oh that we had a book on botany!'[28] she exclaimed. Two years later she was still not able to name all the flowers she saw: 'The vetches are in abundance ...' she wrote. 'That pretty little waxy-looking dial like flower, the speedwell, and some others whose names I do not yet know.'[29]

She might also have wished for a book on ornithology, for, in the same entry, she described 'a pair of stone chats' skimming along the surface of the lake – which stone chats do not do. The behaviour of these birds seems more like that of grey wagtails. Maybe her identification of the skoby rocking in its nest was also inaccurate – though she *sounds* knowledgeable as she uses the colloquial name.

However, Dorothy looked for herself. She was not content to do as Marianne Dashwood does sometimes and keep 'my feelings to myself, because I could find no language to describe them in but what was worn and hackneyed out of all sense and meaning.'[30] She would achieve, over the years, a manner of writing about the natural world which was never worn or hackneyed, but always startling and fresh. She seems to have achieved this by coming to the subject as an outsider, without any pre-conceptions, and without adopting anybody else's prescribed vocabulary. Perhaps sometimes she deliberately avoided names, for a name can be limiting. Once a name is given we can stop looking, in the (perhaps false) belief that we know and understand something entirely.

There is one other slightly odd aspect to Dorothy's writing which must strike anyone who knows the Lake District scenery she described: a kind of blindness. It was particularly evident on 16th June 1800 when she and William strolled into one of the area's most beautiful valleys – and she noted in her journal, 'The vale of Little Langdale looked bare and unlovely.' Little Langdale is a glorious example of a Cumbrian valley, with a beck and a tarn cupped by mountains, whose reflections dive deep into its waters; in June, its fields are bright with flowers, its hedges laced with wild roses. Why should Dorothy dismiss this charming place as 'bare and unlovely' and say not another word about it?

A clue to the mystery may lie in the old spoil heaps and overgrown slate quarries that can still be seen in the valley, and in the remains of a forge on its beck. When Dorothy walked there in 1800 there would have been, mixed with the little smallholdings, grazing sheep and fields of oats and hay, scattered quarry-workings and small-scale industries. This seems to have rendered the whole valley unsuitable for inclusion in her journal.

Yet this would not have been the only place in which Dorothy came across such scenes. There were slate quarries visible even on the fells around Grasmere, and in Ambleside – to which Dorothy walked frequently to collect letters – there were several water mills producing linen and woollen cloth. For centuries the folk of this area had earned their livings in a variety of ways, not just by farming.

Of all this Dorothy says nothing in her journal. Her Lake District is a rural landscape untouched by industrialisation. She observed closely, but selectively, and her selectivity, together with the detailed, almost exaggerated, reality of the things on which she focused, created a Lake District that she wished to see.[31]

The Grasmere house itself – with only three proper rooms on each of its two floors – was very far removed from the grandeur of Racedown and Alfoxton. It had once been an alehouse and it was 'rather too near the road, and from the smallness and the manner in which it is built noises pass from one part of the house to the other.'[32] At the back, the house was half-buried in the hillside. Its downstairs rooms were still panelled with the cheap stained pine of its days as an inn and the place was damp, with cold slate floors.

It was almost empty when they took it and they were only able to furnish it because Uncle Kitt had recently died and proved his affection for Dorothy with a legacy of £100.[33] This little bit of money – one of the very few that Dorothy could call her own – was used to buy the essentials.

This was certainly a more practical choice of home than Alfoxton, the rent being only £8 a year.

Lyrical Ballads had not brought its authors much money, and John Worthen has calculated that – due to bad investments, the expense of the German trip and the necessity of spending rather than investing a large part of the Calvert legacy – 'The Wordsworths could only be sure of just under £20 a year,' at the time they settled in Dove Cottage. He concludes that this 'was really the only kind of place which they could afford; their financial state must have played a considerable role in their decision to go to Grasmere.'[34]

Dorothy's expectations had, perforce, diminished since her first setting up home with William. At Racedown she had not 'any thing to do in the house', except at the time of the monthly wash; but her *Grasmere Journal* with its cooking and mattress-making, its white-washing of walls and 'nailing-up' of bed frames, presents a very different life indeed.

William and Dorothy were now living on the very edge of gentility, poorer even than the marginalised Mrs and Miss Bates whom Jane Austen describes in *Emma*. They can at least afford *one* proper servant; in the early days at Dove Cottage Dorothy had only the help of sixty-year-old Molly Fisher. Writing to Coleridge, soon after their arrival at the house, William (who – as far as we know – had never contemplated his friend's Pantisocratic ideal of shared housework) blithely reported, 'We do not think it will be necessary for us to keep a servant,' and described Molly as, 'a woman who lives in one of the adjoining cottages' who would for two shillings a week attend 'two or three hours a day to light the fires wash dishes etc.' adding generously, 'We could have had this attendance for eighteen pence a week but we added the sixpence for the sake of the poor woman, who is made happy by it.'[35]

Dorothy did not feel diminished or shamed by her poverty as – under similar circumstances – Jane Austen might have done. She did not mourn lost luxuries as Jane did when torn from the ice and French wine of Godmersham, but nor did Dorothy consider herself to be the equal of the cottage-folk who lived around her – though their incomes may not have been dissimilar. Gentry she had been born and gentry she remained.

During the early days at Grasmere she formed close friendships with other genteel folk, such as the Simpsons – the family of a clergyman living close by – and, most notably, the anti-slavery campaigner Thomas Clarkson and his wife Catherine who lived at Eusemere by the side of Ullswater. But there were other neighbours whom she viewed in a different light.

'We are very comfortably situated with respect to neighbours of the lower classes,' she told Mrs Marshall, 'they are excellent people ...attentive to us without servility – if we were sick they would wait upon us night and day.'[36]

She may have had too rosy a view of these lower classes. These same 'excellent' and 'attentive' neighbours were found by the Wordsworths' friend, Thomas De Quincey (who took over the tenancy of Dove Cottage in 1808) to be 'particularly gross and uncharitable.'[37] The inhabitants of Grasmere were no doubt just human, and the truth lay somewhere between these extremes.

They would have been rather more independent folk than the 'lower classes' Jane Austen knew. The mountainous terrain of Cumberland and Westmorland had never taken on the social pattern that the more fertile lowland counties of England had known since Norman times: that of the big estate with the 'Great House' at its centre and large areas of land owned and controlled by one landlord (such as Jane's brother Edward). There were some great landowners in the north (John Wordsworth's employer, James Lowther, for example) but there were also a number of small farmers, owning just enough land to feed their families.

William Wordsworth celebrated these 'independent *proprietors* of land' in many of his poems such as *Michael*. But, as they established themselves in their cottage at Grasmere, he and Dorothy heard with dismay the reports of their neighbours: 'John Fisher ...talked much about the alteration in the times,' wrote Dorothy, 'and observed that in a short time there would be only two ranks of people, the very rich and the very poor, for those who have small estates says he are forced to sell, and all the land goes into one hand.'[38]

Down in Hampshire, Jane's clergyman father was at the heart of an old hierarchy that had its roots deep in the feudal system of medieval days. A large part of his income came from the tithes paid by parishioners, rich and poor, of Steventon; and most of those tithes would continue to be paid to him after he had ceased to live in the parish or conduct services there. Mr Austen was determined to get as much as he could out of this system to fund his retirement. 'My father is doing all in his power to encrease his

Income by raising his tythes etc,'[39] wrote Jane in January 1801.

Mr Austen seems to have felt this was a reasonable thing to do, but when writing *Mansfield Park* his daughter would make her more sympathetic characters critical of absentee clergymen who live off their parishioners and give little in return.

NINETEEN

Exercised to Constraint

On 3rd January 1801, Jane was able to tell her sister that she was becoming 'more and more reconciled to the idea of our removal [to Bath]'[1]. The six surviving letters sent to Cassandra in the first two months of that year are determinedly cheerful.

'We have lived long enough in this neighbourhood, the Basingstoke balls are certainly on the decline,' Jane wrote, over-looking the possibility that it was not the balls themselves that were in decline, but rather her own enthusiasm for them. She was even able to find 'something interesting in the bustle of going away'[2], though the sight of the family possessions – including even her own piano and collection of music – being prepared for auction, must have been painful.

The only truly sour note in these letters is her complaint about the way in which 'everything ...will be seized' by James and his wife. And on 16th January, when the couple held a party to celebrate their wedding anniversary, she remarked grimly, 'I was asked, but declined it.'[3] She might have been reconciled to the move, but she could still not *quite* forgive the relations who, she believed, had forced it upon her.

Where Jane, Cassandra and their parents were to settle in Bath was a matter for intense discussion, with Laura Place, Westgate Buildings and Queen's Square all being canvassed at different times. But Jane had little hope of her own wishes being considered. She favoured Laura Place or its environs but did not 'venture to expect it,'[4] for her mother hankered after Queen's Square. Yet Cassandra's wishes carried some weight in the family. When Mrs Austen was keen to settle in Westgate Buildings (which, incidentally, was to become the rather insalubrious home of Mrs Smith in *Persuasion*) Jane assured her sister that 'your opposition will be without difficulty decisive'[5]. Jane herself deferred to her sister. 'My mother bargains for having no trouble at all in furnishing our house in Bath –' she told Cassandra, '& I have engaged for your willingly undertaking to do it all'.[6]

The plan was to stay with their Uncle and Aunt Leigh-Perrot in their house at Paragon and from there conduct the negotiations for renting their own home in Bath. But who was to move first and when? '*Your* going I consider as indispensably necessary,' Jane wrote to Cassandra, 'and I shall not like being left behind'.[7] There is a hint here of Anne Elliot's situation: the plot of *Persuasion* leaves her behind in the country when the family move because 'nobody will want her in Bath'.[8] Jane's habit of stepping aside and allowing Cassandra to take the lead in practical matters was not changed by this disruption in their lives.

In the end the move was arranged differently. Mrs Austen and both her daughters travelled to Martha Lloyd's home at Ibthorpe at the beginning of May and, on the 4th, Jane and her mother went on alone to stay with the Leigh-Perrots, leaving Cassandra behind. Jane did not want to face the move alone without the support and companionship of her sister, but even that was finally forced upon her.

These letters demonstrate the way in which a 'daughter of the house' was expected to behave: giving up her own desires in the interests of family harmony. Writers of all religious and political colours concurred on this. The conservative Reverend Mr Fordyce declared in his *Sermons to Young Women*, 'Providence designed women for a state of dependence, and consequently of submission.' Priscilla Wakefield warned that, should a woman's 'destination be to remain an inhabitant in her father's house, cheerfulness, good temper, and obliging resignation of her will to that of others, will be there equally her duty, and her interest'.[9] Even the radical thinker Jean-Jacques Rousseau was in agreement. '[Girls] must be thwarted from an early age ...' he wrote in *Emile*. 'They must be exercised to constraint, so that it costs them nothing to stifle all their fantasies to submit them to the will of others.'

Jane did a fair amount of stifling of her fantasies as the Bath scheme was carried into action; she had no choice. As she said to Cassandra, 'I have given up the desire of your going to Bath with my mother and me. There is nothing which energy will not bring one to.'[10]

However, Rousseau – illustrious philosopher though he was – was wrong in supposing that *anyone* could do all that stifling without any personal cost. The cost to Jane was to include eight miserable, barren years during which she wrote hardly anything.

In her new home at Dove Cottage, Dorothy Wordsworth was able to write her best work. *Her* feelings do not appear to be stifled, for they are fearlessly acknowledged from the very beginning of the journal she kept during her early years in Grasmere.

It opens on 14th May 1800. Her younger brother John – now a sailor in merchant ships – had been staying at Dove Cottage and on this day he and William set off to visit the Hutchinson family in Yorkshire. Her first entry has an air of loss and melancholy.

'I left them at the turning of the Low-wood bay under the trees. My heart was so full that I could hardly speak to W. when I gave him a farewell kiss. I sate a long time upon a stone at the margin of the lake, and after a flood of tears my heart was easier. The lake looked to me I knew not why dull and melancholy, and the weltering on the shores seemed a heavy sound.'

After six months in her new home it hurt her to part with both her brothers, but it was William who was uppermost in her mind; her farewell kiss to him was remembered. In the same entry, she explained that she was starting this journal, 'because I will not quarrel with myself, and because I shall give Wm pleasure by it when he comes home again.' It was a way of staying connected to the man she loved by writing down the little observations which, had he been present, might have been spoken aloud.

In the *Grasmere Journal* (which was continued long after William returned from this trip in early June), though she does not use the self-conscious device of addressing her journal as an animate friend, Dorothy *seems* to write as she did to Jane Pollard back in Penrith days, putting down whatever is 'uppermost in my mind'. The result is an eclectic mixture of impressions and concerns, ranging from their many and varied visitors ('Mr Simpson came to tea …We drank tea in the orchard.'[11]) and anxiety about Coleridge and his disintegrating marriage ('We sat a long time under the Wall of a sheep-fold', runs one account of his visits. 'Had some interesting melancholy talk about his private affairs.'[12]), to moonlight on the lake (like 'herrings in the water'[13]) to cookery ('a bad giblet pie' on one occasion[14]) and the illnesses from which both Dorothy and William constantly suffered. 'Birds sang divinely today. Bowels and head bad', runs one line.[15]

The *Grasmere Journal* displays the sensibility of Marianne Dashwood, but also, sometimes, the down-to-earth sense of her elder sister. 'The snow-covered mountains were spotted with rich sunlight, a palish buffish colour. The roads were very dirty …' she wrote on 14th February 1802.

'How can you think of dirt, with such objects before you?' Marianne might have demanded (as she demands of Edward Ferrars when he notices mud in a beautiful scene). But Dorothy could be practical. And now she could be reserved too, a failing Marianne condemns in both Edward and her sister, Elinor. The outpouring of feeling in the journal, though it can create an illusion of closeness to the writer, is oddly impersonal, and, in the end, Dorothy eludes us. Though she may have written *what* she felt, she failed to record *why* she felt it. In fact the only thing which is always unequivocal is the strength of the emotion.

The opening passage, which seems to be a spontaneous expression of feeling, in fact reveals very little. '[M]y heart was so full', she wrote. But full of what? Was she simply distressed at the parting? Or was she upset because William was visiting Mary Hutchinson – the woman he would marry two years later? Was the possibility of marriage already in the air on this May morning, giving to the present separation the threat of future division? Was it the unacceptable emotion of jealousy which put Dorothy in danger of arguing with herself? Or was she match-making? Had she herself persuaded William into this visit? And was she now wondering whether she had done the right thing?

By the time the *Grasmere Journal* opens, something seems to have happened to the young woman who had been so very open about her feelings, something which made her cautious in her expression of emotion.

It is not unreasonable to suspect Dorothy's apparently transparent prose of hiding secrets, for we know that there is one very important secret concealed in the journal. During 1802, when the short suspension of war made communication possible between England and France, letters from William's abandoned mistress, Annette, were received and answered at Dove Cottage. The worry of these letters frequently affected Dorothy's health. On 15th February, for example, a letter arrived from Annette, and Dorothy 'slept badly' that night; on 26th March 'William wrote to Annette' and Dorothy 'was ill and in bad spirits'; on 3rd July another letter came from France and the next day Dorothy was 'sick and ill had been made sleepless by letters.'

She wrote nothing in her journal about the letters' content; she did not mention who Annette was, nor why the letters upset her. It was not from the *Grasmere Journal* – published in 1897 – that the story of William's French love affair was first pieced together by researchers; the Annette from whom these disturbing letters came was not identified until 1913.[16]

Free and unconventional though Dorothy's Grasmere life appears to be by her own account, restraint and silence were being forced upon her. Now that Annette's story is known, we can trace something of that pattern she described herself in which 'any thing that exercised my thoughts or feelings' brought on illness. There are, however, other illnesses, sleepless nights and fits of anxiety in the journal which do not correspond with the arrival of Annette's letters.

The *Grasmere Journal* is many things. It is a compelling account of life in Dove Cottage: an imperfect idyll, punctuated by hard work and illness and inadequately explained bouts of extreme sadness.

Sometimes it was a reference work to which William might turn for ideas. 'He asks me to set down the story of Barbara Wilkinson's Turtle Dove,' Dorothy wrote in January 1800 and then related a story they had probably heard from a neighbour.[17] Scenes and characters from the journal frequently reappear in William's work. For example, 'a very tall woman, tall much beyond the measure of tall women,' who appears in the journal begging at Dove Cottage takes on a romantic air in William's poem *Beggars,* where,

'She towered, fit person for a Queen
To lead those ancient Amazonian files;'

And the woman's 'very long brown cloak' which the journal describes is transmuted by poetry to:

'A mantle to her very feet
Descending with a graceful flow,'

The description might have been embellished by William's imagination, but the story of the woman and her two little boys ('wild figures' in prose, 'joyous vagrants' in poetry) is essentially the same in journal and poem.[18]

The style of the journal was a development of that employed at Alfoxton. There are those absolutely accurate descriptions of her surroundings: 'The valley of its winter yellow, but the bed of the brook still in some places almost shaded with leaves – the oaks brown in general but one that might be almost called green.'[19]

Sometimes now this precision was combined with a gathering together of vivid, disparate impressions which combine in the reader's mind to create something more than a picture – a keen awareness perhaps – of the scene she experienced:

'The moon shone upon the water below Silver-how, and above it hung, combining with Silver how on one side, a Bowl-shaped moon the curve downwards – the white fields, glittering Roof of Thomas Ashburner's house, the dark yew tree, the white fields – gay and beautiful.'[20]

And the manuscripts of the Journal reveal that, unselfconscious though Dorothy's style seems to be, she was, as she wrote, searching for the best form of expression. For example, on 17th March 1802 she described her home valley as 'quiet and fair in the moonlight', but that phrase has been changed to 'fair and quiet in the moonshine'.[21]

The journal also testifies to Dorothy's involvement in William's work. Tracing the tortuous progress of one particular poem, *The Pedlar,* gives an idea of how she contributed, though it still leaves some uncertainty as to whether she would be best described as muse, emotional support, secretary or co-author.

By 2nd February 1802 *The Pedlar* had begun to give William trouble; he 'wished to break off composition, and was unable, and so did himself harm.' Dorothy comforted him by reading aloud from *Paradise Lost.* He took a day off the next day and, on the 4th simply 'thought a little about the Pedlar'. On the 5th he '[s]ate up late at the pedlar', and slept badly that night.

On the 6th Dorothy probably made a fair copy of the poem for him, for on the following day there was a version to be read through. Dorothy thought (probably hoped) that it was now finished – 'but lo…it was uninteresting and must be altered. Poor William.'

Poor Dorothy too! For she now faced not only more copying, but more anxiety over William's health which was always badly affected by composition.

On the 9th William 'fell to work, and made himself unwell.' But he must have been making progress, for on the following day Dorothy was 'writing out the Poem as we hope for a final writing'. Later the same day they 'read the first part of the poem and were delighted with it…' Dorothy must have been relieved! But not for long, for she continued, rather obscurely, ' …but William afterwards got to some ugly places and went to bed tired out.'

Next day he made himself so tired by working on the poem that he had to lie down on a mattress in the sitting room while Dorothy read to him again. He woke refreshed … 'but he got to

work again and went to bed unwell.' On the 12th: 'I almost finished writing The Pedlar, but poor William wore himself and me
out with labour.' It was the first – and only – time she mentioned
feeling weary with the enterprise herself.

On the 14th: 'William left me at work altering some passages
of the Pedlar, and went into the orchard.' He then went away for
a couple of days, so Dorothy had a break from copying, worrying
and recopying. But when he came home on the 16th, 'He ... had
altered the pedlar.' (Oh dear more copying!) He continued to
work on the poem and make himself ill until the 28th when the
journal produces one of its most enigmatic comments. 'Disaster
pedlar' wrote Dorothy – probably too physically and emotionally
exhausted to explain herself further.

Maybe William had detected a flaw in the composition, or
maybe all the changes had made his draft illegible. Whatever
it was, Dorothy would now have faced a dilemma. Should she
encourage him to finish the poem – and so make himself ill?
Her love for the man was in conflict with her love for the poet.
Nothing happened for two days; but then, on 3rd March: 'I was
so unlucky as to propose to rewrite The Pedlar. Wm got to work
and was worn to death.'

William was off on another journey the next day, but he must
have left a new version of the poem because, while he was away,
Dorothy 'wrote the Pedlar, and finished it ...'[22] But there is one,
slightly ambiguous, comment the next day: 'I stitched up the Pedlar'.

Since she had finished copying the poem the previous day it
seems likely that this was a literal stitching – attaching the sheets
of paper to one another. But it is possible that her needlework
was metaphoric, involving a putting together of disparate verses
to make a coherent whole. Whichever it was, there was only one
more reading – and a little more altering – of this troublesome
poem, before William began to talk of publishing it on 10th
March, which must have been a considerable relief to Dorothy.[23]

This saga of anguish and labour shows that a simple country
life dedicated to poetry could be extremely stressful, and contrasts
sharply with serene journal entries such as, ' ... sailed down to
Loughrigg. Read poems on the water, and let the boat take its

own course.'[24] The illness (usually manifesting as a pain in his side), which Wordsworth suffered whenever he wrote, was probably psychosomatic, but it would have been no less debilitating for that – and no less distressing to witness.

The exact role which Dorothy played in the composition of William's poems is difficult to establish; though it would seem that, observing them, local folk had their own views on the subject. 'Well,' recalled one neighbour, 'fwoaks said she was cleverest mon of the two at his job, and he allays went to her when he was puzzelt.' Another provided this memorable image of the two Wordsworths working together: 'Mr Wordsworth went bumming and booming about, and she, Miss Dorothy, kept close behint him, and she picked up the bits as he let 'em fall, and tak'em down, and put 'em on paper for him.'[25]

What is certain is that Dorothy's emotional investment in William's work was immense; and she identified so closely with him that frequently she dropped names and pronouns altogether, writing, for example, on 1st August 1800, 'Altered the Whirlblast etc.' It is not always possible to know what was done by her and what was done by William.

The relationship between brother and sister was an extraordinary one. It had sustained Dorothy for many years, it had made her exquisitely happy, it had energised her, and it had given her the courage to rebel against the restrictions of life with her family. But it seems that, during the years at Grasmere, it began to impose on her its own, terrible restraint.

TWENTY

Our Affections do Rebel

About this time, in the poem *Home at Grasmere*, William Wordsworth captured the completeness and finality of his and Dorothy's union. Once more using her poetic name 'Emma', he wrote:

'Long is it since we met to part no more,
Since I and Emma heard each other's call
And were Companions once again ...'

Dorothy and William were indeed companions now. They were able to share ideas and interests as Dorothy inspired, copied, discussed (and, maybe, contributed to) his poetry. It was a relationship few women were able to have with their husbands (or brothers), for, at this time, the two sexes were expected to inhabit different mental landscapes.

'[Women] are not formed to govern the state, to make war, or to enter into the church,' declared one of the eighteenth century's most popular educational treatises – at a stroke cutting genteel women off from nearly all the interests considered proper for a gentleman. Instead a woman's role was to 'regulate the *minutiae* of domestic affairs'.[1] Indeed many people believed that male and female minds were fundamentally different. 'Male genius fetches its treasures from the depths of science, and the accumulated wisdom of the ages', wrote Laetitia Matilda Hawkins: 'the female

218

finds her's in the lighter regions of fancy and the passing knowledge of the day.'[2]

These attitudes did not encourage true companionship in marriage. Those careers of government, war and church all drew men away from women whose education did not fit them for understanding politics, military tactics or theology. In the winter of 1795/96, as Jane Austen enjoyed Tom Lefroy's company in the ballroom and wrote to her sister about silk stockings, white gloves and pink petticoat material, her brother Francis, Lieutenant on HMS *Glory*, was writing dispassionately in his log: 'Punished P.C. Smith forty-nine lashes for theft.'[3]

A boy returning from foreign travel and war might be breathlessly listened to as William Price is listened to in the drawing room of Mansfield Park, but the vast majority of women would have had nothing to contribute: there could be no discussion. And when Jane Austen wished to display the affection of the Price siblings she turned to their conversations about the shared experiences of childhood.[4]

The *Grasmere Journal* is an account of a shared, companionate life, and also a record of an extremely intense relationship. Affectionate from the very beginning, as Dorothy sits weeping over her separation from her brother, its trajectory is one of ever more freely expressed love. At least it is up until William's marriage in October 1802.

The way in which Dorothy wrote about William changed over the time that she kept her journal. During the first year or two he was usually simply 'William'. But, in the early months of 1802, her language became more charged with emotion. On 2nd February he was 'My William'. On 4th March he was 'my darling' and by 17th March he was 'my Beloved', a term of endearment which characterises the rest of the journal until his wedding.

The overall impression is one of extreme intimacy. Dorothy's happiest times were moments alone with William when they 'sate talking and happy'[5], or were simply together: 'The fire flutters and the watch ticks I hear nothing else save the Breathing of my Beloved and he now and then pushes his book forward and turns over a leaf.'[6]

It is a picture of domestic contentment such as Jane Austen draws to portray a genuinely happy marriage. It is the 'tete-a-tete with the person one feels most agreeable in the world'[7] which Mary Crawford describes in *Mansfield Park*; it is the snug evening, enjoyed by Admiral Croft and his wife in *Persuasion* when they escape from their friends 'and shut ourselves into our lodgings, and draw in our chairs'[8].

Sometimes Dorothy and William's moments of companionship were made more intense by physical contact: 'I read him to sleep – I read Spenser while he leaned on my shoulder.'[9] And: 'After we came in we sate in deep silence at the window – I on a chair and William with his hand on my shoulder. We were deep in Silence and Love, a blessed hour.'[10] And again: 'After dinner we made a pillow of my shoulder, I read to him and my Beloved slept...'[11]

Here were two people very much in love.

When, several years later, Thomas De Quincey reported the gossip about William having been 'intimate' with his sister, he suggested that the rumour had grown up because 'It is Wordsworth's custom whenever he meets or parts with any of the female part of his own relations to kiss them – This he has frequently done when he has met his sister...in roads or on mountains...without heeding whether he was observed or not...'[12]

De Quincey maintained that the rumour was false; but, as Kathleen Jones has pointed out, he may not have been a very good judge of such things for he was also convinced that Lord Nelson's relationship with Lady Hamilton was entirely platonic.[13]

Local gossip would, in fact, have had more to draw on than a few hello-kisses. It is not difficult to see why Dorothy and William's behaviour might have raised some eyebrows in rural Westmorland as it had done in Germany and Somerset. Dorothy did not hide her feelings. After any separation her joy at meeting her brother again was uncontrollable. 'I believe I screamed,'[14] she admitted on one occasion when there were witnesses to the reunion.

There was also their habit – begun in Somerset – of lying down together outdoors. On one occasion: 'William lay, and I lay in the trench under the fence … William heard me breathing and rustling now and then but we both lay still, and unseen by one another.' Their motives were entirely poetic – they were intent on absorbing the sights and sounds of the place; but a passing local, seeing them climb in or out of their trench, might well have wondered what they were up to. On the following day they were prone again: 'We spread the gown, put on each a cloak and there we lay.'[15] It is evident from the description of the view that follows that this was on the open fell-side where anyone might have seen them.

These were not farm-folk or servants sprawling on the hillside and rustling about in trenches: these were a lady and a gentleman. Their status would have added spice to the tittle-tattle, but Dorothy probably did not care what people said, echoing perhaps Marianne Dashwood's opinion of a gossip: 'I value not her censure any more than I should do her commendation.'[16]

There were moments when Dorothy felt an intense physical awareness of her 'darling'. 'His mouth and breath were very cold when he kissed me,' she wrote of one reunion[17] and of another: 'He was cool and fresh…and smelt sweetly – his clothes were wet. We sate together talking till the first dawning of Day – a happy time.'[18]

When he was absent from home she attempted to comfort herself by occupying his bed. 'I slept in Wm's bed, and I slept badly, for my thoughts were full of William.'[19]

It is evident that Dorothy's love for her brother, which had begun in letters during their separation, had changed during the years of proximity. This memorable extract, written when he had just left her for a visit of several days, captures the unsettling intensity of her devotion:

'I will be busy, I will look well and be well when he comes back to me. O the Darling! Here is one of his bitten apples! I can hardly find in my heart to throw it into the fire…I walked round the two Lakes crossed the stepping stones at Rydale Foot. Sate down where we always sit. I was full of thoughts about my darling. Blessings on him …'[20]

There is pain – and a sense almost of confusion – at the separation, a lingering awareness of the beloved's physical presence mixed with sheer adoration in her response to that bitten apple. Dorothy sometimes seems to have been overwhelmed and bewildered by her love: not quite sure what to do about it.

Something was troubling Dorothy deeply at this time, and it is hinted at in these uneasy and not quite happy expressions of love. But she does not say why she must struggle to look well when William returned, nor what the thoughts were that filled her head as she sat by the stepping stones.

There is much left unsaid in the journal. Dorothy seems to have reached a point where she *could not* be honest about her feelings, though she appears unable to stop them spilling onto the page. After all, if this was just a reference book for William, a daily account of events, or an exercise in describing the natural world, there was no particular need for her to say anything at all about her feelings, but out they come. Then, always, having said just so much, she draws back. She is certainly no longer attempting the style of those novels she had enjoyed as a girl, in which every nuance of feeling is explored.

Was she sexually attracted to her brother?

The question must occur. There are those beautiful moments of exquisitely pleasurable connection as her beloved rests his head on her shoulder, moments when they are 'deep in silence and love'; there is Coleridge's jealousy of a closeness which in some way excluded him; there are the doubts which the folk of both Somerset and Germany had had about the title 'sister', and the more definite report that a rumour of incest circulated in Westmorland and London during Dorothy's own lifetime.

De Quincey was quick to deny this rumour. And, in his recollections, he was also careful to make his description of Dorothy sexually unappealing, writing of her 'unsexual awkwardness'[21] and 'her stooping attitude when walking…which gave an ungraceful, and even an unsexual character to her appearance when out of doors.'[22]

It seems as if he wished to assure his readers that here was a typical spinster: as pitiable and inoffensive as Miss Bates in

Emma. This was a common purpose among male writers of the time. There was a great reluctance to think of single women like Dorothy (who had failed to fulfil their 'true' purpose in life) upsetting the social order with their sexuality.

'The great use of Women in a Community,' declared Daniel Defoe, 'is to supply it with Members that may be serviceable, and keep up a Succession.'[23]

Georgian medical texts agreed with this limited view of the female sex. '[S]he is only to Conceive, to give suck, and to breed up Children', said the writer of *An Essay Concerning Human Generation*,[24] while *The Ladies Dispensatory* declared that, 'Being designed by the great Author of Nature for the Vehicle thro' which the human Species should be propagated...it was proper that her Parts should be suited to these Ends'.[25]

Words such as 'use' and 'serviceable' implied that a woman's body and sexuality belonged more to society at large than to the individual herself. So it was with some regret that a writer assuming the pseudonym 'Philogamus' (in a discussion of why so many marriages were unhappy) admitted that 'As Women were principally designed for producing the Species and Men for other greater Ends: we cannot wonder, if their Inclinations and Desires tend chiefly that way.'

He meant that, inconvenient though it was, women enjoyed sex. It just could not be helped. If they didn't they wouldn't supply the babies that the human race needed. Consequently – according to the sage 'Philogamus' – 'The great Concern of every Commonwealth, is to keep them within due bounds.'[26] Male Georgian moralists had not formulated the idea of angelic female innocence which was to prove a great comfort to their Victorian counterparts. 'Every Woman is at Heart a Rake', declared Alexander Pope.[27]

So – 'To counterbalance this violent natural Desire,' wrote Bernard Mandeville, 'all young Women have strong Notions of Honour carefully inculcated into them from their Infancy. Young Girls are taught to hate a *Whore* before they know what the Word means; and when they grow up, they find their worldly Interest entirely depending upon the Reputation of their Chastity.'

223

Or, as Mary Bennet says (having read the pontificating of learned men), 'loss of virtue in a female is irretrievable...one false step involves her in endless ruin ...'[28] Elizabeth may 'lift...up her eyes in amazement' at this. But, that's not because it isn't true; it is just so obvious it does not need to be said.

This anxious, dangerous vision of women as sexually insatiable, held in check only by custom and law, had been around since at least the Middle Ages. It is the foundation of the persistent fiction that women want to be raped. Or, as Mandeville put it: 'Most women ...let them be ever so fully resolv'd to comply, make as great a Shew of Resistance as they can conveniently counterfeit... [I]t is ...a Kind of *Salvo* to her Honour and Conscience, that she never did fully comply, but was in a Manner forc'd into it. This is the plain natural Reason why most Women refuse, to *surrender* upon Treaty, and why they delight so much in being *storm'd*.'[29]

Early marriage was the preferred method of controlling women's violent natural desire. (Defoe even believed that 'no Woman ought to be allowed to marry after her Capacity of Child-bearing has left her'.) Medical men supported the moralists' views with their theories about 'hysterica'.

This dire malady, which was peculiar to women, was remarkable for 'the Variety of Forms, by which it discovers itself.' It could take the form of almost any disease and only a trained physician could recognise it. (Though no cogent method of diagnosis was ever described.)[30]

Dr R. James in his *Medical Dictionary* avoided the indelicacy of directly stating that this mysterious disease was all about a woman's unsatisfied sexual impulses. But his meaning was clear. He said, '[Hysterica] more particularly seizes Virgins before their first menstrual discharge ..., such as are marriageable ... and [those] indulging themselves in generous Wines, and Delicacies, which prove a Stimulus to Venery.' And, he said, 'Reason, Experience, and the Authorities of the greatest Physicians, concur in pronouncing Matrimony highly beneficial in removing hysteric Disorders.'[31]

If marriage was the cure for hysterica, it might be supposed that women such as Dorothy (and Jane) who remained unmarried all their lives would be particularly prone to it. However, Dr James does not mention confirmed spinsters in his list of those most at risk. Perhaps the idea of women having sexual feelings that lasted throughout their lives and were entirely independent of their marital status, was just too frightening for the men who wrote these Georgian texts.

Spinsters were made safe in the popular imagination by the notion that chastity itself triggered an alarming degree of physical decay. Even Lady Mary Wortley Montagu fell into this way of thinking. 'I have a Moral Aversion to be an Old Maid,' she wrote, 'and a decaid oak before my Window, leaveless, half rotten, and shaking its wither'd Top, puts me in mind ...of an Antiquated Virgin, Bald, with Rotten Teeth, and shaking of the Palate.'[32]

It is alarming to find that even such an intelligent woman as Lady Mary could accept the popular confusion of spinsterhood with the disfigurements of old age. Did she really believe that a husband could somehow prevent her body aging, her hair falling out and her teeth rotting?

By 1838 the myth of the decrepit virgin was so widespread that Richard Carlisle was able to declare confidently: 'It is a fact that can hardly have escaped the notice of anyone that women who have never had sexual commerce begin to droop when about twenty-five years of age ...their forms degenerate, their features sink, and the peculiar character of the old maid becomes apparent.'[33] Thus superfluous spinsters were rendered harmless. They were not likely to form sexual relationships of any kind. Their passions could be safely distilled into the 'chagrin and peevishness' which Dr John Gregory attributed to spinsters when, in his *Legacy*, he advised his daughters of the dangers of not marrying.

Thomas De Quincey's description of an 'unsexual' Dorothy is unsettlingly similar to Carlisle's drooping virgin. Perhaps he wished to assure his readers that his admiration was confined entirely to her mind, and that he felt no physical attraction to this stooping little spinster with broken teeth.

But we need not concur with De Quincey and Carlisle. In the twenty-first century there is no reason why such an important part of Dorothy Wordsworth as her sexuality should be dismissed as irrelevant and ugly.

The recent confusing experiences of adults who have been re-united with siblings after separation as children has led to the belief that there is such a phenomenon as Genetic Sexual Attraction. A support group set up to help individuals affected by these issues maintains that as many as fifty per cent of reunited siblings feel some degree of physical attraction to their brother or sister.[34] The evidence is, so far, only anecdotal, but, if it was confirmed, it would mean that reunited siblings are more likely to be attracted to one another than the average couple meeting for the first time. This suggests it is possible that Dorothy was vulnerable to such an attraction because she and William had been separated after the death of their mother.

The 'negative imprinting' – that is a lack of sexual interest in relatives – which deters inbreeding is believed to be caused by intimate contact in childhood rather than by genetic similarity.[35] In other words, we tend to find our close childhood companions unsexy when we meet them later in life. It has been suggested that, because of their early separation, Dorothy and William might have lacked this imprinting.

However, there is a problem with this theory. Investigations into this negative imprinting – which psychologists call the Westermarck Effect – have indicated that the crucial period of contact during which individuals learn to recognise relatives to whom they will later feel sexual aversion is *the first six years of life*.

Dorothy had passed her sixth birthday when she was separated from her brothers.

The Westermarck Effect – which has been observed to be stronger in women than in men – would probably have protected Dorothy, helping her to separate sexual feelings from her deepening love for her brother. However, there may have been other reasons why her peace of mind was disturbed after her arrival in Grasmere.

At twenty-two, eloping with a brother had been an exciting

act of defiance. But Dorothy was now thirty years old; she had reached that time of life at which many women begin to experience a growing pressure from their bodies, as well as from society, to produce children, and she was 'fond of children'.[36] She might never have heard about the ticking of a biological clock, but that would not have stopped her suffering from it. She had learned over the last eight years that her relationship with William was a secure and happy one. She also knew now just how desperately he needed her in order to carry on with the work which she believed was his vocation, and Dorothy needed to be needed. While her hormones were urging her to reproduce, her heart was telling her to stay with William.

Frances Wilson, noting the close identification which Dorothy felt with William has likened their attachment to that of Heathcliff and Cathy, even suggesting that when Emily Brontë wrote *Wuthering Heights* she may have been influenced by the account of the Wordsworths published in *Taits Edinburgh Magazine* in 1839.[37] 'I am Heathcliff', declares Cathy. 'He is more myself than I am.' Wilson believes that the Wordsworths' love, like that of Brontë's characters, was elemental and asexual. 'What Dorothy Wordsworth and Catherine Earnshaw experience is depersonalising, dematerialising, and unsexing', she writes.

However, it is difficult to connect this account of the Wordsworths' relationship with the tender, gradual fall into love which can be traced in the letters Dorothy wrote between 1791 and 1794. Dorothy and William had lived together until Dorothy was six, but after that they were separated. They did not grow up together as Cathy and Heathcliff do; they did not, 'evolve from childhood inseparability into a hybrid...'[38] Their reunion as teenagers was followed by a period of getting to know one another, a period during which William 'courted' Dorothy.

The young man Dorothy described as having 'a sort of violence of Affection ...which demonstrates itself ...when Objects of his affection are present with him, in a thousand almost imperceptible attentions to their wishes,' does not sound much like a Heathcliff! Nor does the 'Delicacy of Manners', which Dorothy also attributed to her brother, call to mind the brutal master of Wuthering

Heights. That rather suggests one of Jane Austen's more sensitive heroes – Colonel Brandon, or Mr Knightley perhaps.

Frances Wilson believes that the 'physical expression [of their love] would have been of no interest' to Dorothy and William.[39] But they were two young, healthy people enjoying a deep companionate love. The evidence of Dorothy's letters and journals suggests that it was a gentle, individual love – not that powerful but disturbing emotion that Brontë's heroine likens to 'the eternal rocks …a source of little visible delight, but necessary.' Dorothy took emotional, intellectual and physical delight in her brother's company.

In 1954 an intrepid scholar (F.W. Bateson) found evidence in William's poetry for an erotic love of the poet for his sister – and the world of literary studies was outraged. It was felt that the suggestion somehow tainted Wordsworth and his work; an interest in it was merely prurient. The idea that Dorothy might have inspired (or felt) desire at Dove Cottage was as abhorrent to mid-twentieth century academics as it would have been to gentlemen of the early nineteenth century, like Carlisle, who preferred to think of unmarried women drooping and degenerating after the age of twenty-five, rather than maintaining a subversive and disturbing sexuality.

In the *Grasmere Journal*, moments of tenderness, happiness and great sadness follow one another, overlaying and transmuting into each other. At times, Dorothy's love for William seems to hurt her.

'Then we sat by the fire', she wrote on one occasion, 'and were happy only our tender thoughts became painful.'[40] And, 'got into sad thoughts,' she wrote on 5th March 1802, 'tried at German but could not go on – read [Lyrical Ballads] – Blessings on that brother of mine!'[41] Then, a few days later: 'William was reading in Ben Jonson – he read me a beautiful poem on Love. We then walked. The first part of our walk was melancholy …'[42]

Dorothy is acknowledging a confusion of feelings, but offering no explanation. On 28th January 1802, the journal says, 'We were both in miserable spirits,' and conjures a picture of unease in Dove Cottage (where sounds carried so easily from one part of the house to another). That night Dorothy tried to sleep in her room downstairs, while the floorboards over her head creaked with her beloved's restlessness: 'William out of spirits and tired. After we went to bed I heard him continually, he called at ¼ past 3 to know the hour.'

William would sleep badly until his marriage – which was why Dorothy frequently read to him: to soothe him into sleep like a restless child. In fact, in most of the moments of physical closeness between the two, Dorothy's role seems to be that of a comforter. One line which startles modern ears occurs on 31st January 1802, when she writes: 'I petted him on the carpet'. But this was one of the many occasions on which William felt unwell, and the word petted, which now has a sexual charge, was probably used in an older sense of cosseted or made a fuss of.

When composition of *The Pedlar* was going badly, Dorothy must read Milton or Spenser until William slept. And, on other occasions, we hear of William resting his head on Dorothy's shoulder, or reaching out to touch her as they sit 'deep in silence and love'. It does not seem to have been Dorothy who needed the reassuring contact, or soothing embrace.

By January 1802 William was keeping his sister awake with his nocturnal pacing and on 17th March he was still restless. On that night, after they had both gone to bed, 'he came down to me and read the Poem to me in bed.'

By the beginning of the summer William's sleep patterns were very irregular. 'I sate up a while after William –' Dorothy wrote on 19th June, 'he then called me down to him[43] ... I read Churchill's Roscaid. Returned again to my writing and did not go to bed till he called to me ...' The passage again conjures a sense of unease and evokes the closeness of the cottage where only floorboards divided their bed-chambers. But this passage ends on a delightful note of tenderness and acceptance: 'In a little time I thought I heard William snoring, so I composed myself to sleep – smiling at my sweet Brother.' It is a very special kind of love which can find a man's snoring endearing!

The next night he needed her again: ' ...Wm went to bed. I sate up about an hour. He then called me to talk to him – he could not fall asleep.'

The picture the journal evokes in the spring of 1802 is of an intense and slightly unstable love, in which William was the needy party who must be reassured by his devoted sister. Those beautiful arrested moments when the couple sat together, touching and silently loving, ordinary life suspended, argue most strongly against a consummated relationship. It is unlikely that a woman in a full sexual relationship would find such deep significance in the resting of a head on her shoulder or the touch of a hand.

It also seems unlikely to me that, had she been racked with physical desire for the man who sat beside her, Dorothy could have found such an exquisite pleasure in these moments, moments which seemed to supply all the physical contact she needed from her beloved.

Something was making Dorothy uneasy and unhappy. For some reason she felt melancholy when William read a love poem to her and the sharing of tender thoughts could become painful. Something, even in the journal's very first entry, had filled her heart to overflowing so that she could find relief only in tears.

I believe there may have been more at work here than Dorothy's growing realisation that her devotion to William and his work meant the sacrifice of her own chance of having children. The clue perhaps lies in the fact that it was *William* who initiated contact on those disturbed, disturbing nights when he and Dorothy, separated in their own rooms, but still keenly aware of one another's presence, lay awake and listening.

Years later, in a very tender love-letter written to his wife during a time of separation, William would write of the sexual longings he suffered at this time and describe how they had made him ill, before gently assuring her that 'I never suffered half as much as during this absence from you'.[44]

As these later letters to his wife, and his impetuous affair in France, prove, William Wordsworth was a man with strong sexual impulses, who found it a hardship to control those impulses. During the early years at Dove Cottage he needed and loved his sister deeply. And I believe that it was *his* sexual feelings, rather than her own, that caused Dorothy's outbursts of weeping and unhappiness.

William also had a problem which has generally been accounted rather unimportant by his biographers. He was anosmic. 'With regard to *Fragrance*,' wrote Christopher Wordsworth in his memoir of his uncle, 'Mr Wordsworth spoke from the testimony of *others*: he himself had *no sense of smell*.'[45] And, 'Wordsworth has no sense of smell ...' wrote Robert Southey in 1822. 'He has often expressed to me his regret for this privation.'[46]

This privation might have been a tragedy for William, not only because it cut him off entirely from one aspect of the natural world which he had now (under Dorothy's influence) grown to love as dearly as he had in boyhood. For most of us it is strange – hard to comprehend – that when he strode the fells he did not catch the scents of peaty earth and damp bracken, enjoy the fragrance of honeysuckle weaving its way through the air on summer evenings, or smell the wet rock and moss of the waterfalls he admired; but there may have been an even more distressing consequence for him – and for Dorothy.

Psychologists researching the Westermarck Effect – that mechanism which usually protects us from sexual attraction to our close kin – have attempted to answer the question: how do we identify the family members to whom we feel sexual aversion? And their research suggests that the trigger is olfactory.[47]

For most of us our close relatives (or those with whom we have lived as children) just do not smell sexy. It is easy to see how useful such a protection might be; it may well be the foundation of taboos against close-kin marriage which occur in nearly all societies. Its absence would be deeply distressing and confusing, not only to an anosmic individual, who had developed a close and sustaining relationship with his sister, but also to the devoted sister with whom he shared his home.

Without this simple, natural protection, William may well have found the moral demands of society in harsh conflict with his own most powerful feelings as, driven by a strong, healthy sexual impulse his thoughts turned naturally to the woman he loved – and were unchecked by the usual control that nature imposes.

Dorothy had achieved a home in which she was central and for the last six years she had struggled to provide all the support William needed. She identified so closely with him that sometimes the boundaries between them blurred. Now he was deeply unhappy. She was, in a sense, the cause of his unhappiness, and yet she could not help him. For them, of course, the problem would have presented itself, not in psychological or scientific terms, but in guilt, confusion and anxiety.

It is possible to see now why that love poem of Ben Jonson's might have been distressing to them both. Stephen Gill has identified the poem which William read to Dorothy on 9th March 1802 – the poem which resulted in a melancholy walk – as the *Epode* which forms part of Ben Jonson's ode *To the Forest* (See Appendix 2).

In this poem Jonson distinguishes chaste love – which is 'gentle' and 'divine' from 'blind desire' which is 'armed with bow, shafts, and fire'. He writes of the danger when 'our affections do rebel', and, forcefully urging chastity upon his readers, he ends with a dire warning:

'Man may securely sin, but safely never.'

Even secret sins are found out. Here was a thought that would certainly be enough to make William and Dorothy's walk melancholy. And this poem which Dorothy listened to at Dove Cottage's fireside, urged a degree of restraint, far beyond that which Elinor Dashwood recommends to her sister. Jonson declared that our physical senses – our most basic impulses – should be subject entirely to our will:

'Tis the securest policy we have
To make our sense our slave.'

This philosophy was a world away from Dorothy's youthful conviction that 'all is contemptible that does not spring immediately out of an affectionate Heart'.

TWENTY-ONE

Very Capable of Loving

Jane Austen – though she was unmarried and had now passed the apparently critical age of twenty-five – was neither drooping nor degenerating. A gentleman who met her about this time described her as 'fair and handsome, slight and elegant, but with cheeks a little too full.'[1] Fulwar William Fowle (the son of one of her father's pupils) would remember her in her early thirties as 'certainly pretty ...lively & full of humor – most amiable – most beloved ...'[2]

It sounds as if she was still a sexually attractive woman, and Jane does not seem to have suffered from Dorothy's notion that men found her unappealing. But she does not seem to have been happy in her new home. Bath was a place in which it would have been particularly difficult to escape from society's expectations of a woman as the 'Vehicle thro' which the human Species should be propagated'. The town was an important stall on the Georgian marriage market and a young woman's business there was to be attractive.

The novelist Tobias Smollett brought his heroes to Bath in search of rich heiresses, while the heroines of many female writers were excruciatingly aware of their role as commodities. Mary Ann Hanway wrote of a young woman ' ...produced for admiration in Bath seasons, dragged from one fashionable watering place to another, evidently to be disposed of to the highest bidder.' The dancing, chatting and 'sitting down together' of a ball, which had

233

delighted Jane at twenty, had their darker side. It depended rather on your point of view. Charlotte Smith wrote in *Montalbert*: 'Dragged to a scene, where she considered herself exposed as an animal in a market to the remarks and purchase of the best bidder, it was with some reluctance that Rosalie entered the ballroom.'[3]

Whether she liked it or not Jane would have been considered open to offers. And, though she was still attractive, now that she had passed the mid-point of her twenties, her options (like Dorothy's) would have seemed to be narrowing. If she was to find a husband, marry and have a family she did not have a great deal of time left. However, before she left Steventon, she had already shown signs of outgrowing her girlish enthusiasm for dances and an impatience with the duty of always looking her best (remember those caps which saved so much time and effort over hairdressing).

Within days of arriving in Bath she was at the penultimate ball of the season having 'dressed myself as well as I could, & had all my finery much admired at home'. She does not say in the description she sent to Cassandra whether she entered the ballroom with reluctance or anticipation, but noted that, though the dance was 'shockingly thin for this place, there were people enough I suppose to have made five or six very pretty Basingstoke assemblies.'[4]

Since her arrival in Bath, Jane had been making an effort to be positive about her new life. Writing to inform her sister that 'Bonnets of Cambric Muslin…are a great deal worn' and lamenting that 'Bath is getting so very empty…', she succeeded in sounding more like a fashionable young lady gone up to the resort town to enjoy herself than a woman transplanted against her will.

This ball's chief interest, however, was that got from observing a 'famous adulteress', Miss Twisleton, who was 'rather quietly & contentedly silly than anything else'. Another entertainment was watching a Mrs Badcock who 'thought herself obliged to …run round the room after her drunken Husband. – His avoidance, & her pursuit with the probable intoxication of both was an amusing scene.'

It sounds as if Jane spent her evening more as a novelist observing and gathering material, than a marriageable young lady on the look-out for attractive men. She does not mention dancing herself.

Perhaps she was not asked. That would have been a painful experience and a reminder that, though she might still be 'fair and handsome', she was too poor to attract much interest from men.

News of the sale of family possessions now going on at Steventon confirmed just how poor she was. 'Mary,' she complained, 'is more minute in her account of their own Gains than in ours.'[5] As the sale of goods brought less than expected, she could not help but compare her own losses with the advantages that Mary and James had got from the retirement arrangements: 'The Whole World is in a conspiracy to enrich one part of our family at the expence of another.'[6]

Her complaints cannot be traced for long. Just two weeks after that ball a silence falls over Jane's life. The next letters that she wrote did not survive Cassandra's censorship, and we do not hear her voice again for more than three years. Then, after just one letter written in 1804, the silence resumes for another year. All that we know about this period in Jane's life is that she continued to live in Bath with her family, taking frequent visits to relations, and spending holidays by the seaside, usually in the late summer or autumn. Since Cassandra destroyed the intervening letters it is reasonable to assume that they contained more complaints. And Jane complained when she was unhappy.

She seems to have kept her spirits up when they first arrived in Bath by hoping she would be able to continue with her novels once the family had found a home of its own. During the early weeks of house-hunting she described one house they looked around (but did not rent) as having an 'apartment over the Drawing-room [which] pleased me particularly, because it is divided into two, the smaller one a very nice sized Dressing-room, which upon occasion might admit a bed.'[7] This little dressing-room, only occasionally used as a bedroom, sounds very much like the writing space at Steventon which she had lost.

These plans came to nothing. Even after she had escaped her aunt's house and was established in a home with just her sister and parents, Jane failed to escape into that world of work and imagination which might have given her some relief from Bath's milieu of balls and husband-hunting.

In his memoir Austen-Leigh writes that 'nothing which the public have seen, was completed' during the time at Bath.[8] Many dedicated writers find that – once established – the habit of writing becomes necessary to their mental well-being. It is easy to see how a downward spiral might have been established, with discontent preventing Jane from writing and the inability to write making her more discontent. The end of all this may well have been depression.

Despite glib talk about 'the Prozac Generation', depression is very far from being a modern illness[9]. It was around in Georgian days under such titles as 'melancholy', 'lowness of spirits' and the ubiquitous 'nervous diseases' to which the physician William Buchan devoted a whole chapter in his popular *Domestic Medicine or the Family Physician* of 1769. A sense of not being in control of one's own life is often cited by counsellors today as a contributing factor in this illness, and a lack of autonomy may have triggered many of those nervous diseases which were endemic among Georgian ladies.

Causes of depression are cited on the NHS website as including 'an upsetting or stressful life event – such as bereavement, divorce, illness, redundancy and job or money worries.' Jane's uprooting from her home would certainly have been a stressful life event; and, as we have seen, it may well have raised anxieties about money and her uncertain financial future. In addition, 'Becoming cut off from your family and friends can increase your risk of depression.' Jane had been taken away from her established support network. 'The sisters had never known any other home but Steventon,' wrote Fanny Caroline, 'and the leaving it involved in a great measure the loss of their dearest friends and connections.'[10]

Among the symptoms of depression listed in this modern analysis are 'Having no motivation or interest in things' and 'not doing well at work' – both of which are evident in the difficulty Jane found in writing during her Bath years. The description of 'not getting any enjoyment out of life' calls to mind the 'stupid' parties of which she complained during her early months in the city, and another symptom, 'feeling irritable and intolerant of others', was certainly a problem for Jane at this time. Her reluctance to make new friends was turning to peevishness; 'I cannot anyhow continue to find people agreeable,' she announced in May 1801.[11]

Then there is that flatness, that lack of excitement, in the assembly room as the penultimate ball of the Bath season played out around her. Was depression the root of that? A 'lack of interest in sex (loss of libido)' is – according to the NHS site – another symptom of depression. Perhaps that is why the beaus of the Bath ballroom roused no flicker of interest in Jane.

The question of why Jane Austen never married is frequently raised, and the answer to it must, of course, be complex: her poverty, her character, her high expectations of marital love, the wars with France which were horrifically diminishing the supply of eligible young men ('...the melancholy part was to see so many dozen young Women standing by without partners...' wrote Jane of a ball in 1808[12]), her devotion to her career – all these things must have played their part.

However, another cause may have been that, during these crucial few years which represented her last chance of forming an alliance, these few years when she was fairly well placed to meet a soul-mate, a crushing, debilitating illness, by robbing her of natural sexual feelings, made it impossible for her to desire a man enough to wish to share his bed.

It was, perhaps, a cruel chance which denied Jane this last opportunity to form the kind of happy, companionate union to which she had made Elizabeth Bennet and Elinor Dashwood aspire: the kind of union which Dorothy had achieved for a while in the wilds of Westmorland.

There is evidence that Jane remained attractive to men throughout her twenties. There is the man who found her 'fair and handsome' and there would be, in the next few years, two proposals of marriage, both of which she might herself have described as unexceptionable. Mr William Digweed (whose attachment some thought had been the cause of the move from Steventon) seems to have remembered Jane with particular affection all his life. 'I knew him as an old man,' recalled Jane's great-niece, 'and certainly fancied there was some charm linked with her name'.

However, after the departure of Tom Lefroy, there is only one report of Jane Austen being attracted to a man, and that is an odd, vague story.

In 1829[13] (twelve years after Jane's death) Cassandra told her niece Caroline of a charming and rather mysterious man that the sisters had met on one of the seaside holidays taken during their Bath years. Caroline believed the meeting might have taken place in Devonshire. 'He seemed greatly attracted by my Aunt Jane,' wrote Caroline, and ' ...when they had to part ...he was urgent to know where they would be next summer, implying or perhaps saying that he should be there also ... [T]he impression left on Aunt Cassandra was that he had fallen in love with her sister, and was quite in earnest. Soon after they heard of his death.' But Cassandra seems to have felt that the unnamed man 'was worthy of her sister ...and also ...that he would have been a successful suitor.'

The story is as blurred and faded as an old sepia photo, and perhaps already a little distorted by the time Caroline recorded it. Over the years it would change again as different members of the family handled it, with the anonymous lover sometimes being confused with the suitor that Mrs Lefroy had encouraged a few years earlier, and taking the name of Mr Blackall.

In the hands of great-niece Fanny Caroline, the essential points of the charming lover and the early death remained, but the location was fixed at Teignmouth and the couple apparently 'parted on the understanding that he was to come to Steventon.' And when, in 1884, the tale was recorded in Lord Brabourne's first edition of Jane Austen's letters the scene had shifted to Sidmouth and the lover now pressed 'to be allowed to join them later on in their tour'.

It is, perhaps, significant that Jane's suitor becomes more ardent with each retelling. In the oldest surviving version of the tale he is content to let a whole year pass before being reunited with the woman with whom he has, apparently, fallen in love – which does not seem very promising. In Fanny Caroline's *Family History* he wishes to come to Steventon to visit Jane, which is odd, since she was now living in Bath[14], but at least he is not willing to postpone their next meeting for twelve months. Finally, in the published version, he is so eager to pursue the affair that he is determined to follow the Austens on their present holiday.

It seems as if the members of Jane's loving and loyal family were making the most of a rather insubstantial story: trying to assert her claim to being worthy of love. Maybe, after more than twenty years, even Cassandra's version of the story was influenced by a desire to raise her sister to the dignity she had achieved herself of having loved and lost.[15] By the tale Jane was saved from the disgrace of never having married because she was never sought but, in case anyone might think she was in danger of succumbing to that 'peevishness and chagrin' which Dr Gregory ascribed to disappointed spinsters, Caroline wished her brother – in his memoir – to let his readers know that 'Aunt Jane never had any attachment that overclouded her happiness, for long. This [the seaside romance] had not gone far enough, to leave misery behind.'[16]

Beyond this hint of a lost love, no reason for Jane's continued celibacy was ever suggested by those who knew her. No friend or member of her family ever suggested that her career (and it is unreasonable to deny that such a dedicated writer had a career) was a justification for remaining single.

However, Thomas de Quincey claimed to know the cause of Miss Wordsworth's single state. '[S]he had rejected all offers of marriage, out of pure sisterly regard to her brother ...' he said, with obvious approval.[17]

The idea of a woman giving up marriage and children to pursue her own vocation as a writer would have seemed unfeminine. As Robert Southey was to tell Charlotte Brontë when she applied to him for advice, 'literature cannot be the business of a woman's life, and it ought not to be.' However, for a woman to sacrifice those personal blessings for the sake of a man's genius was entirely acceptable.

TWENTY-TWO

Marriage: The Settlement We Should Aim At

Dorothy never married. Her soul remained absorbed in her brother's fame and writing for the rest of her life but, by the time the *Grasmere Journal* opens, she seems to have determined that *William* should marry. She promoted the match with Mary Hutchinson at every opportunity.

It is clear that William was experiencing strong sexual feelings in 1802, feelings which made him restless and unhappy. Later – like the good husband that he was – he would assure Mary that these were entirely directed towards her. But the reading of the Jonson poem suggests that there was an element of guilt mixed with his impulses, guilt which a Georgian man would be unlikely to feel about longings for a woman he could honourably marry.

Still single in their early thirties, both William and Dorothy must have been aware of a significant part of their natures unfulfilled, and between 1800 and 1802 there seems to be a growing resolve to find a solution. That the solution they adopted furthered William's happiness rather more than Dorothy's was entirely in keeping with the spirit of self-sacrifice which is evident in other areas of her life. William – who could not adequately support the daughter he already had – was now to have a new partner and start a new family, while Dorothy apparently gave up all thoughts of ever enjoying a physical relationship.

In June 1802, just after William had announced his engagement, Dorothy made clear her own determination to remain single. She wrote then to her brother Richard about her future, in a very revealing letter. In it Dorothy states unequivocally that 'I shall continue to live with my Brother William' – thereby relieving Richard of any anxiety he might have felt that she wished to live with him. However, now he was marrying, William would have 'nothing to spare' and she must ask her other brothers to help her with money. It seems that Christopher and John had already pledged support, and she was sure that Richard too would contribute. The letter displays the old confidence that 'while my brothers have a farthing in their pockets I shall not starve'.

Having explained her needs, Dorothy continued: 'Observe I am speaking now, of a provision or settlement for life, and it would be absurd at my age (30 years) to talk of any thing else.' It seems Dorothy had decided, at the age of thirty, that she would never marry.

In many readers of Jane Austen's novels, the notion of a woman of thirty being past marriageable age may raise a smile, but little surprise. However, although in Georgian fiction women almost invariably marry in their teens or very early twenties, real life was slightly different. Research shows that through the second half of the eighteenth century the average age at first marriage for women was twenty-five[1]. If twenty-five was an average, later marriages must have been quite common, and Dorothy's own experience would certainly not have led her to expect to be 'on the shelf' at thirty. William's intended, Mary Hutchinson, was thirty-two; Aunt Dorothy Cookson was thirty-four when she married; Aunt Threlkeld became a bride for the first time at the age of forty-five.

With these precedents in her close family, it seems unlikely that it was age alone that had led Dorothy to abandon thoughts of marriage. It is more likely that she was too deeply committed to William, too important to him, to consider another close relationship. And, though he had now made up his mind to marry, there is some evidence that William himself clung to his sister and, as the wedding approached, attempted to bind her to him more firmly than ever.

It is not possible to know that Dorothy chose – or helped to choose – Mary Hutchinson as a wife for William, but neither is it possible to imagine a wife who could have fitted with less pain and disruption into the established home at Dove Cottage. She and Dorothy were to live together for a little more than fifty years and in all their correspondence there is no real sign of disagreement.

The Wordsworths had known the Hutchinson sisters since childhood but, when Mary came to stay at Racedown back in 1797, she seems to have come simply as a friend and companion for Dorothy, because William left on a visit to Bristol just after she arrived. She was certainly someone with whom Dorothy felt at ease, as the companionable poem-copying and shirt-sewing of the Racedown visit proved.

Dorothy and William's long stay with the Hutchinsons after their return from Germany would have given William an opportunity to get to know Mary better, and she was the Wordsworths' first visitor at Grasmere, arriving at the end of February 1800 and staying for more than five weeks.

Then, in May 1800 – on the day the *Grasmere Journal* opens – William and John set off to visit Mary at Gallow Hill in Yorkshire where she and her brother were now living, leaving Dorothy weeping beside the lake. For the next three weeks – until William returned on 7th June – Dorothy waited anxiously for news, often troubled by 'my saddest thoughts' and 'the deepest melancholy'.

It is possible that Dorothy began her *Grasmere Journal* because she wished to record a way of life which she knew could not last. The *Alfoxton Journal* was begun soon after she discovered that her home there must be given up; perhaps again at Grasmere she wrote as a defence against change and insecurity: as a way of not 'quarrelling with herself' over the difficult decisions that were being forced upon her.

It was after the intense, claustrophobic time in Germany – and the writing of the first Lucy poems – that Mary Hutchinson had begun to be a more important part of William and Dorothy's lives. Perhaps it was on their return to England that they began to consider admitting a third person into their relationship. Mary was there at Grasmere almost from the start – as if Dorothy was making a trial, finding out what it was like to live with another woman in her ideal home.

What was there about Mary that made her a suitable wife for a great poet, or a suitable third party at Dove Cottage? Some people believed that Mary's intellect was 'not of an active order'. But Wordsworth assured his university-educated friend, Francis Wrangham, that she was someone 'with whom you would converse with great pleasure.' She was so calm and unassuming that Thomas Clarkson claimed she could only say 'God bless you!' But her taste, wit and liveliness were apparent to those who knew her well. Dorothy's journal refers to her reading aloud and to her sense of humour. Consistently loyal to those she loved, Mary was quite capable of making barbed comments about those outside the charmed circle of her affection. '[H]er countenance belies her if her mind is not made of lard ...' she remarked of one acquaintance[2] and the curate of Grasmere was dismissed as having 'a vulgar Presbyterian look with him.'[3]

There was little in her looks to arouse the envy of another woman. She was tall, thin and fair-skinned, had a squint ('an obliquity of vision'[4]) and was generally considered plain; or rather she would have been plain had it not been for 'a sunny benignity – a radiant gracefulness'[5] in her air. Like Mary Lloyd, Mary Hutchinson was 'not either rich or handsome' and she was no longer young when she married. Observers might have regarded both Marys as having been fortunate to make a match at all. But there was a world of difference in the relationships they established with their new sisters-in-law. There was never any danger of Dorothy being squeezed out of the family home as Jane had been, as the Dashwood sisters are, or – if Mary Wollstonecraft and Amanda Vickery are to be believed – rather a lot of Georgian spinster sisters were.

'Mary Hutchinson' reported Dorothy, 'is a most excellent woman – I have known her long, and I know her thoroughly; she has been a dear friend of mine, is deeply attached to William, and is disposed to feel kindly to all his family.'[6] It was usual to praise the prospective bride when an engagement was announced, but the deep attachment of the lady should not have been mentioned – at least not without making it clear that her fiancé felt a reciprocal passion. If a woman should not be in love before she was sure of the gentleman's feelings, it was certainly not polite for her friends to imply a one-sided attachment. But Dorothy says nothing of William's feelings – only her own and Mary's.

Though it is not possible to be certain, I believe that Dorothy was an active force in this courtship. In April 1801 she pressed Mary urgently for another visit: 'My dearest Mary I look forward with joy to seeing you again, you must come in Autumn or before.' In November 1801 Mary responded to the warm invitation and during this visit an attachment seems to have begun to develop.

William's behaviour – or maybe Dorothy's hints – raised a suspicion in Molly Fisher, the Wordsworths' part-time servant who, on 16th November was 'very witty with Mary all day' on the subject of love. Perhaps their unchaperoned walks had aroused her wit. During this visit Dorothy seems to have deliberately made time for Mary and William to be alone together. On 18th November, for example 'Wm and Mary walked to Rydale', while Dorothy stayed at home.

Sometimes she lingered behind as on 30th November: 'We walked round the Lake. Wm and Mary went first over the stepping stones. I remained after them and went into the prospect field above Benson's to sit ...' On 24th November the three started a walk together but – 'I was obliged to return for my fur tippet and Spenser it was so cold.' Perhaps this was a bit of devious plotting on Dorothy's part, like Emma Woodhouse's scheme to leave her friend Harriet alone with the eligible Mr Elton!

Dorothy noticed any signs of happy courtship with approval. On 25th November the couple had been walking alone and 'came in at nine o'clock ...chearful blooming and happy.' On 2nd December, after another tête-à-tête walk, 'They looked fresh and well when they came in.' When they all took a walk together on 12th December, Dorothy allowed them to linger behind. 'I came home first –' she wrote, 'they walked too slow for me.' As Christmas approached Mary took her place quietly in their cosy domesticity: 'We sate snugly round the fire. I read to them ...'

It was after this visit that Dorothy became gradually more outspoken in her journal about her affection for her brother. Perhaps it was the fear of losing him that made the expressions of love spill out; perhaps she felt safer, more able to let her love show, now that they had agreed on their future. It seems likely that, by the time Mary left them, an 'understanding' had been reached.

Her moments of closeness to William became more and more precious to Dorothy as the wedding approached, but, if William needed encouragement to pursue the affair, she was prepared to give it. When he made trips to meet again with Mary (on his own) during the Spring of 1802, Dorothy seems to have sent him off on his mission. On 14th February she remarked with pride, 'off he went in his blue Spenser and a pair of *new* pantaloons fresh from London.' She was clearly pleased that he was looking his best, but William was either reluctant or nervous. 'He turned back when he had got as far as Frank's to ask if he had got his letters safe, then for some apples – then fairly off.'

The letters which were now coming from Annette were a worry and at some point it was decided that Dorothy and William would travel to France to see her and Caroline to warn her of the impending marriage, and to arrange to pay some money for Caroline's maintenance. The trip was made in the summer of that year. The idea that William might marry Annette – now that the short-lived peace with France made such a thing possible – does not seem to have been seriously considered. It is easy to see why Dorothy would prefer a union with her old friend – a friend who had proved she could fit easily and comfortably into their existing life – to an unknown French woman.

Dorothy might have seen the wedding as necessary, but her emotions became more volatile as it drew near. On 13th April when William returned from another visit to Mary (during which the date of the wedding seems to have been decided) Dorothy greeted him rapturously but, the next day: 'I was ill out of spirits – disheartened.'

However, William had brought a present for her: a poem he had written on his journey. *Among All Lovely Things my Love had been* recalled a real act of love he had performed for Dorothy in Somerset, several years earlier – one of those delicate little 'attentions to [her] wishes', that had made her love him so much. Knowing that she had never seen a glow-worm, he brought one home and left it in the garden for her to find. (See Appendix 3 for the full text of this poem.)

The poem itself was a gift to Dorothy now: a reminder of their times together, and his care for her happiness, a reassurance that he still loved and needed her. The next day Dorothy repeated the poem to herself as she walked, as if it were a charm to ward off anxiety about the future. But a few days later she made a copy of this poem to send to the Hutchinson family, and in this copy of the poem the name of the beloved woman was changed. It was no longer Emma (the name William habitually gave to his sister in his poetry). It was Mary.[7]

It is possible that William himself was callous enough to make the alteration – but this would not be consistent with the other evidence of his consideration and tenderness towards Dorothy at this time. It seems more likely that, having taken pleasure in the shared memory, Dorothy felt able to pass on the gift to William's other love. A strange little act of self-sacrifice.

On 16th April Dorothy wrote to Mary and called her 'sister' for the first time. '[D]o not make loving us your business,' she wrote, 'but let your love of us make up the spirit of all the business you have.' William seems to have convinced her that she would be a part of this new alliance, and she implies in her letter that Mary will not only marry William, she will also marry Dorothy. The two cannot be separated.

It appears to be a strange marriage to us. However, Amanda Vickery's research and Mary Wollstonecraft's commentary show that it was far from unusual for an unmarried sister to have to be incorporated *somehow* into a Georgian marriage. The triangular household established by the Wordsworths was kinder, more generous-hearted, than many, but in it Dorothy was to find her feelings checked and restrained as never before. It would produce its own unique suffering.

Down in Bath, Jane Austen was also thinking about marriage in 1802, and in December of that year, prudence and restraint led her into great danger.

Depressed, forced to look upon herself not as an aspiring author, but as a woman launched unsuccessfully on the marriage market, it is perhaps a measure of her despair and low self-esteem that she overcame the girlish imperative of 'Do anything rather that marry without affection', which she had put into the mouth of the highly principled Miss Bennet of *Pride and Prejudice*. Somehow, that year, she made herself believe that gratitude was a sufficient foundation for marriage. She had become used to being 'thwarted', she had learned to stifle her fantasies as Rousseau recommended and finally her belief that individual needs and feelings should give way to the wider interests of family brought her to a humiliating decision.

In December of 1802, Jane and Cassandra went from Bath to stay with their old friends Catherine and Alethea Bigg at Manydown Park in Hampshire. This house – which, sadly, was demolished in 1965 – was an old-fashioned place with a park, an Elizabethan wing, panelled parlours, a sweeping staircase and at least one room grand enough to hold a ball, for Jane had danced there in a large party in 1796. It seems to have been a warm, comfortable place that was pleasant to be in; a later letter describes it as a house 'in which one is tolerably independent of the weather'.[8] It was a familiar place too: only five miles from Steventon, it would have aroused a sense of home and belonging.

On the evening of 2nd December, Jane discovered that this could indeed be her home if she chose. She could escape from Bath for good. Harris Bigg Wither, the brother of Catherine and Alethea, and heir to the entire Manydown estate, asked her to be his wife. She accepted.

There was to be an end to her Bath life: no more 'stupid' card parties, no more painful parading at balls, no more anxiety about her future. She was to live in the country; she was to be rich and independent; she was to be lady of the house and able to offer a permanent home to her beloved sister. The advantages of acceptance are clear. But for Jane, there were drawbacks; there must have been, because the following morning she sought out Harris and withdrew her consent.

'I conjecture,' pondered Jane's niece, Caroline, 'that the advantages he could offer, and her gratitude for his love, and her long friendship with his family, induced my Aunt to decide that she would marry him ...but that having accepted him she found she was miserable and that the place and fortune which would certainly be *his* could not alter the *man*.'

Caroline was sure that the refusal was given because Jane did not love Harris, and she honoured her aunt's integrity. 'All worldly advantages would have been to her – and she was of an age to know *this* quite well – My Aunts had very small fortunes and on their Father's death they and their Mother would be, they were aware, but poorly off – I believe most young women so circumstanced would have taken Mr W. and trusted to love after marriage.'[9]

Harris was six years younger than Jane, a large, rather uncouth figure of a man, afflicted with a stammer which tended to make him unsociable. Though Jane was undoubtedly able to look beyond personal disadvantages to the good sense with which the young man was also credited, it is unlikely that they had much in common – Harris was to become a shooting and hunting kind of country squire – and very doubtful that she could either have loved him at the time of the proposal, or been able to convince herself that her gratitude could blossom into conjugal affection.

It seems likely that Caroline was right: Jane found herself unable to go against her abhorrence of loveless marriage, even for the sake of providing financial security for herself, her sister and their mother. She had given up so much: her first love, her home and the freedom to write. Now she was being asked to surrender her integrity and she could not.

It is also likely that all her family wished her to marry Harris. Certainly the refusal was made 'much to the sorrow of Mrs James Austen who thought the match most desirable'.[10] In the end she seems to have recognised that this was a case in which feeling must come first. It was no time for prudence.

Caroline was probably also right in supposing that Jane's was not the decision which 'most young women so circumstanced' would have taken. However, if she had behaved more like other young women and done as her family wished her to do, she might have become acquainted with Dorothy Wordsworth. In 1808, Harris's sister, Catherine Bigg, married the Reverend Mr Herbert Hill who was an uncle of the poet, Robert Southey, a friend of

William and Dorothy and the brother-in-law of their close friend Samuel Taylor Coleridge.[11]

There was to be no such connection. Jane put the whole episode firmly behind her, returning to Bath as soon as she could, and her next actions were certainly not a common sequel to a broken engagement. Within days she had taken out her manuscripts and begun to work again. Her life had almost been thrown away, her future and her body almost traded in a mercenary transaction. The realisation of the danger she had fallen into seems to have shocked her out of the mental lethargy into which depression had thrown her and made her determined to act for herself.

Dorothy made the second honeymoon journey of her life with William and Mary as they travelled back to Grasmere. On one occasion, when they were all tired, 'William fell asleep, lying upon my breast and I upon Mary.' Many people have noted – and been amused by – the fact that Dorothy was sitting between the newly-weds in the carriage, but Dorothy seems to have seen nothing remarkable in it herself.

Her whole account of the wedding is written in the true style of sensibility. Focusing almost exclusively on her own experience of events, it very rarely enters into the feelings of the bride or groom. Dorothy might have argued this was the only honest way to write, the feelings of others being only imperfectly known to us, while to a more rational mind like Jane Austen's it might have suggested 'a sensibility too tremblingly alive ...to every affliction of my own.'

Dorothy's description of the wedding day (4th October 1802) would have been particularly open to that accusation. It is an extraordinary account and was, early on, deemed so odd that someone (maybe Dorothy herself, or maybe the first editor of her journals) crossed out part of it which has only been recovered by modern analysis. The part given in italics below is that which has been erased in the manuscript.

'At a little after 8 o'clock I saw them go down the avenue towards the Church. William had parted from me upstairs. *I gave him the wedding ring – with how deep a blessing! I took it from my forefinger where I had worn it the whole of the night before – he slipped it again onto my finger and blessed me fervently.* When they were absent my dear little Sara prepared the breakfast. I kept myself as quiet as I could, but when I saw the two men running up the walk, coming to tell us it was over, I could stand it no longer and threw myself on the bed where I lay in stillness, neither hearing or seeing any thing, till Sara came upstairs to me and said 'They are coming'. This forced me from the bed where I lay and I moved I knew not how straight forward, faster than my strength could carry me till I met my beloved William and fell upon his bosom. He and John Hutchinson led me to the house and there I stayed to welcome my dear Mary.'

It is easy to feel impatient with this account; it is so very egocentric with its 'my dear little Sara' and 'my dear Mary'. Dorothy seems to be spoiling the bride's big day by demanding attention with her histrionics and it seems very odd that she should welcome Mary into her own home. The proper, considerate thing to do would be to contain her own feelings and let the bride walk home quietly on her husband's arm.

However, Dorothy was too taken up with her own feelings to care about propriety. The journal again records a complex of emotions, without clearly defining any of them, but the ritual of the wedding ring identifies William as a conscious participant in Dorothy's drama. Again he is taking the initiative as he had done during those haunted sleepless nights in Dove Cottage, and it is easy to see why someone felt this deeply symbolic act ought to be suppressed.

William had entrusted to Dorothy the safekeeping of the ring which was, by tradition, his responsibility. She returned it to him, and gave her blessing to the marriage. But he did not simply take it from her. Just as he had hesitated and returned to her on that February morning when he set off in his new pantaloons to visit Mary, he now paused before leaving for the church and, before he placed that ring on the finger of his bride, put it back on his sister's finger. It was a private ceremony which – to Dorothy at least – had as much significance as the service that was about to take place.

It might be said that William married her before he married

Mary, and that Dorothy was making a promise in that upstairs room very like the one Mary was about to make in church – 'keeping only unto him as long as we both shall live.' Yet William seems to be drawing that promise from her, binding her to him, reminding her that she is still necessary to him. Dorothy sat easily between the newly-weds in the carriage but, if she was at the centre of this marriage, it was William who had placed her there.

Meanwhile, in Bath, Jane was once more a writer. Taking out the manuscript of *Susan* (the proto-*Northanger Abbey*), she began to copy and prepare it for publication.

She had learned something important about herself: she could not accept anything but a love-match; pragmatic though she was, her integrity would not be compromised. Her feelings could not always be suppressed for the advantage of her family. A marriage of convenience was impossible and a marriage of real affection did not seem likely. It may have been this realisation which made her determined to take some steps to provide for herself, for, as Caroline observed, she knew that, on her father's death, she would be 'but poorly off'.

Like Dorothy, with her conviction that it would be 'absurd' for her to think of marriage, Jane seems now to have been considering a future without a husband. They had both turned their backs on that 'settlement in the world we should aim at ...the only way we females have of making ourselves of use to Society'. They had both determined to seek another meaning, another purpose, for their lives.

PART FOUR

TWENTY-THREE

Writing and Publication

Being in the middle of someone else's marriage offered Dorothy reassurance and a kind of security, but it was not a comfortable place to be.

Some weeks before the wedding William and Dorothy had exchanged bedrooms. Dorothy gave up the dark room next to the kitchen, in which she had slept since their arrival at the cottage, and moved into the room above that had been William's bedroom. The downstairs, stone-floored room would have offered a little more privacy for the newly married couple than the room above, from which, we know from the testimony of the Journal, Dorothy could hear William's every move when he was sleepless. But, with sounds carrying too easily throughout the house, the situation cannot have been easy for any of them. Tact, consideration and the kind of forbearance which only comes with real affection would have been necessary.

Dorothy attempted to continue her journal in the months after the wedding, and kept it up until January of the following year. There are some beautiful descriptions in the same style as the earlier entries, but sometimes she went for days without writing and often had to catch up. She had always had periods of catch-up in her journal, but there is a sense of struggle in these later entries that was never present in the days before the wedding.

During Mary's long visit in the winter of 1801 Dorothy had maintained the stream of consciousness and observations that characterise the *Grasmere Journal*, but now Mary had come as a bride, the current of Dove Cottage life no longer flowed freely onto the page. Resolution was necessary in order to carry on as if nothing had happened. In almost the last entry Dorothy wrote with a kind of determination she had not needed before: 'I ...*will* for the future write regularly and, if I can legibly ...'[1]

Like Jane Austen exiled in Bath, Dorothy seems to have lost her creative equilibrium and writing had become a struggle. However, she remained loyal to the companions she loved; she made no complaint and soon there was a new addition to the family to demand her devotion. William's first son, John (usually known as Johnny to distinguish him from his uncle) was born in June 1803. Dorothy's love for this baby was absorbing and unreasoning. 'He has a noble countenance,' she wrote, in one of many long descriptions, to her friend Catherine Clarkson, 'if I were not half afraid of making you laugh at me I should say he looks as if he was not the child of ordinary parents.'

'Indeed,' she concluded, trying to be rational, 'I think if it is possible to tire you with a long story of him you will be tired now.' However, in the next sentence her overwhelming love breaks out again. 'But oh! that you could see him!'[2]

Like many a new mother, she was convinced that everyone shared her fascination: 'It is very affecting', she enthused, '...to see how much John is beloved in the neighbourhood.'[3] And: '...there is something like greatness in his countenance, a noble manliness which makes the first view of him catch hold of every Body and keeps them looking at him.'[4]

There was no danger of this wondrous child being left to cry alone in a distant room as poor little Basil had. A year later, when he sprained his ankle, his devoted aunt explained: '[He] is made a pet, and a little hanger-on about his Mother and me, so that whenever we leave him he cries, which bad habit will make him yet engross much of our time ...'[5]

However, in spite of Johnny's arrival, there were still times when Dorothy could be alone with her brother. On 15th August 1803, less than a year after the wedding, the Concern re-established itself. Dorothy managed to tear herself from baby-worship and accompany William and Coleridge on a tour of Scotland. It was their first journey together since the unsuccessful German trip.

William seems to have felt no reluctance in leaving home at this time. At this point in his marriage he was prepared to be away from his wife for six weeks, to travel in the old style with his sister and his friend. As it turned out, for most of the journey brother and sister were alone – companions as they had been in Germany – for once more the Concern fractured, and, after two weeks, Coleridge left the others. The reason for the division seems to have been Coleridge's unhappiness – the old jealousy he had felt in Germany for his friends' closeness. 'I soon found I was a burden on them' he wrote.[6]

William and Dorothy's devotion could still make a third party feel jealous. This continuation of their relationship – Dorothy's unaltered importance to her brother – seems to fulfil the pledge he had made in the upstairs room before his wedding, as he slipped the ring onto Dorothy's finger. It was a sincere promise; but it was not going to be easy to keep.

In 1803 Jane Austen was once more able to write, and she had enough energy and concentration to complete the new manuscript of *Susan* in three months. However, once it was finished she did not approach a publisher herself. She stepped aside, as a modest young lady should, and allowed a man – her brother Henry – to act for her. It was Henry's agent, William Seymour, who sold the book to Benjamin Crosby and Son, for the sum of £10 (about the equivalent of a housemaid's yearly wage, if board, lodging and clothing are taken into account). After her father's one half-hearted approach to Cadell, Jane relied heavily on Henry to negotiate her way through the world of publishing. And, though this indirect approach may have been the *correct* way for a young lady to conduct business, it was not a wise decision.

Henry Austen was considered to be, 'the handsomest of his family and in the opinion of his own father also the most talented.' But – 'There were others who formed a different estimate and considered his abilities greater in show than in reality'.[7] Jane may have inclined towards her father's opinion, for Henry was her favourite brother; but perhaps on this occasion his knowledge of the business in hand was 'greater in show than reality'. His choice of publisher was almost certainly a mistake. Crosby's business relied heavily on just the kind of Gothic Romances which are ridiculed mercilessly in *Northanger Abbey*. An approach to a rival firm would have been wiser. Crosby may well have felt that £10 was a small price to pay to prevent anyone else from publishing the book.

Henry and Seymour also made the elementary mistake of having no date for publication written into their agreement; only a vague undertaking was made to print the book quite soon. This was disastrous. Crosby did not publish *Susan* himself and when, six years later, Jane attempted to push him into action, he was able to threaten her with legal proceedings if she should renege on their deal and publish the book elsewhere.

Like Dorothy, who had seen her hope of an independent settlement evaporate as William invested the Calvert legacy unwisely, Jane trusted this beloved brother with what was most valuable to her. They would not have been the only women of the time who had to bite their tongues as their business affairs were mishandled by their men-folk.

For now, all that mattered was that the book was sold. The exciting promise of publication was enough to make work possible even amid the distractions of Bath. Writing could earn money. It was important.

Marriage was still on Jane's mind as she began the incomplete novel which is now known as *The Watsons*. She employed again the engine which had driven the plots of her first two books – the poverty of a family of sisters and their need to marry. But there was a marked change in tone for this story. Perhaps affected by the difficult choice which she had recently had to make herself, she presented a much bleaker, more pressing version of the conflict between integrity and prudence than she had in either *Sense and Sensibility* or *Pride and Prejudice*. The Watson sisters are noticeably poorer than the Dashwoods or the Bennets: they labour over laundry and cookery themselves – unable to afford the luxury of having 'nothing to do in the kitchen'. They are also much more explicit in their discussions about marriage.

The two opposing approaches to the subject are stated clearly in the first few pages. Miss Watson starkly declares: 'we must marry ...my father cannot provide for us', but Emma Watson – who seems destined to be the novel's heroine – speaks with the voice of integrity. '[T]o pursue a man merely for the sake of situation – is a sort of thing that shocks me', she says. 'I cannot understand it. Poverty is a great evil, but to a woman of education and feeling it ought not, it cannot be the greatest.'[8]

This may well have been the argument which ran through Jane's head as she agonised overnight at Manydown after her acceptance of Harris.

The world of *The Watsons* is a gloomy one, coloured perhaps by lingering depression. Mr Watson is in his room, dying slowly as the novel begins, and Emma (who is returning to the family after having been brought up by a wealthy aunt) finds her sisters Penelope and Margaret ruthlessly pursuing husbands. The eldest sister Elizabeth is a little more sympathetic, but she does not hide their desperate situation from Emma. When their father dies they will have hardly any income and no home either for, interestingly, Mr Watson is a clergyman and the house in which they live is tied to his job.

Towards the end of the fragment, Emma's brother, Robert, arrives from his legal practice in Croydon, to represent that third alternative to marriage or destitution: a brother's protection. In this case, it is a particularly unpalatable alternative. Robert bemoans the fact that Emma's aunt has married, making no provision for her niece who is now 'returned upon [her family's] hands without a sixpence.' He does not spare Emma's feelings at all as he reflects: 'It will be a sad break-up when [my father] dies. Pity, you can none of you get married! You must come to Croydon as well as the rest and see what you can do there.'[9]

The prospect of living and husband-hunting in Croydon is made even less appealing by Robert's wife, another selfish sister-in-law – rather in the style of Fanny Dashwood – who is 'very pleased with herself for having had ...six thousand pounds, and for being now in possession of a very smart house'.[10]

This was not a book with which Jane was likely to write herself out of depression. It is not surprising that it was abandoned after about 17,000 words. She had chosen a subject which must continually remind her of her own precarious situation. The only way in which her own circumstances were materially better than Emma Watson's was that her father was in good health. Or, at least, he appeared to be.

Dorothy continued to write even though the *Grasmere Journal* had faltered to a close. But, after William's marriage, she turned to a different kind of work: an account of her Scottish Tour. In fact she began to write – as Jane had from her earliest years – for publication. Like Jane she aimed, primarily, to share her work with her family and friends. She claimed, at first, to have no other readership in mind, but in the end she did consider wider publication.

The household's money troubles continued, despite the settlement of the Lowther debt, so it is possible that Dorothy was, in the early years of William's marriage, exploring the possibility of making money with her pen.

In the previous year, after the wedding had become a certainty, she had begun to study German again. 'I read a little in Lessing and the Grammar', she wrote on 8th February 1802, and over the next few months there are intermittent references to work which may have been a revival of her hopes of earning an income from translation: on 9th February 'We did a little of Lessing', on 15th February 'set on to reading German', on 10th March 'I read a little German', etc.

Now that the marriage had taken place, she chose to put her energy into travel writing, a kind of work that was very popular – and saleable – at the time. 'I am not writing a journal,' she explained, 'for we took no notes, but recollections of our Tour in the form of a journal'.[11]

As usual she denigrated her own work, which had the rather cumbersome title of *Recollections of a Tour Made in Scotland: A.D. 1803*. 'I think', she wrote, 'journals of Tours except as far as one is interested in the travellers are very uninteresting things.' However, she intended that this journal, which was not a journal, should be copied and passed about among her friends and relations.

Many of her first audience believed it to be her finest work, but modern readers who have enjoyed the spontaneity of the *Grasmere Journal* often find the more self-conscious, conventional tone of these Scottish recollections disappointing. It is true that some scenes are observed in a business-like way that calls to mind Fanny Price noticing 'the bearings of the roads, the difference of the soil, the state of the harvest, the cottages, the cattle, the children ...'

'[W]e descended towards a broad vale,' wrote Dorothy of the approach to the village of Crawfordjohn, 'children playing, linen bleaching. The vale was open pastures and corn-fields unfenced, the land poor ...the people of the village, who were making hay, all stared at us and our carriage.'[12]

Such descriptions lack the charm of the journals, but Dorothy was still able to bring to her work an accurate eye and make the scenes memorable with details such as the bleaching linen and staring haymakers.

It is worth remembering that, even if all the giblet pies, bowel-troubles and other personal details were lifted out of the *Grasmere Journals*, they would still never have been publishable in Dorothy's lifetime. Today we value their disconnectedness, finding them fresh and quirky, but no publisher of the early nineteenth century would have been enthusiastic about a style of writing so far removed from any genre he knew.

Accounts of journeys, on the other hand, were a recognised and popular form of literature, and Dorothy seems to have determined to try her hand at one. It was three years now since her hopes of earning money by translation had been dashed in Germany, but maybe she was, once more, looking for a way to earn some independence. Perhaps the emotional upheaval of William's marriage was making her look outward for a wider audience and a wider purpose to her life. For Dorothy was a remarkably good travel writer and it seems unlikely that she can have been completely unaware of her own talent. De Quincey believed the *Recollections* to be 'a monument to her power of catching and expressing all the hidden beauties of natural scenery with a felicity of diction, a truth, and strength, that far transcend Gilpin, or professional writers on those subjects.'[13]

Her first qualification for the work was an almost superhuman memory. Reading some of her descriptions it is hard to believe that she was recalling things she had seen, maybe, two years earlier. 'The stone both of the roof and walls is sculptured with leaves and flowers ...' she wrote of the chapel at Roslin, 'and the whole of their groundwork is stained by time with softest colours.'[14]

Her style acknowledges picturesque conventions, connecting her readers with other works in this genre. The wish she had shown in the *Alfoxton Journal* to sometimes improve upon the view that she saw – to compose pictures – is particularly evident in this new project. She described one valley as 'cold and naked, wanting hedgerows and comfortable houses.'[15] and she found that there was in the mountain Ben Lomond 'something ...which disappointed me, – a want of massiveness and simplicity, perhaps from the top being broken into three distinct stages.' [16]

Unlike the *Grasmere Journal*, the *Recollections* look at the scene unflinchingly, not attempting to exclude the un-picturesque. Scotland, Dorothy told her readers repeatedly and unreservedly, was *dirty*. 'Smoke and blackness are the wild growth of a Highland hut',[17] she assured them, and, finding one inn to be, 'exceedingly clean', she exclaimed, 'I could hardly believe we were still in Scotland.'[18]

She allowed herself to express opinions rather more than in the journals and she disapproved of some of the 'improvements' which many owners of large estates were making at this time. Like Fanny Price of *Mansfield Park* Dorothy grieved over the threatened felling of an avenue of trees. 'We were told', she wrote of one great parkland, 'that some improver of pleasure-grounds had advised Lord B. to cut down the trees, and lay the whole open to the lawn ... His own better taste, or that of some other person, I suppose, had saved them from the axe.' [19]

Dorothy's ability to observe closely and respond emotionally to the things that she saw was very effective in travelogue, a form of writing which aims not only to describe but also to evoke a sense of place and foreignness.

Near Loch Lomond she spent the night in a house unlike any most of her readers would ever have encountered. 'It consisted', she explained, 'of three apartments, – the cow-house at one end, the kitchen or house in the middle, and the spence at the other end. The rooms were divided, not up to the rigging, but only to the beginning of the roof, so that there was a free passage for light and smoke from one end of the house to the other.'

This is an efficient enough description, but Dorothy aimed not only to make her reader understand the layout of this building in which light and smoke – and, presumably, the smells from the cow-house – circulated freely, she also evoked the memorable experience of sleeping in it.

'I went to bed some time before the family' she wrote, and though she does not say so, it would seem her bed was in the 'spence'. 'The door was shut between us, and they had a bright fire, which I could not see; but the light it sent up among the varnished rafters and beams...produced the most beautiful effect that can be conceived. It was like what I should suppose an under-ground cave or temple to be...'[20]

Dorothy's pen brought to life not only places, but people too. There was, for example, the minister whom they found working in a hayfield in 'a shabby black coat', who advised William how to mend the broken wheel of their carriage, but did not 'offer to lend any assistance himself ... as if it were more natural for him to dictate, and because he thought it more fit that William should do it himself. He spoke much about the propriety of every man's lending all the assistance in his power to travellers, and with some ostentation or self-praise.'

Sometimes she displayed an almost psychological insight into character. At Jedburgh she described their hostess as, 'a good woman, who, though above seventy years old, moved about as briskly as if she was only seventeen ... She had a quick eye, and keen strong features, and a joyousness in her motions ... I found afterwards,' she continued, 'that she had been subject to fits of dejection and ill-health: we then conjectured that her overflowing gaiety and strength might in part be attributed to the same cause as her former dejection.'[21] Dorothy seems to have recognised what we would now call a bi-polar condition, based, presumably, simply on her own observations since there would have been no such diagnosis at the time.

Perhaps her well-observed characters – together with her vivid evocation of place – might have found their way into novels, had she lived, as Jane Austen did, among people who valued, discussed and experimented with that genre. Like Jane, Dorothy was a critical reader of other people's fiction and certainly understood the importance of characterisation. In 1815 she would write of Scott's novel *Waverley,* 'you care not a farthing for the hero...the Scotch Characters are so outrageously masked by peculiarities that there is no pleasure in contemplating them – indeed in the delineation of character he greatly fails throughout'.[22]

It is unlikely that Dorothy considered writing novels herself. At the very heart of Dove Cottage's little community was poetry. Life there was dedicated to the creation of poems, its philosophy summed up by Samuel Daniel, a seventeenth century poet read at its fireside: Daniel claimed that 'weakness speaks in prose, but pow'r in verse.'

Poetry was considered the highest form of literature. In his *Essay on Morals,* for example, William Wordsworth declared that a mere prose treatise on ethics could never be effective because it would lack the 'power to melt into our affections, to incorporate itself with the blood and juices of our minds'. Only poetry, he believed, could do that. Interestingly, he was claiming for poetry the same moral purpose which Samuel Johnson had demanded of novels.

Wordsworth did not simply defend the traditional value placed on poetry. The philosophy which he and Coleridge had developed was expanding poetry's scope. In the *Advertisement* that accompanied the 1798 edition of *Lyrical Ballads*, William warned that some readers would find the poems to be unlike any others they had read, but he advised that, 'while they are perusing this book, they should ask themselves if it contains a natural delineation of human passions, human characters, and human incidents...'

This is very like Jane Austen's defence of prose fiction: she claimed that novels were works 'in which the most thorough knowledge of human nature, the happiest delineation of its varieties…are conveyed to the world.'

William, as a poet, was laying claim to the territory of the novel. Deferring to him as she did on such matters, it is hardly surprising that Dorothy should have felt her prose to be of little value, and she doubted her ability to write poetry.

'Do not think that I was ever bold enough to hope to compose verses for the pleasure of grown persons', she wrote in one letter. 'Descriptions, Sentiments, or little stories for children was all I could be ambitious of doing and I did try one story, but failed so sadly that I was completely discouraged.'

If only she had persisted with the story, rather than giving up after a single attempt! However, she had little confidence in her own talents – which is slightly odd. She was a self-effacing woman in many ways but, if she had no reliance on her own judgement, she most certainly did trust William's. She had an unshakeable faith in his pronouncements.[23] If *he* had told her that her writing was good – told her repeatedly and encouraged her to write more – is it possible that she would have disbelieved his verdict?

Dorothy continued in her letter, 'no one was ever more inapt at molding words into regular metre. I have often tried,' she wrote, 'when I have been walking alone (muttering to myself as is my Brother's custom) to express my feelings in verse… but prose and rhyme and blank verse were jumbled together and nothing ever came of it.'

It is surprising that she should have failed to shape her words into 'regular metre' because, in several places in her journals, Dorothy's prose seems to fall perfectly naturally into metre. Take this line from the *Alfoxton Journal* for example: 'The crooked arm of the old oak tree points upwards to the moon.' It is an almost perfect two lines of ballad metre.

Passages like this in Dorothy's journals raise two possibilities. Firstly, she may have had an accurate ear for the rhythms in words – been, in fact, a natural poet – but she became too anxious, and struggled too hard to achieve poetry when she tried to imitate her brother's techniques of composition. Secondly, it may be that a larger part of the journals than we suppose is made up of phrases spoken by William and only written down by Dorothy.

However, Dorothy's letter reveals a more fundamental reason why there was no body of literature published under her name during her lifetime: something beyond a lack of facility with metre. '[L]ooking into my mind', she wrote, 'I find nothing there, even if I had the gift of language and numbers, that I could have the vanity to suppose could be of any use beyond our own fireside ...'[24]

It is possible that Dorothy was confessing to a fear that would certainly have undermined her confidence in her own creativity: the fear that she lacked that 'shaping spirit of imagination,' of which Coleridge wrote and which was valued highly by both him and Wordsworth. This rather sad comment raises the question of what Dorothy Wordsworth would have written about in a novel or poetry.

By contrast, Jane Austen seems to have had no difficulty in believing that her mind contained material which was worth writing about. Even her earliest works are full of ideas that the young girl was burning to express. Her opinions of books and people, as well as her adolescent desire to talk on 'indelicate' subjects, developed rapidly into a more mature consideration of the disadvantages under which women like herself (and Dorothy) were placed by their families. There is a strong element of discontent in Jane's work, though it is smoothed over and rendered relatively inoffensive by the lightness of her style. By the time she was in her teens Jane had discovered that a voice and manner which were 'winningly mild' might be used to argue that what was too often perceived as white by her contemporaries, was, in fact, black.

There was no such burning need to express her own opinions driving Dorothy's genius, no impetus beyond one which she probably shared with Jane – the wish to make money. There was no urge to make her voice heard, because she believed that all the important truths were being expressed by her brother.

Also, paradoxically, the suffocating good-manners of the Austens may have driven Jane to take up her pen and create her own worlds in which she could express her ideas. While Dorothy, free to hazard her observations among those with whom she lived, had less motive to write, and would be more tempted to abandon the story that was not turning out quite right, or the verse that would not scan, to put the pen aside and busy herself instead with some task of cooking or sewing for the people she loved, something which seemed more obviously useful.

Just finding time to write her *Recollections of a Tour Made in Scotland* was not easy for Dorothy. She began work soon after she and William returned from their trip, but she was distracted by Coleridge, who had been full of complaints since he parted from them in Scotland; complaints about his health and about his marriage which was becoming increasingly troubled. Dorothy worried about him. 'We had,' she reported anxiously in October, 'a long letter from poor Coleridge written in the languor of the first moments of ease after suffering the various tortures of tooth-ache, teeth drawing, rheumatism, sickness, pains in the Bowels, Diarrhoea and worst of all, a shortness of breath.' (Coleridge could rival Mrs Austen herself in the description of colourful ailments.) Dorothy added admiringly that 'His spirits and strength are yet wonderful.'[25]

Believing Coleridge's tales of 'Ill tempered speeches sent after me when I went out of the House, ill-tempered Speeches on my returns' to be a complete and unbiased account of his domestic troubles, Dorothy was anxious that he and Sarah should agree to live apart. 'Is not it a hopeless case?' she exclaimed and put the blame entirely on Sarah, describing her as 'So insensible and so irritable she never can come to good ...'[26] Dorothy ridiculed Sarah's opposition to a separation, saying that she 'urges continually that one argument ... that this person, and that person, and everybody will talk.'[27]

The talk of this person or that person – or 'the discussion of the neighbourhood'[28] as Jane Austen called it – was an important part of a woman's life and determined her social credit. Dorothy's breezy opinion that if the couple separated, 'there would be a buzz and all would be over,'[29] was naive. Sarah understood the influence of gossip all too well – after all it was the Bristol gossips who had hurried on this marriage which was now proving so painful.

Back in the days when Sarah boldly strode about the countryside with her young man, the question of divorce had been discussed: should the ending of unhappy unions be allowed in the Pantisocratic Utopia they were planning? But that was in the wilds of America among like-minded people; it was not in parochial Keswick where the laws and customs of society were rigid and long established. Like Jane Austen, Sarah Coleridge believed in finding happiness as best she could within the boundaries of the community in which she lived. This was an approach to life which Dorothy regarded with suspicion.

Sarah was not opposed to a separation; she simply wished it to be discreet, for it to appear that work only took her husband away from the marital home. But Dorothy (supported by William and Mary) would not countenance this compromise. She felt that, if the separation was not clear-cut, poor Coleridge would be left with 'something hanging over him.'

Even more surprising is Dorothy's approval and encouragement of Coleridge's notion that he was now in love with Sara Hutchinson, Mary's younger sister. He believed he had found in her his ideal supportive woman and expected his wife to accept the situation without question. 'Permit me, my dear Sara[h]! ...to say' he wrote to his wife, 'that in sex, acquirements, and in the quantity and quality of natural endowments whether of Feeling or of Intellect, you are the inferior. Therefore ...I have a *right* to expect & demand, that you should to a certain degree love, & act kindly to, those whom I deem worthy of my love.' [30]

Though, in part, Coleridge was attacking his wife on the same grounds Dorothy had cited – a lack of feeling – it is interesting that the first instance of inferiority which he mentions is 'sex'. A woman's opinions were intrinsically of less value than his. It is another hint of how he may have regarded Dorothy's role in the Concern.

In December 1803, Coleridge arrived for a month's stay at Dove Cottage; and then even Dorothy's sympathy for him was tested.

She probably began now to suspect that many of his problems were the result of opium addiction. That winter the household was repeatedly woken in the night by his screaming from bad dreams. For carers already suffering disturbed nights with a young baby this would have been extremely trying; and, besides this, he was 'continually wanting coffee, broth or something.'[31]

Towards the end of January Coleridge set off for London on the first stage of a journey which would eventually take him to Malta, having decided that only that nineteenth century panacea-for-all-ills, 'a warmer climate', could cure him. But even when he was gone, Dorothy had little leisure in which to resume her writing because, 'Old Molly ... is still our sole servant though at present not so well fitted for her place as she was'.[32]

Coleridge's needs must still take precedence over her own composition. By March: 'We have been engaged, Mary and I, in making a complete copy of William's Poems for poor Coleridge to be his companions in Italy ... There are about eight thousand lines ...' It must have been a monumental task. 'Judge then how fully we have been employed,' she continued, 'what with nursing, and the ordinary business of the house ...'[33]

Dorothy struggled on, writing her *Recollections* when she could, but, in August 1804, the birth of William's second child, (christened Dorothy after her aunt, but usually called Dora), increased her workload. And then, in February 1805, there was a family tragedy. William and Dorothy's brother John drowned when his ship sank off Portland Bill. 'I had no power of breaking the force of the shock to Dorothy or to Mary', wrote William, 'They are both very ill. Dorothy especially, on whom this loss of her beloved Brother will long take deep hold.'[34] The death of John did indeed take a deep hold on his sister. The final pages of the *Recollections* were written by a grieving Dorothy, seeking solace in her work.

When the manuscript was finished, it was – in its way – published; bound copies were sent to family and to friends.

The whole history of the *Recollections of a Tour Made in Scotland* is a mass of contradictions. It was a journal – and yet it was not a journal. It was, intrinsically, a 'very uninteresting thing' – and yet it was worth a remarkable amount of labour, labour which was carried on in spite of emotional interruptions and endless other demands upon its author's time. It was only of value to friends who were 'interested in the travellers' – and yet, some fifteen years later, the poet Samuel Rogers persuaded Dorothy that the work should be published. The scheme never came to anything, but Dorothy must have agreed to it, for she made a revised copy ready for printing. Maybe wider publication had always been her aim.

She had worked hard on the manuscript. She had deliberately taken up a form of writing that was – unlike her journals – suitable for publication. She seems to have found in her writing a sense of purpose even amid the clamour of William's new family, even in the depths of her grief. The money that the project might have brought would have been extremely useful. Yet she chose not to attempt publication either at the time of finishing the manuscript, or later when she had gone so far as to prepare it for print.

There is a hint of what might have been going on. Towards the end of her Scottish *Recollections*, Dorothy's prose steps deferentially aside to make way for superior poetry; she omits to describe Neidpath Castle, near Peebles, because 'William has done it better than I could do in a sonnet which he wrote the same day'.

The same humility is apparent in the story of another of Dorothy's schemes to publish her work. In 1821 she would write another travelogue about a tour of the continent and 'Crabb Robinson, seeing the journal's market potential, urged her to shorten and publish it.'[35] The reason this scheme failed seems to be that the prose was, so to speak, superseded by poetry. 'William is writing poems to intersperse'[36] with the journal, Mary reported, and a few months later, his work had 'grown to such importance ...' according to Dorothy, 'that I have long ceased to consider it in connection with my own narrative.'[37]

On this occasion the poems were published, but the journal was not. Perhaps a similar thing happened with the Scottish *Recollections*. Perhaps in that case too Dorothy decided that her own work was but an inferior shadow of her brother's: 'Weakness speaks in prose, but pow'r in verse.'

TWENTY-FOUR

My Father Cannot Provide for Us

There are no surviving letters to give us any idea of how long Jane continued to work on *The Watsons*. It is not until January 1805 that we hear her voice again and, for the modern reader attempting to follow her story, the long silence is broken thus: 'My dearest Frank, I have melancholy news to relate...'

Jane was announcing to her brother Francis, the sudden death of their father. He had been carried off after an illness that lasted only a few days. The transition in Cassandra's censorship from complete blackout to allowing her sister's voice to be heard again is shockingly abrupt. Is it connected with the event related in the first surviving letter?

In destroying so many of her sister's letters, Cassandra was almost certainly trying to obliterate criticism which would have hurt other family members, but the letters which she allowed to survive still show *some* evidence of Jane's asperity. In fact, as they stand, Jane's letters criticise, or evince impatience with, nearly everyone, from her brothers and mother to casual acquaintances. She was deeply unhappy in Bath and this seems to have inclined her to hit out at those around her. Describing Jane's letters, Claire Tomalin has said 'mostly you are faced with the hard shell; and sometimes a claw is put out, and a sharp nip is given to whatever offends.'[1]

However, the remarkable thing about the few letters allowed to survive between the time that the move to Bath was mooted and

271

January 1805, is that the claw is *never* extended in Mr Austen's direction. Yet he was the person responsible for Jane's misery. His decisions had taken her from the home she loved and placed her in a position where she was unable to write.

Criticism of a father was particularly shocking to Georgian sensibilities. The duty owed to the head of a household had religious and political overtones, with the family often portrayed as a miniature commonwealth having a divinely appointed 'king' at its head. The political philosophy of Edmund Burke (which was respected by moderate Tories such as the Austens) equated the challenging of the head of the household with revolution in the state – maintaining that when one was allowed, then the other must surely follow. If Jane had written anything at all disrespectful of her father, this would have been more than a little disruption of the smooth sunny surface that the Austen family liked to preserve; it would have been a positive dereliction of Christian duty. It could not be allowed to survive.

I think it is possible that, as her misery deepened during the Bath years, Jane's acerbic wit occasionally turned against her father. Her unhappiness, boredom and frustration at not being able to continue with the career she had chosen may have overcome her love and sense of duty so far as to necessitate occasionally this outlet in letters which were for her sister's eyes alone. The loyal Cassandra would not have risked any hint of such a transgression surviving. Perhaps that is why she deemed it safest to destroy all letters for a long period.

Inadequate and neglectful fathers are common in Jane's fiction, and all three complete novels written after the Bath period feature heroines with deeply unsatisfactory fathers. Mr Woodhouse of *Emma*, Mr Price of *Mansfield Park* and Sir Walter Elliot of *Persuasion*, all fail their daughters in different ways. They are negligent in their duty to their families, but their daughters *never* neglect their duty of respect and forbearance. Emma Woodhouse's patience with her father's 'gentle selfishness' cannot help but win our admiration, even though we might wish she would extend it to other, more deserving, acquaintances. Fanny Price always manages a respectful 'sir' for her rum-sodden father, and, when

Sir Walter Elliot insults the friend of his long-suffering daughter Anne, 'she did long to say a little in defence ...but her sense of personal respect to her father prevented her.'[2]

This was clearly the kind of behaviour which Jane believed to be right; she did not expect her protagonists to win her readers' sympathy without it. But this may have been another point at which she fell short of her own ideals of correct behaviour.

Dorothy Wordsworth, who was outspoken enough to frequently lament the effects that *her* father's decisions had had in separating her from her family, also seems to have maintained a correct degree of respect and never actually blamed her father for the misery he inflicted on her. But all her surviving letters come from the period after his death. It is easier to be respectful and to remember only the good about someone who is dead.

Jane's letters written after 21st January 1805 would not have needed to be so severely censored by Cassandra and some of them have been allowed to survive. The natural and dutiful expressions of grief could be preserved. Jane wrote of her father's 'worth & constant preparation for another World'[3], of his 'tenderness as a father'[4] and the 'sweet benevolent smile which always distinguished him.'[5] Irritated and hurt by his decisions though she may have been, her grief was undoubtedly sincere.

His will would have contained no surprises. Jane almost certainly knew what to expect from it, for it had been drawn up five years before she was born and had not been altered since. Mr Austen left everything of which he died possessed to his wife. It was little enough. His capital, probably amounting to around £4,000,[6] was more or less what he and his wife had brought to the marriage between them, so it was in keeping with the marriage settlement that this amount should now pass to the survivor.

However, there had been no money saved during the marriage to provide even the smallest dowry for his daughters. The Austens had always 'lived up to their income' (to employ another of those useful phrases with which Jane Austen summarises the complex financial affairs of her characters). Their money had all been spent on day to day living and on educating and setting the boys up in the world.[7]

Most of the money which had supported the household in Bath came from Mr Austen's tithes and a small pension which he drew. These ended with his death and there were insufficient funds to support the women he left behind in anything like the comfort they were used to. If he had thought at all about what would happen to his daughters after his death, Mr Austen must have simply assumed that they would – in Mary Wollstonecraft's terms – live on 'the bounty of brothers' for the rest of their lives. And that is what they did.

The family immediately stepped forward to help Mrs Austen and her daughters. Francis offered to pay his mother £100 a year but she would accept only £50. James and Henry also both offered £50 and Henry wrote that, 'If Edward does the least he ought, he will certainly insist on her receiving a £100 from him. So ...' He concluded 'with her own assured property, & Cassandra's, both producing about £210 per ann., She will be in the receipt of a clear £450 pounds per Ann ... I really think that My Mother & Sisters will be to the full as rich as ever.'[8]

This is a revealing summary of the situation. It shows a slight doubt whether Edward will do the least that he ought, and no expectation of him doing more than the minimum. It shows that Cassandra's income – the tiny amount of interest which she received from a £1,000 legacy left by her fiancé, Tom Fowle – was counted by her brother as belonging to her mother. Above all, it makes Jane's situation painfully clear. She was to have nothing of her own, no regular income or allowance. Not one of the Austen brothers seems to have considered making a separate allowance to his sisters. Mrs Austen was to hold the purse strings for the rest of her life.

The loss of her father did not bring any more autonomy to Jane's life and her mother's choices do not seem to have been the ones she would have made. Like Anne Elliot of *Persuasion*, Jane's preference would almost certainly have been for 'another house in the country ... A small house in their own neighbour-hood'.[9] But, like Anne's, her wishes were disregarded. The three women continued to live in Bath, in rented lodgings, and to make long stays with family and friends. It was a disrupted way of life, particularly ill-suited to the demands of writing and, after abandoning *The Watsons*, Jane seems to have once more found herself unable to work.

At the time of Mr Austen's death none of the brothers offered to set the women up in a permanent home. Edward, with his large estates at Chawton and Godmersham, owned several houses suitable to accommodate them, but he does not seem – at this time – to have offered any of them.

The Austen women lost status by Mr Austen's death.

'I believe that my mother [will] remain in this house till Lady Day,' Henry wrote to Francis soon after their bereavement, 'and then probably reduce her establishment to one female Domestic and take furnished lodgings.'[10] In his next letter, he assured his brother (and, probably, himself) that 'a smaller establishment will be as agreeable to them, as it cannot but be feasible.'[11]

Just why he supposed they would find a smaller establishment agreeable, Henry did not say. Despite his cheeriness, it is likely that Jane was distressed by a change which would have had a significant impact on a family of genteel women. The washing, cleaning, cooking, sewing, fire-lighting, coal-carrying, fire-tending, water-carrying, food-preserving, ironing, marketing etc for even the smallest middle-class household could not be accomplished by one person. Living in a one servant family meant that the ladies of the house got their hands dirty – probably very dirty indeed.

One female domestic and furnished lodgings is exactly the situation of Miss Bates in *Emma*. She too is the unmarried daughter of a clergyman living with her widowed mother, and it is clear that Jane does not consider *her* life to be 'agreeable'. She is unequivocally described as 'poor' and 'has sunk from the comforts she was born to'.[12]

Jane cared about money and status. She had always lived among people who cared about them. The attention to financial detail in her books is extreme, and although her novels are undoubtedly love stories, she never gives her sanction to imprudent love matches any more than she does to mercenary, ambitious marriages. In the closing chapters of *Sense and Sensibility*, Elinor Dashwood, sure at last of the affection of her Edward, is still not 'quite enough in love to think that three hundred and fifty pounds a-year would supply them with the comforts of life.'[13] Earlier in the story, Elinor has maintained that with an income less than £1,000 a year 'every kind of external comfort must be wanting'.[14]

Jane Austen would certainly have considered the life Dorothy Wordsworth was leading at this time as wanting every kind of external comfort.

Though she now had a sister-in-law to help with the work in Dove Cottage, any amelioration in Dorothy's daily round of chores did not last long. As at Forncett, the arrival of 'little relations' was soon curtailing their aunt's freedom. 'I really have been overwrought with positive labour' she wrote in May 1804 when Mary was pregnant with her second child. 'Our old Servant...has left us, and we have been engaged in a Whitsuntide cleaning, colouring and painting etc etc ... [F]or the last six weeks ...we have had no servant but a little Girl, therefore, my Sister not being very strong, I was glad to take upon myself the charge of putting things in order.'[15]

However, Dorothy had two advantages over Jane. Firstly, not every family distributed its resources as unevenly as the Austens. By the time Jane was forced to be financially dependent upon a mother with whom she never quite saw eye to eye, Dorothy had at last acquired a little capital of her own.

In 1802 Sir James Lowther, the 'Bad Earl', who had withheld the Wordsworth children's inheritance, died, and, on inheriting, his heir, Sir William Lowther, placed in the *Cumberland Pacquet* an advertisement inviting 'all Persons with any demands on the late Earl' to claim what was due to them. News of this exciting development reached William and Dorothy on 18th June when their friend Captain Luff arrived to tell them of 'Lord Lowther's intention to pay all debts etc'. Predictably the emotional shock gave Dorothy 'a woeful headache' and disturbed her sleep. But she was soon able to enjoy the turn of fortune: two days later she and William 'talked sweetly together about the disposal of our riches.'

Of course, payment took a little while (and several rather

imperious letters were sent to brother Richard who was dealing with the affair). But, by July 1803, Dorothy could write that the total to be paid was 'eight thousand five hundred pounds' and 'The whole of the money is to be paid in a year.' [16]

This sum was to be divided equally between the Wordsworth siblings – 'having no respect to sex or Eldership', to employ the words of Jane Austen's grandfather's will. Dorothy's share was £1,700. It was a little bit of security and it meant a great deal to Dorothy. She referred to it – when discussing its investment with Richard – as 'my independence'[17]. Having money of her own must have been psychologically reassuring. Unlike Jane, she could feel herself the equal of those among whom she lived, even though her 'riches' were not sufficient to substantially change her lifestyle.

However, the second advantage Dorothy had over Jane was her very comforting contempt for the ways of the rich. She gloried in her simple way of life and regarded it as virtuous. On 2nd October 1800 she and some friends could enjoy 'a pleasant conversation about the manners of the rich – avarice, inordinate desires ...'[18] This sort of conversation could help to sustain a woman when she was cooking giblet pies and spring cleaning. Jane had neither such a philosophy, nor the kind of friends with whom she could discuss it. She lived among people who were all richer than herself – some of them very much richer.

Within her own little household she was also the poorest. Even her sister had a tiny income, while Jane remained dependent on her mother and arbitrary gifts from her richer relatives. The only sums she could call her own were that £10 from Crosby and an inheritance of £50 left her by a friend in 1806.[19]

Unable to despise the wealthy, conscious of her own respect for wealth, and suspecting, perhaps, that it was not a very amiable bias, Jane frequently laughed at herself in her letters by playfully conflating good character and riches. '[T]he rich are always respectable'[20], she wrote while enjoying the comforts of Edward's large house; and of Francis she joked, 'he wants nothing but a good Prize [i.e. money paid by the navy for the capture of an enemy vessel] to be a perfect Character.'[21]

The difference lay partly in the two women's upbringing:

Dorothy with her enterprising Aunt Threlkeld and Jane in her genteel rectory where ladies were expected to enter only theoretically into the work going on in the kitchen. But Dorothy's attitude would also have been influenced by that break for freedom she had made in her early twenties, the decision to throw in her lot with a not quite respectable brother, a decision to ignore the opinions of others which restricted her life. Flying in the face of family expectations had meant she *must* accept poverty, and the sense of purpose which she found in supporting William's vocation added a.kind of glamour, or even nobility, to the privations of a cold damp house and an unceasing round of housework.

Jane's itinerant life would not have promoted a sense of purpose. The years after Mr Austen's death were particularly restless; a relatively small amount of time was spent in temporary lodgings in Bath and there was a lot of travelling about with long visits to Godmersham and Steventon, a holiday in Worthing and a brief stay with the Bridges family at Goodnestone.

In Bath invitations (to tea parties in particular) flowed in from friends and relatives. 'What request we are in,' Jane remarked, but she suspected that some of their popularity might arise from pity. 'I think we are just the kind of people & party to be treated about among our relations; – we cannot be supposed to be very rich.'[22]

Being 'treated about' by her richest relations could, of course, be very pleasant. The ice and French wine of Godmersham were always acceptable, and Jane seems to have entered into family life with some spirit. Her niece Fanny recalled in her diary how, during one visit her aunts and Mrs Austen 'played at school with us. Aunt Cassandra was Mrs Teachum the Governess Aunt Jane, Miss Popham the teacher ...Grandmama Betty Jones the Pie woman ... They dressed in character and we had a most delightful day.'[23]

Though Jane may have enjoyed the game, she would also have known that it was her duty to make herself agreeable. A poor relation – as Fanny Price is at Mansfield Park – she would be expected to be obliging and join in. During her stay in the great house, she was constantly reminded by small things of her poverty in comparison to her relations. The visiting hairdresser charged the lady of the house 5s for his services but from the spinster sisters-in-law he asked only 2/6. 'He certainly respects either our Youth or our poverty,' Jane remarked to Cassandra. And then there was the embarrassment of being expected to leave tips for the servants; 'I cannot afford more than ten shillings for Sackree,' she lamented[24].

There was no escaping the knowledge that she was a poor relation, and the overall impression of an account of Jane's life at this time is one of pointless wandering about. The evidence of Jane's earlier letters suggests that she often became weary of visiting and it is difficult not to conclude that an intelligent woman would have found her life at this time a little humiliating and, ultimately, boring.

However, she seems to have refused one chance of gaining a more settled way of life. During her stay at Goodnestone her sister-in-law's younger brother, Edward, was very attentive. 'It is impossible to do justice to the hospitality of his attentions towards me;' she wrote, 'he made a point of ordering toasted cheese for supper entirely on my account.'[25] She was probably as little impressed by this homely mark of affection as Emma Woodhouse is by Robert Martin's riding about the country to get walnuts for her friend, Harriet, but it seems likely that Edward Bridges was enough in love to propose to her about this time.[26] Like Harris Bigg Wither's it was a very respectable offer, but she does not seem to have hesitated this time in refusing.

Her resolution had been taken against a marriage of convenience and that resolution held, even though she was now as 'poorly off' as she had feared to be. It was not marriage which could give her life direction and meaning.

TWENTY-FIVE

Another Exile, Another Homecoming

In October 1806, one of Jane Austen's brothers did provide her, her mother and her sister with a home, but it seems to have been done more for his own convenience than theirs. Francis, having had some success in his naval career, felt himself able to marry and, as he wrote in his memoir, he 'fixed his abode at Southampton making one family with his mother and sisters, a plan equally suited to his love of domestic society and the extent of his income which was somewhat restricted.'[1]

Southampton, conveniently close to the naval base of Portsmouth, was at this time a fashionable resort town, so it would have been considered a suitable place for a family of ladies to settle. It had also been decided that Martha Lloyd, who had recently lost her mother, should join their household. This kind of arrangement seems to have been quite common at the time – spinsters frequently becoming 'co-tenant with other women, related and unrelated.'[2] Sharing a home in this way was certainly economical, but Martha was probably the only friend with whom Jane would have been happy to live.

It was in July that Mrs Austen and her daughters left Bath and Jane, according to her own recollections, experienced 'happy feelings of Escape'. There was then another period of wandering among friends and relations – to Clifton, Adlestrop, Stoneleigh Abbey in Warwickshire, Hamstall Ridware in Staffordshire and Steventon, before they finally settled in lodgings in Southampton.

The amount of travelling done by the Austen women is worthy of note. Travelling was expensive, particularly for women who could not cover long distances on horseback and must always be suitably escorted by male relations or servants. In *Pride and Prejudice* Elizabeth observes that, even though Mr Collins and his wife have a 'comfortable income', it will not 'allow of frequent journeys'[3]. And Dorothy Wordsworth said her greatest ambition as far as wealth went was, 'the liberty of travelling a little and seeing our Friends without caring for the Cost.'[4]

Other members of the family must have helped with the cost and the arrangement of the ladies' incessant travelling about, but at least some of the expense fell on the women themselves. Jane's account of her own expenditure made up at the end of 1807 includes a sum of £1.2s.3d for 'a journey'. But Jane herself would have had little choice about making most of these journeys. Mrs Austen was in control; she chose how their limited budget was spent. It is extremely unlikely that Jane welcomed having to constantly move around. It made writing all but impossible and she would probably have rather the money was spent on a quiet, settled life in a home as comfortable as they could afford to make it.

About this time, she expressed a longing very like Dorothy's for that ideal home in which she could speak her mind freely without censure or ridicule. Writing from Godmersham, she spoke of the 'pleasures of friendship, of unreserved Conversation, of similarity of Taste & Opinion'[5] which she would know with Cassandra and Martha when she returned, and which would make up for the loss of all the luxuries she enjoyed in Edward's grand house.

However, soon after the family 'settled' in Southampton, Cassandra was on the move again – to Godmersham – so when brother James and his wife arrived to spend New Year with them, Jane was responsible for their entertainment. She does not seem to have enjoyed the occasion. 'When you receive this,' she wrote to Cassandra in February, 'our guests will be all gone or going; and I shall be left to the comfortable disposal of my time, to ease of mind from the torments of rice puddings and apple dumplings, and probably to regret that I did not take more pains to please them all.'

The 'smaller establishment' of which Henry had spoken so cheerfully, was impacting on Jane's life; her familiarity with rice puddings and apple dumplings was greater than she had been brought up to consider becoming. And her affection for James's wife was not growing. 'Mrs J. Austen has asked me to return with her to Steventon;' she reported. 'I need not give my answer.' Mary would have been an uncongenial companion for her literate sister-in-law. Reporting on their reading aloud of *The Female Quixote*, by Charlotte Lennox, Jane remarked, 'I believe [Mrs J Austen] has little pleasure from that or any other book.' But a greater cause of friction must have been Mary's tactless lamenting over her and James's poverty – when they were much better off than her sisters-in-law. 'Mrs J.A. does not talk much of poverty now,' remarked Jane ironically, 'though she has no hope of my brother's being able to buy another horse *next* summer.'

Jane seems to have been painfully conscious of being poorer than those around her at this time. This same letter ends with an account of a visit to some new acquaintance in Southampton: 'They live in a handsome style and are rich, and she seemed to like to be rich, and we gave her to understand that we were far from being so; she will soon feel therefore that we are not worth her acquaintance.'[6]

The house in Southampton into which the family moved in March 1807 was pleasantly situated with an attractive garden running up to the old town walls; but the Austen women were no more inclined to stay still after they took possession of it.

Frank's wife, Mary, (usually referred to as Mrs F.A. to distinguish her from the other Mary, James's wife, Mrs J. A.) gave birth to her first child in April, and, soon after, Frank set off on a voyage to the Cape of Good Hope. Then the new mother was off to Ramsgate, and in August Mrs Austen and her daughters went to Edward's big house at Chawton for a month. Most of the first half of 1808 was spent by Jane and Cassandra moving between Steventon, Manydown and Kintbury. In May Jane went with Henry to London and in mid-June her mother joined her there and they travelled to Godmersham, not returning to Southampton until 7th July. Of the sixteen months they had (nominally) been occupying the house in Castle Square, Southampton, Jane had actually lived there for, perhaps, eight.

Cassandra went to Godmersham when Jane left. Edward's wife, Elizabeth, was about to have her eleventh baby and she seems to have particularly valued Cassandra's help on these occasions – unless Cassandra always put herself forward to save Jane from having to bear her company.

Jane's letters to her sister at this time reveal that their residence in Southampton was not expected to last. The arrangement of sharing a home with Frank and his wife does not seem to have been working out very well now that his family was growing (Mrs F.A. was pregnant again); and it may be that Mrs Austen felt unable to accept his £50 a year now that he had a wife and children to support.[7]

As Dorothy was finding up in Westmorland, a growing family of children can make a home feel very crowded indeed.

Another move was under discussion, but Jane still had no control over her own destiny and was only able to observe as someone else took the decisions which controlled her life: 'In general however,' she wrote in October 1808, '[Mrs Austen] thinks more of Alton, & really expects to move there.'[8]

Alton in Hampshire, about fifteen miles from Steventon, was close to Edward's Estate at Chawton and was also a town in which Henry had business interests. The rents would probably be lower there than in fashionable Southampton. But before a suitable house could be found in Alton, tragedy struck. At Godmersham, on 10th October, Elizabeth, though safely delivered of her baby and seeming to make a good recovery, was suddenly taken ill and died within half an hour.

The whole family was shocked. 'We have felt, we do feel for you all,' Jane wrote to Cassandra who was still at Godmersham, '...may the Almighty sustain you all'.[9] Edward, she wrote, 'has a religious Mind to bear him up, & a Disposition that will gradually lead him to comfort.'

Maybe one of the comforts that occurred to Edward was that of helping his poor relations, for, oddly, his grief seems to have reminded him that he owned property not far from Alton:

property which his mother and sisters might be able to make use of. By the end of the year he had offered – and Mrs Austen had accepted – the cottage at Chawton which was to be Jane's final home.

It is impossible to know why this offer was made now, nor why it had not been made years earlier. But it is also impossible not to wonder whether the recent bereavement might be the solution to both puzzles. Jane suspected that (like John Dashwood) her brother James was too much influenced by his wife: 'his Opinions on many points [are] too much copied from his Wife's'[10], she wrote after his visit to Southampton. Perhaps Edward had also been influenced by *his* wife – with whom, according to Anna's recollections, Jane was not a great favourite. Anna wrote that, '[the Godmersham children] were not really fond of her. I believe that their mother was not …'[11] It is not unlikely that Elizabeth's feelings about Jane would have had some influence on her daughters, and this is how Elizabeth's eldest daughter, Fanny, would remember her Aunt Jane in 1869:

'from various circumstances [she was] not so *refined* as she ought to have been from her *talent* … They were not rich & the people around with whom they chiefly mixed, were not at all high bred, or in short anything more than *mediocre* & *they* of course tho' superior in *mental powers* & *cultivation* were on the same level as far as *refinement* goes … Aunt Jane was too clever not to put aside all possible signs of "common-ness" … and teach herself to be more refined, at least in intercourse with people in general. Both the Aunts (Cassandra & Jane) were brought up in the most complete ignorance of the World & its ways … & had it not been for Papa's marriage which brought them into Kent, and the kindness of Mrs Knight, who used often to have one or the other of the sisters staying with her, they would have been, tho' no less clever & agreeable in themselves, very much below par as to good Society & its ways.'[12]

It is a scathing passage, particularly shocking because Jane and Fanny seem (from the evidence of Jane's letters) to have had an affectionate relationship. Jane's anxiety and shame at being looked down on as a poor relation was not a product of her own imagination; other people really did see her that way. This description makes that painfully clear.

Interestingly, there is some evidence to support Fanny's claim that her aunt tried to 'put aside all possible signs of common-ness'. In 1804 Jane wrote disapprovingly to Cassandra of a Mrs Armstrong who 'sat darning a pair of Stockings the whole of my visit – . But', she cautioned, 'I do not mention this at home, lest a warning should act as an example'.[13] Maybe a touch of old-fashioned vulgarity – such as might allow the sight of stockings in a drawing room – was one of the ways in which Mrs Austen offended her daughter.

However, since Fanny's recollection refers to her aunts' upbring-ing and a state of affairs before 'Papa's marriage' – a time which Fanny cannot possibly have known about first-hand – it might well preserve prejudices expressed by her mother. If any part of this was Elizabeth's opinion, then it is easy to see why she might not have wished to have her sisters-in-law settled near her, in a mediocre and unrefined sort of establishment.

It is unpleasant to think of Jane benefitting from, or rejoicing in, anything to do with her brother's terrible loss, and unpleasant to think of Elizabeth as another sister-in-law on her guard against the depredations of impecunious relations. Perhaps Edward's offering the house just at this moment was simply an odd coincidence.

The offer must have pleased Jane very much. She certainly seems to have seen her new home as a place in which she could settle down and write. As the preparations for the move got underway, she began to consider her career and to take action. Hiding behind the assumed name of Mrs Ashton Denis (where did that come from?) she wrote to Crosby and Co about the 'novel in 2 vol entitled Susan [which] was sold to you by a Gentleman of the name of Seymour ... of which I avow myself the authoress'. She reminded them that early publication had been promised and offered to provide a copy if they had lost the original manuscript. 'Should no notice be taken of this Address,' she concluded firmly, 'I shall feel myself at liberty to secure the publication of my work, by applying elsewhere.'[14]

Crosby replied promptly and rudely to say he was not obliged to publish, he would 'take proceedings' against her if she attempted to publish elsewhere, and she could have the manuscript back if she paid the £10 he had originally given for it.

She did not have any money and was unable to do any more about it. The support which her family offered to her writing did not stretch to advancing £10.

The year 1808 was also a time of great change in Westmorland. By the time Jane Austen ended her empty itinerant years and came to rest at last in a real home, Dorothy Wordsworth had lost her beloved home at Dove Cottage.

The small house had become desperately crowded. Sara Hutchinson was living with them for much of the time now and, by 1808, there were three small children (John, Dora and Thomas). Dorothy explained that: '[W]e are never thoroughly [comfortable] till after seven o'clock in the evening, when the children are put to bed, and the business of the house is over; for the kitchen not being ceiled, we can almost hear every word that is spoken when we are in the sitting-room, and every foot that stirs.'[15]

In the summer of 1808 – with Mary expecting a fourth child – the family moved into the large, newly built Allan Bank about a mile from their old home. Standing in its own grounds with elegant, high-ceilinged rooms and glorious views to the lake and woods, their new home must have been a wonderful change (at least until winter set in and it was discovered that the chimneys smoked uncontrollably). But Dorothy's relief was mixed with regret at losing the home she had so long dreamed of possessing, the home which had been – for a short time – so completely *her own*, and the place in which she had written freely. '[B]ut the dear cottage!' she exclaimed as the move was completed. 'I will not talk of it. Today the loveliness of the outside …made me quite sad – and all within how desolate!'[16]

However, this move coincided with a dramatic change in Dorothy's outlook on life.

The truth was that, although the family desperately needed more space, the Wordsworths could not afford the rent or the running of such a home as Allan Bank. Even with the Lowther case settled and some of his work published, Wordsworth could not support his rapidly expanding household.

In the Spring of 1808 he went to London, meaning to raise funds by selling his long poem *The White Doe of Rylstone*. But once he got there, he began to have doubts about its reception; perhaps he would not publish after all. Dorothy's tone was shrill and desperate when she heard this news:

> 'We are exceedingly concerned, to hear that you, William! Have given up all thoughts of publishing your Poem. As to the Outcry against you, I would defy it – what matter, if you get your 100 guineas into your pocket ... without money what *can* we do? New house! New furniture! Such a large family! Two servants and little Sally! We *cannot* go on so another half year; and as Sally will not be fit for another place, we must take her back again into the old one,[17] and dismiss one of the Servants, and work the flesh *off our poor bones*. Do, dearest William! do pluck up your Courage – overcome your disgust to publishing – It is but a *little trouble,* and all will be over, and we shall be wealthy, and at our ease for one year, at least.'[18]

Dorothy's life was no longer a rural idyll of virtuous poverty, in which it was possible to have 'a pleasant conversation' about the inordinate desires of the rich. This frantic anxiety over money and servants and furniture was certainly not the future she had anticipated when she strode off into the Lake District with her brother, gaily washing her feet in streams and defying Aunt Crackenthorpe.

It was domestic cares – the need to look after William's growing family – that had so abruptly narrowed Dorothy's existence and changed her outlook. How different her life might have been if those old Pantisocratic ideas of shared housework had found their way into the revolution fomented in the Quantock Hills! She herself now found it all but impossible to write. Once her account of the Scottish tour was completed it was several years before she attempted anything else like it.

Nor was there much time now for Dorothy to involve herself in

William's work: to listen to him, to discuss ideas and memories, to write as he dictated. And she was no longer writing the journal which had provided sketches from which he could compose poems. So much of that sense of purpose which had once ennobled her poverty and hard labour would have been lost.

The demands of housework and child-care are difficult to reconcile with a creative life. 'I wanted a few days quiet, & exemption from the Thought & contrivances which any sort of company gives,' Jane Austen would write from Chawton in 1816 on one occasion when the house had been full of visitors. 'Composition seems to me Impossible,' she went on to say, 'with a head full of Joints of Mutton & doses of rhubarb.'

Her own experience made Jane wonder about another female author of the day. '[H]ow good Mrs West could have written such Books & collected so many hard words with all her family cares,' she wrote, 'is still more a matter of astonishment.'[19]

Jane West was an extremely conservative writer who produced a large amount of didactic improving novels, poems and advice literature; but who very 'properly' shrank from the idea of being considered an authoress, asserting that, 'my needle always claims the pre-eminence of my pen.'

Though the products of Mrs West's needle may have been extremely useful to her family, those of her pen have long since ceased to charm anyone. Jane Austen's reference to collecting hard words, and the slightly patronising 'good Mrs West', suggest that she was not a great admirer of her fellow author and may have found her attitudes a little smug. For by 1816 Jane herself understood the cost of sustained creative work.

The move to Chawton established her in a home where writing was once more possible – at least when the house was not full of visitors. In 1809, just as Dorothy was exiled from the place where her creativity had flowered, Jane Austen was escaping from her rootless life. As Dorothy's pen fell idle (and her needle, undoubtedly, became more active) Jane was resuming the work which could give meaning to her life.

Chawton Cottage – though it too had once been an inn – was much larger and more comfortable than Dove Cottage. It had two storeys, plus attics and cellars, good-sized gardens, a dining room, a parlour and bedrooms to spare for visitors; it was comfortable, but not grand, and not unlike the old home at Steventon. Standing at the junction of two main roads at the very heart of the village, it would have been as noisy as Dorothy's old home, for 'Before the railroad opened there were 3 coaches passed through for travellers 2 from Winchester, one from Portsmouth. There was a … wagon for luggage or passengers that could not pay coach fare'[20] and all these vehicles would have rattled past the Austen ladies' dining room window.

In this house, according to family recollections, Jane took on the usual role of a genteel, unmarried woman, living 'a very quiet life according to our ideas but they were readers and besides the housekeeping our aunts occupied themselves in working [sewing] for the poor and teaching here and there some boy or girl to read and write.'[21] Amazingly nothing is said in this recollection of the labour which must have occupied a great deal of Jane's waking hours. The picture presented is simply one of a genteel spinster (with her needle as busy as good Mrs West's) leading just the kind of life that was expected of her.

At Chawton the ladies took on the role of patrons to the lower classes. In 1816 Edward Austen Knight paid £10, to 'Miss Austen [probably Cassandra] donation to Chawton poor'. But even as they distributed largesse on behalf of their wealthy brother to those worse off than themselves, Jane, her mother and her sister were the recipients of charity. Now that he had taken his poor relations under his wing, Edward was generous, making several fairly substantial payments to workmen for maintenance or improvements to Chawton Cottage, such as £45.19s.0d. 'Paid [to] John Dyer a Bill for work and materials at Mrs Austen's house', and also supplying firewood from his estate.[22] His generosity meant that theirs was no longer a household with just one female domestic. At Chawton the Austen ladies were able to employ a cook, a maid and a manservant.

Jane's new life was firmly embedded in a traditional landscape that was, at its heart, feudal: Chawton Great House with its satellite cottages and farms. She took her place in this hierarchy, taking an interest in the welfare of the poor, but also beholden herself to the generosity of a wealthy patron: her brother. However, her protective armour of cool detachment – so different from Dorothy's impulsive warmth – now, in her mature years, provided a kind of liberation. The move to Chawton Cottage was not only a homecoming and an escape to the peaceful countryside, it was, more importantly, an escape into creativity, into that infinite space within her head: a place in which she had some element of control.

Once that space was achieved, she was autonomous in a way in which Dorothy could never be. Tied by a network of emotional threads – to William, to his children, to Mary, to Coleridge – her labour given unstintingly to those she loved – Dorothy had no such freedom.

Jane's first undertaking at Chawton was the revision of her two early novels, *Sense and Sensibility* and *Pride and Prejudice* – with their controversial themes.

She liked her new home well enough, was certainly not ungrateful to the brothers she loved, and yet the plots of these two first published books lay bare the injustice of decisions taken by families like her own. They concern girls who are left to the arbitrary benevolence of their brother, girls whose father fails to lay aside money for their support. A poor relation, living on the bounty of her brothers, she might now be, but she had long ago learnt that, obliquely expressed and wrapped up in humour, almost any ideas might be safely expressed.

This was where the decisions of their youth had brought these two women. Jane had succeeded in finding a way of expressing herself and had at last been granted the space and time in which to be creative. She was never the centre of home life at Chawton Cottage – Cassandra adopted that role. When her sister was at home Jane's only part in the housekeeping was making breakfast – after that, she was free to write.

Dorothy, on the other hand, had achieved a home in which she was not only dearly loved and admired but absolutely necessary to those around her. A home in which she gave freely of herself and her energies to those she loved, but a home in which there was little scope for her own creativity.

There seems to have been an uneasiness too about Dorothy as she approached her forties. Since 1793 her greatest wish had been to live a life in which she could honestly and openly express herself. To achieve this ideal she had escaped from Forncett to live with William, enduring poverty and the censure of her family. And yet, when Thomas De Quincey first met her in 1807 – just before the move to Allan Bank – his first impression of her was certainly not that of a woman who appeared to have fully achieved that dream. His description is startling – and rather disturbing.

'[S]ome subtle fire of impassioned intellect apparently burned within her,' he recalled, 'which, being alternately pushed forward into a conspicuous expression by the irrepressible instincts of her temperament, and then immediately checked, in obedience to the decorum of her sex and age, and maidenly condition ...gave to her whole demeanour and to her conversation, an air of embarrassment and even of self-conflict, that was sometimes distressing to witness.'[23]

De Quincey's memories are not always to be trusted, but he was an observant man and there is reason to give this account careful consideration, for Dorothy's own writing suggests that it may have been, in its way, perceptive. There is something familiar about it for anyone who has read the *Grasmere Journal*. In the journal the pattern he describes of impulses imperfectly expressed can be found again and again.

Dorothy may have felt free to express her *opinions* among the people with whom she lived; but *feelings* were a different matter. For example, in her first journal entry there is an acknowledgment of very deep emotion: 'My heart was so full that I could hardly speak ...' But (to use De Quincey's words) it is 'immediately checked', first relieved by a solitary fit of weeping and then given only an incomplete examination. 'The lake looked to me I knew not why dull and melancholy, and the weltering on the shores seemed a heavy sound.' Dorothy 'knew not why' the lake looked dull and melancholy; the sound of the waves on its shore merely *seemed* a heavy sound. She went no further in seeking to understand herself.

Left alone again with her thoughts nearly two years later, she would still write fretfully, 'I *will* be busy,' seeking an escape from introspection, leaving her feelings about her separation from William unresolved.

In her journal Dorothy perfected a form of expression which exposed the power of her emotions but which, almost compulsively, concealed their cause. Perhaps this was an expression of that inner conflict which De Quincey detected. His account suggests that this style was not confined to the words on her page, but characterised her outward appearance and behaviour.

The picture he paints of the mature Dorothy is of an emotionally vital woman full of 'organic sensibility', a busy woman, yet one who was delightfully attentive to the conversation of her friends. He believed that she had 'humanized [her brother] by the gentler charities', but he detected in her an intensity which gave her pain. Others also remarked on it. Noting her uneasiness about Coleridge, Mary wrote 'I wish she would not suffer such things to disturb her so much.'[24] and her friend Catherine Clarkson expressed regret when Dorothy's grief for her brother John's death lingered on, cutting her off from the usual pleasures of life.

By contrast there is an air of ease and contentment in Jane's letters once the move to Chawton was decided upon: a comfortable acceptance of her life. She wrote of a ball in Southampton in December 1808: 'It was the same room in which we danced 15 years ago! – I thought it all over – & inspite of the shame of being so much older, felt with thankfulness that I was quite as happy now as then.'[25]

Once they were settled at Chawton Cottage, the Austen women were no longer in continual motion. Apart from a visit to Manydown, which they made together, Jane and Cassandra stayed at home for the first year. The benefit to Jane of this calm, stationary life is obvious: the rapidity with which she settled to work as soon as it was established, suggests how deeply unpleasant the rootless, wandering years must have been for her.

By 1809, when Dorothy was thirty-seven and Jane thirty-three, we see two unmarried women, apparently living as nineteenth century society expected them to live. But the choices they had made as they grew and matured had, in fact, taken them on widely diverging paths, and ensured that the way in which they would be remembered was very different.

PART FIVE

TWENTY-SIX

Beyond 1809

Jane Austen was, of course, destined to become a published and successful writer. Sometime in 1810 or 1811, she offered *Sense and Sensibility* (again through Henry's mediation) to the publisher Thomas Egerton, who agreed to publish it 'on commission'.

'It was,' according to her nephew's *Memoir*, 'with extreme difficulty that her friends ...could prevail on her to publish her first work'.[1] But this again may be an attempt to portray Jane as a shy, retiring lady uninterested in earning money. It certainly does not match up with the brisk determination of 'Mrs Ashton Denis', taking matters into her own hands and attempting to recover what was her own: attempting to find a way forward for her own career.

Jane's 'friends' (and Austen-Leigh would have included family members in the term) certainly do not seem to have been so urgent or so determined in their attempts to persuade her to publish as to offer much financial backing. 'On commission' meant that the author must cover any losses incurred in publication and Jane, 'actually made a reserve from her very moderate income to meet the expected loss.' With an income of less than £50 a year such a saving could only have been made with extreme difficulty, and it was perhaps only possible because she had at last come to rest in a proper home; while she was flying about the country, it is unlikely such economy would have been within her power.

The move to Chawton had changed Jane's life completely. The

last remnants of depression lifted; she was able to work purposefully and with concentration. Soon she had begun to revise *Pride and Prejudice* and, in 1813, it followed *Sense and Sensibility* out into the world.

Jane was able now to identify herself as a writer – except when she was interrupted by visits from her brothers and her nieces and nephews, bringing with them those demands for Joints of mutton and doses of rhubarb. She enjoyed their visits – and expressed relief when they left. But for Dorothy the very centre of her life was William and his growing family. Her love for the children who soon filled those larger rooms at Allan Bank and the family's subsequent homes at Grasmere Old Rectory and Rydal Mount, was powerful and often obsessive.

For an unmarried woman in Georgian times the children of her siblings were the closest she would come to motherhood. It was an important relationship, as Jane Austen acknowledged in *Emma*; these children provided, 'objects of interest, objects for the affections ...' Emma believes that her nephews and nieces will 'supply every sort of sensation that declining life can need. There will be enough for every hope and every fear'.[2]

Jane herself had begun upon the business of being an aunt much earlier in her life than Dorothy. Her eldest niece, Edward's daughter Fanny, had been born back in January 1793 when Jane was just seventeen years old. The accounts of her nephews and nieces suggest (what is not very apparent in her letters) that she showed them a great deal of affection. '[S]he seemed to love you,' recalled Caroline, 'and you loved her naturally in return.'[3] And, 'Aunt Jane was the general favourite with children;' according to her niece Anna, 'her ways with them being so playful ...'[4]

But, for all this, she would prove, over the years, to be a much more cool, reserved sort of aunt than Dorothy. Aunt Jane was always keenly aware of how quickly children changed; she knew that even the cutest babies could develop in unappealing ways. 'I shall think with tenderness & delight on his beautiful & smiling Countenance & interesting Manners,' she wrote of Edward's third child, George, 'till a few years have turned him into an ungovernable, ungracious fellow.'[5]

In this relationship, as in others, Jane would maintain a distance, think rationally and not allow her feelings to overwhelm her.

Dorothy had no such detachment from William's children; she was completely absorbed in her feelings for little Johnny when he was a baby. 'I feel deeply every hour of life the riches of the Blessing which God has given us,' she wrote to Catherine Clarkson, 'and you who have nursed your own Babe by a cottage fireside know what peace and pleasure, wakefulness and hope there is in attending upon a healthy infant, and that ones thoughts are never tired when so employed.'[6]

She was, in fact, identifying herself with Mrs Clarkson – seeing herself as a mother. Her closeness to William, her daily contact with the baby and her complete faith in the 'rightness' of her own emotional response, perhaps made this inevitable.

This was a line which Jane would never cross; aunts might be important but they were *not* mothers. She was in agreement with Emma Woodhouse who finishes her reflections on the pleasures of nieces and nephews with this reservation: 'though my attachment to none can equal that of a parent, it suits my ideas of comfort better than what is warmer and blinder.' Jane's assessments of her brothers' children were neither warm nor blind. 'Charles is not quite so lovely as he was. Louisa is much as I expected, and Cassandra I find handsomer than I expected,' she wrote from Godmersham. Of James's daughter she wrote, 'Little Caroline looks very plain among her Cousins, & tho' she is not so headstrong or humoursome as they are, I do not think her at all more engaging.'[7] Of Charles's daughter: 'I should be very happy in the idea of seeing little Cassy again too, did not I fear she would disappoint me by some immediate disagreeableness.' [8]

Like Emma she seems to have found comfort in detachment. In fact she did not quite approve of Dorothy's brand of blind enthusiasm for children; even mothers should, in Jane's opinion, show a little restraint. 'Harriot's fondness for her [daughter] seems just what is amiable & natural, & not foolish,'[9] she noted with approval. Dorothy's adoration of Johnny she would certainly have dismissed as 'foolish'.

Dorothy *could* make comparisons between the five nieces and nephews with whom William and Mary eventually provided her – Johnny, Dora, Thomas, Catharine and Willy. But usually she compared only to mark the superiority of the exceptional Johnny, whose primary hold on her heart was never challenged, even when it became apparent that that 'noble countenance' was not linked to a superior intelligence. Little Dora 'grows very like Johnny,' she reported when the children were two and four years old respectively, 'but she is twice as sharp, and when she can talk will utter, I believe, three words for his one.'[10] Only two years later she insisted: 'They are both sweet in their way; but it must be allowed that John is the finer creature'.[11]

Even when Johnny was twelve years old and his schooling was proving extremely problematic, she insisted, not very coherently, on his innate ability: 'His understanding is I am sure very good, as far as he *does* understand; but he is naturally slow ...'[12] This was certainly a kind of blindness.

Perhaps the more cautious Jane took into account the emotional risks of such absolute devotion.

'Nephews and nieces, whilst still young and innocent,' wrote Thomas De Quincey – probably with Dorothy in mind – 'are as good almost as sons and daughters to a fervid and loving heart that has carried them in her arms from the hour they were born.' But, 'after a nephew has grown into a huge bulk of a man, six feet high, and as stout as a bullock ...he ceases to be an object of any very profound sentiment.'[13]

Jane Austen – like many other maiden aunts – had carried her nephews in her arms and taken her part in child-care, but, though she made no comment on their size as young men, nor their like-ness to bullocks, she did sometimes find the boys' habits distinctly unappealing as they grew older The privileged sons of Edward repeatedly upset her with their 'habit[s] of Luxury or some proof of sporting Mania'.[14]

However, Jane seems to have found great pleasure in the society of her older nieces. She sent long letters of advice on matters of the heart to Fanny, and Anna found 'in her aunt Jane ...a sympathy and a companionship which was the delight of her girlhood.'[15] Perhaps Jane had in mind the pleasure she took in the company of these young women when she made Emma Woodhouse look forward to a future in which 'I shall often have a niece with me.'[16]

Rather alarmingly, the letters of both women begin to display an anxiety about the temperaments of their nieces when the children are still very young. While cleverness – or, perhaps, a 'noble manliness' – was looked for in a boy, docility was most highly prized in girls. Jane remarked on the contrasting temperaments of her great-nieces, when both girls were still under three years old: 'Jemima has a very irritable bad Temper…and Julia a very sweet one … I hope [their mother] will give Jemima's disposition the early & steady attention it must require.'[17]

By the time Dora was four, Dorothy was becoming uneasy about this little girl who was 'of the dancing brood'[18] and 'all fun and life'.[19] She could not but confess that 'Her faculties are, I think, quicker,' than John's. Though she maintained that her favourite 'has ten times the thought…and he is knowing and sensible.'[20]

Both children were now attending the little school in Grasmere village where John – who probably suffered from some form of dyslexia – struggled to learn to read. His little sister soon overtook him and, to Dorothy's dismay, Dora was 'proud and not unwilling to display what she can do'.[21] This was definitely not the way in which a little girl ought to behave.

'A woman especially, if she have the misfortune of knowing anything, should conceal it as well as she can', Jane Austen observes wryly in *Northanger Abbey*.[22] And this was a lesson that was taught harshly to poor little Dora Wordsworth very early in her life. Her aunt determined to conquer her 'waywardness', and set about breaking the child's spirit with punishments and imprisonments. Finally, she persuaded (a reluctant) William that Dora should be sent away to boarding school; and, before the poor child reached her fifth birthday, she was dispatched (alone in a public coach) to the care of a Miss Weir in Appleby, more than thirty miles from Grasmere.

In bringing this about Dorothy was almost certainly driven, in part, by her dislike of seeing Johnny eclipsed by his clever sister, but the arguments she put forward reflect the most conventional of conventional attitudes towards the upbringing of girls. 'I fear we shall have great difficulty in subduing her,' she lamented; and the purpose of sending Dora to Miss Weir's school was that she might become a '*useful* girl in the family' (my emphasis).[23] It might have been Hannah More herself speaking.

Dorothy who had, in her youth, not only valued spontaneity, but had also enjoyed a sense of mental superiority over the Miss Custs, was now an advocate for subjection in a girl, valuing her niece chiefly, not for her intellectual abilities, but for her usefulness to the family. This contradiction, this conflict in Dorothy's feelings in her middle life, was not only the source of misery to little Dora – who cried bitterly and clung desperately to her father when he visited her in her exile – it also seems to have caused pain to Dorothy herself.

Mansfield Park, the first novel which Jane Austen wrote entirely at Chawton, suggests that she had changed from the nineteen-year-old who had created Marianne Dashwood.

Like Marianne, Fanny Price (the heroine of *Mansfield Park*) is remarkable for her depth of feeling, yet she is a very different creature. First there is the difference in the way Fanny Price is presented. Much of the story is told from her point of view. We see sensibility from the *inside*. The reader of *Sense and Sensibility* is told about Marianne's behaviour and occasionally the author gives an explanation of that behaviour which is, usually, not very sympathetic – 'Marianne would have thought herself very inexcusable had she been able to sleep at all the first night after parting from Willoughby'[24]. By contrast, the readers of *Mansfield Park* are privy to its heroine's joys and sufferings (mostly sufferings), as they follow the narrative of Fanny's life – her homesickness when she is taken from her parents, her unrequited love for her cousin Edmund, and her uncle's determination that she should marry her rich suitor Henry Crawford. Fanny's feelings, her inner life, are given much more weight than those of Jane's earlier heroines.

This perspective makes it more likely that readers will feel sympathy for, and identify with, Fanny. But she is also a more nuanced and subtly drawn character, one with whom the author herself seems to have more sympathy.

Unlike Marianne, who is rude to others and whose lack of perception makes her indifferent to her sister's suffering, Fanny's sensibility does not make her selfish. She has that ability which Jane had specifically denied to her characters in the early burlesque *Love and Friendship*: the ability to enter imaginatively into the feelings of others.

When her cousin Julia loves and is rebuffed by Henry Crawford, Fanny notices her pain and feels for her. When she hears of her cousin Maria's adultery Fanny is immediately overwhelmed, not only by her own sense of shame and shock but also by the suffering of everyone else in the family – her aunt, her uncle, her other cousins. She is so anxious about other people's feelings that she sometimes attributes to others her own extreme sensibilities. When Mary Crawford has been ridiculing the clergy in her conversation with Edmund, only to discover that he is shortly to be ordained, Fanny 'pitied her. "How distressed she will be at what she said just now," passed across her mind.'[25] In fact, she feels more for Miss Crawford than Miss Crawford feels for herself on the occasion.

Jane was now willing to allow that sensibility was not always selfish and that a being 'tremblingly alive' to her own misfortunes (and Fanny Price does a fair amount of trembling) need not be selfishly indifferent to others' pain.

Like Marianne, Fanny loves and responds to nature, but again there is a striking difference: Fanny not only glories in the natural world, she finds in it a moral tutorship. As she looks out on a starlit night, she declares: 'I feel as if there could be neither wickedness nor sorrow in the world; and there certainly would be less of both if the sublimity of Nature were more attended to, and people were carried more out of themselves by contemplating such a scene.'[26] In fact she has discovered those lessons of 'moral evil and of good' which William Wordsworth believed could be found in the natural world.

The change in Jane Austen's voice as she began upon her later novels is arresting.

William Deresiewicz and other academics believe that Jane Austen's writing – particularly her last three complete novels,

Mansfield Park, Emma and *Persuasion* – displays an awareness of the work of her contemporaries, Wordsworth, Coleridge, Scott and Byron: writers who would, years later, come to be known as 'the Romantics'.[27] Jane mentions reading Walter Scott's novels in her letters, and Byron's poetry is mentioned in her unfinished novel *Sanditon*. It is harder to determine whether she had read anything of Wordsworth's. But Deresiewicz draws attention to an intriguing little echo.

In the East Room – the former school-room of Mansfield Park to which the Bertrams' poor relation, Fanny Price, retreats for solace – there are 'three transparencies, made in a rage for transparencies, for the lower panes of one window, where Tintern Abbey held its station between a cave in Italy, and a moonlight lake in Cumberland'. This, he believes, may have been meant to call to the reader's mind William Wordsworth, the Romantic poet whose name was associated with both Tintern Abbey (about which William wrote one of his most popular poems) and the lakes of Cumberland.[28]

Whether or not Jane had read Wordsworth's work, Fanny Price is a 'Romantic'. The spiritual and moral significance which she finds in nature is at the heart of Romanticism, and she is also possessed of a Romantic's imagination, one which, rather than breeding extravagant fancies, allows an individual to enter into the feelings and experiences of another. These qualities make Fanny very different from Marianne (and Marianne's forerunners in *Love and Friendship*).

It is possible that Jane Austen had independently hit upon two of the central tenets of the literary movement which had been initiated by the Concern and which was, by the time she arrived at Chawton, influencing some of Britain's most popular poets, but it is more likely that, during her long sad exile in Bath, she had been reading poetry. Poetry has a particular appeal for those who are unhappy – as Jane would acknowledge when she created Captain Benwick of *Persuasion*. Perhaps, through William's poetry, she had been touched by that small revolution in thinking that Dorothy had taken part in as she walked with her brother and his friend on the Quantock Hills.

Jane Austen certainly makes *Mansfield Park*'s heroine a whole-hearted devotee of poetry. When it comes to the artistic expression of feeling, Fanny is not like Marianne with her passionate attachment to music, her enthusiasm for her sister's drawing. The beauty of that starlit night makes her exclaim: 'Here's what may leave all Painting, and all Music behind, and what Poetry only can attempt to describe.'

However, though the influence of the Romantic poets may have played its part in the creation of *Mansfield Park*, Fanny Price is more than an embodiment of Romantic notions. When Jane Austen described herself as 'the most unlearned, & uninformed Female who ever dared to be an Authoress',[29] she was, no doubt, being deliberately over-modest, but she was also obliquely saying that her inspiration came from experience and observation as well as literature. The observations and life-experiences which she brought to this new novel were much wider and more complex than those which had informed her earliest work.

In particular, her experience of living as a poor relation is likely to have played its part in the creation of Fanny Price, who shares her author's lack of autonomy. Like Jane, Fanny plays no part in the decisions which most affect her life. 'It can make little difference to you, whether you are in one house or the other', says the insensitive Lady Bertram when Fanny's future is being discussed. [30] When Jane wrote that she may have been remembering her mother's autocratic decisions, and Aunt Norris's admonition of 'Remember, wherever you are, you must be the lowest and last'[31] might contain a bitter memory of her own visits to the grander parts of her family.

While *Sense and Sensibility* is the production of a brilliant girl, *Mansfield Park* is the work of an experienced woman and the mature Jane was able to acknowledge that acute sensitivity need not, necessarily, launch a woman into unguarded behaviour. This is the other great difference between Fanny Price and Marianne Dashwood. Like Marianne, Fanny trusts her own feelings in the most important decisions of her life. But Fanny's reliance on her own emotional truth does not lead to reckless self-gratification; it drives her instead into silence and concealment. Like Elinor

Dashwood, Fanny is presented with a moral dilemma – should she reveal a truth and justify her own actions which are misunderstood by her family, or should she maintain an honourable silence for the sake of others?

The secret Elinor honourably conceals is Lucy Steele's engagement to Edward Ferrars which has been revealed to her in confidence. The secret Fanny elects to keep is her knowledge of Henry Crawford's true character, because the truth can only be told by revealing her cousin Maria's improper behaviour during the play- acting at Mansfield.

Because of her decision to keep silent, Fanny is tormented by Crawford's unwelcome courtship which is given the sanction of her guardians; and her resistance to him is publicly justified only by the revelation of his character when he runs off with her married cousin. It is the combination of extremely deep feeling and almost pathological restraint which makes Fanny Price's story compelling.

Jane Austen, now safely installed at Chawton, stationary at last and able to take up her pen, set about exploring the very complex consequences of deep feeling in the world which she and Dorothy shared: a world in which silence, repression and inaction were sometimes the only honourable course of action; a world in which obligation and loyalty to her family could conflict painfully with a woman's own idea of what was right.

It was a conflict of which she had had personal experience. When Tom Lefroy deceived her, she had submitted and done what was expected of her, what was considered 'right'; she had done her duty to her family and controlled her feelings. Six years later, Harris Bigg Wither's proposal presented a harder test. Here again her duty was plain: she should accept such an unexceptionable offer, provide a home for herself, her sister and her mother. At first she did her duty, but her resolution lasted for only twelve hours. Then she changed her mind and acted for herself.

When asked to sacrifice her principles for the good of her family, Jane had found the strength to make a stand. Now, on her page, Fanny Price was also opposing the wishes of her family out of principle.

'She had been forced into prudence in her youth,' Jane would write of her final heroine – Anne Elliot of *Persuasion* – 'she learned romance as she grew older – the natural sequel of an unnatural beginning.' In the margin of her copy of that novel, Cassandra wrote, after her sister's death, 'Dear dear Jane! This deserves to be written in letters of gold.' Cassandra's endorsement of the sentiment seems to add weight to it, to highlight it as a particularly significant insight. Perhaps Cassandra recognised in it some personal meaning.

Jane Austen's earliest writings had mocked the excesses of young women such as Dorothy Wordsworth who liked to align themselves with the wronged heroines of novels of sensibility, but her mature work would enter imaginatively into the tension which must arise for a woman of deep feeling living in the real world of early nineteenth century Britain. Jane had come to recognise that the choices forced upon women could be complicated: the world was not as simple as her youthful burlesques suggested.

Dorothy too had learned that the impetuosity which had driven her out of her uncle's safe home to accept relative poverty with her beloved brother, the honesty which had fuelled her delightful defiance of Aunt Crackenthorpe, were not always the answers to life's crises. Sometimes self-control and concealment were necessary.

Sarah Coleridge (a woman who might well have won Jane Austen's admiration) had been behaving very much like the heroine of *Mansfield Park*. She had – out of loyalty – been concealing a secret, even though her secrecy meant that her own actions were misunderstood. And within two years of moving to Allan Bank, Dorothy at last, discovered this secret. She learned that Coleridge was a drug addict and came to fully understand the effect this had on his behaviour.

After his return from Malta, Coleridge had taken up residence with the Wordsworths at Dove Cottage, and their search for a new home had been made all the more difficult by the need to find somewhere large enough to accommodate, not only their own family, but also their friend and his two sons. For Coleridge was determined to take advantage of the unjust laws of the day which gave a father complete control over his children. He planned to leave his young daughter with her mother, but to take his two sons to live with him; and this despite the fact that he had spent so much time away from home he can have been little more than a stranger to the two boys, Hartley and Derwent.[32]

Dorothy seems to have felt that this was a reasonable thing to do, and she began with hopes that 'William's conversation and our kind offices may soothe [Coleridge], and bring on tranquillity'.[33] However, once she was sharing a home with him, a thorough understanding of his illnesses, ill-temper and unreliable habits was forced upon her. 'We have no hope of him ...' she wrote in April 1810. 'If he were not under our Roof, he would be just as much the slave of stimulants as ever; and his whole time and thoughts, are employed in deceiving himself, and seeking to deceive others.' She complained that 'He lies in bed, always till after 12 o'clock,' and 'Sometimes he does not speak a word'[34]. It is easy to believe that this was just the kind of behaviour his wife had been enduring for years, and her 'ill-tempered speeches' had not been made without provocation.

Sara Hutchinson was also hurt and disillusioned by Coleridge's behaviour. At Allan Bank she had been attempting to give him the support which he and his friends had believed he needed, writing to his dictation, listening to him, copying his work. But now Dorothy admitted that his love for her was no more than 'a fanciful dream'. It seems likely that Sara had tried to break Coleridge of his opium habit for, said Dorothy, 'when she stood in the way of other gratifications it was all over.'[35] Exhausted by his demands Sara made her escape from Grasmere.

Soon after this letter was written, Coleridge quarrelled with William and left the Lake District for good[36]. It must have been a heavy blow. Though Dorothy had given her love unreservedly to this brilliant, damaged man within days of his arrival in her life, their friendship had proved a source of pain for both of them. Her interference in his marriage had been presumptuous, ill-judged, and, very probably, destructive; and her closer devotion to William had frequently made Coleridge feel jealous and excluded.

Yet Coleridge's affection must have taken its toll on Dorothy just as it did on his wife and on Sara Hutchinson, for Dorothy too had done her best to support him emotionally over the years. His sense of superiority over his wife on the grounds of sex, and the impossible demands he placed on the woman whom he believed he loved, indicate the role which he might have expected his close female friend – the third member of the Concern – to perform. It seems likely that he had been an emotionally draining companion, and improbable that he had done much to encourage Dorothy's confidence in her own talents.

After Coleridge left the Lakes Dorothy continued to worry about him, grieve over him and criticise him. They never met again, but the wounds he inflicted – wounds to which she had laid open her heart more than a decade before – would continue to smart until the oblivion of her final illness.

Just as Jane began upon those mature novels which explore the pain of deep sensibility in early nineteenth century society, Dorothy seems to have been suffering under the checks and curbs which that society imposed on unmarried women – or, as De Quincey put it 'the decorum of her sex and age, and maidenly condition'. These checks, forced upon a woman who had, in her youth, been determined to speak every feeling, and to value only 'an affectionate heart' may well have caused the tension and discomfort – the 'self-conflict' – which he detected.

It is pointless to look for evidence – or explanation – of that inner conflict in Dorothy's own writing. As we have seen, only the power of emotions is revealed there – rarely is the cause, or even the exact nature, of any emotion described. But a remarkable sequence of letters exchanged between William and his wife does throw some light on the landscape of Dorothy's inner feelings as she reached the end of her thirties. There certainly was tension, because the promise of inclusion, of continuing, undiminished love, which William had made to Dorothy as he slipped the wedding ring onto her finger minutes before he gave it his bride, had proved particularly difficult – perhaps impossible – to keep.

Jonson's poem – the one in which Dorothy and William had found solace and pain before his wedding took place – tidily separates sexual desire and tender, companionate love. But one point Jonson does not touch on is that the two are not *always* separable. A couple marrying, as William and Mary seem to have done, on the basis of calm affection, can continue to fall more and more deeply in love as they live together, particularly if they share a happy sex-life.

In 1803 – in the very early days of his marriage – William had, with apparent unconcern, left his wife alone to visit Scotland with Dorothy and Coleridge. But, years later – in 1810 and again in 1812 – he was forced to part from his wife for a few weeks. The letters they exchanged at those times indicate how very much this marriage had changed since the days when William left Mary behind in order to jaunt about the Highlands with his sister.

By 1810 William hated being away from Mary; it was an almost physical pain. 'Nor will I ever,' he promised the woman to whom he had been married eight years and who had borne him five children, 'except from a principle of duty, part from you again, to stay any where more than one week. I cannot bear it ... [I]t seems criminal to me in a high degree, to part from you except from a strong call of unquestionable moral obligation.'[37]

William was convinced that the love he and Mary now shared was rare and precious. 'Every day every hour every moment makes me feel more deeply how blessed we are in each other,' he wrote, indicating that he himself believed their love to have grown and matured since their marriage. ' ... I am persuaded,' he continued, 'that a deep affection is not uncommon in married life, yet I am confident that a lively, gushing, thought-employing, spirit-stirring passion of love is very rare'.

It sounds like a wonderful marriage, and these letters call into question the rather dour picture of William Wordsworth which it is all too easy to gather from later portraits and the more didactic passages of his writing. For Mary's part in the correspondence reveals that she was more in love with him after ten years of marriage than she had been on their wedding day. It throws a very flattering light on his character!

However, being a third party caught in the middle of a 'thought-employing, spirit-stirring passion of love' cannot have been pleasant. William and Mary's letters illuminate the hidden corners of the extraordinary relationship which had developed over the years, and which had to be maintained by the three members of the Wordsworth household. Before his marriage William had been careful to assure Dorothy of his continuing love for her. But now he was involved in a burgeoning sexual love which – if it were allowed – could, by excluding her, hurt her deeply.

'O my William!' exclaimed Mary in delighted response to the above letter. '...it was...so new a thing to see the breathing of thy inmost heart upon paper that I was quite overpowered'.³⁸ It was the first proper love letter she had received from her husband – another indication that their courtship had been less than ardent.

It seems that most letters Mary received from William had to be shared with Dorothy, either before they were sent or after they arrived. But just now circumstances had combined to make it possible for Mary to get a letter which would not be read by her sister-in-law. Dorothy was also away from home at this time, but not with William.

So Mary was able to speak of, 'that love which unites us & which cannot be felt but by ourselves.' In fact, now she had the chance, Mary was quite determined to make a distinction, to let William know that this bond – marital love – had, she believed, the highest claim. In her next letter, she wrote of, 'the blessed bond that binds husband and wife so much closer than the bond of Brotherhood – however dear & affectionate a family of Brothers [&] Sisters may love each other. – ' ³⁹

Her remarks form a kind of counterpoint to Dorothy's declaration: 'I have at all times a deep sympathy with those who know what fraternal affection is. It has been the building up of my being, the light of my path.'

In *Mansfield Park*, Jane Austen's voice would join Dorothy's in what might almost have been a chorus of Georgian spinsters, as she boldly stated that, in some respects, 'the conjugal tie is beneath the fraternal'.⁴⁰

The cool style of Jane's letters is far removed from that of Dorothy's journal. It is certainly impossible to imagine her calling

Edward or Henry 'beloved', but the passage from *Mansfield Park* reveals that she also had made the comparison between *amore* fraternal and *amore* conjugal, and she had considered the conflicting claims of sisters and wives not only in material, but in emotional terms.

Fraternal love could not but be important to women of the insecure, pseudo-gentry class when family circumstances manoeuvred them into celibacy. Brothers, as we have seen, had played a crucial role in the young lives of both Dorothy and Jane. Mary Wollstonecraft's account shows how the dependency of women in Georgian times frequently threw wives and sisters into conflict. Against this background, the household at Grasmere reveals itself as an admirable, affectionate balancing of claims. Mary might, in a private letter, state her belief that the conjugal bond trumps the fraternal, but she does not seem to have urged her point too often, or too forcefully. She loved her sister-in-law and was considerate.

In these love letters, both William and Mary express a longing for privacy beyond what was practicable in their circumstances. William hoped to return home before Dorothy and, if other visitors did not trouble them too much – 'I cannot say my Love with what fondness I feed on the thought of our being together without interruption day or night.'[41]

He also wished – since Dorothy was not with him – to have, 'a letter for myself and of which I need only read parts to the rest of the family'. He was travelling into Wales at the time and would be in company with Mary's sister, Sara, when such a letter reached him, but, he said, 'I know that S[ara] will take no offense' at hearing only part of the letter. This suggests that Dorothy *would* have been offended by his failing to share a letter unreservedly.[42]

It seems she was very touchy about such things, and here we are given an insight into her inner life which it is not possible to glimpse anywhere else. The long-married William and Mary struggled to conceal their passion from their sister, like young lovers hiding their sex-life from their parents.

Dorothy could not even be allowed to suppose that Mary would rather write to William than to her. 'I have yet to write to Dorothy,' Mary confessed, '& ...as I can but write her a short letter; when you write to her…do not give her to understand that you received a longer one – this would make her uneasy.'[43]

Dorothy seems to have found it more painful than any of her own writing shows to share her brother with another woman. Jealousy was unacceptable: it could not be admitted to and maybe the threat of it caused her to quarrel with herself. Her self-image was one of generosity and open-heartedness; it always had been. It is easy to see why there might have been inner conflict.

After years of all living together, Mary and William clearly understood very well the strategies Dorothy had developed to cope with her position as third person in a marriage which was turning out to be exceptionally passionate. Sadly her method seems to have been to turn her face from any show of intimacy.

In another letter, written from London, William told his beloved wife that all the amusements of the city appeared 'worthless and insipid when I think of one sweet smile of thy face, [which] I absolutely pant to behold'. But this delightful expression of affection (so like the things William had once written to his sister – ' so eager is my desire to see you that all obstacles vanish. I see you in a moment running or rather flying to my arms') had to be hidden because he had accidentally put it on a part of the letter which Dorothy would see. At first poor William tried desperately to cross out the passage but, he wrote, 'I fear [it] will still be legible; at all events the very attempt to hide, will I fear give offense.' In the end he was driven to subterfuge – 'I have now blotted the sheet so that it is impossible to make out the obnoxious expressions.'[44]

This extreme caution indicates the lengths to which husband and wife were used to going in order to protect Dorothy from any evidence of an exclusive love. But it also shows how strong were the defences which Dorothy had herself reared against the hurt of feeling left out. A natural, pleasant expression of love between husband and wife would be considered *obnoxious* by her.

The girl who had been as spontaneous as Marianne Dashwood, determined to express her feelings and despise all that did not spring from an affectionate heart, had grown into a woman who must turn her back on intimacy and close her eyes to deep feeling. It seems to have become worse as the years progressed.

When she was young Dorothy had taken an interest in weddings, but, as an older woman, she did not enjoy them. By the time baby Johnny came to marry in 1830, she could describe weddings as 'but a *melancholy* pleasure.' And she explained that 'This wedding, however, was to be a gay one if a large assemblage of affectionately attached Relatives could make any wedding gay.'[45]

Spinsters had ways of protecting themselves against jealousy. Both Dorothy and Jane commented freely on one of marriage's downsides – over fecundity. 'You will be glad to hear that she [Mary] is not with child again', Dorothy wrote to her friend Catherine Clarkson in 1805, '– for her constitution is not strong enough to support the having a child every year.'[46] Jane was, characteristically, more outspoken on the subject. 'Poor Animal,' she remarked on hearing that her niece Anna was pregnant again, 'she will be worn out before she is thirty.'[47]

As they aged both Dorothy and Jane preferred new brides to be discreet. In 1829 Dorothy grudgingly described one bridal pair as 'the most pleasing company I ever had to do with at a time so engrossingly interesting to themselves.'[48] And, after the marriage of her niece Anna in 1814, Jane commented: 'Her letters have been very sensible & satisfactory, with no *parade* of happiness, which I liked them the better for. – I have often known young married Women write in a way I did not like, in that respect.'[49]

What exactly was it about the letters and behaviour of brides that could be unpleasant? Perhaps it was just a general smugness about having achieved the status to which every woman was expected to aspire, or perhaps some of the young wives Jane and Dorothy knew contrived to imply something about the pleasures of sex, or hinted at being 'in on' a secret from which spinsters were excluded.

As she aged, Dorothy's revulsion at marital intimacy would exceed Jane's, for it was not only in life, but in literature too that her tastes and attitudes changed. As a young girl she had eagerly devoured Samuel Richardson's *Clarissa* with all its passionate scenes, but in 1815 she complained that, 'When love begins almost all novels grow tiresome.' And she said of Walter Scott's novel *Waverley* 'as usual the love is sickening.'[50]

Spinster though she was – and more than a little given to cynicism – Jane Austen retained some of the feelings of her youth. She
certainly never went so far as to think a bit of love spoiled a novel!

There is one hint in Dorothy's later letters – an oblique reference to her own past – which suggests her own experience may
have caused her extreme coldness on this matter of love and marriage, a coldness which seems so far removed from the impulsive
affections of her younger self.

In 1829 Dorothy's niece, Dora, acted as bridesmaid to a friend
(Coleridge's daughter), and she too set off to join the newlyweds
on their honeymoon journey – just as Dorothy had, twenty-seven
years earlier. However, Dora's experience would not be quite the
same as her aunt's because another friend was also joining the
party. Dorothy remarked on this difference with approval because,
she said: 'to be solitary in that capacity with a Honey-moon pair
is not quite the most satisfactory thing in the world …'[51]

It is a hint of the hurt and defensiveness which William and
Mary's letters reveal. More than twenty years after she set out on
that honeymoon journey from Yorkshire to Grasmere – a journey
on which she *seemed*, by her own account, to be relaxed and
perfectly at ease – Dorothy still remembered the experience as,
'not quite the most satisfactory thing in the world.'

Dorothy did not entirely abandon journal keeping when she left
Dove Cottage. But the journals which she kept at her final home
Rydal Mount (to which the family moved in 1813) are generally
rather sketchy compared to those of her younger days. They only
became detailed and animated when she went on a journey. As
she remarked in her Scottish *Recollections*, 'On going into a new
country I seem to myself to waken up'.[52]

It seems as if she needed to see *new* sights to arouse her talents.
Even a short tour with William to Coniston and Furness, when she
was fifty-three, was able to produce the same zeal and accuracy
as that with which she first described the green paths down the
hillsides making channels for streams in the opening lines of the
Alfoxton Journal.

'[E]ntrance arched –' she wrote of a well at Lindale 'rather lintelled over with old ash stem – roof arched with stone – green with moss – hung with Adder's Tongue and Geraniums – '[53]

Her talent for observation did not diminish with age, but the plans to publish her travel writing came to nothing. Thomas De Quincey believed that this failure was little short of a tragedy in Dorothy's life. He thought that her 'excess of sensibility' became a source of unhappiness to Dorothy in middle age. 'I fear', he wrote, 'that Miss Wordsworth has suffered …from …an excess of pleasurable excitement and luxurious sensibility, sustained in youth by a constitutional glow from animal causes, but drooping as soon as that was withdrawn.'

Publication of her work, he felt, might have sustained his friend and protected her from 'the sort of suffering which, more or less, ever since the period of her too genial, too radiant youth, I suppose her to have struggled with.' He believed that publication would have given Dorothy hopes for the future as she got older, for 'It is too much to expect of any woman …that her mind should support itself in a pleasurable activity, under the drooping energies of life, by resting on the past or on the present.'[54]

Dorothy never experienced the 'pleasant cares and solicitudes' of authorship which De Quincey believed would have supported her drooping spirits. But Jane's final years were full of hope and excitement; sometimes she even defied the conventional distain for childless spinsters by unashamedly making children of her books. 'As I wish very much to see *your* Jemima,' she wrote to her niece Anna after the birth of her first baby, 'I am sure you will like to see *my* Emma'.[55]

Years ago, deciding that she would rein in her feelings, Jane had reserved for herself an inward life: a safe space where no-one could hurt her. Settled at Chawton she was free to follow what she had always known was the purpose of her existence, to write – and to write. Her tragedy was simply that she did not long enjoy the creative freedom she had won, dying too soon with, perhaps, many books left unwritten.

Dorothy would live all her life – until 25th January 1855 – with William, Mary and their family, working tirelessly for those she loved until illness overtook her. During her life only a few of her poems would be published among her brother's work. There would be no volumes of travel-writing with her name on them, no translations from German or Italian, no novels which might have taught Walter Scott how Scottish characters *ought* to be portrayed.

As William aged, his output of original work decreased, particularly after 1812 when financial pressures on the family brought about a major change. At that point – as William himself expressed it in a letter to the new Lord Lonsdale – he abandoned the hope that 'the profits of my literary labours added to the little which I possessed would have answered to the rational wants of myself and my family.' He asked his Lordship to find a job for him. Lord Lonsdale obliged and, in 1813, Wordsworth was appointed Distributor of Stamps for Westmorland – a tax-collecting role.[56] After this change in lifestyle, Dorothy's importance to her brother as a muse and assistant diminished, and the pressures of family life absorbed more of her attention.

The end of her life was extremely sad. Though she lived to the age of 83, her last twenty years were spent in an upstairs room at the beautiful Rydal Mount, confused and unknowing, her mind completely broken. She became irritable, bad-tempered and irrational, given to making loud sudden noises and uttering obscenities at inappropriate moments, and she had such unreliable habits that her family shielded her from the outside world. De Quincey believed that she had, lacking any worthwhile activity to support her 'drooping energies', 'yielded to that nervous depression which, I grieve to hear, has clouded her latter days.' [57]

It is terrible to think that, in the end, Dorothy's sensibility might have destroyed her sense. Her last illness is now generally believed to have been a form of dementia, compounded by physical weakness in her legs and bowels, and by long-term use of opium to relieve her symptoms. De Quincey – who had only the inaccurate (and, sometimes, positively bizarre) medical theories of the day to inform his judgement – may have been wrong in supposing that her condition was affected by the experiences of her life. It may have sprung entirely from physical causes.

However, Barbara Crossley, in a talk given at the Wordsworth

Trust, Grasmere, has suggested that Dorothy's illness was severe depression, not dementia. She draws attention to three character-istic symptoms of depression which were prominent in Dorothy's case: low energy levels, an inability to experience enjoyment, and low mood. Also, she believes that the pattern of remission and relapse that can be traced in the letters written from Rydal Mount may be significant. For example, in 1850, when William was in his final illness, one friend wrote: 'Miss Wordsworth was as much herself as ever she was in her life time and had absolute command of her own will, does not make noises, is not all self, thinks of the feelings of others, and is tenderly anxious about her brother.' Dementia is generally an unremitting, progressive illness; such periods of lucidity would be unusual.[58]

It may be that, as she aged, and William's children grew up, Dorothy did feel that the family needed her less. All her life, she had held back nothing of herself. Her eagerness had made her give all to those she loved. She lacked an independent interest – such as writing for publication – an interest which could have given her a sense of purpose and achievement.

But, in return for the sacrifices she had undoubtedly made in her life, she was deeply loved. Whatever her final illness was, William and Mary cared for her with uncomplaining affection.

Jane lived the rest of her tragically short life at Chawton, dying on 18th July 1817 at the age of just 41, probably from Addison's Disease (a failure of the adrenal gland).

Though in the memory of her family she lived a typical spin-ster's existence of reading, working for the poor, entertaining her nephews and nieces, and teaching local children to read, the reality was slightly different: there was some success, some recognition of her extraordinary talents in her lifetime. There was increas-ing praise from critics – including Walter Scott. News came to her of her novels being read in Ireland, in Cheltenham and in London, and by the time *Emma*, the last book to be published in her lifetime, appeared she had won the admiration of the Prince of Wales himself.

However, Jane did not embrace the change in lifestyle which was now possible for her. An invitation to a literary soiree which offered the opportunity of meeting the famous Madame de Staël received a firm refusal. For years she had worked alone; now she drew back from conversing with other established writers, published anonymously and preserved that anonymity for as long as she could. She had always been reluctant to form intimate friendships. Perhaps the intimacy of shared ideas, which had attracted Dorothy Wordsworth ever since she was a girl, held no appeal for her.

She seems to have preferred the creative world she had made for herself, living, to all appearances, the quiet life of a typical spinster, while – protected from intrusion by only a creaking door – she wrote three of the greatest novels in the English language.

Jane and Dorothy were two unmarried, childless women who had failed to fulfil the destiny that their society prescribed for their sex. But they had neither drooped nor withered as Carlisle expected, nor developed the chagrin and peevishness which Dr Gregory believed inseparable from their condition. Instead they had forged their own meanings from their lives.

EPILOGUE

A Natural Sequel to an Unnatural Beginning?

By the time Jane and Dorothy reached the end of their thirties, the world in which they lived had changed from that into which they had been born. The long wars against Napoleon had united English hearts against the French. The social changes connected with industrialisation and urbanisation were well underway, and the evangelical teaching which had disturbed Dorothy's peace at Forncett had gained ground among the middle classes. There was a new air of religious seriousness throughout the country.

There had been a subtle change too in the meaning of those opposites of Sense and Sensibility which Jane Austen had, nearly twenty years earlier, ascribed to the two heroines of her first mature novel. The sensibility of eighteenth century novels had been transformed into something more complex and thoughtful by the increasing influence of Wordsworth, Coleridge and other poets who had initiated, 'a revolution in poetic form, diction and subject matter.'[1] Dorothy Wordsworth had been a part of the discussions which began that revolution, and Jane Austen's last great novels – particularly *Mansfield Park* and *Persuasion* – acknowledge that change. The moral complexity of their stories would not be possible without the new ideas.

Jane and Dorothy had both been born into the insecurity of the pseudo-gentry class; they had shared in the inadequacies of an education which did little to prepare women for either poverty or independence. They had both grown up knowing that they were

321

likely to be financially dependent on their brothers in a kind of informal arrangement which would allow them neither security nor dignity. And they had both lived with the contempt which their contemporaries heaped upon spinsters.

They had met these challenges in different ways.

Dorothy Wordsworth had followed her heart when she decided to throw in her lot with her brother. Her love and devotion had saved him and helped him become a great poet. She had achieved with him a true companionship such as few women of her time were able to form with a man. Her friendship with Coleridge had been exhilarating and she had been a part of one of the most exciting intellectual debates of her day. Her courage and belief in the 'rightness' of her own impulses had enabled her to disregard the materialistic standards of her class and live happily in comparative poverty.

However, her open, loving nature bred a spirit of self-sacrifice, and the demands of the 'Romantics' among whom she lived were curiously similar to those of conservative writers like Hannah More who believed a woman's highest achievement was to comfort, counsel and soothe the sorrows of a 'man of sense'. Dorothy's need to be loved tempted her to be the modest retiring female that William admired and perhaps inhibited her from pursuing an independent livelihood. Important though she was in her brother's work, her life with him did not inspire in her a confidence in her own abilities. By 1802, circumstances seem to have conspired to make it impossible for her to continue in the happy partnership which they had established at Dove Cottage. Restraint and silence were forced upon her as she encouraged William to marry, as she taught herself to live as the third party in his marriage.

Jane Austen had given up Tom Lefroy and borne the pain in silence, as Elinor Dashwood bears the distress of losing Edward Ferrars. She had swallowed her resentment when she was torn from her home and work to live an empty life in Bath. But, when her compliance was put to the ultimate test in 1802, and she was forced to contemplate an intimate relationship with a man for whom she felt no attraction, she had found the inner strength to rebel. Her resolution held when, three years later, Edward Bridges' proposal put her again in the position of deciding between feeling and prudence. She seems to have chosen the former with greater ease – even though her financial circumstances had deteriorated since her father's death. Sometimes, Jane discovered, sense *must* give way to sensibility, if a woman is to retain her self-respect.

The reserve which Jane cultivated was founded on the lessons she had learned as a child, and it was as much a protection as a sacrifice. Reading her preposterous early stories aloud to her family she had discovered how to say what she thought without being censored. She had learned too that her inner life was secure against the unfair demands of others around her. In her head, in her imagination, she found an exhilarating freedom, a freedom which produced those novels which have been enjoyed by generations of readers.

This seems to have been a lesson Dorothy never learned, a kind of escape she never achieved. Eager and emotional, responsive to those around her, ever ready to love and accept new friends, it is as if she gave too much of herself away and never developed an inward space, or imaginative life, of her own. Her response to nature was intense, her descriptions exquisite, but imagination did not shape that response. Precision was the end of her endeavour and through it she seems to make a gift, to us her readers, of her experiences. She displays the same unselfconscious generosity of spirit to us as she did to those she loved.

In the society Jane and Dorothy inhabited, both 'eagerness' and 'prudence', both 'sense' and 'sensibility' could bring a woman considerable pain. By following their experiences the sheer weight, the inertia, of the prejudices that pressed upon their lives becomes frighteningly apparent. Dorothy's courageous elopement could not, in the end, free her from domestic labour, for the apparently 'alternative' lifestyle she embraced was rooted in traditional notions about the respective roles of men and women. Equally, Jane's quiet acceptance of the loss of Tom Lefroy only left her in a home where more and more sacrifices would be demanded of her.

However, from within the restricted world of a respectable

Georgian spinster, Jane Austen crafted novels which have appealed to a broader range of readers than almost any other body of literature. From Japan to Canada, to India and Eastern Europe readers have found universal meaning in the stories of love, injustice, kindness, cruelty and personal integrity which she wrote on a tiny table in an ordinary, slightly shabby parlour in Hampshire over two centuries ago.

At first Dorothy's legacy was limited to a small circle of close acquaintances. In 1833, Catherine Clarkson, having read through 'heaps' of her letters exclaimed, 'What a heart and what a head they discover! What puffs we hear of women, and even of men, who have made books and done charities, and all that, but whose doings and thinkings and feelings are not to be compared with hers!'[2]

Dorothy would live in the hearts of her friends until her journals were published in 1897 and she gradually found her way into the consciousness of a grateful public. 'If the written word could cure rheumatism I think hers might,' said Virginia Woolf, 'like a dock leaf laid to a sting'.[3]

The voices of those two fifteen-year-olds – one who sought to lay bare the secrets of her heart, and one who aimed to expose the folly of others – would mature into the work that survives and still speaks to us. And that is because neither the spirit nor the genius of these two women, neither their good sense, nor their deep feelings could be entirely silenced by the suffocating circumstances under which they lived.

Jane and Dorothy were not simply products of their time. They made choices in their lives, and it was those choices which defined them.

APPENDIX 1

These are the stanzas from *The Minstrel* which reminded Dorothy of William.

> And oft he traced the uplands, to survey,
> When o'er the sky advanced the kindling dawn,
> The crimson cloud, blue main, and mountain grey,
> And lake, dim-gleaming on the smoky lawn;
> Far to the west the long, long vale withdrawn,
> Where twilight loves to linger for a while;
> And now he faintly kens the bounding fawn,
> And villager abroad at early toil.
> But, lo! the sun appears! and heaven, earth, ocean, smile.
>
> And oft the craggy cliff he loved to climb,
> When all in mist the world below was lost.
> What dreadful pleasure! there to stand sublime,
> Like shipwrecked mariner on desert coast,
> And view the enormous waste of vapour, tost
> In billows, lengthening to the horizon round,
> Now scooped in gulfs, with mountains now embossed!
> And hear the voice of mirth and song rebound,
> Flocks, herds, and waterfalls, along the hoar profound!
>
> In truth he was a strange and wayward wight,
> Fond of each gentle, and each dreadful scene.
> In darkness, and in storm, he found delight:
> Nor less, than when on ocean-wave serene

The southern sun diffused his dazzling shene.
Even sad vicissitude amused his soul:
And if a sigh would sometimes intervene,
And down his cheek a tear of pity roll,
A sigh, a tear, so sweet, he wished not to controul.

(James Beattie the Minstrel Bk 1 xx to xxii)

The Forest

XI. — EPODE.

Not to know vice at all, and keep true state,
   Is virtue and not fate :
Next to that virtue, is to know vice well,
   And her black spite expel,
Which to effect (since no breast is so sure,
   Or safe, but she'll procure
Some way of entrance) we must plant a guard
   Of thoughts to watch, and ward
At the eye and ear, the ports unto the mind,
   That no strange, or unkind
Object arrive there, but the heart, our spy,
   Give knowledge instantly,
To wakeful reason, our affections' king :
   Who, in th' examining,
Will quickly taste the treason, and commit
   Close, the close cause of it.
'Tis the securest policy we have,
   To make our sense our slave.
But this true course is not embraced by many :   10
   By many ! scarce by any.
For either our affections do rebel,
   Or else the sentinel,
That should ring larum to the heart, doth sleep;
   Or some great thought doth keep

Back the intelligence, and falsely swears,
    They are base, and idle fears
Whereof the loyal conscience so complains,
    Thus, by these subtile trains,
Do several passions invade the mind,   20
    And strike our reason blind,
Of which usurping rank, some have thought love
    The first ; as prone to move
Most frequent tumults, horrors, and unrests,
    In our enflamed breasts :
But this doth from the cloud of error grow,
    Which thus we over-blow.
The thing they here call Love, is blind desire,
    Arm'd with bow, shafts, and fire ;
Inconstant, like the sea, of whence 'tis born,   30
    Rough, swelling, like a storm :
With whom who sails, rides on the surge of fear,
    And boils, as if he were
In a continual tempest. Now, true love
    No such effects doth prove ;
That is an essence far more gentle, fine,
    Pure, perfect, nay divine ;
It is a golden chain let down from heaven,
    Whose links are bright and even,
That falls like sleep on lovers, and combines   40
    The soft, and sweetest minds
In equal knots : this bears no brands, nor darts,
    To murder different hearts,
But in a calm, and god-like unity,
    Preserves community.
O, who is he, that, in this peace, enjoys
    The elixir of all joys ?
A form more fresh than are the Eden bowers,
    And lasting as her flowers :
Richer than Time, and as time's virtue rare   50
    Sober, as saddest care ;

A fixed thought, an eye untaught to glance :
    Who, blest with such high chance
Would, at suggestion of a steep desire,
    Cast himself from the spire
Of all his happiness ? But soft : I hear
    Some vicious fool draw near,
That cries, we dream, and swears there's no such thing,
    As this chaste love we sing.
Peace, Luxury, thou art like one of those   60
    Who, being at sea, suppose,
Because they move, the continent doth so.
    No, Vice, we let thee know,
Though thy wild thoughts with sparrows' wings do flie,
    Turtles can chastly die ;
And yet (in this t' express ourselves more clear)
    We do not number here
Such spirits as are only continent,
    Because lust's means are spent :
Or those, who doubt the common mouth of fame,   70
    And for their place and name,
Cannot so safely sin : their chastity
    Is mere necessity.
Nor mean we those, whom vows and conscience
    Have fill'd with abstinence :
Though we acknowledge, who can so abstain,
    Makes a most blessed gain.
He that for love of goodness hateth ill,
    Is more crown-worthy still,
Than he, which for sin's penalty forbears ;   80
    His heart sins, though he fears.
But we propose a person like our Dove,
    Graced with a Phoenix' love ;
A beauty of that clear and sparkling light,
    Would make a day of night,
And turn the blackest sorrows to bright joys ;
    Whose odorous breath destroys

All taste of bitterness, and makes the air
    As sweet as she is fair.
A body so harmoniously composed,   90
    As if nature disclosed
All her best symmetry in that one feature !
    O, so divine a creature,
Who could be false to? chiefly, when he knows
    How only she bestows
The wealthy treasure of her love on him ;
    Making his fortune swim
In the full flood of her admired perfection ?
    What savage, brute affection,
Would not be fearful to offend a dame   100
    Of this excelling frame ?
Much more a noble, and right generous mind,
    To virtuous moods inclined
That knows the weight of guilt ; he will refrain
    From thoughts of such a strain,
And to his sense object this sentence ever,
    "Man may securely sin, but safely never."

APPENDIX 3

Among all Lovely Things my Love had been

Among all lovely things my Love had been;
    Had noted well the stars, all flowers that grew
About her home; but she had never seen
    A glow-worm, never one, and this I knew.

While riding near her home one stormy night
    A single glow-worm did I chance to espy;
I gave a fervent welcome to the sight,
    And from my horse I leapt; great joy had I.

Upon a leaf the glow-worm did I lay,
    To bear it with me through the stormy night:
And, as before, it shone without dismay;
    Albeit putting forth a fainter light.

When to the dwelling of my Love I came,
    I went into the orchard quietly;
And left the glow-worm, blessing it by name,
    Laid safely by itself, beneath a tree.

The whole next day, I hoped, and hoped with fear;
    At night the glow-worm shone beneath the tree;
I led my Emma to the spot, "Look there,"
    Oh! Joy it was for her, and joy for me!

Notes and References

The following abbreviations are used for frequently cited texts.

Early Years Ernest De Selincourt and Chester L. Shaver (eds), *The Letters of William and Dorothy Wordsworth, Vol 1: The Early Years: 1787-1805 (Second Revised Edition)* (Oxford, 2000)

Middle Years 1 Ernest De Selincourt and Mary Moorman (eds), *The Letters of William and Dorothy Wordsworth, Vol 2: The Middle Years: Part I: 1806-1811 (Second Revised Edition)* (Oxford, 2000)

Middle Years 2 Ernest De Selincourt, Mary Moorman and Alan G. Hill (eds) *The Letters of William and Dorothy Wordsworth, Vol 3: The Middle Years: Part II: 1812-1820 (Second Revised Edition)* (Oxford, 2000)

Later Years 1 Ernest De Selincourt and Alan G. Hill (eds) *The Letters of William and Dorothy Wordsworth, Vol 4: The Later Years: Part I: 1821-1828 (Second Revised Edition)* (Oxford, 2000)

Later Years 2 Ernest De Selincourt and Alan G. Hill (eds) *The Letters of William and Dorothy Wordsworth, Vol 5: The Later Years: Part II: 1829-1834 (Second Revised Edition)* (Oxford, 2000)

Grasmere Journal Pamela Woof (ed) *Dorothy Wordsworth: The Grasmere Journal,* (Oxford, 1991)

Memoir James Edward Austen-Leigh, *A Memoir of Jane Austen and Other Family Recollections* (Oxford 2002)

Austen Papers Richard A. Austen-Leigh, *Austen Papers 1704-1856* (London, 1995)

Letters Deirdre Le Faye, (ed). *Jane Austen's Letters (Third Edition)* (Oxford, 1995)

Note: Where a reference to a letter is made, the number refers to the letter rather than the page; references to Dorothy's *Journals* include a date rather than a page number.

PROLOGUE

1. W.J.B. Owen and Jane Worthington Smyser (eds), *The Prose Works of William Wordsworth* (Oxford 1974) Vol III p.372
2. *Early Years* 1
3. *Early Years* 2
4. *Early Years* 2
5. In 1806, after reading Thomas Clarkson's *History of the Rise and Abolition of the Slave Trade,* Dorothy would write to Mrs Clarkson – as a compliment to her husband's work – 'Clarissa Harlowe was not more interesting when I first read [it] at 14 years of age.' (*Middle Years Part 1* 81)
6. *Early Years* 5
7. Samuel Richardson, *Clarissa, or the History of a Young Lady* (London, 1784) Vol 1 Letter xxiii
8. *Early Years* 1
9. *Clarissa* Names of the Principal Persons
10. The original title of this work, as given in the manuscript notebook *Volume the Second,* was *Love and Freindship*. But the archaism or misspelling was later corrected by Jane Austen herself.
11. All quotations from *Love and Friendship* are taken from Jane Austen *Minor Works* (Oxford, 1988) p.76-109

12. Amanda Vickery, *Behind Closed Doors: At Home in Georgian England,* *(New Haven, 2009)* p.185

13. Emily J. Climenson, *Elisabeth Montagu: The Queen of the Blue-stockings. Her correspondence from 1720 to 1761* (1908) vol 1 p. 113. (Quoted in Bridget Hill, *Women Alone: Spinsters in England 1660-1850* (New Haven, 2001) p. 8)

14. Robert Halsband (ed)*The Complete Letters of Lady Mary Wortley Montagu* (1965) Vol 1 p.112 (quoted in *Women Alone* p.8.)

CHAPTER ONE

1. Jane Austen, *Pride and Prejudice* (London, 2003) p. 337

2. Deirdre Le Faye, *Jane Austen: A Family Record* (Cambridge, 2004) p. 20

3. *Early Years* 277

4. Jane Austen, *Mansfield Park* (London, 2003) p. 225

5. *Memoir* (Oxford, 2002) p. 23

6. William Wordsworth, *The Prelude (1798-99)* (London, 1995) Book I

7. Le Faye, *A Family Record* p. 21

8. *Memoir* p.185

9. *Austen Papers* p. 333. (Mrs Austen's mother died in August 1768)

10. *Pride and Prejudice* p. 79

11. *Letters* p. 24

12. Stephen Gill, *William Wordsworth: A Life,* *(*Oxford, 1990) p. 207

13. See Edward Copeland's chapter *Money* in Edward Copeland and Juliet McMaster (Ed) *The Cambridge Companion to Jane Austen* (Cambridge, 2006)

14. Copeland and McMaster *The Cambridge Companion* p.132

15. Copeland and McMaster *The Cambridge Companion* p.132

16. This extract from Anna Lefroy's manuscript *Notes on Family History* is quoted in Deidre Le Faye's *A Family Record* where there is a full account of Philadelphia's story. See also Deidre Le Faye *Jane Austen's Outlandish Cousin:the Life and Letters of Eliza de Feuillide* (London, 2002) for the equally fascinating life-story of Philadelphia's daughter.

17. Bridget Hill, *Women, Work and Sexual Politics in Eighteenth Century England* (London, 1994) p. 94-95
18. Thomas De Quincey, *Recollections of the Lakes and the Lake Poets* (London, 1970) p. 51
19. Hill, *Women, Work and Sexual Politics* p. 95
20. *Austen Papers* p 64. The comment was made by Philadelphia's husband Tysoe Saul Hancock when, twenty years later, he opposed the plan of his own daughter travelling to India.
21. *Pride and Prejudice* p. 120
22. Mary Wollstonecraft, *A Vindication of the Rights of Woman* (New York, 1996) p.65

CHAPTER TWO

1. *Austen Papers* p.25
2. *Austen Papers* p.31-32
3. *Austen Papers* p.23
4. *Austen Papers* p.132
5. *Austen Papers* p.162
6. *Austen Papers* p. 65-66
7. *Austen Papers* p. 23
8. Fanny Caroline Lefroy *Family History*. Hampshire Record Office 23M93/85/2
9. *Memoir* p.39
10. *Austen Papers* p.29
11. *Memoir* p.39
12. Claire Tomalin *Jane Austen, A Life* (London, 2000) p. 6
13. *Letters* 95
14. *Letters* 93 Another revealing instance of coldness is a small mistake Jane made in a letter of October 1808 (a few years after Mr Austen's death). Cassandra was away in Kent and Jane was at home; she described herself as 'having got into such a way of being alone' that she was not missing the company of their friend, Martha Lloyd. Cassandra – in a reply that has not survived – seems to have picked up the mistake, pointing out that Jane was not alone, their mother was with her. For, when she next wrote, after Martha's return, Jane said, 'Thank you for your letter, which found me at the Breakfast-Table with my *two* companions.' (Emphasis in the original.)

15. *Memoir* p.39
16. *Austen Papers* p. 31.
17. *Early Years* 257
18. *Grasmere Journal* 14th March 1802
19. Mary Moorman, *William Wordsworth: A Biography, The Early Years* (Oxford, 1969) Vol I p.14
20. *Grasmere Journal* 25th June 1802
21. Jane Austen, *Northanger Abbey* (London, 2003) p.15
22. *Northanger Abbey* p.16
23. Tomalin *Jane Austen, A life* p.29
24. *Letters* 50
25. *Early Years* 1
26. *Pride and Prejudice* p. 23
27. John Worthen, *William Wordsworth A Critical Biography*, (London, 2014) p. 6
28. Hannah More *Strictures on the Modern System of Female Education* (London, 1799) p. 95-96 and 99
29. *Memoir* p. 32-33
30. The report of this dance appeared in *The Cumberland Chronicle and Whitehaven Public Advertiser* on 3rd May 1777. Dorothy had had her fifth birthday in December 1776, so she was not under five. The reporter's mistake is another indication that she was small for her age.
31. *Early Years* 293
32. *Mansfield Park* p. 217
33. *Early Years* 257

CHAPTER THREE

1. *Early Years* 50
2. Wordsworth Trust Collection WLMS 16/118 Letter from Elizabeth Threlkeld (niece) to Samuel Ferguson. From Halifax, 14th February 1798.
3. Wordsworth Trust Collection 1993.R2507 *Mrs William Rawson and her Diary* John Wilson, Halifax Antiquarian Society, 4th Feb 1958.
4. *Pride and Prejudice* p. 65
5. Jane Austen, *Sense and Sensibility* (London, 2003) p. 265
6. H. McLachlan *The Story of a Nonconformist Library* (Manchester, 1923) p.11

7. *Early Years* 28
8. *Memoir* p. 71
9. *Memoir* p. 173 (Caroline's recollections).
10. *Memoir* p. 141
11. *Memoir* Notes p.236
12. *Sense and Sensibility* p. 322
13. *Pride and Prejudice* p. 269
14. *Memoir* p. 170
15. Fanny Caroline Lefroy *Family History*. Hampshire Record Office 23M93/85/2
16. Le Faye *A Family Record* p. 45

CHAPTER FOUR

1. Jane Austen, *Persuasion* (London, 2003) p.15
2. Jane Austen, *Lady Susan, The Watsons* and *Sanditon* (London, 2003) p.110
3. Mary Wollstonecraft, *Thoughts on the Education of Daughters* (London, 1787) p.71
4. Jane Austen, *Emma* (London, 2003) p.22
5. Jane must have realised her own danger quite early on. For, sadly, this episode did result in one death in the family. In response to Jane Cooper's letter, her own mother and Mrs Austen both travelled to Southampton to remove their daughters. Mrs Cooper (Mrs Austen's sister) caught the infection and died of it in October 1783.
6. Le Faye *A Family Record* p. 50
7. *Memoir* p. 160
8. Le Faye *A Family Record* p. 52
9. *Reminiscences of Caroline Austen* Hampshire Record Office 23M93/66/4/ (vol. 1)
10. *Memoir.* p. 198
11. *Memoir* p.174
12. *Letters* 50
13. *Letters* 98
14. *Letters* 4
15. *Middle Years* 2 359
16. *Emma* p. 23
17. John Wordsworth's will nominated two guardians for his

children: his own brother Richard Wordsworth and his wife's brother Christopher Cookson.

18. Malcolm Bull, *Calderdale Companion: Schools and Sunday Schools*, online at http://freepages.history.rootsweb.ancestry.com /~calderdale companion/s70_m.html#247. This advertisement announced that the school was expanding, moving into larger premises and becoming a boarding school – so it must have been prospering.
19. Thomas De Quincey *Recollections of the Lakes and the Lake Poets* (London, 1970) p. 132-133
20. *Reminiscences of Caroline Austen* Hampshire Record Office 23M93/66/4/ (vol. 1). Caroline was here recalling the education of her Lloyd aunts, Mary and Martha, who were Jane and Cassandra's friends and contemporaries.
21. *Pride and Prejudice* p. 161
22. Laetitia Matilda Hawkins *Letters on the Female Mind, Its Powers and Pursuits* (Quoted in Vivien Jones (ed) *Women in the Eighteenth Century, Constructions of Femininity* (London, 1990) p. 118)
23. Hannah More, *Strictures on the Modern System of Female Education* (London, 1799) Vol 2 p. 2
24. More, *Strictures* Vol 2, p. 2
25. Wollstonecraft *Thoughts on the Education of Daughters* p. 56
26. Wollstonecraft *Thoughts on the Education of Daughters* p.69
27. Wollstonecraft *Thoughts on the Education of Daughters* p.73
28. Priscilla Wakefield *Reflections on the Present Condition of the Female Sex; with Suggestions for its Improvement* (London,1798) (Quoted in Vivien Jones *Women in the Eighteenth Century* p.123-25)
29. Malcolm Bull, *Calderdale Companion: Schools and Sunday Schools*, online at http://freepages.history.rootsweb.ancestry.com /~calderdale companion/s70_m.html#247
30. *Early Years* 31
31. *Early Years* 36
32. Le Faye *Letters* 132(D)
33. *Memoir* p. 70-71
34. *Early Years* 88
35. *Early Years* 31
36. *Early Years* 280

37. *Early Years* 280
38. Though her niece would remark: 'I doubt whether she cared very much for poetry in *general*'. (*Memoir* p.172.) Caroline also makes the rather surprising comment: 'I did not often see my Aunt with a book in her hand'. Which – in view of the evidence of extensive reading demonstrated by Jane's novels and letters – suggests that the young niece's knowledge of her aunt may have been restricted. It would certainly appear that Jane did not make a parade of her studying in the style of Mary Bennet.
39. *Early Years* 28
40. William Cowper *The Task* Book IV *The Winter Evening*
41. *Memoir* p. 183
42. Gillian Dow and Katie Halsey *Jane Austen's Reading: The Chawton Years* Jane Austen Society of North America. *Persuasions on Line.* V 3 No 2. (Spring 2010)
43. *Early Years* 2
44. If I had to pick out the giver of this book from among Dorothy's brothers I would choose the eldest, Richard – the lad who was to grow up to be a lawyer and who seems to have been least in sympathy with the poet, William. 'Richard's disposition and [William's]' Dorothy wrote in 1793, 'are totally different, and though they never have any quarrels yet there is not that friend-ship between them which can only exist where there is some similarity of taste, or sentiment.' *Early Years* 31.
45. *Memoir* p.34-35
46. *Letters* 145
47. *Pride and Prejudice* p.64
48. *Early Years* 2

CHAPTER FIVE

1. *Early Years* 1
2. *Early Years* 3
3. *Early Years* 2
4. *Early Years* 1
5. *Early Years* 1
6. *Early Years* 2
7. *Early Years* 4

8. Wordsworth Trust MSS 1992.66.46
9. *Early Years* 4
10. Wordsworth Trust MSS 1992 .66.21
11. *Austen Papers* p.118
12. *Austen Papers* p.126.
13. And, since Philly was not present at Steventon and probably relied on the exuberant accounts of Eliza, she might not have been reporting the exact truth.
14. Sometime between 1800 and 1805 Jane Austen did herself write a short play for a family performance; but this was for representation by children, not adults.
15. *Mansfield Park* p. 125
16. *Mansfield Park* p. 152-153
17. *Mansfield Park* p. 115
18. It is possible to speculate further about the feelings of jealousy and self-interest which were exposed by the Steventon theatricals. At this time Cousin Eliza was a pretty, flirtatious young wife; her husband was French and the couple were separated by the troubles in that country. It seems probable that both James and Henry Austen, though considerably younger than their cousin, were attracted to her.
19. Helen Lefroy and Gavin Turner (ed), *The Letters of Mrs Lefroy,* (Winchester, 2007) p. 11
20. *Mansfield Park* p. 131
21. Lefroy and Turner *The Letters of Mrs Lefroy* p.63 and 101
22. Lefroy and Turner *The Letters of Mrs Lefroy* p.107
23. *Austen Papers* p. 181

CHAPTER SIX

1. *Early Years* 6
2. *Early Years* 14
3. *Early Years* 6
4. Wordsworth Trust MSS 1992.66.17
5. *Early Years* 7
6. *Early Years* 31
7. *Early Years* 83
8. *Early Years* 7
9. *Early Years* 8

10. *Emma* p. 427
11. Lefroy and Turner *The Letters of Mrs Lefroy*, p. 60
12. *Early Years* 8
13. *Austen Papers* p.144
14. *Austen Papers* p.142
15. The only evidence of Jane taking any part, or showing any interest, in her friend's educational projects is in a letter of Anne Lefroy's written in October 1803 when the Austens (now resident in Bath) were paying a visit to their connections in Hampshire. Mrs Lefroy wrote: 'Miss Austens have been with me these two or three days . . .I am now writing surrounded by my School & with the three Ladies in the room . . .' *The Letters of Mrs Lefroy* p. 139-140.
16. Jenny Uglow, *In These Times: Living in Britain through Napoleon's Wars, 1793-1815* (London, 2014) p. 426-27
17. This dedication and other quotations from *The Three Sisters* are taken from Jane Austen *Minor Works* p. 57-71
18. Le Faye *A Family Record* p.70
19. *Letters* 17
20. *Letters* 20
21. *Letters* 22
22. *Early Years* 6
23. *Early Years* 8
24. *Early Years* 22
25. Robert Isaac and Samuel Wilberforce *Life of William Wilberforce* (1833) Vol IV p. 167
26. John Witherspoon *A Practical Treatise on Regeneration* (London, 1764) p. 7
27. Evangelicalism was not a fashionable doctrine at the time, but it would gain ground, as part of what was seen as a widespread reformation of manners and morals. Jane Austen would never be entirely comfortable with the doctrine. 'I do not like the Evangelicals,' she wrote in 1809 (*Letters* 66). In 1814, when her niece, Fanny, was half in love with an evangelical young man, she was guarded and diplomatic: 'I am by no means convinced that we ought not all to be Evangelicals,' she wrote to her, '& am at least persuaded that they who are so from Reason and Feeling, must be happiest & safest.' (*Letters* 109) But in 1816, just months before her death, she wrote (probably more honestly)

to Cassandra, 'We do not much like' the published sermons of cousin, Edward Cooper, 'they are fuller of Regeneration and Conversion than ever.' (*Letters* 145).

28. *Early Years* 9
29. *Early Years* 19
30. *Early Years* 205
31. Sarah Trimmer *The Oeconomy of Charity* (London, 1787) vol. 2 p. 20
32. *Early Years* 9
33. *Sense and Sensibility* p.259
34. *Early Years* 19
35. *Early Years* 22

CHAPTER SEVEN

1. *Early Years* 14
2. *Mansfield Park* p. 61
3. Fanny Caroline Lefroy *Family History* Hampshire Records Office 23M93/85/2
4. Le Faye *A Family Record* p. 30
5. *Austen Papers* p. 76
6. *Austen Papers* p.73
7. *Austen Papers* p. 77
8. *Austen Papers* p.75
9. *Austen Papers* p. 79
10. *Austen Papers* p.76
11. Le Faye *A Family Record* p. 38
12. *Mansfield Park* p. 44
13. *Austen Papers* p. 100
14. *Mansfield Park* p. 335
15. *Lady Susan, The Watsons* and *Sanditon* p. 50

CHAPTER EIGHT

1. *Austen Papers* p. 148
2. *Memoir* p.139
3. *Emma* p. 156-157
4. *Memoir* p. 158
5. Laura Boyle *Mary Russell Mitford: Author of Our Village* Published 16th July 2011 on JaneAusten.co.uk

6. *Letters* 2
7. *Letters* 1
8. *Austen Papers* p.150
9. *Early Years* 9
10. *Northanger Abbey* p. 29. Here Jane Austen is referring to a comment made in *Rambler* vol. ii no. 97.
11. *Early Years* 11
12. *Early Years* 12
13. Earl Leslie Griggs (ed) *Collected Letters of Samuel Taylor Coleridge (6 vols)* (Oxford, 1956) vol 1 p. 195
14. *Emma* p. 251
15. *Mansfield Park* p. 334
16. *Letters* 7
17. *Letters* 92
18. *Pride and Prejudice* p.258
19. *Austen Papers* p. 181
20. *Early Years* 12
21. *An Account of the Rise, Progress, and Present State of the Magdalen Hospital, for the reception of Penitent Prostitutes. Together with Dr. Dodd's sermons.* Published 1770. From The Third Sermon preached at the anniversary meeting of the Governors, 18 March 1762.

CHAPTER NINE

1. *Letters* 1
2. *Pride and Prejudice* p. 36
3. *Emma* p. 275-276
4. Thomas Lefroy, *Memoir of the Chief Justice Lefroy* (Dublin 1871) p.6 and 13
5. Lefroy, *Memoir of the Chief Justice Lefroy* p. 8 and 14
6. Lefroy, *Memoir of the Chief Justice Lefroy* p. 13-14
7. *Letters* 2
8. Lefroy, *Memoir of the Chief Justice Lefroy* p. 9
9. *Letters* 1
10. William Roberts, *Memoirs of the Life and Correspondence of Mrs Hannah More,* (London 1835) Vol 1 p.169.
11. *Emma* p. 8
12. *Early Years* 30

13. Robert Gittings and Jo Manton *Dorothy Wordsworth* (Oxford 1988) p. 105
14. *Early Years* 10
15. *Early Years* 14
16. *Early Years* 29
17. *Early Years* 28
18. John Worthen, *William Wordsworth: A Critical Biography* (London, 2014) p. 61
19. *Early Years* Appendix I

CHAPTER TEN

1. *Persuasion* p. 218
2. *Letters* 2
3. Le Faye *A Family Record* p. 93
4. Le Faye *A Family Record* p. 94
5. *Memoir* p. 186
6. *Who was the real Thomas Lefroy?* Online at: www.irishidentity. com/extras/gaels/stories/lefroy.htm
7. Lefroy, *Memoir of the Chief Justice Lefroy* p. 14-15
8. *Persuasion* p.227
9. Jane Austen *Letters* 11.
10. *Who was the real Thomas Lefroy?* Online at: www.irishidentity. com/extras/gaels/stories/lefroy.htm
11. Lefroy and Turner, *The Letters of Mrs Lefroy* p. 148
12. Lefroy and Turner, *The Letters of Mrs Lefroy* p. 170
13. Though a certain solid eloquence can be traced in his writings on legal matters.
14. Lefroy *Memoir of the Chief Justice Lefroy* p. 42
15. Le Faye *Family Record* p.189
16. Gill, *William Wordsworth: A Life* p. 54-55
17. *Early Years* 17
18. Francois de Salignac de la Mothe-Fenelon, trans. Rev T. F. Dibdin, *Treatise on the Education of Daughters,* 1687 (Quoted in Vivien Jones, *Women in the Eighteenth Century,* p. 102)
19. *Early Years* 23
20. *Early Years* 26
21. *Early Years* 19
22. *Early Years* 16

23. *Early Years* 36
24. *Early Years* 31. The original letters have not survived, but these are extracts which Dorothy quoted in her own correspondence with Jane Pollard. She clearly valued the remarks – and was happy to show her friend how much she was loved.
25. *Early Years* 30
26. *Pride and Prejudice* p. 120
27. *Emma* p. 19
28. Vickery, *Behind Closed Doors* p. 24
29. Annette seems to have written several letters to William but none survive except two which never reached him and lay for years disregarded in a French post office; but the whole tenor of these surviving letters can leave the reader in no doubt of her devotion. 'Come my love, my husband, and receive the tender embraces of your wife, of your daughter . . . She grows more like you every day. I seem to be holding you in my arms . . .' (Gill *William Wordsworth, A Life* p. 66)
30. Emile Legouis, *William Wordsworth and Annette Vallon* (London, 1922) p.29
31. Juliet Barker, *William Wordsworth: A Life in Letters* (London, 2003) p.125
32. *Early Years* 30
33. *Early Years* 30
34. Early Years 31
35. Legouis, *William Wordsworth and Annette Vallon,* p. 32
36. This second child was the daughter of William Godwin, an anarchist with whom William Wordsworth had probably been acquainted during his time in London in 1791. The little girl was another Mary, destined to become the wife of poet Percy Bysshe Shelley, and author of *Frankenstein; or, The Modern Prometheus.*
37. Richard Polwhele *The unsex'd female: A Poem* (New York, 1800)
38. *Early Years* 31

CHAPTER ELEVEN

1. *Memoir* p.186
2. *Letters* 4

3. *Letters* 4
4. *Letters* 6
5. *Letters* 4
6. *Letters* 5
7. *Letters* 6
8. *Early Years* 39
9. Mrs Henry Sandford, *Thomas Poole and His Friends* 2 vols. (London 1888) Vol 1 p.128.
10. *Sense and Sensibility* p. 69
11. Vickery, *Behind Closed Doors* p.189
12. The original manuscript of *Elinor and Marianne* is lost and we can only know about it from the book it turned into. But, since the precarious financial circumstances of the Dashwood sisters are crucial to the plot, it is not unreasonable to suppose that they appeared in some form in the earlier version of the tale.
13. *Sense and Sensibility* p. 10
14. William Shakespeare, *King Lear* Act 2 Scene 2. The ruthless but apparently reasonable dialogue from line 407 to 452 in which the sisters reduce their father's number of attendants from a hundred to none follows a similar sequence to John and Fanny's discussion and it is difficult not to believe that Jane had it in mind as she wrote.
15. Wollstonecraft, *A Vindication of the Rights of Woman* p.65-66.

CHAPTER TWELVE

1. *Early Years* 50
2. *Early Years* 50
3. *Wordsworth Trust MS* 1992.66.43
4. *Early Years* 49
5. *Early Years* 5
6. *Early Years* 48
7. For details of the Wordsworths' complex and precarious financial affairs see Worthen, *The Life of William Wordsworth* particularly p. 206.
8. *Early Years* 46
9. *Early Years* 40
10. *Early Years* 42
11. Quoted in De Selincourt's notes to *Early Years* 41

12. *Early Years 41*
13. *Early Years 49*
14. *Letters* 18
15. Wordsworth Trust MS WLMS 16/117
16. John Pinney's biography online at: www.discoveringbristol.org.uk/slavery/learning-journeys/john-pinney/hard-times

CHAPTER THIRTEEN

1. Racedown was a comfortable home suited to a comfortable gentry household such as William and Dorothy had been born into. Dorothy described their common sitting room as having large bookcases, a marble fireplace, and – that most fashionable of contrivances – a Bath stove, such as Catherine Morland discovers in the bedroom of the dead Mrs Tilney in *Northanger Abbey*, and which, by its modernity, helps to dispel her notions of an ancient gothic chamber.
2. *Early Years 55*
3. *Early Years 56*
4. *Early Years 60*
5. *Early Years 65*
6. *Early Years 59*
7. Worthen, *The Life of William Wordsworth* p. 114
8. Worthen, *The Life of William Wordsworth* p. 114.
   Little Basil's father dismissed these accusations saying they originated in 'diseased affections'. But he was in no position to complain about the Wordsworths' care of his son, for he had failed to pay them for much of the time.
9. *Early Years 60*
10. *Early Years 55*
11. The fleet was caught in hurricane force winds in the English Channel after setting sail from Portsmouth in November, with severe loss of life. Fortunately, Tom Fowle had not been on any of these ships; he sailed later on Lord Craven's private yacht.
12. *Early Years 55*
13. Worthen, *The Life of William Wordsworth* p.150
14. Worthen, *The Life of William Wordsworth* p. 116-17
15. William Wordsworth, *Home at Grasmere* L 177-79

Notes and References

CHAPTER FOURTEEN

1. *Memoir* p.140
2. *Letters* 71
3. *Letters* 86
4. *Letters* 10
5. *Letters* 91
6. *Persuasion* p. 48
7. Jane Austen *Minor Works* (Oxford, 1988) p. 456
8. *Sense and Sensibility* p.153
9. *Letters* 79
10. *Memoir* p.81
11. *Pride and Prejudice* p.29
12. *Pride and Prejudice* p.104
13. *Pride and Prejudice* p.292
14. Jon Spence *A Century of Wills from Jane Austen's family 1705 -1806.* (Paddington, 2011). p. 8
15. *Spence* A Century of Wills p. 18
16. *Sense and Sensibility* p.7
17. *Pride and Prejudice* p.161
18. *Letters* 51
19. *Austen Papers* p.157
20. *Pride and Prejudice* p.300
21. *Emma* p. 305
22. Fanny Caroline Lefroy Family History. Hampshire Record Offices 23M93/85/2
23. *Austen Papers* p.159
24. *Letters* 21
25. *Austen Papers* p.226-27
26. *Letters* 15
27. Le Faye *A Family Record* p. 75
28. Named Hastings after her . . .godfather.
29. *Austen Papers* p. 169

CHAPTER FIFTEEN

1. *Early Years* 67
2. Many biographers adopt the distracting convention of referring to Coleridge as STC. This has its origins in a commonplace

teenage dislike which Coleridge developed for his own name. Unlike most adolescents, he did not grow out of the aversion and all his life he liked to be called STC (pronounced something like Esteesee, with the emphasis put, I imagine, on the middle syllable). However, I do not see any reason to indulge this affectation. I shall call him Coleridge.

3. *Early Years* 70
4. *Early Years* 71
5. Gill, *William Wordsworth, A Life* p. 129
6. Gill, *William Wordsworth, A Life* p. 135. Gill's quotation is taken from *The Ruined Cottage*, the poem which William read to Coleridge on his arrival at Racedown and on which he continued to work during the following year.
7. Preface to *Lyrical Ballads,* 1800
8. *Early Years* 72
9. Mary Moorman (ed) *Journals of Dorothy Wordsworth* (Oxford, 1971) *The Alfoxden Journal* 14th and 15th February 1798.
10. Gill, *William Wordsworth, A Life* p. 125
11. Earl Leslie Griggs, *Collected Letters of Samuel Taylor Coleridge* (Oxford, 1959) Vol 2 p.393
12. Griggs, *Coleridge Letters* p.65
13. Richard Holmes, *Coleridge Early Visions,* (London, 1990) p. 75
14. Holmes *Early Visions* p. 75
15. Thomas De Quincey, *Recollections of the Lakes and the Lake Poets* (Harmondsworth, 1970) p.53.
16. *Early Years* 160
17. De Quincey, *Recollections* p.54. The truth of De Quincey's account is supported by a comment Dorothy herself made later, in 1802, when she had been caught in a downpour and was provided with dry clothes by a stranger at an inn: ' . . .there was a young woman . . .who was kindness itself. She did more for me than Mrs Coleridge would do for her own Sister under the like circumstances . . .' (*Early Years* 169)
18. The Coleridges' maid, who is usually referred to as 'poor Nanny', was becoming increasingly unwell at this time and was probably more burden than help.
19. De Quincey *Recollections* p.132-3.
20. Beth Darlington (ed),. *The Love Letters of William and Mary Wordsworth* (London, 1982) p. 110

21. Kathleen Jones, *A Passionate Sisterhood: The Sisters, Wives and Daughters of the Lake Poets* (London, 1997) p. 121
22. This date has been established from sources other than Dorothy's account. Her journal is confused as to dates and she writes of walking with Coleridge on the 3rd 4th and 5th, which cannot have been the case. Her dating would also be inaccurate sometimes in the *Grasmere Journal*. Her mistakes may, in part, have arisen from the practice of 'catching up' which many diarists employ when they have neglected to write for a while, but it probably also reflects a genuine lack of certainty. Living in an isolated place without modern media, and with newspapers arriving several days after publication, it would be easy to lose track of dates. And, as Dorothy and William were not regular church-goers at this time, they would have lacked even the connection with ecclesiastical festivals which would have structured the year for many of their neighbours.
23. William Wordsworth, *The Tables Turned*
24. Meena Alexander, *Women in Romanticism.* (Savage, 1989). p. 7
25. Under the title, *The Ruined Cottage.*
26. I am indebted for both these comparisons to Mary Moorman's editing of the *Alfoxden Journal.*

CHAPTER SIXTEEN

1. *Letters 55*
2. Fanny Caroline Lefroy Family History. Hampshire Records Office 23M93/85/2
3. Fanny Caroline Lefroy Family History. Hampshire Records Office 23M93/85/2
4. *Letters 96*
5. *Letters 8*
6. *Letters 10*
7. *Letters 86*
8. *Letters 11*
9. *Pride and Prejudice* p. 353
10. The uncertainty arises because it is impossible to know whether this particular piece of dialogue belongs to the original draft of *Pride and Prejudice – First Impressions –* or whether it was inserted with later revisions.

11. *Letters* 114
12. *Austen Papers* p.170
13. Uglow, *In These Times* p.168
14. Gill, *William Wordsworth, A Life* p. 127-128
15. Gill, *William Wordsworth, A Life* p. 128
16. Mrs H Sandford, *Thomas Poole and his Friends*, 2 Vols (1888) vol 1 p.242
17. *Early Years* 83
18. *Early Year* 85
19. *Early Years* 93
20. *Early Year* 88
21. *Early Years* 93
22. Lucy Newlyn, *William and Dorothy Wordsworth. All in Each Other* (Oxford, 2013) p. 299
23. *Letters* 14
24. *Northanger Abbey* p. 36-37
25. Incidentally, Egerton Brydges provides a link between the social circles of Jane Austen and Dorothy Wordsworth. He was an acquaintance of William Wordsworth's future son-in-law, Edward Quillinan.
26. *Letters* 12
27. *Memoir* p. 157-8
28. *Memoir* p. 169
29. Hugh Blair *Lectures on Rhetoric and Belles Lettres* (1763; reprint London, 1812) p. 304. Quoted in Eve Tavor Bannet *The Domestic Revolution: Enlightenment Feminisms and the Novel* (Baltimore, 2000) p. 61
30. *Letters* 50
31. David Womersley, *Samuel Johnson Selected Essays (The Rambler* No. 4) (London, 2003) p.13

CHAPTER SEVENTEEN

1. *Early Years* 100
2. *Early Years* 101
3. Gill, *William Wordsworth, A Life* p. 159
4. *Early Years* 109 In his implied contempt for these professions, Wordsworth seems to be forgetting the occupation of his own grandparents.

5. *Early Years* 107
6. Griggs, Coleridge Letters vol 1 270
7. *Early Years* 109
8. William's contempt for conversational competence in a language, was, perhaps, a defence, an excuse for his own failure to achieve even that level of knowledge.
9. *Early Years* 106
10. *Early Years* 103
11. This was the beginning of *The Prelude*. It was the great work of William's life – in two senses: he was to work on it for the rest of his life, and it was about his life, a detailed, dedicated searching of his soul, an attempt to understand himself and the workings of his own mind: an attempt to understand the very nature of creativity itself.
12. *Early Years* 105
13. Robert Gittings and Jo Manton, *Dorothy Wordsworth* (Oxford, 1988) p. 91
14. Worthen, *The Life of William Wordsworth* p. 186
15. *Grasmere Journal* 1st June 1802
16. *Hamlet* II 2
17. *Letters* 11
18. *Letters* 10
19. *Letters* 11
20. *Letters* 14
21. *Letters* 15
22. *Letters* 15
23. *Letters* 18
24. *Letters* 11
25. *Letters* 15
26. *Sense and Sensibility* p.35
27. *Letters* 14
28. This baby was James Edward Austen-Leigh, who was to become Jane's biographer.
29. *Letters* 16
30. *Letters* 21
31. *Letters* 21
32. *Letters* 17
33. *Letters* 10

CHAPTER EIGHTEEN

1. *Early Years* 118
2. *Early Years* 110
3. *Early Years* 125
4. Letter from Emma Austen-Leigh. Hampshire Record Office 23M93/70/3/88
5. Though, of course, the crime was not then given that title.
6. For a full account of this fascinating incident see Susannah Fullerton, *Jane Austen and Crime* (Sydney, 2004) p. 39-43 or Le Faye, *Jane Austen a Family Record* p. 118-25
7. *Austen Papers* p.206
8. *Letters* 23
9. *Letters* 25
10. *Letters* 27
11. Fanny Caroline Lefroy Family History. Hampshire Records Office 23M93/85/2
12. Fanny Caroline Lefroy Family History. Hampshire Records Office 23M93/85/2
13. *Letters* 30
14. *Memoir* p.185
15. Le Faye *Family Record* p.135
16. *Sense and Sensibility* p.92
17. Fanny Caroline Lefroy. Family History. Hampshire Record Office 23M93/85/2
18. *Memoir* p. 140-141
19. *Letters* 19
20. *Sense and Sensibility* p. 95
21. *Mansfield Park* p. 76
22. *Letters* 13
23. *Early Years* 93
24. *Early Years* 49. Her close relationship with the Hutchinson family would eventually teach Dorothy a great deal about the harsh realities of a farmer's life. In September 1826 – following a summer of drought – she wrote of the desperate state of another Hutchinson farm: 'This rain, if warm weather follows . . .may do much towards compensating for bad crops; but Wheat alone is to be depended on for paying rents . . . Mr Hutchinson says that except 60 acres his Farm will yield him nothing . . .Cattle not as

valuable as in Spring . . .' (From Karl H. Ketcham's transcription of Dorothy Wordsworth's Rydal Mount Journals p.17). By now she could rival Mrs Austen herself in a knowledgeable discussion of agriculture.

25. *Grasmere Journal* 22nd December 1801
26. *Grasmere Journal* 17th May 1800
27. *Grasmere Journal* 14th May 1800
28. *Grasmere Journal* 16th May 1800
29. Mary Moorman identifies the waxy, dial-like flower as Yellow Pimpernel. Interestingly, this is not a flower Dorothy would have seen in Norfolk where the Scarlet Pimpernel flourishes instead. That she was unable to identify the Yellow Pimpernel, which is exclusively a product of northern soils (and fairly common in Cumbria), is another indication that her interest in, and knowledge of, flowers was not marked in her childhood and adolescence.
30. *Sense and Sensibility* p.95
31. The same discrimination can be detected in William Wordsworth's poetry. He writes of farmers, of wagoners and leech-gatherers, not of quarrymen, mill-workers and lead-miners.
32. *Early Years* 140
33. '[N]obody else is named in his Will' William informed Dorothy when he wrote to tell her of the legacy. (*Early Years* 125)
34. Worthen, *The Life of William Wordsworth* p. 206
35. *Early Years* 126
36. *Early Years* 140
37. Gittings and Manton, *Dorothy Wordsworth* p. 105
38. '*Grasmere Journal* 18th May 1800
39. *Letters* 29

CHAPTER NINETEEN

1. *Letters* 29
2. *Letters* 29
3. *Letters* 30
4. *Letters* 32
5. *Letters* 31
6. *Letters* 29
7. *Letters* 29

8. *Persuasion* p. 32
9. Vickery, *Behind Closed Doors* p. 188
10. *Letters* 33
11. *Grasmere Journal* 1st August 1800.
12. *Grasmere Journal* 22nd May 1802
13. *Grasmere Journal* 1st November 1800
14. *Grasmere Journal* 29th November 1801
15. *Grasmere Journal* 26th February 1802
16. The sources used included an oral tradition preserved in the Coleridge family, some letters from Dorothy herself to Mrs Clarkson which contained Annette's Paris address, and the birth and marriage certificates of Caroline Wordsworth. (See Legouis, *William Wordsworth and Annette Vallon*. First published 1922, available in *Kessinger Publishing's Rare Reprints*. p. vii – viii)
17. *Grasmere Journal* 30th January 1802
18. *Grasmere Journal* 10th June 1800
19. *Grasmere Journal* 15th November 1801
20. *Grasmere Journal* 12th December 1801
21. From Mary Moorman's editing of the *Grasmere Journal*
22. *Grasmere Journal*, 6th March 1802
23. *The Pedlar* was not published immediately, but a version of it was eventually subsumed into Wordsworth's long poem *The Excursion*
24. *Grasmere Journal* 31st July 1800
25. From *Reminiscences of Wordsworth among the Peasantry of Westmorland*, Compiled by Hardwicke Drummond Rawnsley (London, 1968)

CHAPTER TWENTY

1. Vivien Jones, *Women in the Eighteenth Century* p.102
2. Laetitia Matilda Hawkins *Letters on the Female Mind*. (Quoted in Vivien Jones (ed) *Women in the 18th Century* p. 118)
3. Uglow, *In These Times* p. 176
4. In *Persuasion* Jane would finally portray the ultimate in companionate marriage with the highly improbable Mrs Croft who has somehow – perhaps on account of being childless – contrived to spend almost as much time at sea as her husband, the admiral,

and by so doing seems to have become a kind of honorary officer; while in Bath she is able to join with her husband and male friends in 'a little knot of the navy,' and look 'as intelligent and keen as any of the officers around her'. But real Mrs Crofts, if they existed at all, would have been very rare indeed.

5. *Grasmere Journal* 7th March 1802
6. *Grasmere Journal* 23rd March 1802
7. *Mansfield Park* p.195
8. *Persuasion* p.160
9. *Grasmere Journal* 16th March 1802
10. *Grasmere Journal* 2nd June 1802
11. *The Grasmere Journal,* 17th March 1802
12. Gittings and Manton, *Dorothy Wordsworth,* p. 105-06
13. Kathleen Jones, *Passionate Sisterhood,* p. 98
14. *Early Years* 169
15. *Grasmere Journal* 30th April 1802. The gown in question was probably the 'fur gown' on which Dorothy lay in front of the fire on 14th March 1802. Most likely it was one they had bought to ward off the German cold.
16. *Sense and Sensibility* p.69
17. *Grasmere Journal* 16th February 1802
18. *Grasmere Journal* 25th June 180
19. *Grasmere Journal* 14th February 1802
20. *Grasmere Journal* 4th March 1802
21. De Quincey, *Recollections* p. 203
22. De Quincey, *Recollections* p.132
23. Daniel Defoe, *Some Considerations upon Street-Walkers with A Proposal for lessening the present Number of them (1726)* Extract in Vivien Jones, *Women in the Eighteenth Century* p. 69.
24. *Essay Concerning Human Generation (1740)* Extract in Vivien Jones, *Women in the Eighteenth Century* p. 81
25. *The Ladies Dispensatory* (1740) Extract in Vivien Jones, *Women in the Eighteenth Century* p. 83
26. 'Philogamus' from *The Present State of Matrimony: or, the Real Causes of Conjugal Infidelity and Unhappy Marriages (1793) Extract in* Vivien Jones, *Women in the Eighteenth Century* p. 77-78
27. Alexander Pope, *Moral Essay II*
28. *Pride and Prejudice* p. 275

29. Bernard Mandeville, *A Modest Defence of Public Stews* (1740) Extract in Vivien Jones, *Women in the Eighteenth Century* p. 65

30. The supposed illness of hysterica or hysteria was as old as Plato. He came up with the colourful idea that most of women's ailments were caused by their wombs which had an unpleasant habit of wandering about the abdominal cavity – thus rendering the female sex sickly, unreliable and irrational.

31. R. James, *A Medical Dictionary* (1743) Extract in Vivien Jones, *Women in the Eighteenth Century* p.85-86

32. Hill, *Women Alone* p. 8

33. Hill, *Women Alone p.* 9

34. Alix Kirsta in *The Guardian* 16th May 2003. See also marriage-equality.blogspot.co.uk

35. Irene Bevc and Irwin Silverman, *Early Proximity and Intimacy Between Siblings and Incestuous Behavior: A Test of the Westermarck Theory* Evolution and Human Behavior Vol 14, Issue 3 (1993) p.171-81

36. *Early Years* 50

37. Frances Wilson, *The Ballad of Dorothy Wordsworth* (London, 2008) p. 150-53

38. Wilson, *The Ballad of Dorothy Wordsworth* p. 152

39. Wilson, *The Ballad of Dorothy Wordsworth* p.146

40. *Grasmere Journal* 27th January 1802

41. *Grasmere Journal* 5th March 1802

42. *Grasmere Journal* 9th March 1802.

43. William is now calling Dorothy down *to him*, whereas in March he had come down *to her*. This is because, in the meantime they had exchanged bedrooms.

44. Darlington, *The Love Letters* p.38

45. Christopher Wordsworth, *Memoirs of William Wordsworth 2 vols (1851) Vol 2* p. 322

46. Rowan Boyson, Wordsworth's Anosmia: pleasure, scent and the later poetry. in *Grasmere, 2013. Selected Papers from the Wordsworth Summer Conference.*(Grasmere, 2013)

47. G. E. Weisfeld, T. Czilli, K.A. Phillips, J. A. Gall and C. M. Lichtman *Possible olfaction-based mechanisms in human kin recognition and inbreeding avoidance.* Journal of Experimental Child Psychology Vol 85 (2003) p.279-95

See also M. A. Schneider and L. Hendrix, *Olfactory sexual inhibition and the Westermarck effect* Human Nature Vol. 11, Issue 1 p. 65-91

CHAPTER TWENTY-ONE

1. Le Faye *Family Record* p. 140-141
2. Le Faye *Family Record* p. 165
3. Jennifer Kelsey, *A Voice of Discontent* (Leicester, 2009) p.56
4. *Letters 36*
5. *Letters 36*
6. *Letters 37*
7. *Letters 35*
8. The unfinished *The Watsons* which Jane began, probably, in 1803 had not been published at the time Jane's nephew wrote his memoir.
9. Nor, incidentally, is the attempt to relieve the symptoms of this debilitating disease with drugs likely to be some kind of modern weakness. Judging from the amount of opiates consumed (largely ineffectively) by sufferers from depression in Georgian times, effective antidepressants would have been at least as popular then as they are now.
10. Fanny Caroline Lefroy. Family History. Hampshire Record Office 23M93/85/2
11. *Letters 36*
12. *Letters 62*
13. This date is not absolutely certain but Deirdre Le Faye calculates it to be the most likely.
14. There is no precise date for this romance, but if it took place it must have been between 1801 and 1804 – during a long break in the surviving sequence of Jane's own letters.
15. If this was Cassandra's intention it is easy to see why she might choose to recall this deceased lover, rather than Tom Lefroy who was still alive at the time – and married to another woman.
16. *Memoir* p.188
17. De Quincey, *Recollections* p. 131. There is no evidence – other than this comment – of Dorothy ever having received any offers of marriage.

CHAPTER TWENTY-TWO

1. Vickery, *Behind Closed Doors* p.208
2. Darlington, *The Love Letters* p.79. 15-19 August 1810.
3. Darlington, *The Love Letters* p.48 1-3 August 1810
4. De Quincey, *Recollections* p.131
5. De Quincey, *Recollections* p. 131
6. *Early Years* 171
7. By the time the poem was published the identity of the glow-worm's recipient had changed again. She had now become that dearly loved, but ephemeral woman, Lucy.
8. *Letters* 82
9. Le Faye, *A Family Record* p. 138
10. Fanny Caroline Lefroy Family History. Hampshire Records Office 23M93/85/2
11. It was a family connection which was reinforced in the next generation when Catherine's son (another Herbert) married Bertha Southey – Robert's daughter.

CHAPTER TWENTY-THREE

1. *Grasmere Journal* 11th January 1803
2. *Early Years* 196
3. *Early Years* 196
4. *Early Years* 221
5. *Early Years* 232
6. Holmes, *Early Visions* p. 353
7. Fanny Caroline Lefroy. Family History. Hampshire Record Office 23M93/85/2
8. The contrast between the tone of this discussion and that in the earlier novels is perhaps less obvious to us now, for we have become accustomed to the recent screen adaptations of *Pride and Prejudice* and *Sense and Sensibility* in which the script writers are obliged to make the viewers aware of the heroines' pressing need to marry in as little screen time as possible.
9. *Lady Susan, The Watsons* and *Sanditon* p. 143
10. *Lady Susan, The Watsons* and *Sanditon* p. 139
11. *Early Years* 196

12. Dorothy Wordsworth, *Recollections of a Tour Made in Scotland AD 1803* (New Haven, 1997) 20th August 1803.
13. De Quincey, *Recollections* p.203
14. Dorothy Wordsworth, *Recollections of a Tour Made in Scotland* 17th September 1803
15. Dorothy Wordsworth, *Recollections of a Tour* 31st August 1803
16. Dorothy Wordsworth, *Recollections of a Tour d* 25th August 1803
17. Dorothy Wordsworth, *Recollections of a Tour* 30th August 1803
18. Dorothy Wordsworth, *Recollections of a Tour* 23rd September 1803
19. Dorothy Wordsworth, *Recollections of a Tour* 6th September 1803
20. Dorothy Wordsworth, *Recollections of a Tour* 27th August 1803
21. Dorothy Wordsworth, *Recollections of a Tour* 20th September 1803
22. *Middle Years 2* 350
23. In matters of literature William was *always* right. This is the tirade which poor Sara Hutchinson received from an outraged Dorothy when she had the temerity to gently suggest that William's poem, *Resolution and Independence* might be, perhaps, just a tiny bit . . .tedious:
'Dear Sara When you happen to be displeased with what you suppose to be the tendency or moral of any poem which William writes, ask yourself whether you have hit upon the real tendency and true moral, and above all never think that he writes for no reason but merely because a thing happened – and when you feel any poem of his to be tedious, ask yourself in what spirit it was written – whether merely to tell the tale and be through with it, or to illustrate a particular character or truth etc.' (*Early Years* 172)
24. *Middle Years 1* 14
25. *Early Years* 196
26. *Early Years* 172
27. *Middle Years 1* 57
28. *Mansfield Park* p.188
29. *Middle Years 1* 90
30. Griggs, *Coleridge Letters* 470

31. *Early Years* 200
32. *Early Years* 204
33. *Early Years* 211
34. *Early Years* 244
35. Newlyn, *All in Each Other* p. 244
36. Newlyn, *All in Each Other* p. 244
37. *Later Years I* 104

CHAPTER TWENTY-FOUR

1. Tomalin *Jane Austen A Life* p.6
2. *Persuasion* p. 148
3. *Letters* 40
4. *Letters* 41
5. *Letters* 41
6. This is based on Henry Austen's Letter (*Austen Papers* p.234-35. See below). He calculated that Mrs Austen and Cassandra's 'assured property' would altogether bring them £210 per annum. If the interest was about 4% this would suggest capital of about £5000. Cassandra's legacy from her fiancé Tom Fowle was £1000.
7. The Austen boys paid no fees at Oxford, because they were classed as 'Founder's Kin' but the expense of supporting them there would have been considerable, as would that of equipping Francis and Charles for their careers in the Navy.
8. *Austen Papers* 234-5
9. *Persuasion* p. 14
10. *Austen Papers* p. 233.
11. *Austen Papers* p.235. Henry's belief that this arrangement would be desirable contradicts his previous assertion that his mother and sisters would be more or less as prosperous as they had been before Mr Austen's death.
12. *Emma* p. 351
13. *Sense and Sensibility* p.343
14. *Sense and Sensibility* p. 90
15. *Early Years* 218.
16. Pamela Woof's notes to *Grasmere Journal* p. 240. This sum is rather less than the £10,000 odd claimed. Perhaps legal fees ate up a proportion.

17. *Early Years* 183.
18. *Grasmere Journal,* 2nd October 1800
19. This £50 supplied all her personal spending for a year.
20. *Letters* 53
21. *Letters* 54
22. *Letters* 43
23. Deirdre Le Faye, *Fanny Knight's Diaries* (Winchester, 2000) p. 7.
24. *Letters* 45
25. *Letters* 46
26. In October 1808 Jane would write, in a letter to Cassandra: 'I wish you may be able to accept Lady Bridges's invitation, tho' *I* could not her son Edward's'. (*Letters* 57)

CHAPTER TWENTY-FIVE

1. Le Faye, *A Family Record* p.153
2. Vickery, *Behind Closed Doors* p. 211
3. *Pride and Prejudice* p. 175
4. *Middle Years 1* 112
5. *Letters* 55
6. *Letters* 49
7. Le Faye, *A Family Record* p.168
8. *Letters* 56
9. *Letters* 58
10. *Letters* 50
11. *Memoir* p.158
12. Le Faye, *Fanny Knight's Diaries* p. 38-39.
13. *Letters* 39
14. *Letters* 68 (D)
15. *Middle Years 1* 93
16. *Middle Years 1* 117
17. This Little Sally was Sally Green, a native of Grasmere, for whom the Wordsworths had agreed to take responsibility when she and her brothers and sisters were orphaned. Her parents perished in a snowstorm and the whole community had come together to help the children. For a full account of this sad story see the account which Dorothy herself wrote in order to raise money for the orphans.

18. *Middle Years 1* 102
19. *Letters* 145
20. *Recollections of Chawton.* Hampshire Record Office 28A11/C2
21. Fanny Caroline Lefroy, *Family History.* Hampshire Record Office 23M93/85/2
22. Stewardship Accounts of Edward Austen Knight. Hampshire Record Office 79M78/B211
23. De Quincey, *Recollections* p.131
24. Darlington, *Love Letters* p.251
25. *Letters* 62

CHAPTER TWENTY-SIX

1. *Memoir* p. 140
2. *Emma* p. 83
3. *Memoir* p.169
4. *Memoir* p. 157
5. *Letters* 10.
6. *Early Years* 196
7. *Letters* 53
8. *Letters* 92
9. *Letters* 53
10. *Middle Years 1* 10
11. *Middle Years 1* 135
12. *Middle Years 2* 359
13. De Quincey, *Recollections* p. 205-06.
14. *Letters* 91
15. Fanny Caroline Lefroy Family History. Hampshire Record Office 23M93/85/2
16. *Emma* p.83
17. *Letters* 153
18. *Middle Years 1* 81
19. *Middle Years 1* 95
20. *Middle Years 1* 95
21. *Middle Years 1* 87
22. *Northanger Abbey* p. 106
23. Gittings and Manton *Dorothy Wordsworth* p.179
24. *Sense and Sensibility* p. 83
25. *Mansfield Park* p.83

26. *Mansfield Park* p. 105
27. William Deresiewic, *Jane Austen and the Romantic Poets* (New York, 2004) p. 2-4
28. Deresiewicz, *Jane Austen and the Romantic Poets* p. 9
29. *Letters* 132(D)
30. *Mansfield Park* p. 25
31. *Mansfield Park* p. 205
32. Since the death of little Berkley, Sarah Coleridge had borne a son and a daughter – proof perhaps that her marriage was not as uniformly bleak as Dorothy believed.
33. *Middle Years 1* 48
34. *Middle Years 2* 188
35. Gittings and Manton, *Dorothy Wordsworth* p. 177
36. By now, he had realised he could not look after the children. They remained with their mother.
37. Darlington, *The Love Letters* p. 38
38. Darlington, *The Love Letters* p. 46
39. Darlington, *The Love Letters* p. 82
40. *Mansfield Park* p. 217
41. Darlington, *The Love Letters* p. 85
42. Darlington, *The Love Letters* p. 39
43. Darlington, *The Love Letters* p.53
44. Darlington, *The Love Letters* p. 157 Presumably the blot was passed off as accidental. William was habitually clumsy enough to make this a plausible story.
45. *Later Years 2* 575
46. *Early Years* 243
47. *Letters* 155
48. *Later Years 2* 462
49. *Letters* 109
50. *Middle Years 2* 350
51. *Later Years 2* 462
52. Dorothy Wordsworth, *Recollections of a Tour Made in Scotland* 24th August 1803
53. *Rydal Mount Journals*, Ketcham's transcript p. 8. Wordsworth Trust Collection
54. De Quincey, *Recollections* p. 204
55. *Letters* 135
56. The position was called Distributer of Stamps for Westmorland;

but that is a little misleading. The job had nothing to do with letters or postage stamps.

57. De Quincey, *Recollections* p.204-05
58. From a talk given at *The Wordsworth Trust* 22nd March 2014. Barbara Crossley is a psychiatric social worker with many years' experience of mental health issues.

EPILOGUE

1. Deresiewicz, *Jane Austen and the Romantic Poets* p.2
2. Newlyn, *All in Each Other* p. 298
3. Newlyn, *All in Each Other* p. 312

Select Bibliography

DOROTHY WORDSWORTH

Bateson, F.W. *Wordsworth, a Re-interpretation* (London, 1963)

Darlington, Beth (ed.) *The Love Letters of William and Mary Wordsworth* (London, 1982)

Davis, Hunter, *William Wordsworth* (London, 1980)

De Quincey, Thomas *Recollections of the Lakes and the Lake Poets* (Harmondsworth, 1970)

De Quincey, Thomas, *Confessions of an English Opium Eater* (London, 1997)

De Selincourt, Ernest and Chester L. Shaver (eds), *The Letters of William and Dorothy Wordsworth, Vol 1: The Early Years: 1787-1805 (Second Revised Edition)* (Oxford, 2000)

De Selincourt, Ernest and Mary Moorman (eds), *The Letters of William and Dorothy Wordsworth, Vol 2: The Middle Years: Part I: 1806-1811 (Second Revised Edition)* (Oxford, 2000)

De Selincourt Ernest, Mary Moorman and Alan G. Hill (eds) *The Letters of William and Dorothy Wordsworth, Vol 3: The Middle Years: Part II: 1812-1820 (Second Revised Edition)* (Oxford, 2000)

De Selincourt, Ernest and Alan G. Hill (eds) *The Letters of William and Dorothy Wordsworth, Vol 4: The Later Years: Part I: 1821-1828 (Second Revised Edition)* (Oxford, 2000)

De Selincourt, Ernest and Alan G. Hill (eds) *The Letters of William and Dorothy Wordsworth, Vol 5: The Later Years: Part II: 1829-1834 (Second Revised Edition)* (Oxford, 2000)

Gill, Stephen, *William Wordsworth: A Life* (Oxford, 1990)

Gittings, Robert and Jo Manton, *Dorothy Wordsworth* (Oxford,1988)

Holmes, Richard, *Coleridge Darker Reflections* (London, 1999)

Holmes, Richard, *Coleridge Early Visions* (London, 1990)

Jones, Kathleen, *A Passionate Sisterhood: The Sisters, Wives and Daughters of the Lake Poets* (London, 1997)

Lefebure, Molly, *The Bondage of Love: A Life of Mrs Samuel Taylor Coleridge* (London, 1988)

Legouis, Emile, *William Wordsworth and Annette Vallon* (1922)

Moorman, Mary, *Journals of Dorothy Wordsworth,* (Oxford, 1952)

Newlyn, Lucy, *William and Dorothy Wordsworth. All in Each Other* (Oxford, 2013)

Tomalin, Claire, *The Life and Death of Mary Wollstonecraft* (London, 1974)

Wilson, Frances, *The Ballad of Dorothy Wordsworth* (London, 2008)

Wilson, John, *Mrs William Rawson and her Diary* (Halifax, 1958)

Woof, Pamela, *Dorothy Wordsworth, Wonders of the Everyday* (Grasmere, 2013)

Woof, Pamela, *Dorothy Wordsworth, Writer* (Grasmere, 2013)

Wordsworth, Christopher, *Memoirs of William Wordsworth* (London, 1851)

Wordsworth, Dorothy, *Recollections of a Tour Made in Scotland, A.D. 1803* (New Haven, 1997)

Woof, Pamela (ed.), *Wordsworth, Dorothy, The Grasmere Journal* (Oxford, 1991)

Wordsworth, William, *The Prelude* (London, 1995)

Worthen, John, *The Gang: Coleridge, the Hutchinsons and the Wordsworths in 1802* (New Haven, 2001)

Worthen, John, *William Wordsworth: A Critical Biography* (London, 2014)

Select Bibliography

JANE AUSTEN

Austen, Jane, *Emma* (London, 2003)

Austen, Jane, *Lady Susan, The Watsons* and *Sanditon* (London, 2003)

Austen, Jane, *Mansfield Park* (London, 2003)

Austen, Jane, *Minor Works* (Oxford, 1988)

Austen, Jane, *Northanger Abbey* (London, 2003)

Austen, Jane, *Persuasion* (London, 2003)

Austen, Jane, *Pride and Prejudice* (London, 2003)

Austen, Jane, *Sense and Sensibility* (London, 2003)

Austen-Leigh, James Edward, *A Memoir of Jane Austen and Other Family Recollections* (Oxford, 2002)

Austen-Leigh, Richard A, *Austen Papers 1704-1856* (London, 1995)

Butler, Marilyn, *Jane Austen and the War of Ideas* (Oxford, 2006)

Copeland, Edward and Juliet McMaster, (ed.), *The Cambridge Companion to Jane Austen* (Cambridge, 2006)

Deresiewicz, William, *Jane Austen and the Romantic Poets* (New York, 2004)

Fullerton, Susannah, *Jane Austen and Crime* (Sydney, 2004)

Honan, Park, *Jane Austen Her Life* (New York, 1987)

Johnson, Claudia L, *Jane Austen: Women, Politics, and the Novel* (Chicago, 1990)

Le Faye, Deirdre, ed. *Jane Austen's Letters (Third Edition)* (Oxford, 1995)

Le Faye, Deirdre, *Jane Austen: A Family Record* (Cambridge, 2004)

Le Faye, Deirdre, *Jane Austen's Country Life* (London, 2014)

Le Faye, Deirdre, *Fanny Knight's Diaries* (Winchester, 2000)

Lefroy, Helen and Gavin Turner, *The Letters of Mrs Lefroy* (Winchester, 2007)

Lefroy, Thomas, *Memoir of the Chief Justice Lefroy* (Dublin, 1871) Available on Google Books)

Nicolson, Nigel, *The World of Jane Austen* (London, 1991)

Spence, Jon, *A Century of Wills from Jane Austen's Family 1705-1806* (Sydney, 2011)

Tomalin, Claire, *Jane Austen: A Life* (London, 2000)

BACKGROUND

Alexander, Meena, *Women in Romanticism* (Savage, 1989)

Bannet, Eve Tavor, *The Domestic Revolution: Enlightenment Feminisms and the Novel* (Baltimore, 2000)

Buchan, William, *Domestic Medicine: Or , A Treatise on the Prevention and Cure of Diseases by Regimen and Simple Medicines: With an Appendix Containing a Dispensatory for the use of Private Practitioners* (Edinburgh, 1790. Available on Google Books)

Gregory, John, *A Father's Legacy to His Daughters* (London, 1774) Available on Google Books)

Hill, Bridget, *Women Alone: Spinsters in England 1660-1850* (New Haven, 2001)

Hill, Bridget, *Women, Work and Sexual Politics in Eighteenth Century England* (London, 1994)

Johnson, Samuel, *Selected Essays* (London, 2003)

Jones, Vivien (ed.) *Women in the Eighteenth Century: Constructs of Femininity* (London, 1994)

Jones, Vivien (ed.), *Women and Literature in Britain 1700-1800* (Cambridge, 2000)

Kelsey, Jennifer C, *A Voice of Discontent* (London, 2009)

Knott, Sarah and Barbara Taylor (ed.) *Women, Gender and Enlightenment* (London, 2007)

Uglow, Jenny, *In These Times: Living in Britain through Napoleon's Wars, 1793-1815* (London, 2014)

Vickery, Amanda, *Behind Closed Doors: At Home in Georgian England* (New Haven, 2009)

Vickery, Amanda, *The Gentleman's Daughter: Women's Lives in Georgian England* (New Haven, 2003)

Wilson, Ben, *Decency and Disorder 1789-1837* (London, 2008)

Wollstonecraft, Mary, *A Vindication of the Rights of Woman* (New York, 1996)

Wollstonecraft, Mary, *The Collected Letters* (London, 2004)

Index

Abbey House School, Reading 28
Abercromby, Sir Ralph 139
Abolition of Slavery Bill 130
Affleck, Admiral Sir Edmund 154
Alfoxton House 160, 161, 170, 176, 177
Alfoxton Journal 167-70, 178, 242, 262, 265, 315
Allan Bank 286, 287, 291, 298, 307, 308
amateur theatricals 48-50
Ashe, parish of 50
Austen, Anna (later Lefroy) 2, 3, 150, 152
Austen, Caroline 25, 29, 31, 94, 96, 111, 198, 238, 247, 248, 298
Austen, Cassandra (mother of JA) 4, 11, 21, 27, 50, 78, 151, 195-97, 202, 248, 280-85
  controlling family budget 281
  distant from Jane 13, 14, 151
  financial support 274
  health problems 154, 173, 189, 190, 199
  looking old 78
  moving to Bath 197, 210
  moving to Southampton 280

  not supporting Jane's writing 172
Austen, Cassandra (sister of JA) 6, 12-14, 66, 73, 74, 77, 83, 84, 86, 99, 111-14, 119, 128, 139, 150, 173, 179, 189, 191, 196, 210, 234, 238, 239, 247, 272, 274, 281, 283, 285, 307
  at school 27
  death of Tom Fowle 151, 152
  destroying letters from Jane 29, 197, 235, 271, 273
  engaged to Tom Fowle 75, 112
  frequency of JA's letters 13
  hearing of Jane's writings 144
  memorandum of Jane's writings 142
  seen as prettier than Jane 52, 56
Austen, Charles 6, 51, 74, 128, 175
Austen, Edward (later Knight) 12, 29, 58
Austen, Eliza *see* Feuillide
Austen, Francis or Frank (brother of JA) 6, 113, 114, 143, 154, 175, 219, 271, 274, 275, 280
Austen, Francis (great-uncle of JA) 7

371

Index